# THE HISTORY OF ANDHRA COUNTRY 1000 A.D.

# ADMINISTRATION, LITERAFURE AND SOCIETY

## (2VOLS.)

# THE HISTORY OF ANDHRA COUNTRY 1000 A.D. ADMINISTRATION, LITERAFURE AND SOCIETY

# (2VOLS.)

BY

YASHODA DEVI

GYAN

ISBN : 978-81-212-0438-5(sat)

ISBN : 978-81-212-0485-9(vol 2)

First Published, 1995

*Published by*

Gyan Publishing House
5, Ansari Road
Daryaganj, New Delhi-110002
Phone: 011-47034999, 9811692060
www.gyanbooks.com
E-mail: books@gyanbooks.com

*Printed at:* G. Print Process, Delhi.

# THE HISTORY OF ANDHRA COUNTRY
## PART II
## Administration, Literature and Society

# The History of Andhra Country

## Part II

### Administration, Literature and Society

YASHODA DEVI

GYAN PUBLISHING HOUSE

New Delhi 110 002

## FOREWORD

I deem it as a proud privilege to write Foreword to this enlightening work - History of Andhra Country (A.D. 1000-1500) by my revered Professor Dr. Varanasi Yashoda Devi. This volume on history and culture of a more advanced nature is of primary importance and it exactly fills the void in the medieval history of Andhra. Regional History of this sort is a miniature history of India - and deals with all aspects - administration, both central and provincial, military, transport, trade and commerce, irrigation and agriculture, justice, coins, weights and measures, taxes and tolls, tanks and drama, social life - religion, temple, festivals, etc. The minute details of all the minor dynasties of Andhra are meticulously carved out. This properly projected perspective is bound to make a spectacular dent on the annals of Indian culture. As a proud and privileged\Research\Scholar of the Revered Professor Sri K.A. Nilakantha Sastri, Dr. V. Yashoda Devi publishes this volume as a fitting memorial to this great historian of India.

It is sincerely hoped that this work, besides providing voluminous material to the historians, would also be a valuable reservoir of authentic information to the scholars of various academic disciplines.

**Dr. A. Suryakumari**

Professor and Head
Department of Historical Studies
Mother Teresa Women's University
Kodaikanal

## PREFACE—II

The Volume I has dealt comprehensively with the political history of the subsidiary Dynasties in Medieval Andhradesa, tracing their ancestries, fixing their genealogies and chronology and relations with their de jure suzerains - eg; the Chalukya Cholas the Kakatiyas, the Eastern Gangas, the Gajapatis and so forth, retaining defacto independence in twenty chapters.

The present volume II, based on the findings in the previous volume as told by Richard Hakluyt that geography and chronology are the right eye and left eye of history, gives a detailed account of the Administrative systems - Central, provincial and local, territorial, agricultural, irrigation, coinage and so on in Chapter XX. The next chapter is devoted to a study of the arts in medieval Andhra - namely literature - sanskrit and Telugu, music - classical and temple, musical instruments, and dancing - classical and folk in royal courts and temples, the last and XXII chapter analyses the social, cultural ethos, the religious, caste system, social festivals amusements and women's participation in them. Kota Ganapama Devi, the ruler of the Kota dynasty at Dharanikota was Sister of Queen Rudrama Devi of the Kakatiyas of Warangal. Aravilli Nagamma famous as Nayakuralu was the Prime Minister of the Haihaya Kingdom of Palnad.

I express my deep sense of gratitude to Dr. A. Suryakumari, my student (1960-62) now Professor and Head, Department of Historical Studies, Mother Teresa Women's University, for her determined effort to perceive the two volumes published. I clasp my hands in reverence to the memory of my Professor K.A. Nilakantha Sastri to whose renowned scholarship this volume is dedicated as a humble token. The first volume came out during his birth centenary year (1992-93). I also acknowledge the constant help in my academic activity from my younger brother K. Krishna Mohan, M.A. In fact, the most important to my acknowledgements is sincere gratitude to the Gyan Publishing House for bringing out the two volumes in their excellent and inimitable style.

**V. Yashoda Devi**

## CONTENTS

# 1

# Introduction

## General Introduction

The system of administration that obtained in the Andhra land in medieval times presents complex features. It was a happy blend of indigenous and imposed elements, which neither distinguishable nor separable were a result of the prevalent political phenomena - namely the suzerainty of the major power of South India over Andhra from without and the dominance of the larger kingdoms over smaller ones with in. And no continuity in the growth of the administrative institutions is discernible. The major powers in Andhra like the Velanandu cholas and the Telugu cholas, though owing allegiance to a suzerain power assumed imperialistic prasastis; and even petty powers whose exact political status and extent of territories are not ascertainable in some cases were not free from the temptation of bearing long prasastis.

The Chalukya-cholas, the suzerain lords over Andhradesa, during the major part of this period, exercised the greatest influence over its administration, which was but a replica of the chola system; and remained thus till AD 1500 when the country came under the Gajapatis and the kings of Vijayanagar. The cluster of dynasties in Andhra, which rose towards the end of Chalukya rule is Vengi, later transferred their loyalty to Kulottunga I under whom Vengi became an important Viceroyalty of the Chola empire, entrusted to persons no less than the sons of the emperor. Later the province was left by the Cholas in charge of the Velanandu cholas, their loyal subordinates. For Gonka I ruled Andhra-mandala under the orders of Kulottunga I; and chola I was adopted as son by the Kulottunga I and was conferred with the insignia of his sons and Vengi 16000.[1] Similarly many of the local dynasties and their kingdoms to the chola monarchs. They imbibed thoroughly the chola system, their administration which is reflected in every aspect of their several governments - for instance, the nomenclature of kings, geographical divisions, coinage, temples, tanks, weights, measures and so forth.

Roughly the period of half a millonnium falls into two divisions - 1. The age of Chola suzerainty and Velanandu rule from 1000 to 1200 AD when, to quote Professor Sastri, "Vengi was so closely connected with the Chola kingdom, .... that though its separate political existence continued throughout in all its vigour, for all practical purposes of interstate diplomacy, it counted as more or less as part of the Chola empire."[2] After 1200 AD in which period the Telugu Cholas and the Telgu Pallavas were the important powers, who like the Velanandu Cholas were loyal to the Cholas and deservedly succeeded to everything that was chola in Andhra.

Sources—As for political history, for administration as well, inscriptions - stone and copper plate of all the dynasties form the primary source. Literature, writings of foreign travellers, recorded tradition and references in the records of contemporary dynasties from the supplementary material. In this and the subsequent chapters may be found references to some dynasties, records and literature having a general bearing on the period, not dealt with already.

**Common features:** The kingdoms with wide variances in extent and resources, had some essentials in common. For the government consisted of the king ministers and council though joint rule and dual kingship was not rare. Capitals were located in place of geographical or strategic importance. Army was all important to the state; and military officials played important roles in civil life also. Land and hill fortresses were commoner than water and forest fortresses. The importance of irrigation for purposes of cultivation was realised and tanks and canals were dug. Roads were laid to ease transport and facilitate trade and commerce. Mercantile organisation wielded wide powers over their members; they could offer protection and punish crimes. Foreign trade was encouraged by royal charters promising protection and safty. Industries prospered and many dynastics had their coinage, ports, tolls, measures, weights and so forth.

The growth of administration in "the Telugu country which was for the bulk of the period (850-1270) an appendage of the cola empire'[3] was rendered easy by the decline of the cholas. "The hold of the central administration over the outlying parts of the empire had always been less firm than in the districts nearer the capital.......The growing weakness of the centre rendered necessary new arrangements of more or less feudal character for loal regulation and defence; these arrangements in their turn stood in the way of the centre regaining its former accendency when it attempted to do so. Political compacts among local rulers attest the growth of imperia in imperial until the local imperia burst the shell of the central imperium under whose protection they had at first begin to take shape; and these compacts are now seen to become even more numerous in Kulottunga III's reign than under his predecessor. The sphere of these compacts is coterminous with the territory under the direct rule of Kulottunga.

....By these local alliances therefore the regular functioning of the king's Government must have been seriously hampered: under Kulottunga III, Rajraga III and Rajendra III the forms of administrative procedure present the same appearnce as in the best days of the empire under Rajaraja I and Rajendra I out the spirit behind these forms could no longer have been the same .... The name Golamandalam long survived the cola kingdom itself and was subsequently corrupted into Coramandal."[4]

## The Velanandu choda kingdom

The Velanandu choda kingdom, under the paternal care of the cholas, developed a powerful administrative machinary. Strong army was its backbone. Forts were built, irrigation was cared for, ports were developed, facilities for transport prevailed and trade and commerce were encouraged by the Velanandu chodas. These rulers and chief and provincial capitals, and in the kingdom were current their coins and these of subordinate dynasties. The Velanandus took the cholas as their ideal and the local dynasties had the Velanandus as their model. Thus, the chola system pervaded in Andhradesa as long as in Cholamandala and even after.

Name, extent and divisions of the kingdom: Though the term Velanandu forms a prefix of the kings' names, and lord of shatsahasra to the south of the Krishna i.e. an epithet in their prasasti, the Velanandu kingdom embraaced almost the entire Andhra-desa mentioned thus in records of the Vengi chalukyas, and as Vengi mandala, the region of the rising sun, Andhramandala or Vishaya in inscriptions Velanadu alias Aruvelanadu or shatsahasra was the home province. The assumption of titles indicating lordship over Vengi or Andhra by the Kona Haihayas and Kolamu rulers and other rulers, does not impir Velanandu suzerainty and Venginadu was a province of Andhradesa i.e. Vengimandala.

The Velanandu kingdom comprised many provinces of unequal sizes and resources ruled by viceroys or local dynastics owing allegiance to the Velanandu chodas. They are as follows: Velanandudesa or mandals, Varanandudesa or shatsahasravishaya lies to the south of the Krishna. In Chalukya times, it formed the northern portion of Kammarashtra,[5] corresponding to the eastern portion of the modern Guntur district.[6] It appears as Velinandu in some Kakatiya inscriptions, which was superceded by the popular form Velanandu shatsahasra when it developed into the 6000 country.

2. Kathmandu alias Kammarashtra, Kammadesa and Kammanativishaya, generally corresponds to the southern part of the district of Guntur and the northern part of Nellore. Under the Chalukyas, Kammanadu constituted the southern part of Kammarashtra i.e. Kammakaratha of Ikshvaku times[7] and Karma Karta under the Pallavas. In this period, Kammanadu extended upto Markapur taluq in the west.[8] 3.Kondapalle 300 had its capital at Kondupalle 4. Kondapadumati the giripaschima, saila pratichivishaya, and Sailapaschatyadipa of records in Sanskrit; is the country to the west of the Kondapila hiss. 5. Kotadesa or the tract about Amaravati on the Krishna had its capital at Amaravati. 6. Palnadu or Pallides 300 which lies to the south of the Krishna. 7. Natavadivishaya forms part of the country about Bezvada and Amaravati. 8. Omgerumarga vishaya. 9. Ivanikandravadi, 10. Konakandravadi, 11. Gudrahara or gudrara or Gudravara corresponds to Bandar Gudivada and Kaikalur taluqs[9] (Kistna district). 12. Pakanadu 21000 extending from Mandukur in the north to Kalahasti in the south; comprises parts of Nellore, Cuddapah and Chittoor districts.[10] In Chalukya times, Kavali and Kandukur and a part of northern most taluq (Nellore district) constituted Pakanatisima.[11] 13. Vengi 14000 is the tract between the Krishna and the Godavari. Later on it developed into Vengi 16000. It is mentioned as Venginadu vishaya in the records of the Chalukyas of Vengi. 14. Konamandala Konasima and Konadeva is the deltaic country at the mouth of Godavari and formed a portion of Venginadu. In Reddi time it is called Konasthala and Konasima is applied to a portion of Amalapuram taluq. 15. Kolamu vishaya or Kolamadu corresponds to Ellore and Tanukkur taluqs.[12](West Godavari district) 16. Prolunadu to the country on the southern side of Pithapur and north of the lower Godavari. 17. Guddavati Guddadi or Dughdi includes Razole and Ramachandrapuram taluqs (East Godavari district). 18. Oddadivishaya i.e. Matsya desa. 19. Jantarunanati vishaya i.e. Dantapuranadu 20. Dimile vishaya, Bobbilidesa and so forth in south Kalinga were included in the Velanandu kingdom which extended for a while up to Mahendrachola. Of these provinces, those numbering 300 e.g. I palmed and Kaipalle are the small and Vengi 16000 and Kammanadu 16000 the biggest.

Each Province was subdivided into groups of villages called sthalas or township of variable size. e.g. Siripuram 12. Yanamadala 60. The chief town of the group is referred to as sthala or pura. e.g. Rakudurishthala, Yenamanddasthala, Nelluristhala and of the province were liable to fluctuations consequent on the expansion on contraction dependent on the capacity of kings and governors.

Besides as Andhramandala,[13] the Velanandu kingdom is also mentioned as durendugangagondachodavalandu and Uttamachodavalanadu. The formation of the kingdom was as follows:- Shatsahasrayagati obtained by Malla I from Trinayanapallava was the nucleus and the earliest province of the kingdom and was under the direct rule of the kings. The pair of districts i.e. Gudravaradvaya got by Kudiyavarman II from Vimaladitya, must have been Gudravara and Guddavadi which were later on distinguished thus "gudravara in ancient times must have comprised the sea board between the Krishna and the Godavari and was occasionally applied to both the divisions Gudravar and Tuddavadi." So, Gudravaradvaya comprised the territory between the Krishna and the Gautami. Sindhuyugmantradesa - the country between the pair of rivers - obviously the Krishna and the Godavari was obtained by Vedwra II. Probably Sindhuyugmantara is identical with Gudravaradvaya. Andhramandala was ruled over by GonkaI[14] and Vengi in his time extended form Mahendragiri in the east of Manneru in the south. Vengi 16000 was ruled over by Choda I which is corroborated by a chatu verse mentioning him as the ruler of Andhra 16000 (Andhrabhutalamu-padavurevlu), Lord of Vengi vishaya 16000 was a title of Gonka II[15] in the early part of his reign and in his later records Gonka is mentioned as the lord of Vengi of Andhra. Gonka II, Choda II claims to have ruled the country from Mahendra to Srisailam and was also the lord of 63000, country. Like Gonka II is described as the lord 63000 country, Andhra 16000 the entire Vengi and Andhramandala - bounded by the eastern ocean, Kalahasti hill, Mahendrachola, and Srisailam. Velananduvishaya and Navalaksha - Telugu is nine lakh Telugu country are mentioned by Somanatha.[16] Fifty lakh Andhra country i.e. Panchasatlakshasamkyuktamandhradesam was the country ruled by Gonka [17] (s 1153) of the later Velanandu chodas.

**Central Governments King:** The rulers were warriors and administrators. Joint rule towards the close of each reign and the beginnig of the next was a recurrent phenomenon as in the case of the imperial cholas. According to Hindu concepts, kingship is divine, sacred, and supreme; and the king is sarvabhauma, Prithvipati, performer of Asvamedha and enforcer of law. "The Hindu ideal of sovereign made him the sole repository of sovereignty."[18] The Velanandu chodas strove towards the ideal kingship with rights and duties. Though feudatories, they were not free from the notions of empire and emperor. Manchana in Keyurabhaucharitra describes the king thus - he is lustrous, commands his enemies, fears notoreity, does not displease enemies and gets at faults. He possesses good conduct, is truthful, free from excessive pleasure, pretensions, indifference, fear, anger, and sins and is praised by his good subjects. He knows his kingdom thoroughly, the palace, topography, fertility, necessity of fortresses at certain places, and friends and ememies among neighbouring kings. Free from the seven vices, the king knows the use of the four devices, and protects sapta angas. To him weapon is intelligence, sapta angas are body, work and secret are shoes, ambassadors are looks, people are face and good conduct is life. His country enjoys place and prosperity.[19]

King Indrasena is said to have been bestowed with the regal emblems - a white parasol, gold staff, silkoncanopy, 1\2 of his throne, an suspicious lamp, couches and two beautiful white chauris, by king Yadhistara.[20] Vendura II must have inherited this regalia, and in the presence of all kings in the assembly was conferred with half of his throne by Virchoda. Gonka I, the founder of the kingdom, must have inherited the regal emblems. He was a man of strong will, character, possessing all the requisite qualities as the successful head of the Velanandu power. Records describe him as truthful, friendly and charitable. Choda I was bestowd with the emblems of his sons by Kulottunga I. He strengthened the kingdom, and ruled well. For inscriptions mention him as the possessor of the three powers (saktitraya) and compare his rule with that of Rama.[21] His eyes were beautiful and glittering and the epithets - Vanajavana martanada and Tribhuvanabhirama reflect on his striking personality. He is described to have been resplendent truthful and firm. Described as the ruler of the world protector of earth, patient and prosperous he is compared with Indra and Narayana. Interested in the happiness of his subjects Gonka, mentioned as the incarnation of Dharma, established dharma in his kingdom. His mind was pure consequent on following truth and righteousness. Choda II was handsome, possessing good eyes and all auspicious sign in hands and feet. Described as the lord of the world and equal of the six emperors, he ruled in accordance with dharma. His motto was - *yatodharma statojaya.*[22] This cautious king stored always nine crores of money in his treasury and seventy-five puttis[23] (corn) in Granary. Gonka III and prithvisvara were learned in the royal sciences. Entitled Rajaraja paramesvara, Prithvisvara is compared with Yudhishtara in just rule. His rule was benevolent for the Pithpur pillar inscription says that ended his rule, men did not know the etymology of words meaning enemy and thief.[24]

**Ministers:** In each reign, the number of ministers varied. In some cases, the office was hereditary. Manchana describes a minister thus[25] he must be of good health, and appearance, possess intelligence, courage, thinking and orthodoxy. Free from vices, he must please people, be kind to them, and keep secrets and unravel those of the enemy. He must be of good lineage, playful, heroic and quick in work, and learned in all sciences. The premier is the best among ministers, the bearer of the burden of the kingdom, devoted and friendly to the king, knowing many good devices and destroyer of enemies.

No ministers of Gonka I are heard of. Somanapreggada, son of Vennaya Somayaji was the pradhani of Choda I. Jilla, Narayana and Suraya and the sons of Narayana, all of Ayya family assisted Choda in conquering his enemies and administering his kingdom.[26] Gonka II had many ministers. Govinda preggada, a warrior, was Rajadhyaksha and sandhivigrahi mukhya[27] and is also mentioned as Sandhivigrahi. His father Komma, lord of Apperuvanguru and described as the protector of people, was probably the minister of Gonka I. Another minister was Kumma, grandson of Origandi Ramana.[28] Gantiya preggada alias Kanta was the occupant of the office of Mahaniyogapadavi. His father was minister Sridhara and one of his ancestors was Potana Somayaji the lord of Vanaramu in Vengidesa.[29] Gantiya received a palanguin, pretty parasols, and trampets and ministership from Gonka II. His younger brother Kuppa also was a minister of Gonka II. Amatya Komma, son of Itumanayaka, lord of Kurugallu in Ivanikandravati, was a bhritya, and Vasanapreggada was the pradhani and samasta senadhipati - of Gonka II.[30] Of the predecessors of Amatya Madhava, nama was a minister of Rajendra choda and Soma served king Viraperumandi. Choderaja, a samastabandhu chintamani and mahimechchuganda was another minister of Gonka II.[31] Surya preggada or Suryamatya, lord of Kantapu and son of Kantapuna Viddenapreggada, was the pradhani and rajadhyaksha of Gonka. Interested in the welfare of subjects, he is described as the bearer of the empire - samrajya.[32] Vallana and Isanapreggada, Sejjaprole nayaka, lord of Rajavrole were the ministers, Appana-matya was a Karyakhadgadurandhra, nallasurya preggada mantrirajadhyaksha and Amatyakamma, son of Govinda preggada - sandhivigrahi of Gonka II.[33] Prola, lord of Nelikutsa and an expert in royal polity was conferred with the regalia of a feudatory by the king.[34]

Kammaproadhani a warrior and ruler of Pakanadu 21000 was the chief among the ministers of Choda II.[35] Amritaluri Devana Preggada and Pasayiti Nannyapreggada were the pradhanis. Komma, son of Itamanayaks, and lord of Kurugollu and Damalur was a minister. Boolinayaka, son of Prolinayaka was appointed the minister of Guddavadivishaya by Choda II. Gonka III and Prithvisvara had few ministers. Kotana, son of Komma was a minister of Prithvisvisvara, his grandson Nanduri Gundamantri, is described as the ornament of ministers and praised by kings in courts.[36]

**Other officials:** References to the officials of the government are few till the reign of Gonka II.... Sena preggada was the Chamupati and Kavya Khadgadurandharah, and Muppanayaka was the dhamadhyaksha or bhandaru of Gonka II.[37] Prithari chintamanayaka and his son padihari Muttana and Kamatham Vasenayaka were the bhrityas of Gonka II. Kottari Erramaayaka of Kottaruva Errana, son of Kottari Nidubroli sabvinayaka, was the Koshtadhikari i.e. Koshtarayadhishta of Choda II.[38] Bhundari Mappinayaka and bhandaramu Nagi setti were the treasurer of Choda II.

**The Council:** The king's cabinet of which there is no clear evidence must have consisted of the king, premier, ministers, Cammander-in-chief, treasurer and chief officials at the centre, with the king as the apex. In the reigns of Gonka I and Choda I the interest of the Cholas in the kingdom continued, though not so vigorously afterwards. The kingdom formed a part of the Chola empire and the administration was carried on by viceroys of Vengi efficiently on their responsibility and the Velanandu kings were required to carry on the imperial behests. This explains the existence of few ministers and officials in these reigns. Under Gonka II, the Velanandu kingdom reached its widest limits, and the needs of a growing empire had to be met with a full - fledged system of administration at the centre and the provinces by the employment of several ministers and officials. Some of the official designations are pradhani and preggada, meaning minister and suffixed to names of ministers. Perhaps pradhani is Sanskrit and preggada - Telugu for minister. e.g. Govinda pradhani,Vasenapraggada, Rajyadhyksha or Rajadhyakasha president of the kingdom, perhaps refers to the president of the council. Sandhorigrahi is the minister for war and peace and the term Sandhivigrahimukhya seems to suggest the existence of the Chief Minister for war and peace, equivalent to mahapradhani. Ametya and mantri refer to ordinary ministers - Kanta was the occupant of Mahanipgapadavi - probably the minister in charge of high offices. Karyakhodgadudrandarah is perhaps the minister in charge of civil and military departments, similar to sandhivigrahi. Some minister were in charge of more than one portfolio. For Govindapreggada was the pradhani, rajadhyaksha and sana preggada was chamupati and karyakhadgadurandhara. Dhanadhyakasha, Koshtadhikari, Kottari and Bhandari - all mean superintendent of treasury.

**The Assembly:** Till the reign of Gonka II, the assembly in Vengi was summoned by the Chola emperors and their viceroys. Virachoda and Vikrama choda in their assemblies conferred regal insignia on Gonka I and Choda I and honoured Vedura II with 1/2 the throne - for their services. Generally the assembly met at the instance of the king for making grants, holding religious discourses, and discharge similar work. Choda II, according to the Appikatla inscription[39] assembled all the residents of Kammanativishya - namely the Rashtrakutas, prominent families and so forth and ordered his grant of land in the presence of mantri, purohita, pradhani etc. According to Panditaradhayacharitra,[40] Choda II held his court at Tsandavole, to which were invited people of all religious scholars, philosophers, logicians, experts in Kautilya sastras and so forth. It had been proclaimed in the city that even if one person was caught without going to the sabha, he would be considered disobeyer of the command. Feudatory rulers, amatyas, mantri, samanta, dandadhinatha and so forth, servant, soldiers, dancers, friends, servants, priests, princes, treasurers, cavalry men, slaves - assembled. Such was Rajasabha. The king's assembly which was recast into Brahma sabha-[41] by the king just before the proceedings began. Brahmasabha - perhaps an assembly of scholars, was constituted in this case, by giving more prominence to scholars, which was necesary for the agenda were not political matters but religious topics. Despite this change the public criticised that it was not a proper sabha as it consisted of only royal partisans, and there was no royal sabhapati[42] i.e. president of the assembly. The criticism shows that a sabha in those days was expected to comprise representatives of all parties and the president was to be a non party man. And when the rules were not strictly adhered to, even the king and his sabha did not escape criticism by their subjects. Choda's requisition of the compulsory presence of one and all in Tsandavole in the sabha was laudable practice recognising the rights of people by the king so early as the Velanandu days. The public criticism of the king's sabha speaks for the courage and democratic spirit of the people of the day. King Prithvisvara called together all the inhabitants of the district of Prolunandu, the rashtrakutas, ryots, and others and announced the grant of Navakhandavada by his mother Jayamahadevi to Kuntimadhava of Pithapur, in the presence of ministers, family priest, Commander of forces, heir apparent, doorkeepers and so forth.[43]

**Provincial Government:** The Governmental machinery of a province was a replica of the system at the contra. The provincial head, whether a feudatory chief, viceroy, governor or a prince, was assisted by ministers, council and assembly and officials in administering the province. The appointment as the head of a province was made by the king. Origandi Remana, the minister of Kulottunga I was placed in charge of Kammadesa.[44] In Choda II's reign, Bollinayaka was the minister of Guddavadivishaya. Provincial assemblies were convened sometimes by the king during his visits to some places in the provinces to temples and Brahmins. For instance, Choda II assembled the rashtrakutas and families of Cmginimarga vishya and ordered a grant in the presence of mantri, purohita, pradhani, etc., as noted elsewhere he assembled the people of Katmmànadu.[45]

**Local government:** Village had its officials who discharged their duties in a thorough and efficient manner. The village assembly had an important place in the affairs of its people at large Gramani or Reddi - both meaning headman and talari is watchman were some of the village officials. Jillama reddi was the gramani of Gautamaipura in Velanandu vishaya[46] and his grandson Vasena was the Adhyakaha in the reign of Gonka II Kammanayaka received the raddikam of Davulur from Choda II. Talari Muppa finds mention in record of Gonka II. Probably the village council consisted of the village officials and non-officials all important persons of the village. Mahajanas[47] in records is a reference to the assembly or sabha. The Kotappakada record to choda II records that a grant was entrusted to the mahajanas of Kavuru. His Pamalapadu inscription mentions the samastapraja - the entire population of Pamulapadu in Kondapadumati.[48]

Town in general, and those possessing fort, were ruled over each by a governor. In the reign of Gonka I, Dharani Kota was governed by prolinayaka.. Local groups of persons - military and mercantile - undertook sevaral works of public utility. An endorsement at Chebrole was left in charge of the sthanapati. 300 samis and 300 manis. The Nudurupadu inscription[49] mentions the nayakas of Ramki. The mention of Siripuram as - obviously - a territorial division of 12 villages with siripuram as the head quarters "reminds of the practice of Kannada inscriptions naming the local divisions together with their territorial extent, a practice not so commonly found in Telugu inscription."[50]

**The Capital:** The capital Dhanadapura or Tsandavole 18 miles from Repalle, is celebrated in ancient ballods and poems. It was the capital of the Ikshavakus and was either built or named after Dhanada of the Ikshavakus of Pratipalapura i.e. Pratipalapura in the 5th or 4th century B.C. By the time of the Velanandus, the historical significance of the name is superceded by puranic sanctity for it is often compared with the city of Dhananda i.e. Kubera in prosperity. Manchana speaks about the prosperity of the people of Tsandavole.[51] Srinatha[52] refers to the hall of audience of king. Dhavalasankha i.e. Gonka, at Tsandavole. People say that Tsandavole used to have a large number of temples and tanks. "There are solid masonry foundations of very extensive buildings." The coins found the pillars dug there attest the glory of Tsandavole in the past.

**Military administration:** Efficient army was the mainstay of the kingdom and was a necessary requisite for warfare. The military administration consisted of central, provincial and local departments commanded by a gradation of officials on a feudal basis. Apart from military aggrandisement for fame and acquisition of lands, self - protection was the motive behind army maintenance at any time. Tutered under Cholas, the Velanandus were aware of this principle. Forts were of strategic importance. Almost every village and town had a fort in which was located militia. The capitals chief and provincial were duly fortified. Some of the rains in the area attest the importance of forts as military strong holds in Velanandu times.[53]

**Central:** The kings were warriors, and the glory of a kingdom and prosperity of its people depended on the personal capacities of the rulers. Till the time of Gonka II, the Velanandu armies were maintained at a high level under the vigilant eye of the Imperial cholas. The capital attests Manchana, had good horses, elephants and samantas.[54] The omission of chariots and infantry speaks for their comparative insignificance in this period. Under Choda II the army was alert. For C.P. Charter[55] mentions that choda had the very best of horses and elephants and Manchana says that one hundred elephants always wandered in the nagari of choda and 40,000 swift horses were ever ready in his service.[56] Thus in the four traditional arms of the Indian army, the omnipotence of elephantry and cavalry was well reorganised in this period.

Generals and commanders were given lands as fiefs for their maintenance and lesser officials were allotted lands as salaries. In recognition of meritorious services, some officials were rewarded with regal insignia and lordship over vast tracks of land. Some of the ministers were the head of the army. For Sandhivgrahi Karyakhadgadurandhara and Samastasenadhipati were, obviously the heads of the portfolios in the military department e.g. Vasana preggada was the samastasenadhipati in Gonka II's reign. Some families were heriditarily employed in the army of the Velanandu choda. Of the Ayya family at Kroyyura, jilla, Narayana and Surya were in the service of Choda I. Under king's orders, narayana fortified the Dvipa i.e. Telagadadivi by building huge ramparts to it,[57] and was conferred with the worship over the dvipa and the Gontu villages for his military services. Jilla received from Choda I the dignity of a general and a palquin, parasel and other emblems.

Badapa and Gonkaiyan, brothers-in-law of Gonka II, Choda, Damana, Padavalu Choda, the governor of Shatsahasra and Vengi were some of Gonka II's generals. Sodamu Eriyamaboyadu, was an officer of Gonka II's Bayyapanayaka was the bhatagragmya of Gonka II.

Ministers, were generally warriors. Mandrana[58] gives a graphic description of the fighting capacities of Komma, minister of Choda II. He could pierce with nails, two or three horses at a time, pierce with altalas[59] and thus break the back of kings facing him, kill with his sword elephants as though they were sheep, and behead mohouts by his arrows, and make his elephan walk on their heads and those of kings; and break the heads of elephants in the battlefield. Damma, Muppinayaka, Guddavadi mudiseli Bhiminayaka, mudiseli Narayana preggada, padavalu gonka, mudili Ilundavada Suraph Reddi, Sadama[60] Proliya Boyi were in the army of choda II.

The army in the reign of Prithvisvara was efficient and the king could think of even undertaking expeditions of conquest.

**Provincial and local**: The provincial governor was the military head also. Officials corresponding to sandhivigrah; Karyakhadgadursndhara must have existed in the province also. Local military organisation was modelled after the central and provincial organisations. And similar gradation of officials - with their rights and duties must have existed. The local militia in villages and towns was maintained by the public partly for local defence and by royal subsidies and thus owe service to the king.

In Gonka II' reign, the soldiers (ekkalis) of a village made a grant. General Jaya prior to his subjugation to Ganapati of the kakatiyas, was in the service of the Velanandus. He was appointed the gajasahini, the chief of the elephant forces by Ganapati and conferred with a palanquin, parasol and other emblems of his office. He built a surrounding wall surmounted by towers to chebrole.

Most of the forests within the precincts of the kingdom, at present in ruins were built probably in the regime of the Velanandus. And in several cases, the ages of the forts and their builders are not preserved for us. Recorded tradition Kaifiyats of villages of these parts state that the local forts were built by the cholarajas or in chola regime or in the time of the cholas. That is the general indication for approximately fixing the age of the forts of that description. For with the decline of the Vengi chalukyas about the middle of the 11th century AD, the rule of the Imperial cholas in Andhra began, and all these forts were built under their suzerainty by the Velanandus, to defend the country from the invader, here the chalukyas of Kalyani. Hence Cholaraja, refer to the Imperial cholas.

**Irrigation:** The Velanandu chodas, being aspirants of their chola overlords evinced keen interest in building tanks, digging canals etc, tank building has religious sanctity and is ciphered sixth among the seven good acts of man. Many tanks are dedicated to temples. Tsandavole had many tanks. In Choda I's region Narayana I constructed two tanks.[61] Chodasamudram and Bhimasamudram at Telagadadevi and Vadlakurru. In Telagadadevi, the paddy and sugar cane fields are said to have been inundated by water from tanks in the vicinity. In the reign of Gonka II, Kamma dug many tanks, one of them being the huge tank Dronasamudra with high banks named after his father, at Narnapadur.[62] Maraya panda constructed many tanks. Saranaya, brother-in-law of Gonka II dug a tank at Chevaram, identified with Busavaripalem in Muktasvaram Sivar[63] (Narasaraopet taluq). Choda II donated three tanks. One at Siripuram and two at Marripudi in congini marge to Temple Silacheruvu at Konda Munjalur, Errameruvu at Kaza, Chodasamudram at Savalyapuram are mentioned in Choda II's inscriptions. Prithvisvara caused to be dug many big tanks. Nanduri Gunda mantri built many tanks. At Timmapuram was the tank - Brahmasamudram. The members of the Mandadi family dug many tanks at Sattanapalle. Canals were dug form the rivulets-pateru and Vareru, the tributaries of the Manneru flowing into the Krishna.[64]

**Agriculture:** Land was the primary source of income to the state agriculture was the main occupation of the bulk of the population and cultivators of the soil formed the wealth and man power of the kingdom. Land was classified into arable, pasture, for parks, gardens and so forth; and the arable land into wet, dry lands in accordance with its fertility and for purposes of raising a variety of crops. Lands, garden etc. donated to temples and Brahmins were exempt from taxation.

Prosperity and fertility of the Velanandu kingdom is attested by some records. One record says that the tract sindhuyugmantara possessed plenty of corn fields, fruit treess and another that Velanandu vishaya had many agraharas, corn fields and gardens.[65] The villages in the reign of Prithvisvara, had many fine trees.[66] Tsandavole had several parks, sugarcane gardens, and corn fields[67] laying of a upavana is one of the saptasantanas and this must have given the necessary incentive for people to lay parks. Tulagadadivi had extensive gardens teeming with trees of fruit and flowers, fields of paddy and sugarcane Gautamipura on the Godavari had many parks and gardens.[68] Navakhandavada near Pithapur had many fields and parks.

Fields some with millets and gingelly are mentioned in inscriptions. Gardens of arecanut, betel leaves, cocoanut and palmyra, with the number of trees specified in each case, existed in large numbers at attested by records. Choda II brought a site at Anantarama, sufficient for 100 arecanut trees and one of its bound was the garden of Kottaruvu Errama.[69] Kottaruvu Errana granted a site-pattu of 2000 arecanut trees in Anantarama to Bhimesvara, to be converted into a garden. Nagi sett's arecanut garden of 1500 trees. Ilindavada Surapa Reddi's gardens were in neighbourhood of Draksharama. A mango garden and Errama's garden of Cocoanut trees both at Bapatla Ilindavada Surapa Reddi's garden of 1000 trees to the west of Anantarama are mentioned.[70] All these gardens were in the neighbourhood of Draksharama. A mango garden and Errama's garden of cocoanut trees both at Bapatla and a palmyra grove at Siripuram are mentioned in Choda II's records.

**Transport**: Facilities of transport are esssential for movements of trade and armies. Under the Chola aegis, big trunk roads connecting different provinces of Vengi and Vengi with the chola capital are known as being used. No doubt the Velanandu chodas effected improvements in this direction. For without good roads and facilities of transport, they could not have vanquished the enemies inside and led expeditions of conquest and trade would not have flourished. Andharapathi was the road connecting the Telugu country with the southern kingdoms. Omginimarga, as the name itself suggests must have been a road connecting two provinces and gave its name to Omginimarga province.

**Trade and Commerce**: Trade and Commerce prospered. Important ports and foreign settlements within the kingdom were found; and a regular method of levying and collecting of taxes, tools, customs was followed. Internal and inland trade was organised by country wide merchant and trade gilds. The gilds were organised on communal basis, had rules regulations, held periodical meetings and undertook several activities of utilization nature. Foreign and overseas trade had royal patronage, and transport by water, waterways and mercantile marine must have existed in this period.

In this reign of Gonka II, his subordinates and those of Haihaya Kama, together assigned some taxes to the greatmen of Peddakodamagandla.[71] Probably the village was located on the border line dividing the two kingdoms. A grant of gold realised by selling salt from the salt pans (Uppalamulu) at Peddaganjam, Kondakaganjam, Kadakuduru, Upparatlu, Perali, Vayumdorru, and Kuravada was made by Gonka II and Tribhuvana malla C.M. at Konidena in AD 1152.[72] Thus the Velanandu and Telugu cholas had equal rights over the salt pana and their income in places mentioned above.

As for ports Nangegadda is mentioned in a record of Ganapati (1231 AD). The Ubhayamanadesis of the eighteen vishayas, made a grant at Nangegadda of a large fanam, as income on every boat touching at Nangegadda.[73] As Ubhayananadesi refers to the merchant community as a whole,[74] the translation "various inhabitants of eighteen districts (Vishayas) on both (sides of the Krishna)"[75] is wrong. Oplagangula, must have been another port of importance as suggested by its name. Probably located near Nangegadda, Odapangula was the port where ships could come close to shore, prior to the rise of Motupalli into prominence. Motupalle-- Muttili of Mareopolo[76] was the most important port in the entire coast towards the close of the Velanandu rule and remained thus till the beginning of the 19th century AD. It was the centre of considerable coasting trade and coasting vessels could come in closer to shore than at other ports on the coast.[77] Foreign trade prospered during the hey-day of the Velanandu chodas and contracted in volume, with their decline. Trade is sensitive to changes in political conditions, in any clime at any time the decline of the coastal trade on the fall of the Velanandus is nothing surprising. The causes operating were "the local rulers exacted from them (the traders) all kinds of extortionate dues under one pretext or another and were only too ready to turn their misfortunes to account by seizing whatever they salvaged from wreck."[78] This told adversely on foreign trade which was reduced in the prevalent unsettled political conditions. Merchants were not willing to risk their lives and wares in undertaking overseas voyages. Ganapati of the Kakatiyas by issuing the Motupalli charter[79] in AD 1244 on abhayasasana guaranteeing safety to foreign traders, whose vessels might be wrecked on the coast and promising that nothing but the usual customs duties would be levied on the articles. The traders included those starting for and arriving from all continents, islands, foreign countries, and cities and the cargo consisted of gold, elephants, horses, gems etc. From this time trade on the east coast prospered under the kakatiyas and the Reddis, and Anapotakondavidu issued a trade charter similar to Ganapati's in AD 1353. Peddapalle,[80] 4 miles from Nizampatam and 14 miles south - south-west of Repalle was probably a fort in the Velanandu times. At Ferangidibha or Pranguladibba, 14 miles south-west of Bapatla on the coast, was a foreign settlement Boswell notes[81] the tradition that there used to be a European colony probably Genoese and Venetian as far back as AD 1224 at Farangidibba. A dandakavile says that the portugese (or the Venetians) were at Farangidibba in AD 1240[82] - Sewell observes thus "It has been conjectured though as yet there is no proof forthcoming that previous to the visit of Marcopolo there had been Venetian and Genoese settlements on the coast. At any rate the establishment of a colony of some Europeans on the coast at Franguladibba (or Farangidibba) in very early days seems to be a matter of certainty. They traded in diamonds from the mines on the river west of Bezwada and in fine cloths."[83] Thus during the last years of Velanandu rule and twenty years prior to Ganapati's charter, from AD 1224 to 1244, there was a foreign settlement at Farangidibba. The name Farangidibba or Franguladibba - the mound of foreigners or Europeans i.e. Farangis designated thus by the natives, as Muslims by the name Yavanas, supports the existence of the settlement there. Probably by the time of Marcopolo's visit to Motupalli in AD 1293.[84] Faringidibba lost its importance as it missed his attention.

Partiyala, 17 miles north of Bezwada and some other villages forming a small block are the old diamond villages. At Nalavalle and Boravamcha are some old diamond mines. As Marcopolo refers to trade in diamond and fine cloths at Motupalle, probably these mines were worked in the period.

Some merchants designated as the settis of kings in records were probably required to supply all the articles necessary for the royal house hold. Bhimisetti, Kamanasetti, and Bhattiproli Proli setti were the settis of Gonka II.

**Coinage, weights and measures:** The Velanandu chodas had a good variety in coins, weights and measures, their names, metals used and so forth. The names are significant being those of gods. Titles of kings indicating some events in their lives. In the words of Professor Sastri "Gold gadyana is a coin of 58 grains, the heaviest revealing 60.1 grains, with the growth of the chola empire the currency system of the colas extended over the whole empire including its feudatory provinces. The new standard was adopted for instance in the Vengi country about 1000 AD."[85]

The earliest Velanandu coin we hear of is the Jayamada[86] issued by Gonka I. Its issue was to signify some outstanding victory of his, as the name - victory coin implies or the establishment of the Velanandu kingdom. By Gonka II's time, the number of coins increased. For birudugadyas, Kulottunga gadyas, birudumadas, chamaramadas, gadyas and chinnams are mentioned in his records. Birudugadyas and birudumadas are issued by Gonka II perhaps after some victory. Kullottungagadyas are named after emperor Kulottunga II and the chamaramadas probably are meant to commemorate some donations to temples or king's coronation. Records of Choda II mention rukas, chamaramadas, Tyagigadyas, the last mentioned being the coins of the Chagis, the feudatories of the Velanandus. The Ganapesvaram record issued towards the close of Velanandus - rule mention peddachinnam (large famam).

As for the weight and value of the coins, Chinnam is worth 1/8 of a pagoda or 7 annas, mada is equivalent to a nishka, and is worth 1/2 pagoda or two rupees, 1/2 varsha. The plural of mada Madalu means money-in general.[87] Ruka is a silver coin, sometimes equal to two annas and sometimes to four annas. Generally it refers to two anna piece, and the plural - rukalu means money in general.[88] In the light of Professor Sastri's definition of Gadyamu, cited above, its definition as "an obselete coin like a forthing equal to 1/4 or 1/5 or the paikamu - dinaru, a varaha"[89] is in correct. A study of the Jaya, bimda, Kulottunga and chamara coins could be interesting if they are available.

The chebrole inscription of Gonka I mentions the manike measure named Mahasenamu. Mana, adda and1\2 mana find mention in the records of Gonka II; and Tribhuvanamkusanemana Kottaruvu Nandi Kunchamu, Padi, Talalenidandimanika and so forth are mentioned in Choda II's records. Of these measures Mahasenamu is named after god Kumaraswami at chebrole.

Tribhuvanakusa after one of the titles of chalukya Bhima I, and Kalaleni dandi manika is the big measure with an edge at the top. Mana or Manika is a dry measure equal to 1/16 part of a tum and 1/4 of a Kunchamau. Adda is also a dry measure equal to 2 manikas or 1/8 part of a tum Visamu is 1/16 of any measure Chinnam is 1/30 part of a tola.[90] Putti, Khanduka, na, and tum are the land measures mentioned in records. "The putti is the Indiant on weight equal to 20 tums" "The putti and its fractions also denote the extent of land that produces this quantity of grain"[91] Na may be an abbreviation of Na vama (a fur long). Tum is equal to 4 kunchams." Khandi is form 800 to 1000 seers and ciphered Kha" and Kha or Khandi is a measure called Kandy and an abbreviation of Putti.[92]

Taxes, industries etc; 3/4 the Peddakodamagandla inscription[93] mentions Yerana preggada, the mudisali of Gonka I and the taxes - Vaddaravalamu, perusunkamu, Vaddaravalamu biravalamu Biravelu, Boddana bhimanakolchivasamulu.[94] and biranansuslu all raised with in the bounds of the village (Urivaloyamu). The Voddaravula tax find mention in inscriptions of the chalukyas of Kalyani. In the reign of Vikramaditya VI Anantapala was in charge of Vaddaravela tax of 7(1\2) lakh country[95] Gonka II's record at Visvanathuni Khandrika mentions Bhujabalamuttalu. Parikha parika or Perika is mentioned in Velanandu inscriptions and "is a sack which opens in the middle each end is filled with grain and it is laid across a bullock."[96] Ganapati's Motupalle charter mentions Kupasulka which "perhaps corresponds to modern custom house duties."[97]

Precious metals were used in jewellery and baser metals in industries.

**The Haihaya Kingdom of Konamandala**

The prasasti of the Konamandala Haihayas is imperialistic and they claimed lordship over Vengimandala. Dual kingship lasting for generations together was the unique feature of their administration. Kondamandala or Konasima, the deltaic country of the Godavari is very fertile. Kona[98] means a valley or doab country which is generally fertile and such tract about the

Godavari is the Konasima or mandala. "At Dowleishvaram the Godavari is divided into two large streams- the east flowing past yanam and Nilapalle and falling into Bay of Bengal near Cape Gordewa over Godavari and west flowing nearly due south entering the Bay at point Nursapur. A few miles above this mouth, another large branch separates from the river and falls into the bay near Bendamurlanka forming the island of Nagaram. This rich delta[99] of insular shape constituted Konamandala kingdom of the Kona Haihayas. Mackenzie MS: mention that the strip of land about 12 miles far east of Pittapur dying between the shore of the sea and the villages of Ponnada, Tondangi and Vanavaram which extends in length from north to south about 20 miles and varying in breadth between a mile and two at different places - is called Kona.[100] As the kona rulers[101] made grants in Guddanadinadu and Guddevaivishaya probly Konamandala formed a part of Guddavadinadu.

**Government:Central King** whatmade the Kona Haihayas embark on double rule, deliberately is not clear from their records. It was not a measure to strengthen the kingdom against foreign attacks, for the kingdom is located in an insular corner, far from expeditions: and history reveals that even when liable to foreign attacks, generally kingdoms did not institute dual kingship, though joint rule to strengthen the kingdom in the beginning and end of a reign and at times throughout a reign is not rare. Generally the Kona kings followed bigamy and had many sons. Dual kingship was invented perhaps to prevent fricton between rival brethren for the throne resulting in civil wars ruinous to the kingdom and people. This gains support from the part that race initiated with the rule of two brothers with mothers different, dual kingship rolled on smoothly every time the two kings representing the two lines - elder and younger, whether the particular relationship was that of father son, brother, cousin and son. Thus dual kingship assured safety and prosperity to the kingdom and people freedom from internal struggles and blessed a long lealse of life to the dynasty. According to Hindu idea, a sovereign was entrusted with sovereignty in entirety which was therefore indivisible and divine in origin." This would make it quite impossible to conceive of two kings with equal power each having the right to question and modify the action of the other"....But it was such dual kingship that prevailed in Konamandala for several generations. "Dual kingship may roughly be taken to be the conjoint constitutional exercise of the sovereign power by two persons in a state."[102] The Konamandala kingdom was never divided, for no two dynasties were founded and ruled separately as in the case of the Velamas of Rachekonda after Anapota's reign, the Kotas after Kot II's reign and the Haihayas of Palnad after the reign of Aluguraja. The Pittapur pillar inscription says "Bhima II and Satya I again (?) divided the earth (?) and ruled (it) conjointly. "They were succeeded by Loka and Bhima III who were followed by Mallideva and Vallabha; and they by Mallideva and Manmasatya II whose successors were Rajaparendu II and Bhima III.

The throne, partidhakka, peococks's tail, spear single couch were the regal insigns of the Kona Haihayas. They were conferred by Rajendra choda on the grandfather Kona Rajendra choda. Kona Rajendra choda inherited them and was a good administrator, and enlightened ruler and his subjects were happy. He is said to have acquired the title Haihyaditya by enforcing all the rules of conduct for each of the inhabitants of the kingdom.[103] The rule of Satya I and loka was popular.

**Ministers:** Chodaya, Risiyana preggada and Kesanapreggada, the ministers of Satya I are heard of from a Draksharama epigraph[104].(AD 1150) - Suraps Reddi, son Madhurantaka Singi Reddi and rajadhyakha of Kona Satya II figures in a Palakol inscription of AD 1207.[105] In this period, the ministers were generally Brahmins. But the Kona Haihayas, for reasons not known to us employed non Brahmin ministers.

**Council and assembly:** There was no references to the council of the Kona Haihayas. References to the assembly are few. In AD 1198 Mallideva and Satya II conjointly called together the Rashtrakutas and all the ryots of the district of Guddavadi and ordered their grant of Odiyur free from all taxes in Guddavadi.[106]

**Local Government:** The Kona kingdom was not extensive to have been divided into provinces. Local administration must have been efficient towns and villages were each governed by a head man and the village council and sabha.

**Military administration:** The safe location of the kingdom and the Velanandu suzerainty assuring protection, probably, made it unnecessary to maintain vast army. Dandanayaka Mandana and Dandanayaka chodaya, were the generals[107] of Satya I Bantu (soldier) Kesanaya is known from an inscription of Bhima III. The kona army in the reign of Lika must have been efficient for he undertook expedition of conquest.

**Irrigation and Agriculture:** In this kingdom, land was fertile, nature bountiful and water plentiful. Few tanks find mention in records. Uppucheruvu and Racheruvu are mentioned in a record. Some gardens of the period are known. Satya I granted a garden plot located in the fields of Krundhuti.[108] Odiyuru had plenty of gardens - The garden of Kona Bhimaraja was one of the bounds of the arecanut garden donated by Choda II at Anantarama in the vicinity of Draksharama.

**Coins, weights and measures:** The coins birudumadas are mentioned in a record of Loka at Bapatla and gandamadas in the Palakol inscription of Satya II. The biruda made is obviously a Velanandu Coin as Bapatla was included in the Velanandu kingdom and Gandamadas were issued probably by Satya II.

Tribhuvanamkusanetimana, Nandimanike, and Nanditumu are the measures mentioned in records at Palakol and Draksharama Khandea, Putti and acre were the land measures in vogue. The grants of house sites with dimensions specified is a common feature of the Kona Haihayas records. A palakol epigraph gives the dimensions - length ten mullu and width seven mullu of a house site.[109] Mullu obviously was a measuring rod, whose length is not mentioned in records.

**Taxes and industries:** With Samatayas i.e. all income including antariya and so forth and free from sarvakara i.e. all taxes some land donated in AD 1153.[110] More details about taxes and revenue are not mentioned in the record. Odiyuru with all its houses, fields and gardens was exempt from taxes. Khundapalli was granted free of taxes by Padmavati queen of Bhima, in AD 1228. Industries prospered. Rajavrolu, Jadikuppa and Rajaraja koli[111] are mentioned in a record. Koli is probably a corrupt form of Kolimi i.e. furnace used for melting metals. It was called after Rajaraja, a name borne by the Imperial cholas and the Kona Haihayas.

**The Haihaya Kingdom of Panchadharala**

This Haihaya kingdom was located in Madhyadesa - the country between the Vindhyas and the ocean.[112] In some records Madhyadesa is applied, to the tract between the Ganges and the Jamuna whereas in the Velanandu inscriptions - sindhuyugmantara - also Madhyadesa refers to the tract between the Krishna and the Godavari. Thus Madhyadesa is applied to more than single tract in India and Madhyades of the Haihaya and Velanandu records differ from each other and from the more commonly accepted tract many records in the north and south. The panchadharla kingdom was small and the administrative system was neither elaborate nor significant.

**Government**: The rulers were good warriors and administrators. King choda III entitled Rajarajesvara, was virtuous and spread law in his kingdom. The Panchadharala pillar inscription poetically says that choda displayed the splendour of a Rajahamsa, was praised by the world and under his rule, the earth became an ever blossoming lotus field (and obtained) perpetual joy. This choda III is said to have made perfect use of the four royal sciences in reasoning, fulfilling religious duties, helping people and destroying enemies.[113]

Few ministers of the kingdom are heard of. The Haihayas must have had an adequate army, for king Choda III and Choda III led expeditions of conquest and won victories. Forts must have been cared for. Administration of justice was efficient. Choda III well versed in law was the enforcer of justice in the Kingdom.

Irrigation and agriculture must have received the attention of the government as necessity demanded. Few tanks and parks find mention in records. A part in Panchadharala is said to have contained the Jambila (rose apple), coconut, plantain and mango trees. The Panchadharala pillar inscriptions say that nourished by Choda III, the trees in the part at Panchadharala flourished as if they were five Kalpa trees descended from heaven to witness his liberality.[114] The Coin Gandanada figures in a record of choda III and was current also in the kingdom of Konamandala.

**The Gona kingdom of Vardhamanapura**

The rule of the Gonas was beneficient to the people. The extent of their kingdom is not seen clearly from their records. Probably it comprised part of Nalgonda, Panugal and Mahboobnagar taluqs (Nalagonda district).

**Government King:** The Gonas ruled righteously for the local of the people. Obviously their government was modelled on that of their over lords - the kakatiyas. Their ideal was Rama and Ramarajya and they rendered the entire Ramayana into Telugu. Ranganatha Ramayana says that Dasaratha was the ruler of people and that if was the dharma of a king to protect the world.[115] Sri Rama, even as Yuvaraja ruled in the interest of the people. Buddha Reddi describes the fitness of Rama to rule when Dasaratha decided on his enthronement pattabhisheka. In the questionnaire of Rama to Bharata[116] about Government we get all the requisites of a good government - that a king should respect his parents, teachers, protect fires at twilight times, know the behaviour of ministers, use of mantra, think of money daily at midnight, behave properly before people, and use force when the people are in the wrong. The Commander of the armies should be a devotee of the king, salaries to the servants should be disbursed regularly in their presence, get at the news about provinces and enemies through spies listen to the complaints of people with patience and humility, punish thiefs, chaturangabala should be ever ready, Gadidurgas - forts should be ever fall with money, corn, articles and soldiers, taxation on tillers of the soil should not be heavy, no money - not even 1/2 visa - should be taken from the agraharas, desire the welfare of Brahmins and cows and should possess, saktitaraya, shadguna, panchangu, chaturupaya, know the 14 sins of his subjects reach him, untimely deaths occur in the kingdom, and when he does not punish the suppressor of dharma, he gets one fourth of his sins and goes to hell.[117]

Of the Gonas, Kata was a warrior whose feet are said to have been worshipped by his foes. King Rudra was a Rudra in valour, purity and mind. Buddha I was courageous and prosperous. Vithala is described as a manumurti, kind, rich, dutiful, a sun to the eastern hill and moon to the milk ocean i.e. Gananvaya, verses in sama, bheda, etc. and enjoyer of regal splendour. He is said to have been praised in the courts of Kuru, Kuntala, Avanti, Ghurjara, and Dravila, bore the epithets arigandabhairava, and misaraganda and was a great warrior.[118] Inscriptions show that he also known as Ganna ruling from Vardhamanapura was bold, charitable daring, bore the pendara anklet and was a Revanka in horsemanship. Buddha II was a soldier and scholar, versed in puranas, and arts and pleaser of his subjects.[119] Of Kancha and Vithala, Kacha bore the title - Misaraganda, like his father.

**Ministers:** According to Ranganatha Ramayana, Dasaratha had eight ministers who acted together and protected people. It says that a king acting with the approval of his ministers would reap good results.[120] Gona Ganna's chief ministers was Vithala his own brother. Vithala is described as the rajyarakshamani, the jewel amulet of his kingdom, protector of people, aware of his duties, possessor of good qualities and the ruler of the kingdom of Raichur.[121]

**Assembly:** One or two references to the sabha in the Gona kingdom are found. In the Raichur inscription, Ganna is described as holding pleasant conversations with his feudatories at Vardhamanapura. The sabha of Vithala comprised as cholas in puranas, Sastras, Kanyas, and dramas, favourites, minister, priests, subordinates, princes and feudatory chiefs.[122] Vithala is described as Rajasarvajnor Rajasimha and Rajasiromani.

**Military administration**

The military administration of the Gonas was adequate, for as feudatories of the Kakatiyas they had to constitute substantively in men and money to their overlords. An epithet of Ganna is equipper of the kakatiya army. Vithala was the commander-in-chief of Gona armies and conquered the forts of Advani, Tumbulam, Manuva and Haluva.[123]

The importance of forts was realised by the Gonas. For Vithala built a fort at Raichur for the protection of the people of all the provinces in the kingdom Buddha in Ramayana mentions four kinds of arms and seven kind of forts.[124]

The Gonas were learned in the ethics of war. Buddha explains it in the words of Rama. Rama says[125] that Kshatriayas while on move bear arms to protect those who ask for it, an immoral person and an enemy of his friend could be killed and that ranadhàrama demands that the persons in hinding, those who flee, blow, admit defeat, eat grass lose their weapons, and are asleep, should not be attacked and their safety should not be desired by the enemy.

The weapons used in war mentioned in the Ramayana[126] are - parasu, tomara, kumba, pattanuprasa, parighosha, mudgura, sakti, musala, pattisa, trisula, karavala, bhindivala, pisa, chakra, sula, sriya, ankusa, sabalam, parigna, pattan etc. These names show that there was a good variety in swords, spears, lances, clubs and so forth.

**Justice**: In administering Justice, the Gonas were inspired by high ideals. Uttara Ramayana says that the king's right of punishment is supreme and there is no punishment even by yama over that of the king i.e. Jagatisa (lord of the world). People load righteous lives out of fear of king's punishment, and when they deviate from dharma, they should be punished. Dharma demands the protection of the sinner though a good person need not be protected. An ambassador enjoys freedom of speech.[127]

**Irrigation and agriculture**: Tanks were dug in this period and agriculture was cared for. Malyala Gundaya built a tank in the vicinity of Budapur in AD 1259, and called it Bassamudram after his mother Bachasani.[128] In AD 1262 he built a tank locally and named it Ganapasamudram after Ganapati of the Kakatiyas. Kuppasamudram mentioned in the Budapur record of AD 1256, is obviously named after Kuppama.

Probably the coinage of the Kakatiyas their weights and measures were in vogue in the Gona kingdom. Buddha in Ranganatha Ramayana mentions Visa and arevisa,[129] the coins - In the Gona kingdom, perhaps land surveys for assessment of revenue, on the Kakatiya model were conducted.

### The Haihaya kingdom of Palnad

The administration of the Haihaya kingdom of Palnad presents some unique features namely dual kingship as in the case of Konamandala Kaihayas, division of the kingdom between brothers as in the case of the Kotas, a lady minister at the head of the kingdom and the heriditary ministers were sudras. The tract where the Haihaya kingdom flourished, commonly known as Palnad, appears as Palinadu, Palinadu, Pallidesa and Palnad. In Telugu literature, the form Palnadu is common, except in a chatuverse of Srinatha mentioning Pallenatisima.[130] The explanations offered so for the names are thus - 1. as it has several small villages it came to be known as Pallenadu[131] 2. Milk land-Palanadu - because of abundance of light cream coloured marble. 3. Palunadu[132] as it has many kinds of soil. 4. as the tract was surrounded by high hills, in the middle it was of low level and so was known as Pallunadu, which changed into Palmnad, Palanadu and Palnadi.[133] 5. it became famous as Pallavanadu when occupied by the Pallavas during the rule of Andhras, and later on came to be known as Palnadu and Palnadu.[134] All the explanations are based on the considerations of topography of the country and are partially true. But none of them is fully correct for the forms Palanadu and Pallavanadu are not found, the third view is poetical and the fourth, if to be accepted, the term ought to have been Pallapunadu as Pallapugudravara and so forth and not Pallunadu. The first mentioned view is most sensible. Virabhadra mentions Palnad five desas which suggests that it probably comprised five divisions.

**Government King:** Rajaraja and Beta II exercised joint sway till AD 1129 and afterwards Beta II ruled singly till AD 1134. Ahuguraja adopted as son Badaraja alias Peddanna, son of minister Doddanayadu and married a princess of Kshatriya lineage to him. After the birth of several sons to Alugu, the right of succession of Bada was set aside in favour of Virakama or Nalagama,[136] the eldest of Anugu's sons. Nalagama was crowned by Brahmanayadu, second son of Dodda, on the death of Anuga, which was a murder according to one version and ruled for forty years. So far the kingdom of Palnad was one, ruled by the Haihayas with capital at Gurizala. Sometime in the reign of Nalagama the kingdom was divided into two consequent on the rivalry between Brahma and Naqakuralu, the ministers of Nalagama more than the rivalry between the step brothers. For Brahma favoured mallidevas. Peda, Pina and Bala and secured part of the kingdom for them, built Macherla - the capital and ruled till the princes were of ripe age. Then he enthroned Pedamallideva who thus became the first ruler of the Macherla kingdom. Yerakama and his three[136] brothers stayed away at Gurizala with Nalagama.

These Haihayas rulers were great warriors and enlightened administrators. By benificent rule and sacrificing their lives in the fratricidal war, they became endeared to the people, commanded their administration, and deified by them who built towns, temples, drew pictures and wrote songs. Their administration was of the first order and people could approach rulers with their grievances and get them redressed.

**Ministers:** The number of ministers was small, which factor must have strengthened the position of the family of hereditary ministers, who unlike in other kingdoms, were the defacto rulers and were responsible for everything that happened in the kingdom - good and evil. The kings did according to the wishes or dictates of the ministers.

The Kuntala family or Recharla gotra and velama community[137] among the sudras were the hereditary ministers of the Haihayas of Palnad. The earliest member known so far as Jatinayudu. His son Doddanayadu, was the minister of Alugurya and a warrior. One day with Teppalinayadu, Dodda went on an hunting expedition and halted in the vicinity of Narlakonda. A cultivator there presented them some seods to be given to the king. Palnativiracharitra says[138] that the king gave them to the queens, who wanted more and so Teppali raided the field, and got many more and returned to Gurizala. The ryotas complained to their lord who sent a threatening letter to the king. Then Dodda and Teppali invaded Narlakonda, fought a battle, killed the chief, occupied the country and returned victorious to Gurizala. Dodda brought about Alugu with the Velanandu princes. His two sons were Badanna and Brahmanayadu. By securing the favour of the king, Navakaralu became the opponent of Dodda. Prompted by her, Alugu quarelled with Dodda who resigned his premiership in favour of Brahma. On the death of Alugu and Dodda, Brahma became the Chief person in the kingdom of Nalagama. Another version mentions Narasimha,[139] the second son of Bhurama as the successor. Brahma is said to have installed him, probably as crown prince and anointed Nelagama as king. In the kingdom, Narasimha was second only to Nalagama, and this explains Virabhadra's frequent references to him as king and the kingdom as that of Narasimha. Nayatiuralu became the chief adviser of Nelagama and Narasimha and made them distrust Brahma.

Brahmanayadu was a warrior and administrator of great capacities. Vira charitra describes some of his achievements. He vanquished at Aranagandla the kings of eight directions, who challenged him, took their Kuntam and received tributes from them.[140] This battle is said to have been fought between Uttaresvara, king of Dharanikota the kings supporting him and Aruguraja[141] and Brahma fighting on Alugu's behalf proved victorious. Aranagandla is in the neighbourhood of Amaravati and king Uttarasvara is yet to be identified for Dharanikota in this period was the capital of the Kotas. Brahma, is said to have accompanied Virasamesvara of Kalyani in the expedition against king Sivagangaraju of Sivapuri, captured the Citadel, carried off the pillar - Bhutaratsthambha and installed it at Tripurantakam.[142]

Brahma administered the kingdom in the interest of his subjects. When Nayakuralu began misgoverning to the detriment of the people, he threw off allegiance to the kingdom and left Gurizala with Mallideva brothers and the inhabitants of ninety villages built Macherla, divided the kingdom between the brothers and became their joint minister with full powers. He was truthful, frank and wise and was victim of the vicious plots of Nagamma many times. Brahma's visit to Gurizala was to give presents to Nalagama and his brothers, as Alugu prior to his death entrusted all his children to Brahma. But Nayakuralu poisoned him, enraged him to become a party to cock fight and by a trick managed these Brahma's cock was defeated. According to the terms of the wager, the vanquished should spend seven years in exile. So Brahma left Macherla with Mallideva brothers, settled at Mandali where he carved out a kingdom for Pedamallideva. Even there they were not free from Nagamma's tricks. So they left it, reached Srisailam secured a lease some villages from the Bikshavaittis, the rulers Srisailam tracts, built Viramedapi and spent their exile there.[143] According to one version, Brahma told his history to Makaraja, ruler of Sri Sailasimas, and asked for a loan of one crore of gold coins by mortgaging his sword. Makaraja did not agree to it but instead gave 23 villages for rent,[144] all of which are located in the eastern portion of Markapur taluq (Kurnool district) some being Markapuram, Dupadu, Chepalamadugu, Kolakulam, Ambasamudram, Ganapavaram, Tripurantakam and Medapi. On the expiry of the period of exile, Brahma sent an ambassador to Gurizala, demanding Macherla kingdom, which was refused and the ambassador was killed by Nagamma's plots. Then followed the civil war. As minister of Pedamallideva Brahma did everything on his own responsibility. For during his visit to Gurizala, in the wager he started the kingdom and there is nothing to indicate that Mallideva was aware of it or questioned Brahma on his return. Probably Brahma, a veteran minister and statesman was entrusted by the king and people with full powers in internal dealings and foreign policy of the kingdom. Ultimately Brahma won the battle of Karempudi, killed corruption, enthroned Nalagama, established dharma and won immortal fame. By his wife Itamma, of the Gandu family.[145] Brahma had a son Balachandra. He had another son Kannamadas.

Aravilli Nagamma, celebrated as Nayakuralu was the daughter of Chandari Rani Reddi of Jittagamalapadu on the banks of Nagileru. She was wealthy and gained influence in the court of Alugu. She came round Narasimha by a clever trick. She plased him by providing comforts when he was tired after a hunting expedition. She desired to rule the kingdom for a few hours which request the king conceded. So on their return to Gurizala, she ruled for a while, issued secret orders, plundered the country side, got plenty and told the king that sum he should receive if the kingdom was properly governed.[146] She made Narasimha decree the death of Mallideva and his brothers, brought about the division of the kingdom, sent bands of robbers to rob the Macherla kingdom and managed the banishment of the princes and sent robbers even to Mandadi. Six months after the expiry of exile when Alaraja was sent to demand Macherla kingdom with six months tax due to them,[147] the terms were refused and the ambassador was killed in a Brahmin house at Chelagudipadu on his return journey, as prearranged by Nagamma. Thus she brought about the final battle at Karempudi. But just before it began, she sent an embassy to Brahma asking for terms of peace and promising to surrender Narasimha whom Brahma's partisans had sworn to kill in the battle. But then it was too late for treaty making for though the elders were hesitating, the youngsters are determined on war.[148] The end is not known. Some that she lost her life in the battle, others that she was vanquished and committed suicide or fled and was pardoned by Brahma.

We hear of few other ministers and no references to the council and assembly in the two Haihaya kingdoms are available.

**Kings Court:** King's Court is held daily perhaps at fixed hours do discharge daily duties and at other times when necessity demanded e.g. to receive embassies. When the king on move and on the eve of battle, court is held at places other than the capital and in military camp. Irinatha describes Nalagama's court at Gurizala which was summoned to receive Ranabhattu,[149] the ambassador of Pedamallideva. The ambassador informed the king of his arrival. At the king's instance, the court was decorated and a gemstudded golden throne was kept in it. The king gargeously dressed, accompanied by music came and sat on the throne, Narasinga sat next to him, and Nagamma was humble on one side. King's relatives sat second to him and next were seated priests and scholars and ministers of other kingdoms were seated in front. After enjoying dance and music, the king sent for the ambassador who came riding on a horse, elighted, stood in front of the king addressed him sentioning his titles, explained him the object of his visit and advised him to conclude peace with Mallideva by surrendering Narasimha. When Nalagama replied that he would give back the Macherla kingdom, Nagamma whispered the king they should accept the challenga for battle, for there should not be two kings in one kingdom.[150] Then Nalagama spoke to Ranabhattu underestimating the armies of Mallideva, and Ranabhattu replied asserting the strength of Mallideva's troops.

Nayakurala threatened to kill the ambassador and asked him to inform Mallideva that they werereadyforbattle.[151]Mallideva in the military camp at Karempudi assembled the court to receive the embassy comprising Kanche Annamaraju, Madugula Vira Reddi, Chintapalli Reddi and Kota Keta - the elders and confidential advisers of Nalagana led by Keta. The ambassadors on their arrival at Mallideva's court, took their seats at the request of the king and Keta explained the object of their visit when asked by Brahma.[152] The heroes wanted war but were convinced by Manmaraja that an offer of peace should never be rejected. Then suddenly Balachandra appeared in the court, wanted to see the king, and when not given way jumped over the seated and bowed to the king who turned away. Then Bala exclaimed whether he was in the wrong. Then Kannama stoop up, she sheathed his sword, addressed the sabha disapproving the way Bala entered the court and asked him to quit. Bala replied that in his anxiety to see the king he was right in using his force.[153] He questioned the propriety of their arrival into the midst of the enemy, and bringing the king with them, and pacified Kannama. The king forgot his statement that he would avenge the enemy with in three months and wandering in forests and eating green vegetables in plenty after the loss of the kingdom he was tired, green juice reached his eyes and so unable to speak was in need of good medicine. Gandukannamand, father-in-law of Bala, said that both parties were in the wrong having committed five mistakes each and the king not be blamed as he did not commit them. Bala addressed the heroes one by one asking them to get ready for the battle.[154] Then Brahma stood up, welcomed his son mates and explained them the treaty terms. Kannama said it is a sin to kill an enemy in their hands. When all decided on concluding a treaty and cement it by interdining, the sabha was dissolved.

**Espionage:** Spies employed by the Government existed in both the kingdoms in Macherla. Vegulavandru and Kettikandru moving with the armies were spies. Nayakuralu sent Ellidú to spy the kingdom of Macherla. He was taken to the court of Mallideva, was shown round the kingdom and set free by Brahma. On returning to Gurizala, the spy gave glowing accounts of the Macherla kingdom.[155] There was an Erukalasani at the battle field whocouldpredict[156]and was met by Brahma and Kannama.

**Polity and public opinion:** Ethics of war and peace demand complete protection to the ambassador, for he is free from political bias and spirit of partisanship harm an ambassador is the greatest sin it is on that point that usually wars are declared e.g. Palnad war. Obviously aware of his sure position, that generally ambassadors indulge in speeches of ethics of war and peace and display their wisdom, tact and knowledge in bringing about treaties. Ranabhattu explains rajaniti thus[157] many people increase enmity but none suppress it. So surrender Narasinga and rule in enity. War is never good, for the country gets ruined, people destroyed or the treasury becomes bankrupt, armies lifeless, small servants demand fat salaries, the relationship of master and servant gets lost, and they do not discharge their duties well.[158]

**Village Sabhas:** The village sabhas besides deciding on matters on local importance participated in affairs ofsupreme importtance to the state e.g., war and peace and led representations to the King. When Nalagama going to Karempudi[159] halted for the night at Kadamagandla, the citizen of the villages, and the big Reddis of neighbouring villages and the Vaisyas led a deputation to the king requesting him to give up fight. They said, "To rule with no enmity is strength to your happiness to people, and reduces the number of enemies. You have been protecting us as though we were your children, and if you fight and die in the battle foreigners would sway us. Under your rule, evil doers are scared, good people are happy, lives are safe, and taxes are taken at high rates." The king asked them to return homes and be happy. This representation of people shows that people had a right of questioning the action of the king, and he had to give them a patient hearing and reply suitably. Mention of the boundaries of Miriyala and Chintapalle[160] shows that the villages in Palnad had clearly marked boundaries.

**Military administration:** Army was all important to the Haihayas. Viakama's title - Rajadhiraja, rajavesyavitaprabhava prakara, and gandaraganda attest to his capacities as warrior. Nagamma, minister of Viragama had confidence in her capacities and the strength of the armies of Gurizala kingdom. When she underestimates the strength of the enemy, Nalagama says that they should get ready with huge armies for enemies when weak and poor risk their lives and fight hard.

As for the military resources of the kingdom,[161] treasuries and granaries were full, and armies were huge and strong consisting of soldiers, manna chiefs feudatories, mercenary troops cultivators, huants men; bowmen, cavalry men and so forth. With Nagamma, Nalagama visited the stables and inspected the horses which were decked with mails, arrows quivers, swords and bows all hung in their necks, besides knobs, tessels, and gold bells anklets on feet and velvet pattas on faces. The king ordered the classification of the houses, and presented pretty cloths to the horsemen. He inspected elephants also and arranged that huge chances were to be carried in carts, and heavy articles and tents by oxen, camels, and donkeys.

On the advise of Nagamma, Nalagamma sent invitations to several kings asking them to come and join with their armies at Karempudi to fight Brahma to whom they were paying tribute. Vir charitra sasys[162] that the invitees that together and decided to side Nalagam as a he promised to remit the payment of further tribute. The movement of Nalagama and his armies is well described by Ṣrinatha. The armies occupied a space of 100 dandas. The elephants and horses were on the flank of the king, and Nagamma was on his right riding on a horse. On reaching Karempudi, tents were raised for the armies. A pillar with a golden lion at its top was held in front of the king when he took his seat in the sabha there. The armies were located in the valley bounded by hillson all sides with Nagileru in the vicinity. The bounds of the camp were the villages. Gurvalakallu and Sannagandla on the east, Nagileru and southern portion of Nalgonda on the south, Voppicherla on the west, Kodamagundla and prajala melimidimtapalle on the north. Some important places on the boundaries were - temples of Jannidevara, mansion of Savanala, tank of Singabhupati, temples of Sangadi, Uttaresvara, pillar of swing, and so forth. The armies touched all these points and Nalaganda and Nagileru.[163] The army generals were - Banjala Brahma on the west, Sankoji Ganapati on the east Nayakuralu on the south Andala Rama, Mummadi Reddi and Voramalla on north.[164]

At Macherla, as soon as decision of war was taken, the crown prince Bahmallideva was crowned king at Medapi with Balachandra as Minister. Anapolu as chief officer. Huge armies carrying tents, boxes, cots, planks, spittoons, parasols and treasures were carried with the armies. Pedamalle, his brothers,

Kanma, Allavarajulu, and kings of solar lineage and Brahma marched and were followed by the chiefs of several families. Then moved elephantry, cavalry and soldiers holding Bhisvata swords. The armies halted at Mellavagu and from there Brahma ordered the movements of the infantry, cavalry an elephantry in the four directions towards Karempudi. Pedamallideva with army generals walking in a circle round him, followed by brothers, Brahma and relatives, moved in a palanquin.[165]

At Karempudi, the pillar was installed by Brahma with due religious rites. Size of armies, weight of weapons and good leadership were considered important by Nayakuralu, whereas Ramabhattu opined that capacities had to be counted on. Speaking about war Brahma says that for any one having confidence in his own capacities, the strength of the enemy appears cheap and as it is rajadharma to religh fighting, they should be thoroughly prepared for it mentally and physically.[166] Balachandra, about war says, that battle is food for warriors, they should fight in accordance with the dharmas explained by Manu and Krishna to Arjuna "When people are in difficulties, God scatters his heroism, when the country is occupied by other kings, he gathers all his strength, when the tree of empire is on the point of getting dried, he makes it bear new leaves and war is happiness to servants of the king."[167] The heroes wanted to fight so that people may not dub them cowards, but Kunnaraja pacified them saying that offering protection is tantamount to killing Mallideva's armies encamped in the adjacent open space of Revanta adjacent to the Nagileru on its western bank.[168]

The kings and princes were aware of the public opinion about their activities. Before taking any measure they pondered whether people would favour and support them. Balachandra before he entered Nalagama court consulted his mates as to how his move would react on the king, his father, the heroes and the armies, whether they and the people would curse him as the perpetrator of enmity and preventer of the conclusion of treaty.[169] Later events show that Bala was right in his forecast. He encouraged all to fight. When elders ask him not to plunge into battle, he retorted that youngsters are stronger than elders, far at times elders lose sense, ambition and courage, and so for fame or noteriety, responsibility lies with youngsters. Brahma to his son says "battle field is the garden bed for valour, path to heaven, means to happiness in this and the other world, a ladder to salvation, playground for warriors shed their blood to protect dharma."[170] As it was maiden fight for Bala, Brahma asks him not to get a fright of the enemy, to act boldly and steadily and not to feel excited when the enemy is disturbed. Narasimha with his armies came to the battle field. The armies attacked Balachandra section by section and were vanquished and began to flee. Narasimha, by asking them to sacrifice impermanent bodies in favour of permanent fame, and thus retain their employment in this world and salvation in the other. Afterwards in single combat, Bala killed Narasinga, gave head to his partisans and thus avenged the death of Alaraja, went to the battlefield again with his mates and died fighting.[171]

Srinatha gives a lost list of weapons used in the battle, quite common in such descriptions. They are sword, spear, axe, mace, club, lance, disens, knife, arrows, swords with several ends and a good variety in all these weapons.[172] In the temple of heroes at Karempudi, are some iron weapons, which according to tradition belong to the heroes of Palnad. "These are six in number of most extraordinary shapes; spears with ends two or three feet long and with dozens of blades sticking out at various angles and adorned with jingling bells. The biggest of those is called Navudu's spear and the smallest is Baludu's.[173]

Many forts of the area, probably built in this period are in ruins. Srinatha refers to the fort at Gurizala. At Dochapalle, 20 miles north-west of the town are many ruined forts. There is a cluster of old small stone forts now in ruins at a distance of 1/2 miles from Dachepalle. At Goli, Kambhampadu, Kavelapalle, Tangeda, are old forts ruined. At Pidugurala, 12 miles south east of Dachopalle, is "a circular mound, a square composed of stone and earth, the former predominating. It appears to be the remains of a fortification round the village site. Many mounds here, forming a large circle which people believe to be remain of an old fort."[174] Strong forts at Macherla, Mandad, and Medapi - the capitals of Mallideva, must have existed for forts in capitals were a form of defence.

**The Capital:** The Chief capital Gurizala lies 6 miles west of Nagileru and 8 miles south west of Dachepalle. Built by Aluguraja, it owes its name to the abundance of Gurugana creepers in the locality. Gurizala is also known as Gurindalastha and Madhavipattana. It is opined that Gurizala signifies "diamond city"[175] Macherla is located in the centre of Palnad, on the banks of the chandravanka i.e. Chandrabhagu of inscriptions and literature. Viracharitra mentions Macherla as Machapuram, Balamachapuram and says that the first halling place - majili - of Mallideva, after he left Gurizala came to be known as Macherla.[176] But from inscriptions mentioning it as Mahadevicherla, Madevicherla and Mahadevtataka it is clear the Mahadevicherla got corrupted into Macherla. Macherla lies 14 miles south west of Gurizala, six miles south of Tunnikota and 21 miles south west of Dachopalle.

**Irrigation and agriculture:** Mahadevitataka must have a bema tank of some importance. Naganadi and Chandrabhaga, the principal rivers in Palnad are the tributaries of the Krishna flowing from south to north disemboging into it. Nagileru for most part of its course flows deep in a rocky bed, and is wide and standy near karempudi. The Krishna at the west of Palnad to the south of the river is called Peddavagu, running to the south of Devarakonda (Nizam's Dominions) - Yelosvaram over Peddavagu, and Dommaralarevu and Dommarlagundi at the junction of R.Dindi with the Krishna are the fords, the latter over the Krishna.[177]. Brahma is said to have crossed the Krishna at Domarlarevu.

Many tanks were dug under the Haihaya region and some are seen to this day. As the country was rocky, mostly, only dry crops could be raised. Sri natha, visiting Palnad in the 14th century AD, described the country, people, prosperity, crops and so forth.

**Taxes and industries:** The taxes - perusunka, Vaddaravala, birava, Kollivisa, and the officials Prolamaraju, Erayama preggada and Bitanamu Bollama appear in the Peddakodamaganda inscription.[178] In the days of the chalukyas of Vengi, the officer in charge of Vaddaravulamu etc. important taxes is called vaddavyavahar.[179]

Lending money for interest was practised. Nagamma is said to have increased her wealth by this method.[180] Palnad was the centre of commerce and industries. Metals in abundance are found in mines in Palnad. Boswell says "....lead is found in considerable quantities near Karempudi in Palnad .... Copper is found both in Palnad and Vinukonda taluqs"[181] positive signs of big furnaces used for melting from iron in the past and iron stones, are seen to this day in some villages in Palnad. A portion of the village Guttikonda is known as Kolumulapalem where the place where furnaces were kept, iron stones, and minerals are seen. The hill called Indupakonda i.e. Iron hill is in that village.[182] Several mines of stone - white marble, granite or quartzite used for building temples e.g. Amaravati etc. are in large numbers. Palnad was also famous for its diamond mines." Along the eastern edge of the Tumrukota range, there are traces of old diamond workings, more decidedly around Mallavaram, on the right bank of the Krishna where the lime stones lapping round the base of the hill have been regularly undermined to get at the quartzite beneath them containing diamonds. Here these certainly seems good proof of the existence of a set of diamond bearing beds perfectly distinguishable from the quartzite of which the rest of the range is mainly made for the debris and other evidence of the old workings are strictly confined to the edge of the lime stones..."[183] Probably these mines were worked in Haihaya times. Kohinoor is from the mines in Palnad. The name diamond city of Gurizala supports that the mines were worked under the Haihayas, for it was of no importance after the fall of the Haihayas, and so perhaps it got the name as diamonds were preserved in the capital.

**The Chagi Kingdoms**

The Chagis were, as the implies were selfless and beneficient rulers. The extent of the kingdom is not clearly seen in records. Parts of Vishayas of Natavadi, Vajayavati, Kondapadumati and Tolukattalanadu, formed its divisions.

**Governments:** The only instance of joint rule was that of Manmapota and Ganapati. The Chagis[184] e.g. Manma, Dora and Muppa were bestowed with the regal insignia-bhale (forehead plate), bheri (Kettle drum), anaka (couch), Kehala (kabors), arayatapattakam, golden palanquin, canopy resembling the sky with stars parasol, chamis and golden staff by king Rajendra Chola i.e. Kulottunga I.

King Pota I a rajasimha, expert in polity, possessing 3 saktis, is said to have established Dharma which is compared with a bull standing on four feet, protected the samrajaya and pleased his subjects by good rule. Dora II alias royagi ruled in Dharma marge - Gannama of the Chagis of Vinukonda had the title Gandabhernuda and his inscription at Vinukonda bears the figure of that bird lifting up two elephants with his two hands.[185]

**Minister:** Narasimhapreggada was the minister of Dora. Mallanamatya and his son Kavaliya Singana preggada were the ministers of Pota. This family were the hereditary minister of the chagis.

Maranam Ketaraju, a village official figures in a record at Bezwada. Mandadi Revinayaka a subordinate of Doraya Beta, was lord of Mallavrolupura.

**Military administration:** The kings were good warriors. The titles - puliya markoluganda, and Karaval bhairava of Gannama attest his valour. Kanma chamupa and his son Mankachamupa of the reign of Manmapota, figure in a Muppale inscription. The prefix Gajabala to the name of Mali Reddi of the reign of Manma Chagi[186] may moan either that he was of strong physique like an elephant or he was in charge of the elephantry of the Chagis. Surapa Reddi, son of Konnatudi Gandhasiri Bolli Reddi was the soldier of Dora.

The main army must have been stationed on the frontiers of the kingdom. The local chieftains had to maintain armies for local defence and respond to orders from the centre. Forts were important for defence. At Vedadri, 10 miles west by north of Nadigama are ramparts of an old fort. At Vinukonda the hill fort was constructed by Chagi Gannama.[187]

**Irrigation and agriculture:** The Chagis constructed tanks, laid parks and dug canals. Pota II constructed chagi Potasamudram for Narasimha at Simhachalam. At Anumanchipalle, Pota II dug a canal resembling Cauveri, from River Krishna.[188] Munna mentioned in a record is perhaps same as Munneru which with its tributaries Puteru and Vaireru flows from north and enters Krishna.[189]

In Pota II's reign capital Gudimetta, is described to have many gardens having coconut, jack, sugarcane, areas palm, blackish red sugercane and corn fields. In AD 1212 Pota granted Potavura agrahara with Gorulanka for gograsa.

**Transport, trade and commerce:** Trade and Commerce were encouraged Ganapaya had the epithet. Prithvisetti attesting his interest in trade activities. Gudimetta was a centre of trade for several merchants, trade gilds and commercial bodies met and made grant there. In AD 1230 the last year of Pota II and the first year of Dora and Ganapa, a grant of tools and incomes by trade gilds and commercial bodies - namely (gilds) of thirty-six towns of Pakanadu 21,000 twelve settis of Nelluristhala, Ubhayanana desis of Gudimettasthala, Chalumulas amastagavares, gundisetti Nandyapa setti, Gadudula Brammisetti, Vallamari setti, Gunda Bramisetti, Kalisetti brammi setti and mummadi dandas, to the god at Gudi metta, as seen from a record at Chintapalle.[190] All the persons assembled as a Mahanandu, for making the gift - magana mera of tools etc. for the merit of Chagi Dora and Ganapati. The assembly is reffered to also as Pekkandru (the many). The prasasti of these merchants is similar to that borne by their merchant gilds. The epithets-protectors of Virabalanjyadharma, recipsents of boons from the mandate of the five hundred (panchasatavirasarana), truthful, pure, possessing many good qualities, and having Garuda on their banner." The five hundred mentioned here evidently identical with five hundred swamis of Ayyavole (Aihole in hungund taluq of Bijapur district) who superintended the transactions of Virabalanjaya chambers of commerce all over the Deccan and south India from the 6th century onwards. Since the portion enumerating the various trade gilds is written in Kannada with mixture of Telugu expressions, it is possible that the headquarters of the central chamber of commerce were located in the Kannada country presumably at Aihole, whose language was evidently adopted by the subordinate bodies as a mark of affiliation to the central organisation. The Gavares, Nanadesis and Mummasidandasara very frequently mentioned in inscriptions from Bombay carnatic."[191]. An undated inscription mentions a gift similar to the above by trade for the merit of Boraya.

**Coins, weight and measures:** The standard coin current in the kingdom was the Tyagigadyana or gadya.[192] Ruka and na find mention in records. Visá, adda, manike and aduvu were the weights and measures in vogue. Some of their names are - sambatimanike, Kolayapati kha, and Madu - visa is a viss if 40; alams, adda is 1/2 Kuncham, and manke is equal to 4 Solas.

**Taxes and tolls:** Sarvayamu - All income including sunkamu-tolls, figure in a chagi record at Amaravati. The Chintapalle epigraph[193] gives the schedule of tolls on various articles which is follows:

| | | | |
|---|---|---|---|
| Ginelly 1 cart load | 1/4 | Yarns (Kandu) bundle (mopu) 1/16 | |
| Cotton 1 cart load | 1/4 | Ribbed gourds (sharp angled on bundle cumbers) 1/8 | |
| Kolachubhandi" | 1/8 | Ginger bundle | 1/16 |
| Mula perka" | | 1/16 Green grown 1 ruka | |
| Arecanuts asibe | 1/8 | Garlicks (Tulli) | 1/8 |
| "perka | 1/8 | Salt, Kolchu rice "7 on each | |
| Yarn esibe" | 1/8 | Yarn malava | 1/4 |
| Turmeric" | 1/16 | pepper asibe | 1/8 |
| "perka | 1/8 | "perka | 1/4 |
| Gaggery - cartload | 1/4 | mustard asibe | 1/16 |
| Dried ginger" | 1/4 | Sandal wood (Srigandhamu), musk camphor, chandu. javadi (civet) - on these articles - on each bundle - ruka 1 | |
| "perka | 1/8 | | |

Kolachu[194] mentioned in the record means grain or rice. Nelavarti was perhaps a place wellknown for arecanuts or a particular variety in them so as to give its name to them. The words used to denote fractions are padika for 1/4, parka for 1/8, and visamu for 1/16. The quantities and earnings mentioned are - bundle, perka, asibe, mopu, malva etc. Of these bhandis, carts, mopu is bundle, peruka is a bag with opening in the middle laid across a donkey, and asibe is a bag placed on bullock to carry things. The schedule shows that except in the case of Nelavarti arecanuts, green gram, salt, Kolchurice, sandal wood, musk, camphor, and chandu, for all other articles, a fraction is given as toll for a particular quantity both specified in every case. But unfortunately, what the fraction indicates, whether of quantity or a coin is not mentioned in the record. Despite the prevalence of payment of taxes in kind in this period, here the fraction cannot mean part of quantities which instead of referring to the total in each case, are specified. So it must refer to some coin either ruka or more probably Tyagigadya current in chagi and Velanandu kingdoms as far as Simhachalam. It may be that the composer or inscriber of the record considered it unnecessary to mention the Tyagigadya, which was too common and so just gave the fractions.

**The Kondapadumati kingdom**

The Kondapadumati kingdom with capital at Nadundla is also mentioned as Giripratichi and Sailaparchatyadipa i.e. the light to the west of the hill i.e. the Kondaviduranga; giripratichi is mentioned as a tract of 73 villages in a record. As Kondapadumati Buddhavarman claims to have received the 6000 country from Trinayanapallava, it is clear that Kondapadumati was included in the 6000 country. Giriparchimasasana is a epithet in the Kondapadumati prasasti and the Kondavidu hills from a portion of the southern boundary of the kingdom.

**Government:** Joint rule towards the close of a region and the beginning of the next was a recurrent phenomenon in the kingdom. Two sets of joint kings a Buddhavarman and Ganda, Bhuddaraja IV and Manda IV ruled the kingdom. Manda I, says his prasasti, was the ornament of kings, an Indra in wealth, a Rama in the battlefield, Karna in the vruthfulves,

Bhishma in purity, Brahma in wisdom, Revanta in horse manship, nine of virtues and support of virtuous men.[195] Buddha III's prasasti is similar to that of Manda I with the difference that Buddha is compared with Harichandra in truthfulness, Parasurama in keeping vows, taking delight in making gifts and fighting battles and a Vatsaraja in the management of horses.[196]

Ministers: Sura, the mahapradhani of Manda I received the insignia - parasols, and palanquin from him and was interested in the improvement of the kingdom. Sonanapreggada was the minister and general of Mana II. He was the lord of Irralur, son of Badana and of the lineage of Venayabhatta somayaji.[197]

Local Government functioned well. The Nadudla inscription of AD 1132 mentions the mahajanas for whom chodaraja made a grant.

**Military administrations:** Kings and minister were generals of merit. Kapa of the family of the feudatories of the Kondapadumatis is stated to have received the feudal insignia - betel pouch, palanquin, parasols, bugles, and presents from Buddhavarman. By his services to Manda I Kapa earned the title - Mandanagandhavaruna (i.e. the mast elephant of manda).[198]

The Kondapadamatis must have enjoyed the support of the Velanandu chodas. Elephantry and Cavalry formed important sections of the army. We hear of few forts in the kingdom. A family of treasurees were in the sergice of the Kondapadunatis. Bhandaramu Proliyapreggada was the son of Gundenapreggada. His son was Bhandarama Erranapreggada, the treasurer of Manderaja.[199]

**Irrigation and agriculture:** Several tanks were constructed in this period. King Manda built the Mallasamudram tank after his father Malla[200] on the north west of Nadendla. Gundannadevi, queen of Buddharaja constructed the Gundasamudram tank on the south east of Nadendla.[201] Somana mantri constructed a tank on the southern side of Irralur. Phraya dug a tank at Nadendla. The ponds-Gopanagunta and Batta danekunta and the tank Musiyanacheruvu figure in a Nadendla inscription of choderaja.

**Trade and Industries:** Trade and industries must have flourished. Telukula Kammana Gadiyanalu bearing the usual Yamaniyama prasasti of the Teluki merchants made a grant Poligarma kendamara, adhyaksha Indana, tantrapale Nankc, poyigaramupani Kendamarakonnoju and Kasyavana (mas. MS) find mention in records.[202] Polygaramu probably indicates the profession of the family. Adhyaksha and tatrapala,as the names- - indicate were probably strict officials.

**Coin, weights and measures:** Birudugadyas and Gandhavarana modas were current in the kingdom Gandhavaramanada'.[203] was issued by the Kondapadumatis, and the currency of birudagadya in their kingdom indicates their allegiance to the Velanandu chodas. Mana, Odda and Kha are the measures mentiioned in records.

**Taxes and tolls:** In AD 1138, Mahmamanda granted a few taxes levied at Nachinipadu, namely nonchinipati perusunkamu, gotivisamu, godlu visamu, Gomarasisamu, biranam, sadam etc. Biranam and perusunkam were in vogue in the Haihaya kingdom of Palnad also and the other taxes are new probably the taxes - Joti - Visamu, godhivisamu and ganaravisamu - mean 1/16 of each - whereas their meanings are not clear. Godhu probably mean cattle.

**Justice:** According to the Kaifiyat of Tsandavole, "when a vessel essential for the daily worship by Mallikarjuna pandita, was stolen by the Buddhists and Pandita's pupils killed the thief. Buddha sent his men to Pandita prior he came to know of him to ask him the punishment for murder according to dharma. Pandita replied that removal of thè eyes was the prescribed punishment. Accordingly by king's order pandita was blinded who cursed the king and left Tsandavole. Though all this may not be true for Somanatha's accounts differ from this. Pandita visited the kingdom of the Kondapadamatis.

**The Kotas**

The Kotas were good administrators and their good rule is borne out by writings - contemporary and later, their activities of public utility and buildings. Their kingdom comprising the Amaravati country on the Krishna, was later on popularly known as Kotasima and figures as one of the 14 divisions of Kondavidu and is said to consist of 106 village according to MACK MSS[204] and sixty villages according to dandakavile.[205] In old Telugu writings the Amaravati tract appears as Kromadu or the new country.[206] Shatsahasra, Konnatavadi (western portion of Sattenapalle taluq) Kondravadi, Kondapadumati, Kondanatavadi and Doddikandravadi figure in records.

**Government King**: The division of the kingdom between ket II and Rudra who ruled separately with capitals at Amaravati and Yenamadala, and the remarkably beneficient rule by the lady rulers are the two significant features of the Kota administration. Till the division was effected, kingship was vested in a single individual, and after division Devaraja and Mummadi at Amaravati and Beta and Ganapama at Yenamadala exercised joint sway. One of the epithets in the Kota prasasti is - protectors of the earth surrounded by the oceans.

King Bhima II was a warrior and administrator. He sent prince Keta at the head of the Kota armies to participate in the battle of Karempudi. Keta led the embassy to Mallideva, and his words in that connection attest his capacities as a diplomat[207] Kota II acquired the title jagamechchugandi by his popular rule. Records describe him as righteous, charitable, free from avarice, and fear, truthful, powerful like Indra and valiant like Ravana.[208] He contracted alliances of marriages with the rulers of congini marga. Konakandravadi, Kondapodumati and the Kakatiyas. Bhima III was a good adminstrator. Records say that he overcame the 6 bad qualities, secured chaturvarga and protected even enemies when they surrendered themselves.[209] He followed dharma marga and gave plenty in charity. Beta, was brilliant in appearnce, victorious worshipped by subordinates and satisfied the needy by his wealth. During the period of joint rule when Beta was away on expeditions, Ganapama administered with great care. A record says that standing at the head of a kingdom, she was of excellent character, prudent, prosperous, courteous, humble and munificent. Her rule was just and peaceful. She styled herself mahamandalesvara Ganapamadeviyammangaru. As pointed out elsewhere, it is a mistake to think that she was the queen referred to by Marco polo. Queen Vennemadevi or Venneladevamma had the epithets- - lord of Dhanyakatakupura.

**Ministers**: Mahapradhani Uddandanayaka prolinayaka is mentioned in a record of Kota Ganapati.

The emblem of the Kota as that of the Chagis of Vinukonda, was gandabherunda. It is engraved on the seal of the Kota e.p. charter and also in some stone records. And Gandabheruna is a title in the kota prasasti. It has been said[210] that the kotas bore the figure of Gandabherunda on their breasts. This kota crest was borne by the chalukyas and the Hoysalas and later on was the ensign of the Nandyala and Gobburi chiefs. The same emblem has been adopted by the Odayars of Mysore and is represented on their royal seal.[211] The banner of the kotas had the garuda - eagle on it and one of their epithets is Garudadhvaja. At the top of an inscription, the garuda is carved along with the sun, cow with her calf, discus, couch, hanuman and crescent.[212]

**Local Government**: Local government was efficient. Records often mention towns. Yenamadacasthala and the sixty villages connected with it find mention in one record.[213] The representatives of Lavadur, the mahajanas of Gorandla, and a grant by the former to the latter are recorded in an Amravati inscription. The mahajanas of Guragapadu[214] appear in a record. The mahajanas constituted the village assembly. A record refers to a village and its assembly i.e. sabha.

**Military administration**: Kings and ministers were warriors of mark. A family of generals in the service of the kotas is known from the Bejatapuram inscription (AD 1238) or the region of Kota Ganapati. Uddandanayaka a general, suggested by the name itself had three sons - dandanayaka katinayaka, Uddandanayaka Prolinayaka and Basinayaka.[215] Jogannasenani and Sadamu Maramaraju, lord of Amutunur were in the service of the Yenamadala Kotas.

Dharani kota on the Krishna, 20 miles north of Guntur and 1 mile west of Amaravati is the ancient Dhanakachaka, where the fort is fabled to have been built by Mukkanti.[216] A massive wall marks the square outline of the fort to this day. At Ketavaram, 12 miles north west of Krosuru on the Krishna and probably named after Keta II, is an old fort.[217] The fort at Errabalem is called Kammalakota. At Chintapalle, Kochorla, and Rampicherla are ruined forts.

**Irrigation and Agriculture:** Many tanks were constructed in this period. Kota Gonka is said to have built many tanks. Kota II constructed many tanks and dug ponds in gardens. Rampicherla appears as Rampicheruvu and Pankatatakapura in records. Probably after some big tank in its vicinity.[218] At Pedaganjam is the tank Tamaracheruvu, where tradition has it, the elephants of Udayana chakravarti used to drink water.[219]

By granting agraharas and laying out gardens the Kotas encouraged agriculture. The agraharas were named either after themselves, Their relatives or after their titles. He granted twelve villages in the district of Gondanatavadi, Kondapadumati and Doddikandrávadi, converted them into four towns - Subbambikapuram, Bhimavaram, chodavaram and jagame chchugandapuram, after his mother, brother, father and a title of himself. Keta II granted twenty four agraharas and seventy agraharas on the banks of the Krishna Keta II and Ganayama donated agraharas. Keta II planted many gardens. He built alm houses, and ganapama planted two flower gardens at Yenamadala Benadevi was fertile with all kinds of grains.

**Transport, trade and commerce:** Indland trade prospered under the Kotas, as under the chagis, Foreign settlements in the kingdom attest the flourishing condition of trade. Keta II granted villages with all its revenues including tolls. Kota Ganapati granted the remission of taxes - ayasunka due from temple servants. At Nadendla in Ganapati's region, a grant of two Kesarivishlu on each mopu (bundle) realised on the wholesale disposal of certain articles at Nadendla.[220] In AD 1216 at Velpur the kings Bhima and Rudra on one side and love priests and samis on the other entered into an agreement about the meras and sunkamsjas in money and taxes - granted to temples, at the time of the partition of the kingdom.[221] In AD 1258, Ganapama remitted some taxes. Her record at Yenamadala[222] gives a schedule of tolls on articles granted by the merchant community - the Ubhayananadesipekkonedru - On all articles they buy - 4 arecanuts.

1 bundle leaves - 50 leaves.

1 boddu of cotton - lost- Ganapama made a grant of marriage fees in the village to some people whose names are lost in the record. From that income the donces made a further grant of some rukas.

In AD 1246 at Kalkani, the great men of the village made a fight of tolls (magama).[223] In AD 1250 the mahajanas of Garayapadu transferred to the temple the marriage fees granted to them by Ganapaura.[224] The merchants of Yenamadala assigned some tolls. A grant of tolls at Rampicherla was made in AD 1265. In AD 1269 the merchant gild of Yenamadalasthala, the lords of Pakanadu 21,000 Vengi 16,000 and of Amma kondapattanasthala - bearing the usual Virabalayya prasasti granted amagana the details of which are as follows:[225]

1 peruka of arecanuts - Kesaripati Ka 2.

1 bundle " - Visas 2.

1 cart kiad (bhandi) of oil seeds (gingelly or sesame) - Kesaripaka 1.

1 Kolachubhavdi (i.e. cart load of paddy) - visas 2.

1 boddu of cotton - Kesaripaka 1.

1 Kolchuperuka (i.e. peruka of paddy) - Visamu 1.

1 bundle of leaves (betel) - 50 leaves.

1 peruka oil - visas 2.

1 bundle carried on the head - visas 1.

1 miscellaneous (bundle of) -visas 2.

Oil measured by a spoon - spoon 1.

For daily service - Simanu Kesari addugu.

Ankavula pattam - Kesari patika 1 - This is the grant by the Ubhayananadesis.

In this record of the quantities given boddu is a stein or bunch of threads.[226] Kesaripadu is obviously a village probably identical with Kisara, which is also known as Kisarapadu.[227] The land measures - Kesari puti kolata and Singampati Kotla are in vogue. Singampati is the measure used for measuring corn, in Nellore district. Mallam is the section in Kshatraganita of his work Pavuluriganita a Telugu rendering of Ganitasarasamgraha in sanskrit by Mahaviradharya, speak about the ksaripati manamm or kolata, measurment of Kisarapada. [228] Some call it Kesari patikolata. This supports the inscriptional evidence for the form Kesaripalu. So it is just possible that Kisaripadu gradually got corrupted into Kesarapadu and so, as is suggested Kesaripadu need not to be another name for Singampadu.[229] It follows that like the standard land measure, the standard coin in this period was Kesaripatika, the mention Kesaripaka is a mistake for Kesaripatika. In the case of oil measured by a spoon, the quantity is not specified. Probably Addugu is same adduvu of chagi records and adduga which means a two anna piece according to Brown. If so, Kesari addugu is a coin in vogue, after Kesaripadu, and perhaps with a lion represented on it. The meaning of Ankavulepattam is not clear.

In this period, there was a settlement of foreigners at Pedaganjam Mack Mss say that in the region of Ganapati of the Kakatiyas, parangis (foreigners) from foreign lands or islands, built a town extending over a square piece of land of four Kuchchalu[230] at a distance of 2 miles north-west of the village. There the foreigners were carrying trade by sea and were powerful. In s 1146, svabhanu, asvija, ba 3, Monday (ba 13 is Monday) (AD 1224), the sea came upon the village and washed away everything except a few houses and a temple. The quarters of the foreigners remained merely a (sandy) mound. So the settlement was there till 2 1146 (AD 1224). How and when it originated is not known. Later in AD 1274, Sriranga Sappan officer of Ganapati, made a grant of a town of land at Koliparru and three salt pans at Pedaganjam, Kalvakuduru and Chinaganjam, one at each place reserved the customs duty called addavatta at Pedaganjam and exempted the tax on grass.[231]

**Coins, weights and measures**: Visas, rukas, Kesarivisas, Chinnam, Kesari addugu, Kesaripati ka and amadas are the Coins mentioned in records. Khandka, mana, marturu, kuchchela and tum were the measures in vogue. Mana according to Brown is 1/16 of a tum Kuchchela "is a land measure which in Guntur district is 29 acres or 33 3/16 guntas. It is nearly the same as a Katti of land."[232] The mention of tum, putti, as land measures shows that same measures were used for measuring corn and land.

**Taxes and tolls:** Yenamadala and sixty villages connected with it were exempted from all taxes. In AD 1263 all the Kapus made a grant of a chinnam of gold madas. [233] Sunkam, Kara, magana, mera, ayasunka and Addavatta are the terms used for taxes.

## The Parichchadi kingdom

The parichchadi kingdom comprised Omgerumarga traya[234] i.e. the three districts of Omgeru marga. The name Omgeru marge indicates its location for R.Omkara, popularly known as Ogeru, taking its birth in Chejerla (Narasaraopet taluq) flowing through Narasaraopet and Bapatla taluqs into the sea[235] i.e. Bay of Bengal, and obviously the country on both sides of the river came to be known as Omgerumargai.e.,the way for Omgeru another form of Omgeru. Inscriptions mention the form Omginimarge and refer to the rulers which must be taken to refer to the Parichchodi kingdom and its rulers.

**Government King:** There were two instances of joint rule e.g. Bhima and Uttama Bhima and Alludanatha and Bhima. Nambiraja is described as joyous, prosperous and famous possessing all good qualities. King Bhima was interested in the welfare of his subjects. Allada claimed lordship over the 1000 country to the south of the Krishna and Kollipaka 9000 country. Kollipaka, the capital, prior it came under the parichchodis, was a provincial capital of the chalukyas of Kalyani, and after the decline of the Parichchadis was included in the kakatiya kingdom.

**Coins, weights and measures:** Uttamaganda or Uttamaganda made was probably issued by Uttambhimaraja. The measures Tribhuvanamkusa netimana and mahasenamat[236] figure in the records at Draksharama and chebrole. Kesaripati Kha, bharanas and martus were the land measure in use. As Kha or Khandi is same as putti, and also perhaps Kunta, here it is the measure fixed in accordance with kesari poti manamu. The unit of Kisariputi manama is an inch, the length of which should be equal to three corn seeds, or1/2 the circumference of the middle portion of the thumb or the third finger. Twelve inches of such length make one span, thirty-two spans make one gada (pole) four square gadas make one Kunta.[237]

**The Natavadi Kingdom**

The kingdom comprised the tract about Bezvada and Amaravati on the Krishna. King Buddha was a good administrator and diplomat and contracted marriage alliances with the Kotas. Rudra I as suggested by his epithet Vathadimalla was a warrior of merit and allied himself with the kakatiyas by marriages. The Natavadis must have had an adequate army. The tanks Rudrasamudram, Ratta Samudram and a point are mentioned in the Nudurupadu inscription. Trade propsered. Nandivana manna stamped with a nandi is mentioned in a inscription. Muppandumu, putti, marturu or marta figure in records.

**The Malaya Kingdom**

Malayana Suraparaju is mentioned as the ruler of good people and Banka as truthful.

The Malayas had good army. Padavalu Nadupunayaka and the four generals - dandena, Ketana, Potana and Kannama figure in a record. The Malaya seal[238] has a row of ganda birds, holding snakes in their claws, the Malaya banner was garuda and a mirror for one of the titles mentions that their flags are decorated by a row of garuda birds - So the Malaya emblem was eagle and mirror indicates purity.

Gavacheruvulu[239] i.e. the tanks, marking the bounds of an agrahara, and Regula cheruvu find mention in e.p. charter[240] (AD 1018). Some tanks are mentioned in the records at Gudimetla and Penumatla. The four generals, mentioned were the officers incharge - (Adhipatis) of the tanks. Trade prospered. The Rajahmundry inscription of Malayamu Ganapati[241] records a grant of taxes - angadisunkamu and the village Nandamuru, nagartila chinnamu, Kanatla Varakavisamu, Vendasunka pa 1,

Kunchedu for cart load and manedu for one pen. Angadisunkamu is the tax on shops, Nagarti is perhaps a large quantity on which one chinnam is taken as tax, visamu i.e. 1/16 is taken on every pareka of the (articles) of the merchants (komatis). The meaning of Vendasunka. Obviously tax is not known. Pa perhaps is shortened form for panam and paraka is the name of traction of 1/18 of a rupee.

Chinnam and visamu are the coins and mana is the measure mentioned in records. The Malayas granted agraharas e.g. Tadipudi, Chandrapuri, Mashepuri[242] and so forth. The imprecations at the end of the e.g. grant are noteworthy, saying that the protection of this dharma equals the merit of visiting a thousand tanks, a thousand Kapila cows and a thousand temples on a Uttarayana Sankranti day.[243] This is a singular instance of such imprecations in the telugu country.

## The Kondravadi Kingdoms

Ivani Kondravadi and Konakandravadi together constituted the Kondravadi or Doddi Kondravadi. Desati Kondaya was a warrior. Bhima II and Pota ruled together and contracted marriage alliances with the Natavadhi and the Kotas. Bhima of the second Kona Kandravadi dynasty is described as a warrior, a chankya in polity, mahendra in prosperity and a manikya to Andhra mandala.[244]

Mana and Judya are the coins, putti, Kunchana and Kha are the measures mentioned in records.

## The Kolamu Kingdom

The kingdom comprised the country in the vicinity of Kolleru lake to the east of Vengipura, and Renduluru vishaya. Kolami Katama's prasasti has the epithets. Bhujabala bhima, and dharmaputra.[245] King Kesava is described as truthful, selfless, valiant, abode of all kings, the best among Manniya chiefs, kind, bright, a Nanninarayana, charitable and courted by all people.[246] The rule of the Saronathas was popular. They followed the motto - where dharma prevails, victory rules - yet dharma state jayam or jangu W, with which their reads at Palakol, Draksharama and Ellore ind.

Ministers Sridhara preggada and his son Kolani Bhima preggada are mentioned in a Palakol inscription. Anantapreggada and his son Mallapreggada were ministers of Kesava and his son. As Malla preggada was well known, Mallapreggada became the family name of his descendants.[247]

The rulers and ministers were warriors. Armies were adequate. The soldiers in the employ of Kesava, and Anapoti Keti the best of them find mention in records.[248] The fort at Ellore, remains of which are seen today in the northern part of Ellore was in good condition in this period. The capital is variously known as Kolamu, Kulam, and is located in the middle of a lake in Vengi mandala, Natives call it Uppu Ellure of Salt Ellore.[249]

The country was fertile because of the rivers and lakes and agriculture prospered. Kesava granted an agrahara with a varisatra (water house) in it. Katama built many embankments,[250] villages and palaces. Kolleru, lying between the Krishna and the Godavari, is the largest fresh water lake in India. It receives innumerable streams between the two rivers that do not disembogue into them, and disembogues itself into the sea by the Upputeru, near the western mouth of the Godavari.[251]

Trade prospered Katama exempted the Brahmins, ascetics, their women cattle and all their belongings from the tolls in the wharf at Yendapi. Sunkam - toll etc. Yendapirevu is mentioned in records.[252]

Bhujabalamada, current in the kingdom was probably issued by the Kolamu rulers after a title of theirs - Bhujabalabhima. Tribhuvanamkusa netimana, at Draksharama, saniyam batinetimana at Ellore and Palakol, and Mummadibhimanika at Dettika find mention in Kolamu inscriptions of those places. [300] Palams of metal is mentioned in a record.

**The Second Kolamu Kingdom**

The kingdom extended from Warangal to Simhachalam and Ellore, Induluri, Anna bore the regalia - parasal of five colours arthakathari and chanis. His banner has an elephant and a lion represented on it. Rudra shifted the capital to Kolumuvidu, the best among Jaldurgas[253] i.e. water fortresses.

The Government must have been conducted on the model of the Kakatiyas. These Induluri rulers maintained a strong army. Annaya is described as the lord of five lakhs of army, and ruler the fortresses of Betavole, Colacherla and Rajahmundry.[254] A title of his Sthalagirivanadurgajalakotamallu. 12000 cavalry, 5 lakhs of infantry, 6000 swords and lances was the strength of the army. Annaya stationed his relatives in all the forts, as guards. His elephant had a pultilata and five bells Rudra - baha Haridurga built many forest fortresses. General Nagamantri of this family was in the service of the Chalukyas of Nidadavole.

**Tanks and parks**: Annaya constructed many tanks and parks, in the country between the Mahendra and the Krishna, from Amaravati and the sea. [255] Probably the Kakatiya coins were current in the kingdom.

**The Chalukya Kingdom of Pithapur**

The kingdom comprised the Prolunandu tract to the north of the Godavari. Pattisapunadu probably formed a part of the kingdom. The kings were capable rulers. Satyasraya and Vijayaditya II contracted alliances of marriage with the Gangas, the Haihayas and the Telugu cholas. Mallapa II is described as the abode of firmness birthplace of royal splendour, mine of valour and a wrestler with all his enemies in the world. Vijayaditya III was a protector of his subjects and rejoicer of life. He is described to have been daring like Bhima, victorious like Arjuna, virtuous like Dharmaraja and devoted to his family like Nakula.[256] Mallapa III entitled Rajaparamesvara, is spoken of as a second Vishnu, Vasudeva, the greatest of all rulers, an Indra among kings, a Kubera in charity and Dharmaraja in truth speaking. His coronation took place in AD 1202 in the temple of Kuntinendhava at Pithapur.[257] The epithets Sarvalokasraya, Vishnuvardhana, Maharaja andChakravarti and Rajaparamesvara, show that the rulers ever cherished the ideals of empire.

Kondiya preggada was a minister. There is a single reference to the assembly. For Mallapa III, on the occasion of his anointment, assembled the Rashtrakutas, ryots of the district of Prolunandu and commanded thus "Be it known to you that we have given Gudivada in the district of Prolunandu with exemption from all taxes to Kuntimadhava of Pithapur."[258]

**Military Administration:** The chalukyas were good warriors. Puraravi - dipasudapanayaka, Muthigi Maguturi Madi Nayaka and Pampadivirangaka were the generals in the kingdom. Forts were in good condition. In AD 1158, chalukya maharaja built a fort at a distance of 1200 yards from the Bhimesvara temple at Bhimavaram.[259] Mallaparaja's name occurs in connection with the fortifications at Morukonda.[260]

The embankments of Konareru - a local stream, a sluice at the field of Polana of Kolamu, chanka and garuvu lands[261] find mention in inscriptions. Akkasala Potaju is mentioned in a record. Akkasala which is Telugu for Shakshasala means either a mint, Tribhuvanam kusanemana, rajamanamu,[262] saniyambatinetimana,[263] Gundramu kunchamu and the mummadibhimamanika are mentioned in records, the first at Draksharama and the others at Bhimavaram. Gundarama Kunchamu is a circular measure. Rutti and Kha are the land measures in vogue.

**The Chalukya Kingdom of Elamanchili**

The kingdom extended over a portion of the Vizagapatam district. Peddana styles Visvesvara as the lord of Andhra and defines Trilingadesa as the country bounded by Srisailam, Kalesvaram (i.e. Kalahasti) and Draksharama.[264] The title is an exaggeration, for the chalukya arms never reached these limits.

**Government:** Mallapa II entitled - Sarvalokasraya, rajanarayana, dharanivarcha and rajagandagopala, is said to have borne the earth other wise borne by the elephants, tortoise, mountains and the boar. Koppa was learned in polity. Upendra III was interested in the welfare of his subjects. Upendra IV was the follower of Kshatriyadharama. Visvesvara, according to Peddana, followed dharma, Ardha and Kama, was learned in polity, was patient, thoughtful, courageous, prosperous and truthful - some of his titles were Rajanarayana, chalukya pati, Sarvajna, Vajasekhara, Sarvalokasraya, chakravarti, Dharanivaraha, rayagandagopala and hresvarabhirama and hrabhupagraganya and Karavalabhairava. His subjects were happy. Peddana says that Visvesvara performed sacrifices, people worshipped Gods, Indra gave rains, cultivater produced and so the earth was prospereous. He says, when he bore the earth like the boar, dharma, till then standing on a single foot, stood on four feet like our elephant at the beginning of the Kalinga.[265] Visvesvara is said to have acquired his riches in Mitimargadharma by good name, arthe by dharma, strength by money and victory and prosperity by strength.[266]

References to the local Government occur in record. Rakuduristhala the east of Pendalamiriti is mentioned in a record.[267] Perhaps Rakuduru was the seat of headman ruling over a few villages. Another record mentions the raddikam of Pandravadaalamu.

**Military Administration**: The ruler were experts in the theory and practice of warfare. They possessed adequate army, for Visvesvara acquired many victories. Visvesvara was an expert elephant and horse rider and is compared with Lakshmana in hitting targets and Vishnu in the use of Sudarsana.[268] Before undertaking expeditions of conquest, Visvesvara used to consider the Panchangas i.e. five elements - beginning strength, money, country, time and movement and result for defeat and success. And he used to send embassies to try methods of peace. Peddana says that Visvesvara's armies, move with swords in hands, with Bhairava on their flags, holding shinning weapons and raising dust by their machines.[269] The king directed the armies and his enemies become his subordinates bearing varchanka on their heads and breasts.

The capital Elamanchili, six miles to the north of Sarvasiddhi has a fort.[270] Irrigation and agriculture received royal encouragement. The king built many tanks and granted agraharas. Upendra II constituted the chodamallagrahara after his parents and constructed a huge tank after his father.[271] Upendra IV formed Upendravara agrahara Narasimha constituted an agarhara after himself, and dug Virasagara tank near Panchadharala after his wife Viramba. Visvesvara constituted Upendras agrahara. Many villages were named after kings.

In the reign of Upendra III, his court poet did a work in Telugu on agriculture dealing with soils, rains, variety of crops, and so forth,[272] A plot of land for laying a flower garden, and wet land (Jalakshetra) are mentioned in inscriptions. Trade and industries prospered. Silver was used for coinage and iron for casting pillars Padmanidhigandas, madas and Sasukani (silver)tankas[273]were the coins in vogue. The mention of silver tankas in the records of the Telugu country is not common as gold coins. The present instance is a rare case. Tumu, Pandumu, putti and Kunchamu are the measures mentioned in records. A record mentions - pudulekh - a particular method of land measurment.

### The Chalukya Kingdom of Sri Kurmam

The kingdom was small confined to the vicinity of Sri Kurmam. Rajaraja I is compared with Brahma in wisdom, ruled well and was loved by his subjects. Vijayaditya II was virtuous, victorious, righteous and grateful. Rajaraja I was a minister of king Narasimha of the Gangas.[274]

The kings were warriors. The capital sri Kurmam is 6 miles to the east of chicacole (Ganjam District). The crest of the chalukyas of Sri Kurmam and Elamanchili was the boar, engraved at the top of a record.[275] Nishkas, and gandamadas are mentioned in records. Perhaps nishka and mada are equal in value and similarly gandamada and 1/2 pagoda.

### The Chalukya Kingdom of Nidadavole

The capital of this kingdom were Vengi in the beginning and Nidadavole afterwards. The limits of the kingdom are not clear. Gonka I was truthful and Gonka II was a warrior entitled manyasimha.

Two families of ministers in the service of the Chalukyas are known. In Brahma's lineage was born Nandamiya, a resident of Karemchedu agrahara. In his lineage was born minister Narayana, whose son was Amatya Bolla and grandson was Anantapreggada, are expert in polity. Among his sons, mantrisekhara Malla was courageous, and Venga entitled sabha mechachuganda and sajjanandhaketakabharana was devoted to king Vengisa. Vengana preggada, Mallaya preggada, Devanapreggada, son of Bollaya preggada were in the service of king Vengisvarar.[276] The members of the family Induluri family - of the lineage of Kritipati of Sivayagasara were the hereditary ministers of the chalukyas. Nukanarya, was well known in Venginadu, and was an ornament of good people. His son Balla preggada was an amatya of the chalukyas. Naga mantri, son of Balla, is described as courageous, bold and the minister - the bearer of the burden of the kingdom of Nidadavole.[277] This family is related to the Indukura family of the author of Sivayogasara.

Army organisation was adequate, chandesvara was the samastasenadhipati of King Vengisvara.[278] Kumarinayaka was a soldier of King Mahadeva. Nidadavole, 6 miles to the south-west of Rajahmundry has the remains of an old fort.[279] Bikkavole, Biradanda vayapura of earlier records was perhaps a military strong hold in this period at Arugolu is an old fort.

The tank Bhima Samudram is mentioned in a record. Potinayaka in the reign of Induskhara dug a channel. Vamsadhara at Kollipaka.[280] It is significant that grihakshetras are not only specified by limits like tanks, trees, fields, but regular dimensions are given. The Dendulur inscription specified a house site thus - 35 pratimuras on the west with the measuring rod of four jenalamura i.e. a cubit of 4 spans, 32 pratimuras on the north, 30 on the east and 25 on the south similar specifications of four more house sites are mentioned in the record.

**Trade prospered**: According to the Dendulur record, the educated of barahakoti and the Kanati settis of Dendulur record, the educated of barahakoti and the Konati settis of Dendulur should sacrifice one tirupahindi - a coin and give it as salary whether they perform one or many marriages in a year. Industries progressed. The Dendulur record mentions palurdikoli - the furnace where gold is melted and gargunta i.e. the chuvam grinder.

Penugola or the big rod at Bezvada,[281] nandimana at Tadikalapudi, nanditum and 4 Jenatamura kola (the rod measuring a cubit of 4 spans) mura, Jena, Pratimura, Na, Putti, saniyambatimana, at Ganapavaram[282] Tubadukesaraindumanika are the measures mentioned in records. A record at Draksharama mention Attilivishayas.

**The Pallava Kingdom of Guntur**

The extent of the kingdom is not clearly seen from records. There were to instances of joint rule. e.g. Bedd and Bhima, Bhima and Naga. Keta and Tammulangi are described as dutiful, prosperous and delighters of people. Tammulangi was a warrior and Tammubhima did the saptasantanas and all the duties (Dharmas) prescribed in the days of yore.

**Ministers**: Nagadeva was the Adhyaksha i.e. superintendent in the reign of Boddanor Somana Preggada, son of Dattenamatya, was the lord of Origandi, and Sandhivigruhi of Bhima.[283] His son Dattena was the pradhani of Narayana and mahapradhani of Dorapahanayaka.[284] Kuchena preggada was also the pradhani of Narayana.[285] The brothers Marana and Devana were the best of ministers of Nagadeva. They were the grandsons of Potana and sons of Vishnu and had an elder brother Vishnu.[286] Prola of Vatesanvaya father of Kuchene preggada was also in the service of these Pallavas.

Mallepradhani is the premier. Sandhivigrahi is minister for and peace and adhyaksha is perhaps the president of the council. Army was adequate. Rayanapreggada was the samastasenadhipati of the reign of Odayaraju. He was the grandson of mantri Kalyanadeva of Vengi and son of Bollana. He possessed the six good qualities and was good at devices.[287] Potanamatya, son of Chennamatya was the Samastasenadhipati of Nagadeva. Sureboyadu was the Eruvadhyakha of Nagadeva.[288]

**What Eruvdhyaksha meant is not clear.**

The rulers encouraged tank building and killing of the soil. Sandhivigrahi Somana preggada dug many tanks at Guntur. Viddaraja Cheruvu (tank) is mentioned in a record. Nandiman and Bezvada manika were the measures in vogue.

**The Pallava Kingdom of Nellore**

The extent of this kingdom varied frequently. It formed a part of the cholamandalam at Jayangondacholamandalam,[289] and Panginadu and Pakanadu. Mulikanadu and the three pattais formed part of Pakanadu, partly comprised in modern Nellore district.[290] Vikramasolávalanadu alias Pulalkottam, Melnadu, Vedagaral Vallanadu, Elumartadarrudinadu, Vimdarajabhayankaravalanadu, Tenpaiyur kottam, Kaliyur kottam, Vengunra kottam, Urrukhottukkottam, Kulatturkottam, Paiyurilan kottam, Tenkarai damal kottam, Puliyur kottam are mentioned in records. Of these nadus and kottams correspond to provinces and district respectively. Tyagasamudrapattai, Rajarajapattai, Kulottugasolapattai, Damaranadu, Tyagavallinadu, Venganadu, Andainadu, Padanadu alias devaperumalanallur, Perumadu and Tamarurnadu wer sub-divisions of districts.

**Government Central King;** Dorapa was a good Horseman. Nandivarana's crowning took place at chodapuram. Inumadideva claims to have been a protector of the world, and a Bhirava characterised by firmness of character.[291] Vijayagandagopal was the peithet - Jagadagopala i.e. ruler of the world. M.P. prefixed to his name in a record implies some victory of his over the Telugu cholas and not his identity with Gandagopala of the Nellore cholas - Vijayagandagopala made a grant at conjeevaram with the purest mind aspiring for the highest good (dharma).[292]

Few ministers are heard of but many of Vijayagandagopal's feudatories were holding high posts in the Government.Pillaiyar Rajarajasembuvaraga, Alagiyasola Sambuvaraya Panchanadivananilaganga rayar are some such officials. Murya, son of Devaya and servant of Bandiivarma, Kemerayaka and Devi nayaka sons of Golapundi Kesinayaka in the service of Vijayagandagopala, Ammaiyappan alias Annanperumal priyan, were some of the lesser officials in the state.

**Provincial and Local Government:** Records from the Tamil and under the sway of Vijayagandagopala bear testimony to local assemblies and their activities. A record from Tiruppukkali[293] mentions that the assembly of Kattanur - devadana of the temple gave an agreement to the temple authorities stating that the puramu of the village had not been sold by them to anybody, and that they shall not sell, mortgage or present that puramu under any circumstances. If it ever be rumered that they intended selling the lands instead of giving them to the temple, they shall commit the sin of offending god and become liable to a fine. Vorugandagopala confirmed this grant. Another record at Tiruppukkuli records an agreement by the great assembly of Kottanur alias Uttama chola chaturvedimangalam about temple treasures.[294] The assembly of Tiraiyanur is mentioned in a record at Tenneri recording the sale of the village Vet Kaipukkam alias Nayakkan Kuppam by this assembly to Varadam, a merchant living in Vikrama, cholapettai at Kanchipura and to seven men of Vellala caste for 380 panam each.[295] Another mention of a local assembly is in the inscription at Avilda[296] dated in the 18th year of Vijayagandagopala. In that year, the nadu i.e. district assembly convened its meeting in the mandaya perhaps at Kalahasti, to consider the question of sivalinga chalane in the temple. The assembly brought this to the notice of the mehesvaras of the temple and after obtaining the requisite, tirumugam, sadhanam and sattimugam, got it reconstructed.

A few local officials are heard of. The village accountant of Talimangalam is mentioned in a record of the 29th year of Vijayagandagopala. The army and its personnel must have been strong, as the rulers led expeditions of conquest.

**Irrigation and agriculture:** The rulers emulated the great pallavas in their attention bestowed on irrigation. Nandivarma dug a tank Poda samudram, excavated a channel named after himself and built a sluice to the tank.[297] Allutikka constructed a tank named after his father Damaravarma, at Gandavaram.[298] Ganapasamudram is mentioned in the epigraph of Vijayagandagopala at Tripurantakam Kanicheruvu and a channel are mentioned in a record.

Land was divided into several classes on the basis of fertility and yield. The records mention Kilparna, Melparru of the silakam (land), high level fields in wet lands, a block of land called Kancharanga, dry land in the field called Peumani in Graddagantarevata. A record specifies that the Kapus should cultivate the paddy fields given to the temple for its share, 1/2 share in the third crop paddy, they should raise gingelly, flex, Karujonna (a variety in maize) and green gram on dry fields. The kapus should not allow the land to lie waste.[299] Nandavaram planted a flower garden.[300]

**Transport, Tradeand Commerce**: Trade progresssed which presupposes the prevalence of facilities of transport. In the 3rd year of Vijayagandagopala, the Devakanmis of Situdavur agreed to pay a specified rate of Kadamai on the produce of lands - Sirudavur and arrur. In the 15th year of Vijayagandagopala an assembly of merchants - local (nagarathar) and foreign (paradesis) met in the temple of Tiruppalaivanamudaiyar in Tiruppalaivanam and fixed the seigniorage (makanmai) on many articles of merchandise. They record the assignments of magamai taxes by Sri Karyam Pallavaraiyar in the meeting of the nagarattar and paradesis of many mandalas[301] i.e. districts.

Some merchants are heard of. Amarakon, son of Vanjyan (merchant) Kahari was a resident of Narayanapuram. Varadan, a merchant living in Vikramasolapettai in Kanchipura, and another merchant living in Rajaraju perumderuva in Kanchipura are heard of from records[302] Tennari and Big Conjeevaram.

**Taxes and tolls**: Some new taxes come to light from records. The Kaikkalur temple servants granted Tiruvadi mokam pon magadai for a daily service - nimandam - at Tirumala, and provided for the supply of articles (mukkarpu) and coin (kasu). The order every year for the issue of articles had to be written up and the articles to be received into Sri Bhandara. Tiruvenkatamadaiyan, the chief of Vikramadevipuram granted three mandai into the Sri bhandara as poliyuttu i.e. interest yielding capital.[303] On the lands endowed by Rajaraja Sambuvaraya to the temple at Atti, the donee was permitted to collect all dues on the lands such as income in paddy (nnayam), and in coin (Kasyayam) Kasu Kandamai etc. excepting padikaval --the fee paid for "the protection of the padi from outsiders."[304] An order of Alagiya Sambuvaraya at Tiruvallam says,"if taxes and revenue due to us are levied, (these) taxes and revenue have to be levied after remission of 1/16 and 1/15 to the extent of full amount which had not been levied in former times." Kudalur, the southern hamlet of Uttiramerur alias Gandegopala chaturvedi mangalam, with all its taxes was granted as Tiruvidaiyattam by Madhursudana Pallava. Vijayagandagopala exempted Tiruppalaivanam and Paniappakam from the payment of several taxes both in coin and kind, of which Sirpasunkam was one. "Sirpasunkam may have been of the nature of a small profession tax on artisans engaged in architectural work, both secular and sacredotal."[305] Several taxes including makanmai seigniorage are enumerated in another inscription.[306] The remission of taxes on Devadana lands, and the proceeds of certain tolls are mentioned in records[307] at Simudavur and Sulurpet. A native of Kanchipura redeemed temple lands previously mortgaged.

**Coins, weights and measures:** Madai, Varchapanam, gandagopalamadai, gandagopala pudumadai, Palampulimadai, kasu, Kalanju, 3/4 madai, palamguligaipanam, palavannamadai, panam, old kasu and so forth are the coins mentioned in records. Of them, madai evidently was a gold coin, and the madai issued by Vijayagandagopala was named Gandagopala madai,[308] and a new issue of it was designated gandagopala pudumadai. In contrast with the new coin of Gandagopala, the old coin with the old marks, probably issued by the earlier members of the dynasty came to be known as Palampulli madai.[309] the madai i.e. coin with old Pulli i.e. (mark) which was equivalent to7(1\2)varshapanam as attested by a record.[310] The gold coin contained pure metal and was current through out the province and Jayangondacholamandalam.[311] The coin Palanguligaipanam[312] suggested the currency of a new issue of it, perhaps with the name pudupuanam, side by side with the old one. Similarly palavannamadai[313] indicates the currency of a new coin puduvanna madai, perhaps old kesu[314] was superseded by a new issue of it called pudukasu.

Tumbu, vatti or putti, the chelukki (measure), Uchchaiyila ninra narayanan (i.e. god Vishnu who stands on the top of the hill) ninran (measure), kalam, 22 murala kola (a pole or rod of 22 cubits), kuli, veli, are the several measures and weights current in the kingdom. Tumbu was the standard of grain measure, and vatti or putti was a multiple of it.[315] Chelukki of Chelukyanarayanakkal a variant of Malaikiniye ninra peruamal was the measure in vogue at Tirupati for measuring rice. Uchchaiyi ninra narayanan marakkal, more commonly called Malikiniyaninrankal in later inscriptions was the measure common at Tirumala.[316] The letter was the double capacity of the former. Kalam and ninran are used for measuring rice.[317] The weight of gold jewels is specified in terms of Kalanju. Mention of 13 terms of land shows that tum was also a land measure like kuli and veli. The phrases tumedu nela (land of 1 tum) and Kunchedu nela (land of 1 kuncham) are commonly used in Telugu land to this day. The pole of 22 spans of the standard land measure of Maraiyur was used to measure land some kulis at Sulurpet.[318]

Madhyastha a mediator or umpire - was perhaps a village official. For Vijayagandagopala's record at Pulipakkam mention a local Madhyastha. In some grant to temples, certain amount of money was set apart to serve as capital as a lamp and the interest on it was to be spent for its maintenance. A conjeevaram record mentions that the money - 17 gandagopalamadai - was held in trust by residents of Amur.[319]

## The Pallava Kingdom of Cuddapah

The kingdom comprised Mulikindadu i.e. part of modern proddutur taluq (Cuddapah District) - king Chiddanadeva is described as truthful, sweet in speech, pleasant and the greatest of all the kings in the world and establisher of Dharma.[320]

In a record of the Pentrla Pallavas, Manneru, and Indum channel are mentioned - 13 barala kolagola i.e. the measuring pole of thirteen fathoms was used in measuring land.[321] All the Telugu pallavas had common insignia. Khetvanga a banner, Vrishabha as lanchana and Koduvaya pave Irum.

**The dynasties in South Kalinga - The Matsya Kingdom of Oddudi**

The Matsya kingdom comprised Matsyadesa i.e. Oddadirajya or Vishaya in modern Viazagapatam district. Eruvasima and Jembiyanadu find mention in Matsya inscriptions. In Matsya history was a single instance of joint rule e.g. Jayanta II and Jayantika. Jaytenta II was charitable, courageous, prosperous and famous.[322] Arjuna II and Arjuna III were distinguished warriors.

**Ministers:** Several ministers are known. Srirangapreggada, son of Prayaga Manchana was the minister of Arjuna. Varadana preggada, son of Oddadi Peddana preggada was the minister of Arjuna II and bore the epithets - mantrisikhamani, Gunanidhi,and Maharajyaikodhurya.[323] Oddadimantri Prole preggada and his son of Chaturvedi Gundayapreggada, and his son Narasimha preggada, Erayapreggada were some of the ministers of the Matsya kingdom. Of them Bhimanamakya is described as the Mantrisikhanand of Oddadi kingdom and Narasimha preggada as an expert in the use of the three powers[324] Surayapreggada was the pradhani of Oddadi kingdom in the region of Arjuna III.[325] It is noteworthy that unlike in the case of other dynasties, the name of the kingdom - Oddadi is prefixed to the names of ministers and not kings.

Some of the other officers in the kingdom were Tirpari, chief treasurer, Commander-in-chief and so forth. Tirpari Chingamanayadu is mentioned in a record.

**Military administration:** The army of the Matsya was excellent manned by generals of mark. Many generals are heard of from inscriptions. Chandrasenapati and his son-in-law Chitrukhillari, Tipurakhillari son of Rachchasenapati, Chennasinga Senapati and his son[326] were in the service of

Arjuna II. The records of Prataparjuna reveal the names of several of his generals e.g. Vallayajpadalu and so forth. An army officer is mentioned as the friend of King Vallabha.

Forts existed in all important places in the kingdom. The Matsya emblem fish is found in many records. The seal of the Dibbida plates bears two fish in relief. An epigraph is planked by figures of fish carved on pedestals with parasols above them.[327] The Matsya banner had fish figured on it.

Local Government functioned well. King Vallabha granted a Gollapakakam which the same suggests was a settlement of Shepherds on river side. The committee of Vallabharaya temple is mentioned in a record at Chodavaram.[328] The records contain references to village committees and their working. This is rare for generally in records of the period, we get references to village or assemblies.

The tank of Mankaditya, the tank of low caste people and their embankments figure among the bands of Jayantanarayana agrahara.[329] A plot for a flower garden, five plots of land names Jantaraju-gattu, the garden plot of Sripakadasula purayinayaka, a garden of flowers and fruits are mentioned in records.

Facilities for transport prevailed and trade prospered. The Drubbidi plates mention the village artisans, carpenter, goldsmith, barber, blacksmith, sesamum grinder and the services or taxes due from them. Kasimahanti, Kankani mahanti and the merchants of the salt skull at Oddadi granted a salt gadya as a grant at Chodavarm.[330] The blacksmithswere to pay a tax at the rate of a duggadi i.e. a pice on four entries per day. A record at Oddadi mentions the salt stall - Oddadi Uppusala.

Taxes and toll: The taxes on village artisans are enumerated above. The merchants at Chodavaram were to pay two dandis (2 pice) on salt gadyana. Gadya or Gudyana generally refers to a coin or salt pan-probably the former. So on every gadyana the merchants get by trading in salt, they pay a tax of 2 pice. A tax known as Vedipananu[331] at the rate of 2 duggadi i.e. 4

pice per day at 4 entries from blacksmiths and others. This works up to 1 pice at one entry per day.

**Coins weights measures:** Mada, damdi, duggani, gadya, ruka, gandamada, chinnam and silver tankas are the coins mentioned in inscriptions. Gandamadas are also mentioned as gandas and tankas figure in records. As it is to-day dandi or pice was the smallest coin possessing the least value even in Matsya times, and duggani is the next coin having the value of two pice. Besides, there were the Matsya panams and panams - both with two fish represented on their obverse.[332]

Vise or nagarivise were the weights in vogue. Vise is Viss and nagarivisa is the standard viss, probably larger than the usual viss, in vogue in nagar. The capital is Oddadi. 1/2 sola, putti, kuncham, prasada kuncha, adda and dram were the measure used. Prasada kuncha is probably the kuncha, perhaps larger than the usual ones used in palace i.e. capital where the palace is located. Drona is measure used for measuring corn and land for "Drone is as much land as is sown with a drone of corn."[333]

### The Pallava Kingdom of Virakuta

This kingdom comprised Prakkinadu in South Kalinga. Virakuta is Biragottam in Vizagapatam District. The emblem of these Pallavas is the bull. At the end of an epigraph at Srikurmam the figures of a couch, two umbrellas, discus and a seated bull below them[334] are found. Gadya, eragadya and gandamada are mentioned in records. Eragadya is 1/2 gadya. Savukubumi, the measures addeniyada and putti, and the metals - gold, silver, brass and bell metal used in industries are mentioned in inscriptions.

### The Ganga Kingdom of Jantarnadu

The bounds of the kingdom are not clear. Lakkavarapukota was included in it. The identity of Jantarnadu with Dentapuranadu[335] and Jalantradurga[336] is suggested. The kings - Singa and Pratapa Kurna ruled together. The kingdom possessed a good army. Sankaradasu was the mahesenapati of Gangaraju.[337] Three generals of Pratapasinga are mentioned in a record. Gandamadas, Manika putti and Kuncha are mentioned in records.

**The Sila Kingdom of Nandapura**

The Silas attached some importance to forts and army. Three generals of Pratapaganga are mentioned in an inscription. They were given 5 puttis of land - three in Krampa in Bobbilidesa and two in Bobbilisima as salary. The capital Nandapura has relics of past glory and a mud fort which enclosed the whole place.

The tank of Silapanadu, silver tanks, putti, pandum and large pearls set in jewels are mentioned in records.

The records from Narayanapuram mention madas. Aharupakanadu gattu[338] is mentioned in inscriptions of Ruparti chiefs. Visvanatha patnam was included in the area under the rule of the Ruparties. The fort at chikati was a strong one. The coins - ganda or gandamada, gandaparkamada,[339] ruka, gadyas of the weight of ganda and precious stones, sapphires pearls and emeralds are mentioned in record from chikati. As parke means 1/8, gandaparkamada is a coin perhaps of 1/8 of gandamada. As gadyas of the weight of ganda are mentioned, it may be that generally gadyas and gandamadas are coin of different value Gandamadas appear also in Konda kamati inscriptions. Tola and adda, gold, copper and brass are the weights, measures and metals mentioned in records of the Palakonda chiefs. Add is a dry measure equal to two manicas or 1/2 kuncha. Tola is a weight of one rupee or palam.

Some of the important ports in this period in South Kalinga were - Kalingapatam at the mouth of vamsadhara, Srikakulam (chicacobe) Baruva or baraha also known as Barahasasnam[340] and Venkatayi, and Rambha. The sea from Gunjan to Rambha is said to resemble a parrot in shape and so is known as chilkasamudram. The area near Rambha is called chilkasaras, the Kahirambhonidhi of Srinatha. The forts were the fort

Dantavarapukota 1 mile to the south of Purushottapuram and 13 miles to the north of Chicacole, the forts at Sringavarapukota, Potnuru, and chodavaram. The fort at Chodavarm was probably built by pratapavallabha in AD 1467. [341] In the vicinity of Sringavarupukota are found many gold coins and bars of gold. Some of the called nandiparakas have the figure of a bull. Nandi on one side and some small letters on the other. Some coins are of the size of a brinjal seed with a small edge round it, was a big clot surrounded by small dots on one side and called vangaparaka[342] Sastulanikankas, Tyagi mada, chinnam, kuncham, narasimhamanika,[343] narasimha kuncham[344] are mentioned in inscriptions. Probably the value of Nandi and Vangaparakas is 1/8 of a mada. Vyagimada is identical with Tyagi gadyana and the donors Elamanchi Chendrisetti and Narasimhanayaka, Karanam of Ganmakota, were no doubt feuddatories of the chagis. The record at Dakamarri[345] mentions the Mahajanas. Madaaraja entitled Pakanadu chola mahamandelesvara and sikadandapathara was the Commander of Aska Region.

## The Yadava Kingdom of Addanki

Durgasima or navellasima and Kalarayanandu were included in this Yadava kingdom. Sarngadhara II's succession was perhaps due to the minority of Singadeva, son of Singaladeva. Sarangadhara was a popular ruler. His motto was dharma is victorious[346] king Madhava is described as truthful, charitable, pure, pleasant mericful, of good conduct. Mayi preggada was the mahapradhani and sarvadhikari in the region of Singala. He was honourable and had the three royal attributes - lordship, counsel and courage. He was wealthy, a destroyer of enemies and was skilled in managing the affairs of the kingdom. He was appointed mahamatya i.e. premier to rule the whole kingdom.[347] Govinda nayaka was the pradhani of sarngadhara.[348]

Provincial and local government functioned well. The procedure in vogue in fixing the boundaries of any grant in this kingdom was as follows - In the reign of Madhava, Dammu Madeva nayaka, Gangaraju, Chanduri Bairapanayaka and the

Reddis of the eight families of Arulur and Pellursthalas, walked along the boundary line of Ongole and Murikinunti podu. With the consent of these persons, Bottavidu Proli Reddi walked over the boundary line of Ongole. The king granted a vritti to all of them.[349] The trustees - narasasanas were four Reddis whose names are mentioned in the record and Manchinayaka. In another grant, the trustees were six Reddis.

The kings and ministers were warriors. They had an adequate army. In singala's reign Mayipreggada was the Commander-in-chief. Addanki, no doubt was well fortified in this period, though the origin of the present fort in ruins is attributed to Haripalaka, son of Prataparudra.[350] The hill adjoining Kanigiri was well fortified and the remain of some of the batteries still exist. Tradition has it that was captured by Prataparudra.

The emblem of these Yadavas was the boar which together with courch and discus is figured on the first plate of the Sarngapuram charter, and with discus on the last plate.[351] Koddipaticheruvu, a flower garden in Kurijalur, mango tope in the rear of Peddakolanakhandrika, dry and wet lands are mentioned in records.

Probably taxes were few, for Sarngapani says that imposition of taxes on lands free from tax equal sin of killing 1000 cows where as remission of taxes on lands gives the merit of protecting crores of cows[352] - Guntas or Kuntas, puttis, nivartanas and gocharma are the land measure in use. The e.p. grant gives the measurement thus:- one gocharma equals 10 nivartanas and each nivartana equals 30 rods (dandam) measured with a rod of 10 cubits (hasta).[353] A gocharma is a square of 45,000 feet. The lands are measured by a pole of 12 fathoms (i.e.baralu).[354]

### The Yadava Kingdom of Panugal

The administration must have been similar to that of the kakatiyas. The tanks - Tammasamudram and Udayasamudram, land - wet and measure marturu are mentioned in inscriptions.[355]

### The Yadava Kingdoms of Alavulapadu and Erragaddapadu

The kings were heroes. Few ministers are heard of. They possessed plenty of cattle. Refusal to pay tresspass of pasturage on the part of the Yadavas brought them into conflict with the

Telugu Cholas of Nellore. The stream Nerellavagu is in the vicinity of Panchalingulakonda, and the heroes are said to have washed their swords in it and pierced them in the vicinity of the banyan tree on its banks.[356] Fourteen kinds of grain were raised in Marella sima - Chamalu (millets), Ulavalu (horse gram), Sajjalu, Kandulu (red gram), arigalu, Pesalu (green gram), amudalu (castor oil seeds), minugulu (black gram), Jonnalu, ragulu, chollu, bobbarlu (black species of pulses) patti (cotton), and chandalu (pulses got from a leguminous plant)[357]

### The Naga Kingdom of Darsi

Gonkaraju wore a jewelled diadam and lalatapatta. He is described as the protector of refugees and unborn children.[358] Asnadesa in his court used to converse pleasantly with his feudatories. The Naga emblems were - the elephant, crocodile, serpent, boar and moon adorned with serpent. Gonka had a trial of umbrellas with white handles. Asnadeva granted the agraharas - Pinapantada and Pada pantadu to the mahajanas (elders) in the presence of Bayyaraju, Naraparaju, and Mantriraja, and his agrahara at the junction of Darsi and Chandalur in the presence of Siddhavarapu Kalgosa Malayasingaraju. Jakkapudi ganga mantriraju, and Pondaraju agrahara and two others.[359]

Asnedeva built many tanks. In the black cotton soil of Darsi he built the tank Papiravigunta in the name of his son Nunkaraja and a tank after his mother Lakshyamadevi. Idara tank is in the village of that name.[360] A field yielding a sama crop at the junction of Tangedu vancha and Chirumanagada is mentioned in Asnadeva's inscription. The front portion of a garden donated to Chilukuri Annamaraja and Bhairavayya is mentioned in the same record. Gorru is the land measure in vogue.

### The Naga Kingdom of Nellore

A mango tope, flower garden, soma land and the measure putti are mentioned in Nagadeva's inscriptions.[361] The records of the Nagas of Pottapi mention Nadupuru as the vrittir of the Nagas, Potadamaradlapudi as Pattapu nelavu (capital) and Udpubhumi Cultivable land and measure - putti. Of the coins - uramada and Mulavisa mentioned in records from tripurantakam, the former is probably the mada current in

Urua i.e. town. The merchants mentioned in those records belonged to Manmakula and followed Nirabalanjya doctrine.[362]

**The Bana Kingdom**

The epithet Perbana borne by these Banas is hereditary. For their power was never extensive. Parabana is "Perumbanappadi applied to the tract of territory with Sri Sailam in the north, Kolar and punganur in the west and the river Palar in the south."[363] And "Parigipura or Parivi, the traditional capital of these Banas in the Hindupur taluq of the Anantapur district, may be said to be the nucleus of their kingdom, from which they spread towards each and from north to south - the country they thus occupied." [364] The Bana emblem was black buck represented on their banner, and the crest was the bull. The Banas humbly state that they were appointed as the door keepers by god Paramesvara.[365] Revadu bhumi and Putti are mentioned in records.

**The Vaidumba Kingdom**

The records are in Tamil jand the rulers did not bear a prasasti. Kuli - a land measure is mentioned in records.[366]

**The Saluva Kingdom of Podile.**

These Saluvas encouraged irrigation and agriculture. Queen Tippalidevi constructed a tank near Ankepalle for the merit of her husband and both the families of her parents and consecreed.[367] Saluva Maparusayya built some tanks at Jammalamadugu and granted lands - one Kuncha for the tanks and wet land - 100 Kuntas as sarvamanya.

**The Saluva Kingdom of Guntur**

Tirumale of this live enjoyed na, ankara of Nutulapadu.[368] Nayankara was a kind of military tenure in Vijayanagar times. Palamraja Tipparaja, an officer (adhikari) of Teleguraya constructed a tank between Nukulapadu and punur.

Parvataraja of the Saluvas of Tirupati built the tanks Gangasamudram at Siddapura, and Siddhasamudram at Sri Sailam.[369] Tirumalaraya remitted certain taxes through the agency of his subordinate Nagayanayaka. Not less than 66 items of taxation are enumerated. Consequent on the levy of unauthorised excessive taxes on the people of Tenkarainadu, the people migrated from the country and represented their grievances to chikka Parvata who ordained that the old custom should prevail in future.[370] In AD 1598 Teluguraya cancelled all marriage duties. Panam and gadya are mentioned in records.[371]

**The Kayastha Kingdom**

The division of the kingdom were Renadu, Ghandikota, Mulikinadu, Pottapinadu, Marjavadi, Merpakkainadu i.e. Paschimapakanadu, a subdivision of Jayangondacholamandalam, Sakali, Eruva, Penabadi, Perlakallu, Palinadu, Punginadu. Bhurajadi and Mulpakanada are probably corrupt forms of Marjavadi and Merpakkainadu. The government was modelled after that of kakatiyas.

Gangayasahini was the sarvadhikari and saingadhyaksha of Ganapati. He is said to have acquired the titles[372] - Brahmarakshasa and Raddesa Ganga by keeping the feudatories under control and being the head of the seventy - Two offices was known as Bahattariniyogadhipati. But Rakkesa Ganga is the name of the western ganga ruler and not a title of Gangaya. Several ministers were in the employ of the Kayasthas. Saranganayaka was the minister of Gangayasahini. Nagarasa was the minister of Ganniga and probably also of Tripurari. Gangadevaya and Ghoderaya were the pradhanis of Ambadeva. In AD 1290, Gangadevayamgara settled the boundary dispute between the villagers of Ravula Kollu and Bodaya cheruvu, and set up an inscription to that effect at the meeting place of the three villages - Revulakollu, Bodayacheruvu and Brahmanapalle.

Provincial Government was a replica of the central Government. There is a single reference to the provincial assembly of Pottapinadu. The Attirala inscription of Ambadeva dated AD 1274 says that the residents of Pottapinadu met in the Chittramelimandapa and decided to raise one madai from every village in the district to construct an embankment on the south of the river (cheyyeru) and prevent any possible danger from floods to the local temple. Thus every village in Pottapinadu had a share and interest in the construction of the embankment to cheyyeru at Attirala. Possibly each village had its representatives in this assembly of Pottapinadu.

Local administration was efficient. The Kayastha inscriptions mention Kampana - evidently a territorial division - perhaps an equivalent of sima comprising a group of villages. Amanakalamri Kampana and Tripurantaka, chalamartigandapuram are mentioned in a record at Gangavaram.[373] The District of Dupali Kampana is mentioned in a record of Gangaya sahini.[374] Thus perhaps, Kampana perhaps applies to a larger division also besides sima corresponding to modern district and taluq Sthala is another territorial division - probably a subdivision of Kampana. According to one record alavalapadu is located in Poligandasthala.[375] The mahajanas of Nandalur figure in a record of Prataparudra.

**Military administration**: Some of the titles in the prasasti of the kayasthas, for instance Rayasahasramalla, attest their capacities as warriors. Ministers were generally warriors of merit. The kayasthas must have had an excellent army without which they could not have acquired so many victories. There was a gradation of officials in the army. Gajasahini Manmaganapati maharaja,[376] was probably a kayastha prince in charge of the elephantry and cavalry. The Kayasthas themselves were good horsemen as their titles and the term sahani suffixed to their names show. The provincial and local army organisation worked well. There was a good network of forts in the kingdom e.g. Gandi kota, Vallur.

**Irrigation and Agriculture**; Irrigation received due attention at the hands of the rulers. Ambadeva accomplished several irrigational works. For under his orders Peddinayaka dug a canal - Rayasahasramalla kalwa at Lambaka, gandapendarakalwa at tadapaka and many tanks bearing the name Ambasamudra.[377] In the same reign, Katama Reddi of Proli constructed a canal from antara Ganga, called Rayasahasramalla Kaluva and gandapendara kaluva at Tadapaka. In Odili and utukur, he built two tanks named Ambasamudram. Ambadeva and his pradhani Ghoderaya dug many tanks and canals at Poli.[378] At utukur, the Reddis of Odumur dug a tank in their settlement, when it became dilapidated, Ambadeva effected repairs to it and renamed it Amasamudram. At Tripurantakam chalamarti Reddi and Nimma Reddi made a grant of gold coins for digging tanks.[379]

The Kayasthas fostered agriculture. Under the orders of Ambadeva Peddinayaka carried on the land survey of Pottapinadu. Local histories give the detail of the survey thus - the lands were measured and divided into variouss categories and on the basis of their fertility, taxes were levied and collected. Ghoderaya, planted a coconut garden round the temple at Attirala. He conducted the survey of lands in pottapinadu. In Kaduvagudi, he founded the agraharas of Ambapura and Buddadevarapadu.[380] Peddi —3 nayaka founded many villages and named them Ambapura after Ambadeva.

**Taxes and tolls:** Ambayadeva Maharaja granted taxes or tolls (sunka) accruing from Satrasala to the deity.[381] In AD 1287 Choderaya Gangaya paid magama and sunkam collected from the people of the land. In AD 1290, Ambadeva remitted all the taxes on the villages round about Tripurantakam on the representation made by Nandasiva.[382] In AD 1304 Gandapendara Tippayadeva granted Varrikunta with all taxes and customs, including sade, sunkam and the six kinds of income (aya). A few noteworthy details in the grant were - 4 madas for clothe for three months, 1 palam of green beans, wheat, doll, pepper (isola), 50 uncutnuts for one month and 100 betel leaves.[383]

On the whole taxation seems to have been heavy for in AD 1309 Prataparudra issued the following proclamation[384] to the mahajanas of Nandalur "Previous rulers claimed sunkam, sadam, etc which formed avanayas, from Nandalur and its four hamlets. The collection of these dues is unjest. We have exempted you from the payment of the avanayas". The taxes referred to in this were taken by the Kayasthas and this gesture of Pratapa rudra reminds us of Ganapati's trade charter abheyasasana to merchants (AD 1244).

**Regalia, coins, weights and measures:** The Kayasthas adopted the varaha - boar emblem of their overlords. Some coins which may have been issued by Ambadeva are of gold, 16 carats fine, weighing 55 grains and with a diameter .78 to .82". On the coin is a mark representing the crown and the legent Rayasamu. On palacographical grounds the coins may be attributed to the time of Ambadeva. It has been said that Ambadeva had for his model the coins of the chalukyas of

Kalyani or the legends were impressed on western chalukya coins.[385] On some gold coins, is the figure of the boar in the centre with two lotuses and the legend iruvadisapetta, a title of Ambadeva. So the coins were issued by Ambadeva. Four coins of this type at Bezvada and a fifth at Prabhuvulavindu were found. Three gold coins found at Kavaliyadavalli were of 13 carats fine with the legend rayasima.[386] Madai and ga (varaha weight) are mentioned in records. Ga is probably gadya. Palam, putti, sola and kunta are the measues mentioned. For measuring land, Penumbaka manadandamu was well known in this period. Minister Ghoderaya fixed the length of the measuring rod which was 32 feet according to the foot.[387]

**The Telugu Chola Kingdom of Konidena**

The kingdom comprised Kammanadu - a part of the Telugu land to the south of the Krishna - the tract from Ongole in southern part of Guntur district to Kavali in northern part of Bellore district. The original tract of Kammanadu consisted of part of Sattenapalle, Narasaraopet and Vinukonda taluqs, and at one time spread beyond the Krishna on the north, beyond Gundlakamma upto Srisailam on the west, into Guntur district on the east, and Velanandu, Pakanadu and Addanki sima on the south. Its bounds were Palnadu and Aruvelanadu on the north, Velanandu on the east and Velanandu Pakanadu and Addankisima on the south.[388]

Government: Overlapping of the reigns as among the Imperial cholas at the beginning and the close of each reign was common. Pottapi Kama and Tribhuvanamalla Pottapi choda dated together Nannichoda describes king thus - he should be free from seven vices six bad qualities, possess six good qualities, seven devices patience, move closely with the ministers, improve the kingdom and rule for the welfare of the people.[389]

Several ministers are known from records. Mara was the minister of Kennaradeva. Keta and his son Viddana were the ministers of Tribhuvana malla Arinnaya preggada was the Mallapradhani of Tribhuvana malla.[390] Mallayapreggada, the sarvadhyaksha of Tribhuvanamalla is probably same as Mallayapreggada, son of Viddanapreggada and rajadhyaksha of Tribhuvana malla. Kavaliya Annaya was the nagaradhyaksha[391] and Gundayapreggada, the mudiseli in the reign of Tribhuvana malla.

The offices of Rajadhyaksha and Sarvadhyaksha are perhaps identical. Nagaradhyaksha is the minister in charge of the capital. Local administration was efficient. kammanatisthala[392] ! is mentioned in a record. The meaning of thalashere is indefinite. Another record[393] mentions the mahajanas of Dayyalavayeru. They are said to have possessed all good qualities and practiced Yamu, niyama, sandhya dhyana and samadhi. Here mahajanas is a class reference to the village assembly.

**Military Administration**: Nannichoda describes was thus - The king with the help of his army, when country, time, strength and devine will are favourable, conquers the enemy in the battle when the enemy has all these, he must be won by sama and dana. Unity is essential, and several weak persons together could defeat a strong man. Only friends should be appointed to watch over women's quarters, the four arms are protected from the sun by parasols and flags held above allowing no spaces between them, armies adore carriages and weapons, prior to their start from camps to the battlefield.[394] The army officers were anantamandalika, mahasamanta and dandanayaka indicating their rank. In the battle, van should be sent to capture the van of the enemy cavalry should accompany treasury, there should be no connection in front ranks and the elephants should be on the move.[395] Nannichoda mentions[396] the weapons boundivala (arrow or dart thrown from a tube) kanara (iron club or lance), Mudgara (mace or club) bakkera, Kattalamu, shield, broad headed arrow or spear, trident, club and so forth.

The capital— Konidena is called pattana (town) in Kammanadu some of the officials in the army are heard of. Beiraya, son of Sadamu Eriyama was the chief soldier (peddabantu) and Peddli tarapuliyamanayaka was a soldier of Tribuvanamalla choda.[397] Forts in the kingdom were in good condition.

**Irrigation and Agriculture**: Several tanks were dug in this period. In the reign of Kannara, at Koppagrama minister Mara dug two tanks, and Isvaranayaka two tanks and a pond.[398]

Pisalaya Ketaya built a tank near the boundary of kotya down and Koppagramma in the reign of Tribhuvanamalla; and Kosanayasetti constructed a tank on the west of Konidena. The setti of Nannichoda built a bank to the south east of Konidena.[399] There was still another tank at Konidena. Ammapudicheruvu, Yekaraju cheruvu, and Pulicheruvu in Kamuparti, are mentioned in inscriptions. Wet and dry lands fields sown with millets and pannasa chenu are mentioned. Perhaps Pannasa refers to a kind of land tenure. Nannichoda refer to payment to servants in corn.[400]

Trade flourished. The merchant community of Teliki Thousand, the rulers of Bezvada and bearers of Yamaniyama prasasti, made some grant at Bapatla. Nilisetti, son of Jagadobbaganda Venni setti, was the setti of Kannara. Uppugondaru in Pallametta in Kanmanadu with its four bounds, and the salt pans at Pedaganjam Kondakudura, Kuravada, Ambayaderru, and Pinaganjam are mentioned in a record of Kama choda.[401] On these a grant of peruka in Gadyama is made. The salt pan at Songherevelu (village, was granted by Tribhuvanamalla.

Taxes and tolls: Addavatta Sunkarlu - the collector of the tax called addavatta are mentioned in a record at Konidena.[402] Probably addavatta is the tax on exports and imports into Kammanadu, at the place for this purpose called Kammanatisthala. The mahajanas and several merchants of bhojanam a village made a grant the details of which are thus:-[403]

Woven saree - 1 bhandikatta - Adduvu

1 talakatta - padika.

On every saree sold in this shandy - gadyama and visamu

Arecanuts - 1 peruka - 100 nuts.

damaged - 1 peruka - adda.

On garlicks, turmeric, dried ginger, jaggery etc. 1 bundle borne on head - 1 peruka. On nemulama and Kanchu (bell metal) - one gaddena - 1 Kani. Nela (varti) arecanuts peruka - visamu.

Three servants of Tribhuvanamalla made a grant which is as follows:-[404]

Of Pinta sunkamu - 1 padika

(vivi) turmeric peruka - padika

dried ginger " Visamu

garlicks " "

jaggery " "

In the same reign, the princes (rachakodkulu), mandallu, umanayakulu of Mammanandu and other princes, disatlu, mandallu and nukanayakalu assembled together and made the grant:-[405]

On each village 1 ruka

L vari (paddy) - padika

In the reign of Kannara, suraparaja granted some tolls besides land. The tax of Gadyana and visamu on every woven saree sold in the shandy, is rather too heavy. Bhojanama in this period, must have been an important centre of trade where large shandis were held at regular intervals.

**Coins, weights and measures:** Brimdumadas,[406] chamaramada[407]gadayam or gaddena, ruka, visamu, adduvu, kani, padika are coins in vogue in this kingdom. Probably birudamadas were victory coins, and chamarumadas temple coins. The value of adduvu is not known. Padika in this reerence 1/4 of adduva. Kani is perhaps same as modern Kani in Telugu denoting one fourth of an anna i.e. 3 pice. If so like damdi and duggani denoting one and two pice kani also was known as early as the 12th century AD.

Bhandiketta is cart load and talakatta is bundle borne on the head. Pentasunkamu means the toll in penta (town). The meaning of nemulamu is not clear. Mandallu, desatly and mukanayakulu possible represent gradation of army officials.

**The Telugu Chola Kingdom of Pottapi**

The kingdom included Pottapinadu, mulikinadu, Renadu and part of Pakanadu.Pottapi nadu, finding mention in

Periyapuranam, is included in the southern part of the district of Jayangondacholamandalam, and according to another in Merpakkanadu in Adhirajendracholamandalam.[408] Local records say that Pottapinadu is the country about Kalahasti - the region of Chinnavarampadu, extending as far as the Bahuda and on both sides of it for ten miles at some points and five miles at others on the north and south. Rollamadugu on the west and Koduru on the east were the limits. [409] Mulikinadu was the region to the south of Siddhavatam and included Siddhout cuddapah, chennur, Kamalapuram, Duvvur, Chintakunta, Ghandikota and Jammalamadugu taluqs. Renadu is the track to the north of Cuddapah and Ghandikota. Pokanadu extends from Kandukur in the north to Kalahasti in the south.

The kings were warriors and administrations. Local Government functioned well. The chief of the Renedu 70 districts was a feudatory of Atyamachoda.[410] Peddana chola was the ruler of the tract of fifteen villages including paleru under the away of Atyamachola. Mahajanas of villages are mentioned in records.

Army was adequate. Forts were is good condition. The kaifiyat of Palur, says that it was in the reigns of many kings under military tenures till Atyana chola was appointed its ruler. Vallurapattana,8 miles from Cuddapah was the capital of Nalasiddhanadeva C.M. Some of the important places mentioned in records were Lepaka, Kalahasti, Nandalur and Attirala. Lepaka or Lembaka is mentioned as Nenpakkam or Nenpakka in Tamil records. Paka of some records is a shortened form of Lepaka. Kalahasti was called Mummadicholapuram in the reign of Rajaraja I and retained it till the 16th century A.D.[411] Nandalur was also known as Nirantanur, Nirandanur alias Brahmagiri, and Sri-Kulottunga chola charturvedi mangalam was the agarabrahmadega of Nandalur. Attirala is also mentioned as Araturevula and Tiruvaratturai in inscriptions. [412]

In the reign of Mallideva, a tank was dug at Chilamakur (Cuddapah District) king Balliya chola granted Siddhayam in the villages. Inumlroli, Mandara and Paka and in addition broli - Pannasa - pasimdi i.e. gold (padimdi) of the pannasa of Broli. Broli is shortened for Inumbroli which is also known as Poli alias, Pudoli near Nandalur. In chola inscriptions, it appears as Pudoli and Impaloli, puloli could have changed into Puroli or Proli - Pannasa[413] refers to a kind of land tenure [414] and not to a unit of measurement. Siddhayam is the income in gold same as Suvarnadayam. [415] "The use of Pannasa pasimdi along with siddhayam indicates that it probably referred to a certain kind of income which was not included in the general category of siddhayam and was only peculiar to a certain kind of tenure."[416]

**The Telugu Chola Kingdom of Nellore**

The kingdom formed a part of the chola empire mentioned as Jayangondacholamandalam, Rahendracholamandalam, and Adhirajendracholamandalam and cholamandalam in records. It together with the Konidene and Pottapi kingdoms made substantial contributions to the contemporary administrative history of the Andhra land. The several topographical names referring to the kingdom and its divisions occurring in records are Merpakkainadu, Nellurnadu, Angadipattanadu, Pakanadu, Chedikulamanikkavalanadu, Punginadu, Mundainadu, Melpakkaiyandadu, Pottapinadu, Tonkakuduru nadu, Melaipattaiyanadu, Paddainadu, Perurnadu, Poritinadu, Perattinadu, Mungalarattinadu, Kadaisinganadu, Tongaipunulanadu, chakalanadu, Pongainadu, Chedupulinadu, Singattainadu, Tyagasamudrapattainadu, pettainandu, Kilaipattaiyanadu, Melaipattiyanadu, Kaliyurnadu, Nagaminadu, Nayarunadu, Kakkulurnadu, Suratturnadu, Virpadunadu, Vikramasolavalavanadu alias Pulal kottam, Pavittiri kottam Puliyur kottam, Paiyurilangottam, Paduvurkottam, Eyur kottam, Ikkattukottam, Kaliyurkottam, Tiruvadi kavalillu, Dudduravishaya, Batavishaya Malaimandalam alias Mehmandalam and so forth. Of these Pavattirikottam is same as Kadalkondapavattirikottam, chedikula manikkavalanadu as chedikulavalandadu, Padainadu as Pidainadu, Pakanadu as Pakkainadu and Merpakkainadu as Melpakkainadu. Nadu Vishaya and mandala probably formed major terrotorial divisions like provinces and Kottams were sub divisions like districts Tiruvadi Kavalillu was a province which Tonkakadurnadu was a district.

**Government Central King**: Rule of a single king, double kingship, joint rule towards the close of a reign and the beginning of the next, and rule of even three different kings at a time different parts of the kingdom were quite common features of this kingdom. The reigns of Manmasiddha I (AD 1175 -1192) Nallasiddha I (AD 1187 - 1214) Errasiddha (AD 1195 - 1217), Manmasiddha II (AD 1198 - 1210) and Tammusiddha (AD 1209 - 1209) overlapped partly one another. Tikka I associated in the governance of the kingdom by Manmasiddha II, ruled singly the entire kingdom for thrity years.After him, the kingdom became divided between Manmasiddha III and Allutikka.. After Allutikka, his kingdom also was ruled over by the successors of Manmasiddha III at Nellore. Literature of the period speaks about king[417] thus - if he lacks sense of duty, the kingdom would reach a dutiful king. Free from anger and greediness, a king should extend his kingdom, with the help of his Brahmin ministers. Tikkana in connection with Rama's giving up of Sita, says that the mouths of the people could not be shut and a king shall not deviate from virtuous conduct and respect. When Rama had to kill Sudraka, Tikkana says that king's duty was mean and sacred kindness in the interests of his people.[418] Tikkana gives the qualifications of an ideal king and emperor - sarvabhanma jagatisa in his pictures of Dharmaraja. In the words of Krishna and Dharmaraja, he says that conscious of that non-violence (ahimsa) and satya is the dharma, it is the apparent duty of king to sage war to free the worlds from sinners.[419] Tikkana says that it is rajdharma to fight and it is adharma for many together to kill one person. Dharma requires that one asleep, without weapons vahana, admits defeat, loses head dress, should not be killed.[420]

The Nellore cholas claim to have ruled justly in the interests of the people. Inscriptions say that after Manu many kings laid down the principles of just policy, Errasiddhi is said to have established dharma and driven away the kali (age) from the world, as though to prevent its return, piled up his fame like a wall at the end of the quarters. [421] Timmusiddha, crowned at Nellore, was learned in all sciences, kind, charitable, and of pleasant disposition and speech. He is said to have appeared the torments of kali. His orders are said to have been borne by all kings and the closing part of a record mentions "this road of piety should be carefully preserved by all of you."

Thus Tammusiddhi requests the future kings with "(his) head being lowly bent (but) not his bow."[422] Tikka I was a unique personality. Some of his titles are - Tribhuvanirayapendaru the bearer of the anklet Tribhuvaniraya, emperor of the three worlds, advai bharadhaureyadikkarindra - the eight elephants in bearing the burden of the earth, an Anjaneya in destroying enemies, a Bihama in selfessness, a meru in courage and karna in charity. His title Parivarsannaha[423] attests the kind treatment metted to servants. A record says that Tikka was passing his time at Vodalagattu pleasantly conversing with his minister and considering what dharma (virtue) and adharma (vice). Manmasiddha III a rayavesyabhujanga, was valiant, intelligent, prosperous of good conduct and attentive in piling up dharma.[424]

**Ministers:** Many ministers are heard of Gollapudi Bomma nayaka, brother or Biyyapanayaka, the protector, pratipalaka- of the kingdom of Erasiddhanadeva O.M. was the mahapradhani, commander-in-chief and the acquirer of great wealth.[425] He is mentioned as the hero praised by the people and the establisher of the kingdom of Cholamaharaja Padiyari Vaigirappanayaka was the mahapradhani of Errasiddha. The Linganapalem inscription mentions a minister of Errasiddha.[426] Tikkana was the hereditary occupant of the ministership of the kingdom in the reign of Manumasiddha II. His insignia were -palanquin, parasola, adapa, chauris, double conches, Kambagatlu and royal offices.[427] He was a chankya in polly, expert in sama etc. devices, mankya among the ministers of Manumasiddha III. He was handsome, clever, intelligent, possessed great capacities, and a warrior. He could purge the pride of the enemies and could hit correctly difficult targets of the enemy. He is described to have enjoyed regal prosperity and happiness and bearer of the kingdom of Manumasiddhi. The familiarity between Tikkana and Manumasiddha is clear from the fact of the latter addressing the former as mama (uncle).

Tikkana hailed from a family of ministers. Among his ancestors Bhaskara was a follower of dharmamarga, and interested in helping and protecting the needy. He could curse and retrieve curses. Of his four sons - Ketana, Mallana, Siddhana and Kammana, the first learned in polity, had three sons.

Bhaskara, Gundamantri and Nallasiddhi. Bhaskara mantri had sons - Ketana and Marana, a great warrior Gunda, brother of Bhaskara had four sons Mallama, Kamana, Siddhana and Ketana. Malla was a warrior and Siddha, a general. Among Ketana and Siddhana, sons of Nallasiddha Siddhana was strong, prosperous, lustrous and an ornament to the people.[428] Of his sons, Manmasidha was kind, charitable and learned in polity and general siddhi was the establisher of the king of solar lineage i.e.Telugu choda on the throne a Brihaspati in polity and confidential minister of Choda Tikka. Siddhi's sons were Tikkana, Bhaskara, Ketana, Mallana the wrestler, Mallana entitled Dohattanarayana, Pinbhaskara and Pemmana. Among them Tikkana was valiant and truthful and bore the title gandhavarma.[429] Siddhaya Tikka's sons were - siddhana. Kanma, Immadi and Muammadi, Siddhaya Bhaskara was courageous and valiant, and Malla was to be sun to the clouds i.e. the work of the ministers of enemy kings. A chaukattanarayana, we learned in sciences administrative and military. Kottarum Kommana, younger brother of Siddhana, was like the spring to the garden is the kingdom of the Cholas. He was the lord of Guntur and father of Tikkana, Sanayagi, Ketanamantri was the lord of Ventirala agrahara in Vengivishaya and brother-in-law of Bhandaru Keta, probably identical with Bhandaru Keta mantri who is said to have never a defeat in battle, never uttered a lie an expert ruler of a kingdom.[430]

**The Council:** No references to the council are found in inscriptions. Literature of the period says [431] that strength of the king's sabha varied from three to seven - all Brahmins and a king's representative. Its duties were - when the king deviates from the path of virtue it checks him, and punishes even the members when they astray from virtue either due to fear or want of money. The king and sabha decide disputes of people. Settlements should be recorded.

Some of the important officers in the kingdom were Sripatinayaka and Tukkanayaka were subordinates of Tikka I. Tukkanayaka was the younger brother of Podiyari Kosanianayaka andgrandson of Vaigirappanayaka, and padihari of the king.[432] Badapanayaka, brother-in-law of Karangi Siddappanyaka, was the pratihari of Nallasiddhi.[433] or Rayapparasar Tikkarasan was the agent of M.P. Chola Peddinayaka was the director of seventy-two offices in the reign of Allutikka.[434]

**Provincial Government**: We have no direct references to provincial government. Tikkana says that Rama made Satrugana the ruler of Madhura and gave him ministers, servants, learned men, vaisyas, women, regal machinery, insignia and money. Satrughna imposed the rashtra, happiness of people, and was devoted to Brahmins.[435] The provinces in the kingdom must have been governed in a similar position. Mahimadur was the capital of Tonkakudurnadu. Manavira was the governor of Kanchi.

**Local Government**: Village was the unit of administration. The village officials of Tiraiyanur received orders from Rajapparasar Tikkarasan in the reign of Allutikka. Kararu Manmararmandu, ruler of Muranpura was virtuous and protected people. Talari Denimi Janayaka is mentioned in a record.

Nadus, town, hills and mandalams are mentioned in the Kistnapatam inscription. Chilakapati Kampanagalam - the territorial division Kampana corresponding to district is mentioned in Yapilagunta record. Obviously chilakapadu was the capital. References to local assemblies, are known. A record at Conjeevaram mentions the assembly of Jayangonda-cholamandalam.[436] The village officer and accountant of Danavamurari chaturvedimangalam alias Tenneri - people are warned not to deviate from virtue by invoking God as witnesses. The Chiramana record says that the sun, moon, wind, fire, sky, earth, water, heart yama, day and night, the two twilights, and dharma know the disposition of man.[437]

**Military Administration**: Adequate army and strong forts were the backbone of the kingdom. Kings and ministers were warriors of merit. Manmasiddha III was a Ubhayabalavira[438] - hero of both kinds of armies. Probably elephantry and cavalry. Tikkana says that kings vanquished by him lay prostrate, bits their fingers go to forests and flee in all directions with such perfection that they must have learnt these in childhood while crawling, playing and so forth. In the battle field Manmasiddhi kills elephants approaches horsemen, kills soldiers, cuts parasols and so forth. Free from passion he remains unchanged, while immense quantities of gems, hopes and elephants were given as tribute by enemy kings, and when the ambassador announces that the next day was to take place the battle.[439]

Nellore is described as the home of elephants, horses and soldiers. In the battle infantry fights infantry. And afterwards the three arms fight seriously.[440] Senangulam, son of Deva of Nallrui Kota, was the chief soldier of Tikka I Aramur was given as the fief-jivita marga for the military services of both father and son.[441] Tikkana mentions Kaijitagendra[442] (hired troops)

Tikka I was a great warrior. Poet Tikkana was a general of merit. Rama Tikkana, a renowned warrior is compared with Rama Parasurama, Bhima and Kana. A Chetu verse says that when he died, gods sent their conveyances - Sivanandi, Vishnu Gardda, and Indra Iravata to welcome him to heaven. [443]

There were many forts in the kingdom. At Kesavaram, in the locality called Kotakattalamitta, at distance of 1/2 mile from Timmasamudram. Zuvvaladina had once a fort, and through the village was a military route. [444] At Vadapalem is a fort called Gudikali now in ruins - At Rapur is a ruined fort with a ditch round it. At Vodlapudi are the remains of mud walls of an old fort. Chennadandalur on the Penna in Marikinarasimha was originally known as Virulapadu. When king chola maharaja of Nellore while proceeding on an expedition against Ghandi kotarajya along the route halted for a while at Virulapadu, with his army (dandu). The traders of a neighbouring villages set up their shops in the vicinity and provided them with the necessary supplies. Several people were attracted to the place and gradually a small trading village grew there which on account of its proximity to the army came to be called Dandalur i.e. army town. The villagers of Voralapadu emigrated to Dandalur. [445]

Tikkana mentions the usual weapons of war [446] - asi, mudgara suriya, kolu, kanta, bhusundi, tomara, gada, sakti, prasara, kishurika, parasvatha, musala palaka and a great variety in them.

**Irrigation and Agriculture:** These Cholas bestowed attention on irrigation by building tanks and digging canals. Nellore had many tanks. There is the Penna with canals dug form it, svarnala cheruvu, Tamaraimaduvu alias Chitramalingallur forteen wells, vemalasetti bavi or Vemalaniyi on the south and a huge tank on the north.[447] Perangandura had a tank. The chirmana record mentions Eradi Tank to which Gollapdu nayakar provided a supply channel.[448] At Chirmana was also the Mandu tank. At Kavali was Recheruvu (Kavali tank), Velpuncheruvu and a water course. At Timmasamudram were Chintacheruvu and Elamanchingunta. At Utukar, Virmarasan Poyan, Tikkarasan of Andur Devapoyindan, Nallappa Reddi Pudoli Reddi and Muppidi Reddi dug a tank in the north of the village. Tande tank is mentioned in the Ayyavaripalle inscription. At Chepalapalle, Kamala mahadevi of Yadavaraya family dug a tank called Deviyareri, Kamalamahadevi eri alias Kamala mahadevi putteri.[449] Rajamalla Yadavaraya dug a tank called Vishyasamudra alias Puruvulakkel (evidently a reservoir) at Chepalapalle. [450] In the same village were the Tondaiman tank and the big channel named after Kamala mahadevi. In AD 1265 at Tondamand Tikkayadeva built a tank sluice. [451]

Fertile soil and good water supply resulted in bumper crops. Nellore was the home of money and corn. Because of the canals from the Penna, three crops in a year were always raised. [452] Towards the east in the capital was a mango garden. Prabhumanyam at Annamasamudram, mentionedi..arecord of Allutikka possessed paddy fields, dry and Koru dry lands. Prabhumanyam "perhaps means land granted by the state for the private use of a subordinate ruler. [453] The record ordains that the lease was to continue, irrespective of the vicissitudes of season acts of kings, and god and excess of rain and drought. The chiramana epigraph mentions fields sown with millets under Mandu tank and that the diety's land was to be cultivated with a second crop. At Chepalpalle in 220 kuli of land, was to be raised a hot weather crop.[454] Koru land, wet and dry lands are mentioned in Navuru record, which says that the wet land in the rear of mattivadacheruvu was of medium soil among wet fields. [455] Some gardens are mentioned in records. To the south of the temple at Totapalligudur was 1500 kuli of arecanut plantation raised by Pichchaiyan Udaiyan. At Chepelapalle Rajamalla yadavarya raised a flower garden called after Rajamalla in a plot of land measuring 100 kuli and a mango tope in 200 kuli of land and jack fruit tope in land measuring 20 kuli.[456] At Reddipalem were garden lands.

**Trade**: Transport facilities prevailed, and trade prospered under royal patronage, private initiative, and mercantile organisations like trade gilds. In AD 1207 Tammusiddhi granted Kaivandur to the delight of merchants of the town. [457] Records of the period give us many instances of the gilds, their meetings, activities and rules that bound them. In the reign of Tammusiddha, the merchant communities of Nellore Narayanapuram, Ankadu, Mayilappur, Tiruvorriyur, Pandamali, Nadumpirai Damana Kachcheri. Perungalur and Tiruniru Co-operated together in acquiring a whole village and giving it as a devadan-to Tiruppasury temple. The merchants left the village in charge of Tammasiddhi. A few years earlier, in AD 1197 at Nellur chitrameli promulgated an edict of the benefit of the world. The inhabitants of the Nadus-padai, peratti, Mungalaratti, Kadaisinga, pungai, Tongaipunala, Chakala, and Pottapi in Jayangondacholamandalam, assembled at Chittamelimandapav in Tirupparkar chittiramelivinnager,[458] and made a grant. The signatures of those who consented to grant were appended to the record. At Kistnapattam in AD 1256 all the men of the town Kolliturai alias Gandagopala pttana, and the foreigners of the eighteen countries assembled together at the sacred flower garden of Desnayakam attached to the temple of Chandirattirai pillaiyar and granted money to Manumasiddhisvara temple to be spent as follow:

1/4 chainnam for upper and lower female cloths.

1 madai for a vessel

1 madai for sacred ashes.

1/4 madai for cloth.

1/4 for vidava [459]

1/4 for Kalava [460]

1/2 chinnam for Kamarasavalli.

The total amount is not clear owing to mutilation. What the last three items mean is not clear. The grant was the permanent agreement among the townsmen of Gandagopalapattana and the foreigners of the eighteen countries.[461] In AD 1279, in the reign of Immadi Tikka, the merchants of the nadus, towns, hills and the five mandalams and all the 500 foreigners (coming from) other countries (residing in) Kolluttura alias Gandagopalapattana, assembled at Tirukkavanam and made the following grant - 1/4% on the appraised cost of all bags exported and imported at the port - Kistanapatam to the deity.[462] In Tikka II's reign, the incoming and outgoing bags (of grain) in certain villages granted by the king were impressed with Gandagopala seal for purposes of tolls. An order of M.P.C. levied a tax on merchants Saliya weavers, and other people residing in the streets of Arumolidevaperundaruva, Rajarajapperunderuvum, Nigarilisolapperunderuvu, alias Gandagopalapperunderuvu and Kuraivaniyapperudaeruvu at Conjeevaram.[463]

A c.p. grant dated AD 1304 from Nellore district, sheds lime light on the life of the merchants at the time. The merchants of that part of the country too combined to make certain rules for trade. One member among them Kurnadeva taitor and was murdered. This trades union gave the charter document to the murderer allowing him to carry on his merchandise in future free of duty, thus expressing their gratitude to him. [464] It is clear from another e.p. grant of AD 1328 also from Nellore district that the same trades union, publicly recorded another man for having murdered two toll-collectors by presenting him a document of permanent nature and thus shown their satisfaction and approval.[465] Many merchants of the period are mentioned in records. In AD. 1300 at Virannakanupur, Tirukachchanam of the merchant street at Nellore made some grants. At Nellore Kitti Alavam, the goldsmith of Kuvam made a grant, and another goldsmith gave 1 madi to-be lent on interest. At Conjeevaram, a merchant from Malaimandalam made a grant. A record at Conjeevaram, supplies the names of several public streets of the town - Mummadi Chola perunderuvu etc. and the merchant community known as Vaniyanagarather. Some names of the streets are after the chola emperors, Nellore cholas and Provincial Governors. Kandaravirapettai alias Gandagopala chaturdimangalam in Conjeevaram is mentioned in a record of Tikka [466].

Ketana says that when merchants do a wrong they should compensate for it, their gold, precious stones and so forth should be confiscated and they should be treated separately from good people in the town. Perhaps this method was followed in the Nellore chola kingdom.

**Suppression of Rebellions and Administration of Justice:** In the reign of Manmasiddha III, about AD 1258, there occurred some local disturbances in the Nellore district and a revolt was put down by the king. [467] About AD 1288 occurred some disturbances in the Chingleput district and Jatavarman Sundarapandya in his 13th year claims to have quelled some disturbances in the locality. The persons injured in the disturbances, appealed to Pottapiraja, evidently a Telugu chola, and the property of the offenders was confiscated.[468] Incidentally this attests the spread of Pandyam influence northwards along the east coast.[469]

Though small disputes of minor importantce were settled by the local authorities like the village panchayats and big disputes of an importants nature brought to the notice of the king, to whom the parties concerned appealed. The king as the highest authority and enforcer of justice, administered it with the help of various tests - like evidence, witnesses, oreals, and so forth, and the complete proceedings, and decisions in the case were recorded, and some on stone. A record at Nandalur registers the decision of Manmasiddha III in an important dispute with all its details. [470] The Brahmin donees of Perungandura got into trouble with the Vellalas, and royal intervention was necessary to set matters right. The Brahmins represented their grievances to Manmasiddhi III saying that the grant had been made to them in fifty two shares by Mukkanti Kaduvetti - Obviously they had been enjoying Perunganduru for a long time. The villagers of Sakalikodur immigrated at a later period, settled in the land to the north of the village tank as there was some disturbance (kalaha) in their country and they were forced to emigrate. The Vellalar (cultivators) had to leave their village on account of plague marijuana and put up some huts in the fields of Perungandura and agreed to pay compensation amounting to the total produce (arikoru) on the fields under their occupation. Subsequently there was famine in the village caused by astronomical conjuction called Minasani. [471] The Brahmins left the village on this occasion and returned after the disappearance of the famine. In the meanswhile the huts under Velama occupation came to be called Koduru and the Velemas did not give the stipulated arikoru to the Brahmins. The original grant made by the Pallava king was losty and the lands attached to the king - Mammasiddha III.

Manmasiddha III on the representations of the Brahmins, sent for the cultivators of Inumbroli, enquired with the help of the residents of Pakanadu district about the allegations made by the Brahmins and found the Vellalas to have been enjoying the village Kolur by force for some time. He seems to have askeed both the Brahmins and the Vellalas to adduce proof by oreal in support of their contention. The proof was not quite convincing and the village was restored to Brahmins to whom it had belonged in times of Yore. Besides, the king, granted Kodure for the merit of his father (Annajiyya) Tikka I.[472] Perhaps this Koduru is identical with Kodur in Pullampet taluq of Cuddapah district. The occurrence of plague or some epidamic resembling it in a portion of the Cuddapah district in the 13th century AD and the recognition by the people of the necessity for evacuating their permanent abodes and living in huts in open fields is worth noting and speaks for the high sense of public health and hygiene. [473] Tikkana mentions the spread of Mari plague in this Bharata. [474] The famine caused by Minasani must have been severe as it led to the running away of all the Brahmins to other provinces. Such famines might have occurred even prior to the 13th century AD. The nature of the disturbance that brought about the emigration of the villagers of Sakdlikodurto Perungandurur, is not mentioned in the record. The word valasa [475] used to dentoe emigration implies the invasion of a hostile army intothe village. The hostile armies must have been those of the pandyas who sent conquring expeditions which encroached on the kingdom of Nellore. This gains support from the abundance of Pandyan records in Tamil in Cuddapah district, at Nandalur, Lepaka and Attirala [476] and so forth.

Some crimes and punishments are known from the works of the period. Ketana's story of a woman [477] who born a child in secret and sent it to be left in the burning ghat through a nurse who while returning was cought by watchmen who extracting the truth from her related to the king who ordered her arrest and awarded capital punishment, shows that decapitation was the punishment for child murder. In Vijnanesvara Ketana says [478] that Brahmins should stick to their customs, while residing in other countries. He enumerates fines thus: the king takes 100 panam as niti danduvu for abuse of teacher, mother and father without reason : 8000 panam for the abuse of king, god and Brahmins, 100 panam for abuse of Brahmins and languages - murikinativaru and Aravavaru-Brahmins were exempt form capital punishment. Fines were levied for trade tricks, abusive speech, beating, selling of false diamonds, and 1000 panam for prophesy of evil to the king and kingdom. [479] The punishments range from simple fine to mutilation of limbs and decapitation. Adultery and misbehavious were punished. Sunkapu tindlue i.e. customs or toll houses are mentioned [480] and 1/20 of income on sale of articles taken. Four kinds of interest loans, and bonds are enumerated. Property apportionment among family members boundary disputes, sorting of the soil bused on fertility, witnesses, their nature, instructions to them, on this and punishments for wrong evidence are described in the works.

**Taxes and tolls:** Grants free of all taxes and also grants of taxes were made to temples and Brahmins. Tammasiddhi made a gift of all taxes due to him - uripagrahayam ayam - in Triuppalaivanam.[481] At Tiruppasur, he made a grant of revenues due to him from temple villages. A Conjeevaram inscription mentions Kadamai due on each veli of land at Paiyanur as Tiruppardevadana tituvidaiyattam, Pallichehandam, agaripparru, and Vaniyapparru. Velur was granted free of all taxes - small and big - Cholvari and peruvari. [482] Some land in Nellore was given as exclusive property - sarvamanya i.e. free of all taxes. At Kodavalur, the temple treasurer Annapillai collected money at the rate of 1/2 a chinnan for month on every loom.[483] In the reign of Tikka I, Tikkinayaka made a grant of all leviable taxes. He deposited some money for interest which was donated by three brothers at Linganapalem. At Tummuru provision was made for a lamp with the interest accruing from 1 madi at the rate of 1/2 a chinan for month. "The rate is 150% per annum the chinnam being 1/4 of a madai." [484] Taxes on Vemugar, house front (doors), on looms, goldsmiths, and temple dues garden lands are mentioned in a Reddipalem inscription. At Tiruvaorriyur, Manavijava remitted certain taxes payable by some shepherds. Some taxes were levied on oil merchants in Mummadicholaperunderuvu at Conjeevaram. In some case gold was kept as capital the interest on which was to be utilised for provision of a lamp. Though records use the term - all taxes - frequently, none of them give the details of taxes. The tax peruvari is probably same as perjunka or hejjunka, a tax on articles of big merchandise and chilvari same as Kirukulasunka a tax on articles of small mercahndise - both mentioned in records of the Vengichalukyas.[485]

Pasture lands were leased out for Grazing on payment of tax called Pulari "Under this (pullari system) a lump sum of grazing tax was levied on each village by the state. Pullari is really the Tamil Pulavari i.e. grass tax and appears to be ancient origin. Manu prescribes a large extent of free grazing ground for each village for its cattle, that anything in excess of its requirement was liable to be taxed for the benefit of the state."[486] Payments by villagers were called Kalavasamu or mera. Vignanesvara gives the schedule [487] of fines for tresspass thus she buffalo 1\4; cow 1\8, and for sheep 1\6 and double the should be demanded, if the owner aware of that his cattle were grazing in other fields. Sets them free again. He lays down the condition that fine should be taken only when the cattle graze fields and villages properly fenes. For grazing on pathways; and unfenced fields, the king should not demand a fine. A person purposely making his cattle graze other's fields, forfeits the produce of his fields to the owner of other fields and pays a fine to the king. Implements of soldiers, musicians and carpenters should not be taken as fines.[488]

Both Ketana and Tikkana mention ships, boats and voyages. Vijnanaesvara defines the wages for loading and unloading a ship as follows:- horse - 1 panam, man 1/2 panam and women panam.[489]

**Coins, weights and measures:** Madia 1/2 madai 1/4 madai, chinnam ruka, panam, pon, Nellore pudumadai, Nellore Madai, gandagopala madai, gandagopalapudumadai, [490] and bhujeabalamadai are the coins mentioned in records - Nellore madai and Nellore pudumadai find mention in Allu Tikka's records. [491] Probably Nellore madai was issued by Allutikka's predecessors, and Allutikka struck a new coin and called in Pudumadai. The name Nellore madas is obviously after the capital Nellore where must have been located the royal mint gandagopala madai and gandagopala pudumadai of the

Telugupallavas were current in the kingdom. A mada is equal to two rupees. "Pon is a gold coin of variable value." Chinnam is 1/4 of a madai and ruka is a silver coin worth five annas 8 pies. Vignanesvara says that a panam is 1/8 of a mada.[492]

Patti, 20 span pole, the pole of 26 spans, kuli, gunta, kani, Vala vandan kol are the measures mentioned in records. Of these 20 span pole is used for measuring wet government land in Annamasamudram,[493] and pole of 26 spans for measuring dry land in the Bame village. Pattai or Patti, kuli, gunta, and kani were the land measures. The measuring rod at Tirupalaivanam in the reignof Rajagandagopala was known as Valavandan kol.

**The capital:** From early times, Nellore was an important centre in South India forming the northern most limit of the kingdoms of the south and usually the southern limit of the kingdoms of the north. For nearly three centuries from the 12th to the 14th it was the capital of the Telugu cholas. Watered by the Pinakini, the country is fertile and Nellore bore many names and as many explanations [494] for them. The traditional explanation of the name and town is that it originated from the Nelli tree. The second explanation is that in the 13th and the 14th centuries, the Pandyas and their vassals obtained large quantities of paddy from Nellore and the surronding villages and consequently called it Nelliyuru - paddy village. Thirdly the fertility of the country in general and the convenience it offered to the Pandyan kings must have attracted their attention and acquired the name - Nallayuru - good village. Nellore was also known as Lingpuri, Dhanyapuri and Simhapuri. Of these Dhanyapuri supports the second explanation given above - Nelliyuru - paddy village. In records and literature of the Telugu cholas, it apperas as Nellurupattana Vikramasimhakhyanagara, Trivikrama simhapura, Vikramasingupta and Vikramasimhanagara. The most common form is Nellore alias Vikramasimhapattana like the traditional explanation of the origin of Nellore from Nelli tree, the name Simhapuri or Vikramasimhapura derives its beginnings from tradition that lions ever keep watch on the city day and night, and never go to sleep. It is just possible that Nellore came to be called Vikremasingapura after the emblem of thec early cholas of the Telugu country. Three streets of Nellore alias

Vikramasimhapattana are mentioned in a record of the 10th year of Kulottunga I. As Tikkana refers to it as a city, to say that it comprised only three streets is mistaken.

Some of the important places in the Nellore chola kingdom were - Kistnapatam, a flourishing town and seaport till after the time of Krishnaraya and Nagapudol, also mentioned as Rajachaturvedimangalam [495] and demaracted on four sides with stones as a separate city. It is probably identical with Naga rule (Venkatagiri taluq). The origin of the place Kottur is as follows - The residents approached the revenue officers of the range which was subject to the kings of Nellore and requested them to grant them a lease on certain terms. For the first two or three days nothing was demanded. The lease deed was granted to the residents and consequently the place was called Kottur. [496] In the kingdom rest houses were found. At Nandipadu, Allutikka issued an edict for providing rest houses for travellers visiting Siddhanathadeva. This was to be done by Gandararam Proli Reddi, Atmakur Desahi, Duvvurisurama Reddi who agreed among themselves and obtained the permission of the king for providing rest houses.[497]

**The Eruva Chola Kingdom**

In the reign of Tondaya, the royal officer was Tammadhandani, the donor of some land free of all taxes and Koru in the presence of six witnesses. [498] In AD 1322 at Tallaproddutur, Deva C.M. constructed the Ganga Samudram in memory of his parents.[498] The tract came under Achyutaraya of Vijayanagar, for in AD 1512 he donated Potavaram in Tamatamkonda in Eruvasima.[500]

**The Eruva Kingdom of Rajahmundry**

These cholas as the prefix Eruva to their names suggests must have belonged to the same stock as the Eruvas in Cuddapah District. Kamaraja alias Bhattiraja founded the City of Kalyana alias Kanapuri, described as the crest jewel of the Andhra country. [501] Under the rule of Annadeva choda, his subjects were happy, said to have been sporting in the sugur cane fields and arecapalm groves. This attests the fertility of the kingdom. Mummadi Prola varam was a wealthy city described as the crestjewel of the kingdom. It was a resort to merchants from all quarters. Annadeva founded Uttamaganda chodadevannavaram in Visaranadu at the confluence of the rivers - Ganga and Pinnasani.[502] He also granted Annadevavaram near the Ganga in the vicinity of Pulleru to the Mahajanas.

**The Telugu Chola kingdom of Kanduru**

Kavaliya Bhimaya preggada was the minister of Gokarnachoda and was given the lordship over Maduvulu 30 badi of Kukkutamu. Bhandaru Govinda preggada was the minister of king Udaya.

The rulers took interest in digging tanks. In AD 1124 Mallambika's record registering the grant of Chodabhimanarayanapura as agrabara, mentions two tanks - chodasamudram and Bhimasamudram[503], evidently after two rulers of the line. Namisetti cheruvu is mentioned in another record. Trade progressed. In C.V. 84 the three rulers, Bhima, Gikarna, and Singama [504] made a grant the details of which are as follows:

Salt - Baruva 1

Millets - Cart load - p.a.24.

Millets - Giraka - vi 2 ku 1

va dumnira barava.

Leaves bej. paraka - ru 25.

Leaves bundle - 1 mroku (bundle) - pa 2.

Leave 1 bundle arecanuts - 1 cart load - karu (each crop) - 8 arecanuts.

— ru -pa 4 arecanuts.

Pepper - 1 cart load - 22 rarugi

druggapa - a Kakasa saka - 2.

ginger - Patupali - visses 2.

for peruka - ru 2.

Rurmeric, cotton, jaggery, sarees, - 1 viss 1 saree - ru 2.

For Kunkuma and so forth - vi ramu. Whoever brings chodem into the town (Nakaramu) - Panugal and drinks pays surataddi (a tax). Of omgadi siddhayamu to the deity and 1/2 to the mahajanas, of 30 puttis of paddy, belonging to the army. The record is damaged in ports and several terms in it are unintelligible. Baruva equals 20 maunds. What load giraka [505] implies is not known and the same with patupali. pa is palam vi is viss, ku is kunchamu, ru is probably ruka. The meaning of rurugi is unknown. Sura addi is obviously a tax on drink.

Regular toll officers were employed taxes on many articles of merchandise and tolls are certain places were collected. In Udayama's reign, the toll collectors were Kibbette Melvatte Dandanayaka and Nallasiddhamayya, made a grant out of tolls collected at Gangavaram. [506] So they were in charge of that place. They ordained that who ever was in charge of this shhala, sunka, should give five rukas every month. Angadisiddhayamu is the fixed revenue from shops, and sulka is the toll, duty or customs duty levied at ferries, passes and roads. As it is true of silks even now, the value of sarees was fixed by their weight and taxes were levied accordingly.

Besides ruka, gokarna singa ruka is mentioned in records.[507] Provbably it was issued by king Gokarna and loin-the emblem of the early Telugu cholas is represented on it.

## The other Chola Kingdoms

Sambhuchoda assembled all the chief provincial officers to make a grant. [508] Nitisara [509] of Baddena gives a mine of information on royal polity. It defines that an ambassador should be of good caste possess good position the handsome, an expert in nitisastras and praised by all. About the relationship between master and servant, he says a servant of the king, if he gets angry with his lord, he is ruined, and if he makes the lord get angry, even then he suffers. The servant should adopt the same religion as the master and should not get angry with him in rajasabha, though he may be rich and a favourite of the king. About forts, he says, if the fort is not properly guarded, even Indra cannot rule the earth. So forts must be well guarded day in and day out at the gates, watchmen Kotapalem - should remain at the proper place, guard should be provided at karumatla — : passes and central hall, and watchmen should keep going round the palace and side paths, daily the guards must be made to keep watch with lamps in hands under observation and king should see that there exist no difference between the soldiers. Baddena speaks about 15 paddhatis in his work - rajaniti, asadraja, mantri, adhikara, niyoga, karyavichara, upaya, rajyaraksha, arajaka, hitasevaka, dushtasevaka, danasila and Lokaniti.

## The Yadavaraya Kingdom

The Yadavarayas, the feudatories of the chalukyas of Kalyani and the Telugu cholas of Nellore claimed lordship over Vengi as their titles Vengi vallabha and Vengi mahanayaka[510] in their prasasti indicate. Another title in their prasasti, shows that their capital was Kamuparapura or Kankkharipura, Kamuppakapura and Kamucharappura probably identical with Kamupparru on the Godavari. Kunuparti in Guntur district is also mentioned as Kanakapuri and Kosambikapuri i.e. city of gold.[511]

## The Telugu Chola Kingdom of Hemavati

In administration the kings were helped by ministers council and assembly. Hiriya Tantrapala was the minister and senior councillor of Mallideva and his elder brother — Bammana , was the Varamantri of Mallideva. His grandfather belonged to Kottidena. The Hemavati kingdom included Naravadi 500 i.e. Nalavadi vishaya (a portion of Kurnool district). [512]

Severals tanks and canals and wells were built. At Hemavati, Tribhuvanamalla Mallideva C.M. made improvements to a well, originally dug by Periyaluva Setti, son of Alahiya manaval and Andamma of Siduke and a resident of Akur in Rajarajavelanadu, a district to the south of the vauveri.[513] Thus amerchant from the Tamil country dug a well at Henjoru. Trade flourished and mercantile organisations made many grants to temples. Tribhuvana mallachola and the desi merchants of four dialects (Tamil, Telugu, Canarese and Malayalam) together with nakaras of Henjeru made a gift of a fixed fee on all articles with they traded such as must, saffron, yak toil, cus-cus cotton thread, beads, scaling wax, rock salt, wax, rasin, hemp, wool, camphor, sandal, silk thread, tiger skin, sarees and tin. "This long list of articles put into market, and the volume of exchange that such a trade should have involved in order to make the merchants endow a part of the profits thereon, evidently indicates an advanced state of commercial progress and economic prosperity." In the reign of Jagadekamalla, the merchant community assembled and granted one delavisa on each Kammota with in the house, and one haga for a month, on each Kammota in the street. [514] Kanmata is the small movable [514] furnace, used by goldsmith's for melting gold and silver. Trilokyamalla Mallideva granted 2 visas on dala in the mint where coins were minted. [515]

**Weight and measures** : Mattar-the land measure is equivalent of martar marturu of Telugu inscriptions. In Kakatiya times and after well land was measured by martus and dry land by puttis.[516] Martu is an equivalent of nivartana. [517] Oil mills in place of cows and sheep invariably mentioned in records from other parts of the Telugu country, are denoted to temples, for lamp lighting in this part of the country. Thus oil is substituted for ghee. The town Kottitone, also mentioned as Karti Keyapura, corresponding to modern Kudatani [518] (Bellary District) is mentioned in records of these cholas.

In the records from Ghantasala and Masulipatam between the years AD 1128 to 1148, Ghantasala appears as Chola-Pandyapura. At Nagavaram a chola king had founded an agrahara and dug a tank - Brahmana cheruvu to its south east. The donee Mahesvara Somayajulu dig canals from the tank and brought many fields under cultivation. [519] In later times, more canals were dug. In AD 1290 at Bhimavaram, Chodallideva granted land where four puttis and 10 tums could be sown.

## REFERENCES


1. E.I. IV No. 4 v 34.
2. The Colas II - I.
3. The Colas II - I p. 210
4. The Colas II - pp. 83, 170, 171.
5. C.V.Rao. His. of Andh. V p. 355.
6. Rajarajasanchika p. 185.
7. His. of Andh. I p. 156; V p.27.
8. 277 of 1905.
9. J.A.H.I.C.I. p. 45: Bharati I No. 1 p. 98.
10. Bharati III No. 4 p. 84.
11. Rajarajasanchika p. 185.
12. J.A.H. & C.I. p.45.
13. 180 as - Andhramahitala, Vengivasundhara.
14. Lord of 1300 district - Tripurantakam Inscription (s. 1028).
15. He appears as the lord of 480 in a record. This territorial division must have been different from Shatsahasra and was the original tract before the Velanandus became lords of Shatsahasra.
16. Panditaradhyacharitra II p. 415. Bharati I p. 96-K.V. Rao suggest that the number of 9 lakhs refers to the original population of the country.
17. 392 of 1936-37.
18. J.A.H.R.C. XII p. 129.
19. Cants IV vv 200 - 207.
20. E.I. IV No. 4 v 3.
21. E.I. IV No. v 4 48.
22. 168 of 1893: S.I.I. IV 993.
23. Keyurabahucharitra I vv 65, 66.

24. E.I. IV No. 4 p. 52 verse 58.
25. Keyurabahucharitra I vv 65, 66.
26. E.II III No. 15 verse 29.
27. Keyurabahucharitra I vv 21, 22.
28. 314 of 1932-33.
29. 296, 225 of 1892: S.I.L. IV 664, 675.
30. 231 of 1892: 240, 298 of 1893: S.I.L. IV, 1087, 1169.
31. 345 of 1893: S.I.I. IV 1228.
32. 378 & 384 of 1893: S.I.I. IV 1287, 1293.
33. 395 of 1893: 219 of 1897: S.I.I. IV 1316: S.I.I. VI 219.
34. 228-A of 1893: S.I.I. IV 107 a.
35. Keyurabahucharitra I v 29.
36. Keyurabahucharitra I vv 31, 35, 37, 42.
37. 247, 265-B of 1897: S.I.I. VI 211, 240.
38. 124 of 1897: S.I.I. VI 164.
39. 124 of 1897: S.I.I. VI 164.
40. II pp. 506 - 509.
41. Panditaradhyacharitra II p. 509.
42. - do - pp. 520 - 521.
43. E.I. IV No. 4.
44. 314 of 1932-33.
45. 164 of 1897: S.I.I. VI 124.
46. 265 of 1897: S.I.I. VI 238.
47. Upper classes, a multitude of people the masses - Brown. Tel. Eng. Dictionary.
48. 119 of 1917.
49. J.A.H. & C.I P.67.

50. A.R. 1933 II p. 61 para 14.
51. Keyurabahucharitra I v 19.
52. Palnativiracharitra.
53. Kistna Dt. Manual pp. 209-210.
54. Keyurabahuchritra IV 16.
56. 23 of 1916-17.
56. Keyurabahuchritra I v 24.
57. E.I. III No. 15 v 22.
58. Keyurabahuchritra I vv 29-30.
59. A short spear, a lance with a three sided point Brown: Tel. Eng. Dictionary.
60. Probably connected with the word Sadi - a coachman, charioteer, elephant driver, horse soldier.
61. E.I. III No. 15 vv 23, 25.
62. 314 of 1932-33.
63. 443 of 1915 p. 48 of Kandavitisamrajyama.
64. Kistna District Manual p. 170.
65. 265-A of 1897: S.I.I. VI 239.
66. E.I. IV No. 4 v 61.
67. Keyurabahuchritra I v 18.
68. 265 of 1897 S.I.I. VI 265.
69. 259-A od 1893: S.I.I. IV 1115.
70. 246-A od 1893: S.I.I. IV 1099.
71. 144 of 1913.
72. 164 of 1897: A.I.I. VI 606.
73. E.I. III No. 15 p. 89 I 122.
74. Hyd. Arch. Series 13. Telingana inscns. part II p. 211.
75. E.I. III No. 15 p. 92.
76. Prof. K.A.N. Sastri: The Foreign notices of S. India p. 174.

77. J.G.R. VIII p. 316.
78. J.Gr.R VIII p. 316.
79. E.I. XII No. 22.
80. His. of Antiquities I p. 80.
81. His of Antiquities I p. 82.
82. Kistna Dt. Manual p. 206.
83. Antiquities I p. 42.
84. Prof. K.A.N. Sastri: Foreign notices of S. India pp. 174-176.
85. - d - The Colas II (p. 451).
86. 151 of 1897: S.I.I. VI 109.
87. Brown: Tel Eng. Dictionary.
88. -do-
89. Hyd. Arch. Series B. Telingana Inscs. II p.203
90. Brown: Tel. Eng. Dictionary.
91. E.I. III No. 15 p. 92 fn. 1;Brown: Tel. Eng. Dictionary.
92. Hyd. Arch. Series p. 3 II p. 209: Brown Tel. Eng. Dictionary.
93. 144 of 1913.
94. Kollivisa instituted by Boddasa Bhimana.
95. A.R. 1919 II p. 102 para 31.
96. Hyd. Arch. Series 13-II p 209.
97. A.R. 1910 - II p 97 para 45.
98. A Dell or glade or gorge in the hills. a recess, a corner, a narrow place, garden, Konasimha the place of gardens of forest: Brown Tel. Eng. Dictionary.
99. H. Morris: Godavari Dt. p. 5.
100. 15-3-16.
101. E.I. IB No. 17: Bharati XV-Part I - Kodikuppa inscription.
102. J.A.H.R.S. XII p. 125.

103. E.I. IV No. 17 v 12.
104. 249 & 250 of 1893: S.I.I. IV 1102, 1104.
105. 517 of 1893: S.I.I. V 113.
106. E.I. IV No. 17.
107. 240 & 259 of 1893: S.I.I. IV 1102, 1104.
108. 246 of 1893: S.I.I. IV 1098.
109. 513 of 1893: S.I.I. V 128.
110. E.I.I. IV No. 17.
111. 520 of 1893: S.I.I V 150.
112. E.I. XIX No. 25 vv 3 & 8.
113. E.I. XIX No. 25 vv 14 & 15.
114. E.I. XIX No. 25 vv 16.
115. Ranganatha Ramayana Text pp. 10, 25.
116. -do- p. 154-155.
117. Uttara Ramayana pp. 133-134, 150, 151, 152, 157.
118. Ranganatha Ramayana pp. 3, 91.
119. Nizam's Arch. Rep. 1920-30 p.7.
120. Ranganatha Ramayana p. 454.
121. Nizam's Arch. Rep. 1929-30 p.7.
122. Ranganatha Ramayana pp. 3-4.
123. Nizam's Arich. Rep. 1929-30 p.7.
124. Ranganatha Ramayana p. 325, App.2 p. 751.
125. Ranganatha Ramayana pp. 170, 244-245, 406.
126. Purva and Uttara.
127. Ranganatha Ramayana p. 310.
128. Hyd. Arch. Series 13 - II No. 20. Telingana inscns. I No. 20.
129. Ranganatha Ramayana p. 155.
130. Palnativiracharitra - Introduction p. 16 - The verse is cited.
131. Palnativiracharitra - Introduction p. 17.

132. Palantiviracharitra—Introduction p. 17
133. - do- p. 17.
134. C.V. Rao: His. Andhras V p. 170 fn. 1.
135. Srinatha : P. Virach. Introd. p. 46-47.
136. Srinatha : P. Virach. Introd, p.8.
137. - do - text p. 60 s 89, p. 10 v 410.
138. C.V. Rao: History of Andhras V pp. 176, 177.
139. His. of Antiquities I App. A p. 5.
140. Palnaviracharitra Text.p. 23.
141. - do- fn.
142. - do- pp. 6 and 231 fn. fr. p.6.
143. Palnativiracharitra Text.p. 40.
144. C.V. Rao: Hist. of Andhras V p. 86 fn. 1.
145. Palnativiracharitra Text.p. 40.
146. Sewell: Antiquities I App A p. 6.
147. Srinatha P. Virach. Introduction p. 9.
148. Srinatha P. Virach. Text. p. 100-101.
149. Srinath P. Virach. Text.p. 16-24.
150. Palnativiracharitra Text.p. 21-22.
151. Palnativiracharitra Text. p. 24.
152. - do - p. 83.
153. - do - p. 91
154. - do - p. 92.
155. Antiquities I App A p. 7.
156. Palnativiracharitra Text. p. 10-11.
157. Palnativiracharitra Text. p. 20.
158. Palnativiracharitra Text. p. 85.
159. Palnativiracharitra Text. p. 32.
160. -do- p. 33.

161. Palnativiracharitra Text. p. 24, 28, 31.

162. - do - p. 26, 27.

163. Palnativiracharitra Text p. 86.

164. Palnativiracharitra Text p. 87.

165. - do - p.14, 15.

166. - do - p. 35-36.

167. Palnativiracharitra p. 60.

168. Palnativiracharitra p. 86.

169. - do- 88.

170. - do- 106.

171. Palnativiracharitra Text p. 117.

172. - do - Text p. 105.

173. Antiquities I pp. 14-15.

174. Antiquities I p. 62.

175. Antiquities-I App. A p. 5 fn. 3.

176. Palnativiracharitra Int. p. 49.

177. Antiquties I App. A p. 7 fn. 4, p-4.

178. 133 of 1913.

179. Rajarajasanchika p. 133.

180. Sewell: Antiquties I App. A p. 5.

181. Report cited on p. 14 of Introduction Pal. Virach.

182. Palnativiracharitra Introduction p. 14: Kaktiyasanchika p. 144.

183. Memoirs of Geological Survey of India Vol. 8 p. 10.

184. 313 of 1924: 253 of 1897: S.I.I. VI 218.

185. 528 of 1913.

186. 259 of 1924.

187. Antiquities p. 67: inscns. cited on p. 2-3 of App. F of Kondavitsamrajyamu.

188. 284 of 1924.

189. 279 of 1924: Kistna Dt. Manual p. 222.

190. 277 of 1934-35.

191. A.R. 1934 II para 33 pp. 67-68.

192. —do—

193. 277 of 1934-35.

194. Brown: Tel. Eng. Dictionary.

195. 227 of 1892: E.I. VI p. 275: S.I.I. IV 667.

196. E.I. VI No. 26.

197. 110 of 1893: S.I.I. VI 927.

198. 441 of 1915.

199. 236 & 237 of 1892: S.I.I. IV 687 & 688.

200. 234 of 1892: S.I.I. IV 685.

201. 233-A of 1892: S.I.I IV 684.

202. 215, 227 of 1892: S.I.I. IV 668, 667.

203. 232 of 1897: S.I.I. VI 195.

204. 15-6-40: 15-6-45.

205. Kondavitisamrajyamu p. 15.

206. Kistna Dt. Manual p. 12.

207. Palnativiracharitra Text p. 83-85.

208. E.I. VI No. 15-A.

209. 262 of 1897: S.I.I VI 230: J.A.H. & C.R. p. 94-98 Velpur.

210. Nellore Dt. Gazeteer p. 42.

211. Tirupati Report II p. 140.

212. 122 of 1893: S.I.L. 739.

213. E.I. III No. 16 p. 96 No. 4.

214. 142 of 1913.

215. 65 of 1917.

216. Kistna Dt. Manual p.163.

217. Antiquities I p.65.

218. 299 of 1915.

219. Mack MS 15-6-44 Ms p.44.

220. 391 of 1915.

221. 585 of 1925.

222. 122 of 1893: S.I.I. IV 939.

223. 312 of 1915.

224. 142 of 1913.

225. 118 of 1893: S.I.I. IV 935.

226. Brown: Tel Eng. Dictionary.

227. Bharati Vol. I No. p.31.

228. Bharati Vol. I No. pp. 29-31.

229. - do -31.

230. 1 Kuchchalu = 32 kuntas (Sabdaratnakara).

231. Mack MS 15-6-40 p.51.

232. Brown: Tel. Eng. Dictionary.

233. S.I.I. IV 934: Mack 15-6-21.

234. 146 of 1897: S.I.I. VI 103.

235. Sarada Vol. II (1924) No. 6 p. 656.

236. 146 of 1897: S.I.I. VI 103.

237. Pavuluri Mallana: Pavuluri Gantian-Kshaetra ganitam - Bharati I No. 2 p. 31.

238. e.p. I of 1921.22.

239. Gavanu = City gate: Vavanulu or Gavakulu fort gate: gave is shrotened form for gavance.

240. Eduvadalapalepu Sasanamu. Rajarajasanchika p. 189 Text.
241. 117 of 1917.
242. A.R. 1917 - II p. 121 para 29.
243. Text Rajarajasanchika p. 189.
244. 289 of 1893: S.I.I. 1153.
245. 243 of 1953 -36.
246. 527, 529 of 1829: S.I.I. V 167, 175.
247. Hist. of Andh. V p. 389.
248. 530, 532, of 1893: S.I.I. V 176, 186.
249. Morris: Godavari Dt. p. 35.
250. 243 of 1935-36.
251. I.A. 18 p. 61.
252. 243 of 1935-36.
253. Sivayogasara v 54.
254. Sivayogasara v 77.
255. Sivayogasara v 48.
256. E.I. IV No. 33.
257. E.I. IV No. 31 85.
258. E.I. IV No. 33 p. 242.
259. Antiquities I p. 24.
260. Taylor: Mack. Cont. III p. 538.
261. E.I. IV No. 33 1 90.
262. 482-B of 1893: S.I.I. V 75.
263. 485 of 1893: S.I.I. V 89.
264. Kavyalankarachodamani IX v 5.
265. Kavyalankarachodamani IV v 30.
266. E.I. IV No. 33 p.242.
267. Taylor: Mack, cut III p.538.
268. E.I. IV No. 33 1 90.

269. 482-D of 1893: S.I.I. V 75.

270. 485 of 1893: S.I.I. V 89.

271. E.I. XIX No. 26 v 15.

272. Bharati.

273. Antiquities 1 p. 21 - According to Brown Suskani is a coin worth about 8 pies.

274. E.I. V No. 4 A v. 7.

275. E.I. V No. 4 p.35 fn 3.

276. 113-A of 1902: S.I.I. VII 737.

277. Sivayogasara verses cited on p.470 of Hist. of Andhras V.

278. 113 A of 1902: S.I.I. VII 737.

279. Antiquities 1 p.37.

280. Kakativasanchika App p.78 No. 30.

281. 280 of 1902: S.I.I. VII 735.

282. 308 of 1920.

283. 295 of 1892: S.I.I. IV 749.

284. 300 of 1892: S.I.I. IV 753.

285. 263 of 1892: S.I.I. IV 715.

286. 311 of 1892. S.I.I. IV 764.

287. 260 of 1892: S.I.I. IV 712.

288. 302 of 1892: S.I.I. IV 153.

289. 8 of 1911, 287 of 1912: 520 of 1908.

290. Tirupati inscriptions I p.88.

291. Nell. Ins. II Kanigiri 24.

292. E.I.

293. 128. of 1916: A.R. 1916 II p.151 para 81.

294. 128. of 1916: A.R. 1916 II p. 151 para 81.

295. 230 of 1922.

296. 187 of 1937-38 A.R. 1938 p. II para 54.

297. Nell. Ins. III 46.

297. Nell. Ins. II Nell. 15.

299. Nell. Ins. I A 25.

300. Nell. Ins. III 106.

301. 372 of 1928-29: A.R. 1928 II p.79 para 51.

302. 230 of 1922: 40 of 1921.

303. Tirupati inscns. I No. 61 (127-G.T.).

304. 302 of 1912: A.R. II p.126 para 75.

305. A.R. 1928 II p. 79 para 41 375 of 1928.

306. 372 of 1928.

307. Nell. Ins. III, Sulurpet 3.

308. 351. of 1928-29: 428 of 1919. Tirupati inscn. I No. 62.

309. Tiruati inscns. I No.77 (126 TT).

310. 126 TT. Tirupati inscn. I p.89.

311. 129 TT. p.89.

312. 40 of 1921.

313. 433 of 1922.

314. 333 of 1909.

315. Tirupati inscn. I p.89.

316. Tirupati inscn. 68 (137 TT).

317. Tirupati Ins. 174 (652 TT).

318. Nell. Ins. III Nell. No. 21.

319. 428 of 1919.

Maksya

320. 287 if 1899: S.I.I. VI 867.

321. 282 - do - 797.

Pallava

322. 321 of 1905: S.I.I. IX 275.

323. 282 of 1899 S.I.I. VI 797.

324. 284 of 314-E of 1899: S.I.I. VI 839, 973.

325. 288-C of 1899: S.I.I. VI 871.

326. 305-C - do - 946.

327. 322 - do o 937.

328. Mack MSS Elliot's Tel. Inscn. s 15-6-26 No. 61.

329. E.I. V No. 14 M 52 - 64.

330. Mack MS 15-6-26 No. 61.

331. - do -

332. Proceedings 4th Or. conference pp. 171-174.

333. E.I. V. No. 14 p. 109 fn. 4.

334. 275 and 276 of 1896. S.I.I. V 1154, 1155.

335. E.I. XXI No. 41.

336. Bharati X part II p. 735.

337. 252 of 1899: S.I.I. VI 714.

338. 241 of 1899: S.I.I. VI 692.

339. 358 of 1896: S.I.I. 1240.

340. Bharati X - II p. 755.

341. Vizagapatam gazetteer p. 319.

342. Bharati X - II pp. 753, 755.

343. 364 of 1899: S.I.I. VI 1166.

344. 365-X of 1899 S.I.I. VI 1177.

345. Elliot's Colln. 15-6-20 No. 80.

346. Nell. Ins. III O 150.

347. Nell. Ins. III O 151.

348. Nell. Ins. II O 27.

349. Nell. Ins. III O 109.

350. Antiquities I p.138.

351. Nell. Ins. I.e.p. No. 17.

352. Nell. Ins. III O 89.

353. Nell. Ins I. e.p. No 17 v 28. But according to Sukrani Fisara 4 or 5 karas make one dandam and 25 dandams 1 nivartana. Citation on p.64 of Rajarajasanchika.

354. Nell. Ins. II O 28.

355. Tellingana Insn. I No. 34.

356. Bharati V - II p. 799.

357. Bharati X - I p.400.

358. Nell. Ins. II Darsi, 13.

359. Nell. Ins. II Darsi. 13.

360. Nell. Ins. II Darsi. 13.

361. Nell. Ins. II Darsi. 13.

362. 180, 275. of 1905.

363. J. Gr. R.

364. G.V. Ramamurti Pantulu commemoration vol. No. 1 Eng. Sec. p.135.

365. 194 of 1899: S.I.I. Vi 640.

366. Ins. Mad. Pres. II NL. 633.

367. Nell. Ins. II Podile 30.

368. 756 of 1992.

369. 33 of 1922.

370. 103 of 1918.

371. Mack MS. 15-4-4 Ms p. 235.

372. Hist. of Andhras V.

373. Nell. Ins. I D 35.

374. Nell. Ins. I D 35.

375. Nell. Ins. I Darsi. I.

376. Record from Chandur.

377. Mack MS 15-3-8 p. 67 No. 2: 406 of. 1911.

378. Mack MS 15-3-22.

379. Make MS 15-3-25 Insn. No. 10.

380. Mack MS 15-3-8 p. 67 No. 2.

381. 314 of 1930-31.

382. 268 of 1906.

383. Mack MS 15-4-28.

384. Mack MS 15-3-8.

385. Proceedings 4th Or. Conf. p. 149: I.A. 56 p. 191.

386. Proceedings 4th Or. Conf. p. 149: I.A. 56 p. 191.

387. Mack MS 15-3-9 Ms p. 67 No.2 Attirala - 406 of 1911.

388. G. Tel. AC IX p. 203: C.V. Rao His. of Andh. II pp. 354-355.

389. Kev. Sambhava Cono X VV 546-550.

390. 222 of 18999: S.I.I. VI 643.

391. 167 of 1899: S.I.I. VI.

392. 173 of 1899: S.I.I. VI 617.

393. Nell. Ins. II O 19 - Dayyalareyurusasanamu Asosnamahajanamu.

394. XI vv 595, 603, 620, 630.

395. XI v 575.

396. XI vv 679, 704, XII vv 784, 786.

397. 168 of 1899: S.I.I. VI 611.

398. 316, 327 of 1915.

399. 199 of 1899: S.I.I. VI 613.

400. Critique M. Nannichoda's Ku. Sambhava p. 163.

401. 164 of 1899: S.I.I. VI 606.

402. 173 of 1899: S.I.I. VI 617.

403. 191 of 1899: S.I.I. VI 191.

404. 192 of 1899: S.I.I. VI 638.

405. 193 of 1899: S.I.I. VI 639.

406. 188 & 1899: S.I.I. VI 148, 149.

407. 210 of 1897: S.I.I. VI 170.

408. 572 of 1907.

409. Mack MS 15-4-17.

410. 350 of 1950.

411. 302 of 1904: A.R. 1905 p. 43 para 11.

412. 395 of 1904.

413. Pannasa or Pannasa appears to be a kanerese word and same as panneya or panya in kannada meaning a kind of tenure by which land rented to a cultivator by the king and taken back by whenever he liked; and pannai in Tamil meaning agriculture is a kind of land tenurebhuni bhoga. Rajarajsanchika pp. 62-63.

414. J. Ind. His. 15 p. 46.

415. - do - p. 46.

416. J. Ind. His. 15 p.46.

417. Ketana: Dasa Ku Xi v 86.

418. Nirvachama Ra. VIII v 120, X v 75.

419. Andhra Mahabharata III - Virata I vv 67, 185, 186, 188, 192, Udyaga I vv 31-49, 63, I 335, 343.

420. Andhra Mahabharata IV Bhishma III v 110, Drona II 134, Vol v Sanptika I 82.

421. E.I. VII No. 17 Av 16.

422. E.I. VII No. 17A vv 22-23 p. 126.

423. Nir. Ra. I v 32.

424. N. Ramayana III v19 VII vi, Dasaka ch. In 19.

425. Nell. Ins. I A.R. 38.

426. Nell. Ins. III Rapur 38.

427. Dasaku I v 21.

428. Dasaku I v 57.

429. Dasaku I v 66.

430. Chatupadyamanimahajari p. 92.

431. Vijnanesvara Kanda vv 2-18. Dasaku II v 4.

432. Nell. Ins. III R 8.

433. Nell. Ins. III R 36.

434. Nell. Ins. II Karali 25.

435. N. Ramayana XI 94-100 X vv 24-36.

436. 556 of 1919.

437. Nell. Ins. I A.R. 24.

438. N. Ramayana I v 35.

439. N. Ramayana I vv 41, 42.

440. Dasaku II v 8.

441. Nell. Ins. II KR 29.

442. Andhra Mahabharata VR II asramavasa I v 73.

443. Chatupadyamanimanjari p. 27.

444. Nellore Dt. Gazeteer p. 335.

445. Mack MSS.

446. Andhra Mahabharata III Virata I vv 171, 211, III v, 6: Vol. IV Bhishma I vv 272, 283, II v 172, 191, Drona I v 353, II v 95, III 196, IV v 101, V vv 71, 89, 135. Vol. V Karna I vv 132, 178, Salya 1 201, 211, Sanchika 1 v 111.

447. Chatupadyamanimanjari pp. 28-29 Nell. Ins. II Nell. 72.

448. Nell. Ins. I AR 26.

449. Nell. Ins. III Venkatagiri 3.

450. Nell. Ins. III Ven. 16.

451. 233 of 1903: S.I.I. VIII 532.

452. Chatupadyamanimanjari p. 28.

453. Nell. Ins. I AR 7.

454. Nell. Ins. III Venkatagiri 3.

455. Nell. Ins I A 45.

456. Nell. Ins. Venkatagiri 13.

457. E.I. VII No. 17-A.
458. Nell. Ins II Nell. 55.
459. Vidavali = a kind of grass for thatching the roofs of houses: Brown Tel. Eng. Dictionary.
460. Mixture of Sand and Chunnam.
461. Nell. Ins. I Gudur 39.
462. Nell. Ins. I Gudur 44.
463. 609 of 1919.
464. e.p. 10 of App. A of 1918-19: Hist. Inscns. of S.India p. 166.
465. - do - 1908-9
466. 413 of 1919.
467. Sewell: Hist. Inscns. of S India p. 153.
468. 315 of 1919-Hist. Ins. of S India p. 166.
469. There are six pandyan records at Nandalur dated between 1286 and 1293 AD (588-594 of 1907).
470. 580 of 1907.
471. AR 1908 pp. 70-72 paras 72.77.
472. 580 of 1907.
473. AR 1908 II p. 72 para 76.
474. IV. Bhishma III v 119.
475. AR 1908 II para 77: Brown: Tel. Eng. Dictionary.
476. The Pandyan emperor was J. Sundara Pandya I who ascended the throne in AD 1251-The Pandyan kingdom p.259.
477. Dasakau VIII vv 20-24.
478. v 33 Prayaschittakanda vv 43, 49, 52, 54,
479. Prayaschittakanda vv 65-80 137.
480. Prayaschitta kanda v 85.
481. AR 1908 II p. 78, para 40, No.343.
482. Nell. Ins.IGundur 34.

483. Nell. Ins. II Nell. 31.

484. NI. Ins. III Sulurpet 7.

485. Rajarajasanchika p. 133.

486. Nellore Dt. Gazetteer pp. 143, 246.

487. Prayaschittakanda vv 306.

488. Prayaschittakanda v 135.

489. Prayaschittakanda v 86.

490. Nell. Ins. II KR 56.

491. 441 of 1919.

492. Prayaschittkanda v 8.

493. Nell. Ins. I AR 7.

494. Nellore Dt. Gazetteer p. 353: Nellore Dt. Manual.

495. Nell. Ins. III Venkatagiri I Chapalapalle.

496. Mack MS 15-4-33 Kaifiyat of Kottur.

497. Nell. Ins. III U No. 14.

498. Nell. Ins. II Podiles 22.

499. 308 of 1935-36.

500. Mack MS 15-3-11 No. 3.

501. E.I. XXVI No. 2 Rajahmundry Museum plated of Annadeva.

502. E.I. XXVI No. 2. Rajahmundry Museum plates of Annadeva.

503. Hyd. Arch. Series 13. II No. 36.

504. Telingana inscriptions Misc. No. 18.

505. Pully - Brown Tel. Eng. Dictionary.

506. Telingana inscns. Misc. No. 6.

507. -do-

508. e.p. 4 of 1918.

509. V.P. Sastri: Prabandharatnavali vv 303-308.

510. Tirupati inscriptions II O 86.

511. Nell. Ins. II O 85.

512. A.R. 1935-36 II p. 67 para 24.

513. 15 of 1917.

514. 16 of 1917: AR 1917 II p. 113.

515. 8 of 1917 - naga = 1/4 panam, 1/256 nishkam - Rajarajasanchika p. 185 fn.

516. 499. of 1915: S.I.I. IX 228.

517. Rajarajasanchika p. 63.

518. Ganapati's Pakhal inscriptions.

519. A.R. 1918 p. 135 para 7.

# 2

# The Arts

**General Introduction**: In the domain of arts, as in other spheres, the period of half a millonnium from 1000 AD, Constitutes the most creative epoch in the history of the Andhra land. Political security, peace and prosperity under the aegis of the Chalukya-cholas and the popular religious movements in the earlier centuries and the sway of the Reddis, the Velemas, and the kings of Vijayanagar during the 14th and 15th centuries were responsible for the tremendous activity in literature, art, architecture, sculpture, dance, drama, music and learning resulting in their full fledged growth - with political security as the background, the religions fervour of the times supplied the motive force for the acceleration of the progressive movements of the arts. The democratic spirit instilled into literature and arts by the religious movements widened the scope of their respective spheres, so as to embrace not only the high flown Sanskrit and Telugu works meant for the learned few, but also works written in easy Telugu and Kannada for the untutored - the masses. Thus literature flourished under royal patronage and private munificence. Generally the poet enjoying regal support rendered into Andhrabhasha - Telugu the national epics and the puranas,[1] where as poets with a religious bent wrote works mostly dealing with the lives of religious teachers and their tents,[2] in easy style - janu tenuga-in suitable for popular literature of the period e.g. ballads[3] with which its characteristic features flourished throughout.

Sanskrit was not neglected in this epoch and on the other hand occupied a high pedastal in the realm of literature. It was deva bhasha - the language of gods in contrast with desabhasha - the language of the people. Sanskrit was for the privileged few, scholars and patrons, and the high standard in the sanskrit works and the great regard commanded by their authors may be guaged roughly from the volume of works covering a wide range of subjects from poetics and ethics to Isvasatras and their intrinsic merit. In this period it was the ambition of all poets to qualify themselves as Ubhayabhashapravina - scholarship in two languages - Sanskrit and Telugu - at least one each. Thus poets in Andhra Bhasha were poets in Sanskrit as well, for scholarship in Sanskrit forms a pre requisite for mastery in Telugu. Even when they did not compose works in Sanskrit, their knowledge in that language and works in it is mirrored in their Telugu works.

Telugu literature prior to 1000 AD is practically nil. Except inscriptions no literary composition of merit are heard of prior to that date. The period after 1000 AD gaveMahabharata to the Andhras. Nannaya's Bharata written under the patronage of the Vengi chalukyas the earliese extant work in Telugu falls in this period; and was completed by Tikkana and Errapreggada under the aegis of the Telugu cholas of Nellore and the Reddis of Kondavidu. With Nannaya as the apex, works in Telugu on a large variety of subjects were written dedicated to kings, ministers, generals, religious preceptors and deities. The first works in Telugu grammer, poetics, ethics, mathematics, prosody drama, dance, music, were the gifts of this age. In this epoch of the Bharata Kavitraya and Srinatha, not only Kavya but prabandha literature also had its beginnings,[4] to be perfected later on in the age of Krishnaraya of Vijayanagar. Some of the royal authors were Nannichoda, Baddena, Buddha, Kacha and Vithala, besides some of the kings of the Kakatiya the Reddi and the Velama dynasties. General Jaya was an authority on Natyasastra Bhaskara, Ketana, Peddana, Machana, Potana, Ganrana, Jakkana, Ananta, Somanatha and the Panditaraya were some of the poets of the period, besides a host of minor poets. The genealogies of poets show that generally their predecessors were generals and scholars and some times authors of merit. Works on medicine and sciences were rendered into Telugu and commentaries in Sanskrit were written. Poet Mallana, grandfather of Pavuluri Mallana, the translator of Ganitasarasamgraha of Jina Mahaviraharya, into Telugu, lived in the court of Rajaraja Narendra and received Nava-Khandavada from him.[5]

Inscriptions reveal the growth of language, literature, art of writing, script and language used and capacities of the composer, engraver, mason and so forth. The high place given to Sanskrit is seen in the long copper plate charters which are invariably in Sanskrit from beginning to the end, though in some cases the script employed in telugu, and the stone records which are entirely in Sanskrit, some enumerating the boundaries in Telugu - Desabhasha for the knowledge of the ordinary man, as mentioned in the records. But most of the records of the period are in Sanskrit and Telugu the latter script being commonly adopted for both the languages. Several of the Telugu records - both in language and script - are generally brief and in simple prose. In the sanskrit records verse is employed, sometimes very ornate and high flown with double meanings. The long prasastis of the many dynasties, emulating their chalukya - chola overlords consist largely of Sanskrit epithets with an admixture of a few Telugu and Kannada titles. Telugu verse vigorous in style, rich in diction flowing and beautiful is employed in some Telugu records. In few cases, the name of the composer finds place in the inscription and comparatively the engraver is more careful in affixing his name towards the end of it. In the words of Professor Sastri, " Stone masons and copper smiths were to be found every where to engrave on stone and copper, a work which was sometimes done with remarkable accuracy and art. The corrupt and colloquial forms of words and phrases in several inscriptions show that the work was generally entrusted to men who were just literate but were no scholars. "[6] Some of the Telugu records are small poems or Kavyas with verses interposed between prose passages Champu. Some records in which the Sanskrit employed is difficult each verse having three or four interprestations, are complete compositions like Kanyas.

Records in Grantha and Tamil both in language and script are avilable in the Telugu country from Cuddapahto Guntur. Some records are in Grantha Throughtout, some in Tamil, some in Sanskrit and Tamil, and some others in Sanskrit language and grantha script.[7] These Tamil records are in faultless prose and present all the features of the Tamil records in Tamil land, issued by the Cholas and Pandyas and so forth. Similarly the Kannada records of the period are either in Kannada completely or in Kannada and Telugu. The script is Kannada and the presence of Tamil and Kannada scholars in the country. Unfortunately very few of the composers of the Tamil and Kannada records of high literary merit, took care to append their names to their compositions and we are poorer on that count. The masons, engravers or inscribers must have migrated from the Tamil and Kannada countries in the wake of the expeditions and expension of the chola and chalukyn empires into the Andhra country and settled there, or the Telugu scholars and inscribers learnt the languages and executed the records.

This period witnessed the birth of many an original work[8] in Telugu, some of which were rendered into Kannada and Sanskrit by later poets. Some of the Telugu renderings of the Sanskrit epics formed the originals[9] for translations into Kannada, instead of the sanskrit originals. Some poets wrote in Kannada, besides in Sanskrit and Telugu. Somanatha was a poet in eight languages. Several works on law and justice were written and translated into Telugu.

Art and architecture flourished. Temples were raised in honour of kings, heroes and sagas and the sculptures and panels on walls, pillars and roof and so forth in temples and mandapas, about a variety of subjects from epics to Kamasastras-executed under the patronage of local dynasties attest the progress of arts in this period. The advance of music, dance and drama, was closely allied with the festivities of temples and royal courts. Books were written on these subjects, and temple grants included provision for architects, musicians, dancers and so forth besides priests and other members of the temple establishment. King's court had a definite place for musicians, dancers actors, besides poets and scholars, who must have had permanent remunerations. Bharatanatyasastra wastranslated into Telugu including the chapters on music and dance.[10] Dance, music and dramatic performances in temples and courts were in strict adherence to the rules in the texts of the sastras. Sometimes, the authors of works on music and dance were acquainted with the practice of those arts, besides theory. Temple grants making regular provision for various artists in the period prior to 1300 AD were elaborate and detailed, modelled on those of the cholas, though greater attention was bestowed on writings works on these subjects after that date. Some of the titles in regal prasastis show that music formed an essential part of regalia. War music was not neglected which is attested by references in inscriptions and literature and the variety of instruments sounded at the beginning of expeditions and on winning victories.

The education and learning of the populace was looked after by temples and maths. The recitation and exposition of puranas in temples, maths attached to them and or screens, boards and walls formed one way of mass education, besides the wandering mendicants who went about singing ballads.

### The Valanandu Chodas

Literature and arts made great strides of progress in the Velanandu kingdom fostered by its enlightened rulers. Similar situation prevailed in local kingdoms recognising Velanandu suzerainty. The religious movements - Virasaiva and Viravaishnava - affered scope for works like Somanathal, as Janu Telugu and ballads like that of Palnad Heroes. Works like Keyurabahu charitra rendered from Sanskrit into telugu, have plenty of Originality and local clouring in them. Sataka literature had its origins[11] in this age and some of the best original works in Telugu were written. Mallikarjuna Panditaradhya, the great Virasaiva religious teacher lived in this age and visited the court of Choda II. The part played by music and dance in the religious revival is attested by Velanandu inscriptions, and references and descriptions of concerts and performances in royal courts and temples like that of Sri Sailam. A vast variety in songs, dances, and musical instruments, especially the vina were in vogue and nothing except their names are preserved for us in literature. The growth of architecture and sculpture is seen in the temples. Literature shows that carving, drawing and painting were practised. Ladies played a significant role in encouraging and practising poetry, music and dance. In temples provision was made for expounding epics, holding religious discourses, as a mesaure for mass education.

**Literature** : Some of the rulers were scholars, patronised literature and held literary discourses in their courts. The title Sishteshtavanajavana martanda i.e. a sun to the group of lotuses i.e. poets, favourites and pupils in the Velanandu prasasti indicates the rulers patronage extended to scholars. Gonka I bore the title - Sishtesstuchintamani.[12] Gundama, queen of Choda I patronised poets. Gonka II gave plenty to scholars and is described as a moon to the bees on the lotus i.e. scholars. His uncle Panda pleased schoalrs Choda II was a scholar, learned in all sciences and praised by the assembly of scholars. He gave plenty to scholars and the e.p. grant mentions him as Kavipundarikanikara pradyotana.[13] In his court - brahmasabha- Mallikarjuna Panditaradhya and Banddhapadacharya held discussions open to the public.[14] Among the staff of the Ramesvara temple at Siripuram were Eraya, a devarakavi i.e. a poet attached to the god and Kuma, a devi kavi "who from the name must have been woman and was evidently a poetess attached to the Goddess."[15] This provison was made by Choda II in AD 1165. Prithvisvara made grant to scholars.

Ministers, generals and officers patronised poets. In the of Choda 1, Bhimavatha was an expert in the knowledge of the Vedas and Sana was a patron of poets Govinda pradhani of the region of Gonka II was an orator and writer of Kavyas.[16] treasure kanta was well versed in literature and patronised learned man. Minister Surya and Kattamba, wife of Padala choda patrnised schoalrs. In the reign of choda II, Drona was versed in the agamas, and Kanma made a grant to devarabrahmapurulu who were eleven, one of whom was an astronomer.[17] Sebbaya and his son Bhandari Erramanayaka gave plenty to poets. Sajjaprolenayaka is described as a kalpa tree to scholars and poets. Sokkama, the dasi of the Pandisvara temple at Tsandavole patronised schoalrs, poets and brahmins.[18] General Jaya was a poet and an orotor. His chebrole inscription records grants to the superintendent of edicts and the emperor of poets, astrologer, doctor.[19] and so forth - Nanduri - Bhimaya Gundaya was a scholar and expert story teller. Even in the company of scholars, he presented them with palanquin etc. vehicles, he was interested in the meetings of scholars and literary discourses. He could write works, and decipher read and write all script as methodically and vigorously as Andhra characters.[20] Munchama says that Tsandavole was the home of scholars and poets.

**Poets and their works:** Of the composers of the Velanandu inscriptions only single person is known namely Ayyapillarya, the composer of Pithapur pillar epigraph.[21] (AD 1186)

**Mallikarjun Panditaradhya:** A poet of distinction, versatile, scholar and religious teacher, Mallikarjuna pandita was a unique personality of his age. He was the last of the Pandita traya, the other two being - Sripati Pandita and Sivalanka Manchana Pandita. Sripati Paudital Guru of Anantapala, the celebrated chalukya general and ruler of Kondepallinadu with capital at Bezvada, was the author of Sivatatvasara, Panditaradhyacharitra and Sivalhaktavijaya.[22] Manchana pandita lived about AD 1160 and his writings are 131 in total, some of which are dedicated to Isanyamarti Mallikarjunadeva.[23] Mallikarjuna Pandita, the heor of Somanatha's Panditaradhyacharitra and similar works in the ensuing centuries, was the pivot of Virasaiva religion and literature of his times. The main field of his activities was Andhra desa and the chief vehicle of his writings was easy flowing Telugu, easily understood by the masses, though he did write some works in Mannada. He could command a following of the masses and his pupils, devotees and admirers were innumerable. Due to his influence, that the last vestiges of Buddhism in Andhra land ended. Buddhist teachers and thier influence became discredited in the courts of the Velanandus the Kondapadumatis and the Kotas. On the other hand, efficacy and belief in Hinduism became reassured.

**Date and early life:** The chronology of Mallikarjuna Pandita may be settled approximately because of his contemporaneous with several kings of Telugu and Kannada lands. His bography written forty years after his death shows that Basava, the originator of Virasaivism, and minister of Bijjala of the Kaluchuris and killed in AD 1168 by Bijja's ministers, Velanandu choda II, king Udaya of Panugal [24] (AD 1162) and Buddha of the Kondapadumatis (AD 1178) were contemporary with M.Pandita. Pandita was much younger than Basava and lived up to old age. For after he settled at Vellatur he sent Donayya to do circumambulation to Srisailam, reach the top of the hill and complete his vrata instead of himself and Siva to Donayya appeared as an old man in his dream. After completing the vrata when Pandita with his wife and children became one with the linga about AD 1190 at Vellatur,[25] he must been about seventy. If so his date of birth falls about AD 1120.

M. Pandita, son of Bhimana, priest in the Bhimasvara temple at Draksharama and Gauramba, born after their prayers and visit to Mallikarjuna of Srisailam, was a Rigveda and Gautamax gotra. His guru was Aradhyadeva of Kotipalli in the vicinity of Draksharama, from whom he received Sivadiksha, acquired a knowledge of the implications of Saivism, and practised them,[26] when the Brahmins began to deride him, he convinced them establishing the greatness of Siva by explaining sacred ashes, rudraksha, guru padodaka linga workship, eating of offered things, and narrating the stories of Ghantakarna etc. ancient saints. Pandita wrote Sivatatvasara explaining the Viramahesvaramarga and regulated his life accordingly. Then he left the neighbourhood of the Godavari with his devotees to propagate his religion.

Pandita resided at Tsandavole for a while, accepted the challenge to his religion from Choda II and his Buddhist preceptor, and in the Brahmasabha, asserted the superiority of Saivism over Buddhism by his orations attesting his marvellous knowledge in Virasaiva tenets.[27] He announced that he would remove his eyes thrice and got them back by the grace of Siva. He did accordingly and, when he removed his eyeballs for the third time, by king's order poison was put in his eyes Pandita cursed the king and the kingdom, left Tsandavote with - determination not to get back his sight till went beyond its precincts, reached Amaravati, by praying to Amaresvara got his sight and received the sacred ashes sent by Basava. According to another version, the king was Kondapadumati Buddha, Pandita's halting place was Buddham (near Tsandavole), and the Buddhist jealous of Pandita connives for the stealing of a vessel in the articles of his worship, and pupils of Pandita killed those Buddhists without his knowledge. The king through his men found from Pandita that removal of eyes was the punishment for murder and ordered the removal of his eyes as he took on himself the crime of his pupils.From these narrations which may not be true in their entirely, it is clear that Pandita was persecuted by the Velanandus and the Kondapadumatis.

At Amravati, Pandita composed some poems in Kannada and started out to go to Basava, halted at Idugudumala, then at Panugal, reached Vanipuram, where he heard the news of Basava's death. From there he moved towards Srisailam, halted at Vellatur, sent Donayya to fulfil his mission of pilgrimage to Srisailam.

**His knowledge and works:** N. Pandita's knowledge comprised the entire range of all religions, tenets and works on them.[28] In the sabha of choda II, he discredited with citations from scutis, smritis and puranas, the Vedavada karmavada, kalavada, vedanta, sankhyavada, Panchavatra, yogavada, charvaka vada, banddhavada, Gainavada and several other controversies. When Bauddhacharya criticised that Indudharma, Brahmamukha virbhava, Kapilsthimalacharma dharma, umpatitva, Bikshatava gangadharva, trivikramas khandana, hariharabheda, garaladharana, nagnatra, dakshadhvaredhvamsa do not establish that Siva was the greatest of the Gods, Pandita expounded how the very same point assert Siva's greatness and described Siva's pranayalila and mahatandavalila, and was praised and applauded by audience. Pandita had perfect knowledge of all sciences, was pure in mind and thought and possessed good character and appearance. On their way to the king's court, Pandita's devotees were said to have been singing.[29] dakshadhvara, Vyasashtaka, ganadansbara, sarabha, scrutipanchagadyamala, rudramahima, sivatatvasara, samsara mayastavam, rudrasakkas from rigveda, saying by Pancha brahma in Yajurveda, praise of Siva in Samaveda pramatha suktas, basava suktas, sravanatakandalila, dundubji dundilangula, manduka, sakala, maitrayaniya, vaineya, vaidheya, vartantaveya, sannaki, mandgalaya, samkhyayaniya, sapya, sakteya, supayaniya, kapila, bashkala, galava, kanva, dantavatyatparata,brahmodapradanta, khalval devadarsi, jabili, karaha kanghiya,vajasanetya, narayaniya, janapahardaivya, parakramenanta bandheya, viradha, parakrami, brahmapansha khandika, asuraniya alias Mulakathaya, vasuraniya, Katyayani, etc. sukhas, nyayasutras, amnayas, their divisions, sutras, Kaivalya, Kainesha, Jabala, rudra, manavajaigisha, marutamnaya narayana, brahman, sivasankalpa, srirudra charya, brihadaranya garbha-hamsa etc upanishads. Obviously panditha mastered these, taught them to his devotees, and wrote on some of them if not all in easy Telugu.

Sivatatvasara is the best of Pandita's works that have come down to us. It is the first of the satakas in Telugu literature, mentioned thus in Panditaradya charitra. Pandita's authorship of it is clear in the work.[30] The verses in Sivatatvasara generally end with the makuta Siva, though occasionally with aja, rudra and umhesa. Consisting of 1139 verses, the work describes briefly the stories of Sai vaite devotees which were dealt with elaborately and in good style by Somanatha, in his Basava purana and Panditaradhyacharitra. In Panditaradhya charitra, Somanatha 'included the essense of the verses in Sivatatvasara as far as possible in the original words.[31] Some of the Prakaranas of Sivatatvasara are found in Panditaradhya charitra. For instance; advaitakhandana of the former appears as Vedantavadakhandana in vadaprakarna of the latter, dakshadhvaradhvamasa of the former as dakshadhavaraprasamas of the letter, the description and his last prayer to Siva as his last desire in Parvataprakara,[32] Pandita and his pupils are said to have been reciting

Sivatanvasara frequently. The work was popular among Saivaites in the days of Pandita and Somana. It formed the basis and essence for the later works of Saiva poets. Sivatatvasara has some language peculiarities not found in the work of the kavitraya. Pandita adopted old style in it, mentions the ancient poets - Bana, Mayura and Kalidasa and says that a poet may tell his lord to worship Siva.

The names of a few works of Pandita, not extent find mention in Panditaradhya charitra. Pandita did Srimukhadarsanagadya in Sanskrit, Ganasahasranama Kavya,[33] Basvagita and Ishtalingastotra in Kannada. Of his Vachanagala also in Kannada, some are dedicated to Amaragundada Mallikarjuna by which M. Pandita was known for he halted at Amaravati.[34] Banapadya, Uksharagadya, Panchagadya, Varnadembaram, Vyasashtakam, Srinilakantha stavam, Srirudrakavacham, Sarabhem, mayura staram, halayudham, anamayam, malabanam, mahimastavam, malayarajiyam, manidandakam, mahastotrasutramulu, satskam, dipakalika, mahanatakam, udhaharammulu, rudramahima, mukkakavelulu, gitasuktamulu, bhiringastavamulu, ashtakas by sages of yore - were the works of Pandita. Pandita is popularly known as Sivakavi Naliayya.

Pandita had two sons who received a grant from Malla, minister of Ganapati of the Kakatiyas.[35] Vibhuti Ganraya of Machirajupalle near Warangal was a pupil of Pandita.

**Palkuriki Somanatha**: Somanatha, holds a unique place in the history of religion and literature of teh Andhra and Kannada lands. The greatest of the Siva kavis, his could write poetry in eight languages. Of his several works, the majority are in Telugu desi style and a few in Kannada and Sanskrit. Of his writings in other languages only the passages in Tamil, Marathi in Panditaradhyacharitra are extant. Somanatha was the hero of the work - Palkuriki Somesvarapuranas. His genius is revealed in his works, which showed the way to contemporary and later poets in many respects language, style subject matter.

**His date and early life**: Somanatha lived towards the close of the 12th and beginning of the 13the century AD. Some of his contemporaries were Rudra I of the Kakatiyas and grandsons of M. Pandita. His place of birth is a matter of controversy, like that of Bammera Potana of a later date. As his family name is Palkuriki probably he belonged to Palkuriki village in Warangal district[36] (of Nizam's dominions) than to Halkuriki in Tamkur taluq (of Mysore state) and 20 miles from Madakasira taluq[37] (Anantapur district). He was a Brahmin and not a Tangama, as has been wrongly supposed by some,[38] and parents were Vishnyu Ramideva and Sriyadevi. He learnt to write poetry from his guru Karasthali Visvanatha. While still young, Somanatha went to Srisailam and spent his time till old age there. He became one with the got at Kalikana near Sivaganga in Kannada land.

**His works**: As many as seventeen works of Somanatha are enumerated by Pidupari Basavana in his Basavapurana. Of his Telugu writings, the major works are Basavapurana and Panditaradhyacharitra written in dvipada or couplet metre peculiar to the Telugu language "A dvipada is a couplet with prasa or some consonant but not necessarily in combination with the same vowel of the second place of the two lines of the couplet, and either an ordianry gati which in Telugu stands for the same consonant plus a corresponding vowel occurring at the place next to that of the ordinary yat. Therefore, each line in advipada as three [Indra ganas (nala, bhor, ra, ta, sala) and a Surya gana (na, ha, or galat)]."[39]

1. Somana's Basava purana, deals mainly with the life of Basavesvara though the lives of many devotees of Siva - Maratha, Andhra and Karnataka are described in the course of the narrative. The poet gathered his material from old men, writings and songs of old saints, and Basavasvara.[40] Written about thirty years after the death of Basava, Basava purana froms one of the most reliable sources for the history of Basava. It has seven cantos. Being the first of Somanatha's works, it gives us a few details about the author. In dealing with the lives of the Tamil saints, Somana may have consulted Periyapurana by Sekkizar, a Sivakavi in the 12th Century AD. He took the lives of same saints from Sivatatvasara. Somana said that he would purify himself by describing the lives of the saints which writing Basavapurana and Panditaradhyacharitra. He closely followed Nannichoda in his work, which was rendered into sanskrit, Kannada[41] and Tamil by later poets.

2. Mallikarjuna Panditaradhyacharitra : This is the biggest of Somana's works, in which "Somanatha's erudition and poetical excellence find their highest and finest expression in it. It contains a mine of information about many topics."[42] In size and style Panditaradhyacharitra rises above Basavapurana. The stories of Saiva saints not found in Basavapurana, are described in this work. Portions of Basavasvaracharitra, not included in Basavapurana find place in this. Virasaiva dharma, siddhanta, nitimarga are described in it. The author infused rasas at appropriate places, and while describing the pilgrimage of Pandita to Srisailam in referring to the pilgrims hailing from various parts of the country - Kannada, Aredera,and Aravadesa- made them in speak in their languages - Karnata, Maharashtra, Dravida, and besides them in Samskrita in fairly big passages about the greatness of Mallikarjuna, sanctity of the place etc. He styled himself Ashtabhashakavitavisarada, and his poetry in five languges is extent.

Panditaradhyacharitra has several prakaranas or chapters. His knowledge in Marathi is attested by the passages in Marathi. He calls the maratha country Areadera and the Marathi languge as Arebhashta "by which names they are still known in the Telugu country." He "curtailed and condensed Maratha forms to make them suit this (dvipada) metre."[43] Similarly his proficiency in writing poetry in Kannada, Tamil and Sanskrit, is seen from the passages in those languages but all in Telugu script, in the work. We may say that work-Sivatatvasara survives in this work in a different guise. The chapters on music and dance in Bharata's natyasastra are translated in this work. Though written in desiyachchandarsu, the work teems with Sanskrit words, sayings, and quotations though a few of Kannada and Tamil words also are found in it.

Panditaradhyacharitra was translated into Sanskrit by Gururaja Kavi. The translation is literal linc by linc, but the Marathi passage is omitted completely which speaks for his ignorance of the language Srinatha rendered Aradhyacharitra as a padya kavya in Telugu in the 14th century AD. The work was rendered into Kannada by poet Nilakantha in the 15th century AD (AD 1485). Nilakanthacharya was an expert in Sanskrit and Kannada, was a pupil of Gangadharacharya and was patronised by Viranarijendra of Ummattur (AD 1482-1494), entitled Gayaventakara.[44] His work has five prakaranas.[45] sandhis and 3067 verses. He said in the work that he was rendering into Kannada Panditaradhyacharitra written in Andhra by Palkuriki Somesvara, a devotee of Srigiri.

Among the other works of Somanatha, Chaturvedasara, Anubhavasara, chenna malla, Isamulu, Vrishadhipa sataka, and Basavodaharana are in Telugu. Somanathabhashya alias Basavarajiya, Rudrabhashya, Basavodaharana, Namaskaragadya, Panchaprakaragadya, aksharankagadya, ashtottaras atanamagadya, Vrishabhashtaka, Pancharatna and Basavashtaka are in Sanskrit. Basava ragada, Gangoppati regada alias Gangadaya Kavya, Sribasvadya ragada, sadgurunragada, silasampadana, Somesvarasataka, alias Sanaraskya sataka, Sahasra gananma, panchatita etc. are in Kannada.[45] Somanatha's Kannada works "now extant do not bear the stamp of genius exhibited by him in his Telugu works" - Somana's works were models for those of later writers e.g. Tikkana Nachena Somanatha and Gauranamatya. His Vrishadhipa sataka was the model for later Sataka literature, for Pandita's Sivatatvasara did not follow the limits regarding number, and makuta and so forth. Two verses in Badena's Sumatisataka bear close resemblance to two verses in Basavapurana, and Panditaradhyacharitra, one in each work. His Panditaradhyacharitra eclipsed the usage of Sivatatvasara - Somanatha brought into forefront the type of poetry janu tenugu as distinct from works learning with Sanskrit words. Palkuriki Somesvara purana in Kannada dealing with the lives of Somanatha and some of his contemporaries was the work of Viraktatantedarya about AD 1560.[46]

3. Manchana C AD 1350 :- Manchana may be placed about the middle of the 14th century AD. His native place must have been in the vicinity of Tsandavole the place of Nanduri Gundamuntri to whom he dedicated his keyurababu charitra, the only extant work of the poet. Manchana rendered in chempukarya in Telugu, the story of Viddhasalabhanjika a drama in Sanskrit by Mahakavi Rajasikhara. He made some changes in the story. In the original. He king was Vidyadhara malla, the hero was Keyuravarsha yuvarajadeva, and the capital was Ujyapuri. In the Telugu rendering the king is Keyurabahu

and the capited Tripuri.47 Manchana omitted the stories of Mekhala and Kuvalaya vati and changed the story of the marriage of a vidushaka in woman's robes with another Vidushaka into the marriage of a woman dressed in man's robes to another woman. Keyurabahu charitra has four cantos and has plenty of moral tales.

Manchana's style is good, sweet and plesant. He orders Lakshmi, Ganapati, Brahma, Viloma, and poets, Vyasa, Kalidasa, Nannaya, Tikkana and Chanakya Yaugandhara and says that Gunda, one day while listening to strange stories, and discussing them saw Manchana his favourite companion praised his poetical capacities as one who could write poetry in both ways - Ubhayakavyasarani[48] and asked him to dedicate a work to him as poetry of the seven meritorious acts, spreads other gifts all over. Further he said "As you are a genius in writing Kavyas, write Keyurabahu - charitra with Sringara as the main theme and teeming with stories illustrating morals." At this stage Manchana in the verse "balarasalasale" generally attributed to Potana says that instead of dedicating good works to underserving people and eat that food, good poets may remain cultivators and live on roots to protest their families." The poet hates underserving persons and likes deservingn ones. In the colophons Manchana styles himself Sakala sukavijanavidhya and the kavya Mahaprabaudha. Probably he wrote some works in desi style for writing poetry in two ways may mean - marge and desi or Sanskrit and Telugu.

**Art and Architecture** : The architecture of the period is seen in temple building and sculpture in them. In some temple grants shares were allotted to the architects or masons along with other temple servants. The method of building and naming the temples, the Velanandu chodas imitated the cholas. Engraving and carving were well known. Generally the emblems of the dynasty are engraved at the top, some times below the inscription, on the seals and first and last plates of e.p. charters by the stone cutters or coppersmiths. The earliest record of Gonka I from Chebbrole was written by Chandanacharya.[49] and Choda I's records by Peddanacharya at Draksharama. The engravers of Gonka II's records by Peddanacharya (1139 AD to 1153 AD) and Suracharya (from AD 1153) at Draksharama and Kapachari at Avanigadda. In one of Gonka II's records a share was set apart for its writer.[50] Of Choda II's records at Draksharama, some were written by Peddanacharya and some by Suracharya. Prithvisvara's Pithapur pillar inscription was written by Kantacharya. As for painting, Somanatha refers to printed pictures bring used in presentment of plays in the Mallikarjuna temple at Srisailam during the Sivaratri celebrations. Pictures were made either of card board or light wood and a colourful variety of combinations of colours were used in painting pictures, and dressing persons for the stage.

**Music, dance and drama** : Inscriptions and literature attest the growth of the allied arts of music, dance and drama. Royal Court and temple - especially on festive occasions were the chief places where these arts were displayed. Under religious impetus, a large variety of popular songs were written and sung. Several musical instruments were in vogue. Of the several kinds of Vina and music used while staging dramas and in concerts only names are preserved for us.

King's ministers and generals, some of whom were authors of works on arts, patronised musicians and dancers in their courts and provided for the anga ranga bhoga, bodily and theatrical enjoyment of the deities and in some cases for Gitavadyan vitta i.e. music - vocal and instrumental and dance in temples. In several temple grants were specified the name, duties, and shares allotted to each of the vocal musicians, instrumentalists, dance master.

The kings, perhaps, were never free from music, while starting on and returning from expeditions of conquest in the bettlefield while in court and during royal processions. The Velanandu choda prasasti like those of some of the earlier dynasties including the Vengi chalukyas, and many of the subsidiary dynasties of the period begins with Samadhigatapanchamahàsbda which means that the bearer was entitled to go about with the accompaniment of the band consisting of the five great musical sounds emanating from the five great musical instruments - the panchamahavadyas - the born, tabor, couch, shell, kettledrum and a gong,[51] or as some opine from the five main sources of music - leather, orifice , strings metal and the human voice, the lst having become out of use.[52] The latter view is very improbable.

The regal insignia of Indrasena had an suspicious lamp praised by the sounds of many musical instruments and couches. Gonka I provided for the angaranga bhoga of the deity at Tripurantakam and in his region the temple at Chebrole had 300 dancing girls attached to it. In choda I's region, the temple of Palakol had 500 sanis serving in it. Gonka II made grants to the dancing girls at Inimella. One dancer - nattavabhose and two drummers - maddaliyadeva and Maddaliyaketa at Chirumamilla and left a grant in charge of 300 dancing girls attached to the temple at Penuguduru padu.[53] His record at Moparru gives the names of dancing girls appointed to serve in the temple. Sani Nunkama, daughter of Modamamba a narabi-Karambha and Muttana son Padiharichintamanayaka was attached to the temple of Chodanarayana at Avanigadda and is described as a beauty - manushyalokasundari.[54] Sani Banambika, mother of Bayyapa a servant of Gonka II, was attached to Pandisvara temple at Tsandavole. Sakkama daughter of Pota, lord of Dubavadu, surpassing Rambha, Urvasi and Menaka in beauty, was a nartaki in the sevice of Pandisvara. Her daughter Kamidevi was the queen of Gonka II and sons Kanna and Seranaya was in the king's sevice. The Mupaghanta granted by Saranaya to the Deity at Timmapuram.[55] produces five great sounds i.e. panchamahasabdapranavamulu. Saranaya granted 1 Kha to the temple couch blower. The details of Manminayaka's grant to the temple at Davulur are thus :- dancing girls for dancing at the rate of 2 kha each; 2 puttis and panduru for mankhari, drummer Dokha, two kha to avajakadu 8 kha to dancers, kha 2 to kolakadu and pandum to couch blower etc. Avajakadu is the player on avjamu - a brazen kattledrum and Kolakadu is the holder of a staff of danda. At Tubadu, kapa, a servant of Gonka II granted 6 kha to dancer Keta, 6 kha for drummers, and 3 kha to padi Edami - vocal musician. The record ordains that dance and instruments should form accompaniments to the song i.e. raga.[56]

Choda II at Palakol made a grant to sani 300 and their nayaka. Mallama redu for nattava and avja.[57] Two of his records at Yenikapadu register grants to dancing girls and Gajapati Hamvira's renewal of Choda's grant to the temple at Bezvada. The latter mentions dancing girls, painters, men who ring the bell, couch blowers etc. among temple servants. The nayaka of Rank[58] made a grant to the sanis one of whom was sani Brahnaka

Kanojus, and brahmapuris and for devabhoga of the deity. Among the dances figure - natti mallamddamarayadu, mokari Malla, two drummers, and the sanis - brahamasura, nangama, parvati, Kanaraka, Maraka, Koppula marak, Goraka, Ganga, Prolaka Bimmaka, and Bhumaka. Except in the case of Koopulamaraka, Sankumalla, Darabhima, Gotama Marani, and Golla Kusumani, sani is prefixed to the names of the dancing girls. A record of choda mentions that a vessel who taken round the circle of sani vada - the quarters of dancing girls at Srikakulam and was left in charge of 300 sanis.[59] This indicates the location of the quarters of dancing girls round the temple.

Prithvisvara provided for festivals, singing and dancing and music in the Kuntimadhava temple. General Jaya himself was a musician, poet and dancer and naturally evinced keen interest in these subjects. He composed Sangitaratnavali, a work on music about AD 1240.[60] Another work with same name was done by a different author. Jaya is described as Sakala natyavaidika gramani and kavi sabha sikhamani. He composed the work - Silpakala kalapavishaya.[61] The best of Jayana's works is Nrittaratnatecture (silpa) and dance bearing special reference to the Kakatiya kingdom. The date of the composition was kali 4355 Ananda in the reing of Ganapati. The author divided nritya into marga and desi modes, and treated each separately in four chapters following Abhinvagupta for the marga and matonga for desi. "The author traces the chitragandeli dance to the aesthetic conceptions of Bhulokamalla Somesvara"[62] In AD 1215 at chebrole, Jaya made a grant to the temple the details of which are thus[63] among the 300 sanies two kha to each of all those who serve in the temple from the age of eight years, and the following persons were given two kha each - dancing master, one who beats the big drum, one who beats the small drum, vasekanu, one who blows the trumpet, one who plays the gaurau, one who beats the kettledrum, the Jajadvadu, one who beats, the gong, one who decorates the temple, garland maker, and piligaragavadu. Vasekanu means simply a flutist or the flutist named Kanu. Gauru is Kahali.[64] a musical instrument. In AD 1235, at Chebrole, Jaya erected two rows of double storeyed houses for sixteen female attendants (jani kas) and provided for the angarangabhoga of the deity.

Minister Gunda at Tsandavole honoured musicians and presented them with palanquins etc. vehicles. He is compared with Bharata in the science of music and was good at dancing. Tsandavole was the home of arts and artists. The court of Choda II had several dancers and musicians. Many kinds of songs were in vogue. Somanatha says that among the devotees who accompanied Mallikarjuna Pandita, were the multitude of musicians singing songs about several ancient devotees. Some of the songs were - tummedapadas, prbhatapadas, parvatapadas, anandapadas, sankarapadas, nivalapadas, vatesu-padas, gobbipadas, vennelapadas, snajavarnana and ganavarnanapadas[65] - Gobbipadas may salutali songs or gobbi songs singing which girls perform a king of dance Gobbi dance - which according to one writer is some of the garbha dance performed by women in Gujarat and gobbi is a corrupt form at Garbha.[66] There are many kinds of gobbi songs. Among the devotees climbing Srisailam to witness the Sivaratri festival, according to and some reciting beautifully as elas Basava purana and the lives of Dasayya and the 63 saints (aruvattu muvaru), some singing aloud in sweet songs in Gita mantra the lives of ancient saints and Basava dandanathagitas.

The Sivaratri festival at Srisailam witnessed by Donayya, during his visit to fulfil M. Pandita's unission, presents a marvellous and harmonious blending of the music and dance of the period and the very high degree attained in them and the stage Somanatha's description, besides expounding the manifold celebrations, the variety in dramas, dances, songs, actors and actresses exhibits the excitement, enjoyment, and happiness of the devotees who contributed to the success of the festivities. Each of the dramas, dances, music concerts, group dance, was being performed at a separate place in the temple at the same time; and so not only natya and ranga mantapas as on usual festival days in temples, every part in the temple bore festive and gay appearnace thousands of devotees congregating and witnessing the festivals. Though religion was the motive force for this activity, the staging of the puranas, Bhagavatas and Bharata attest that Virasaiva fervour was not rampat. The details of the mahotsava during the night of Sivaratri were thus :- some were reading Sivatatvasara and Basavapurana, some dancing in strange ways, some humming and playing Kodangi dances, some Kannakodangi dances in clever ways, and in their own languages some performing ramana panchandi and perai dances while bimmaras[67] salas, and bayakas were shining, some staging many dramas the lives of Pramathas and saints of distant yore, some doing Veddanga dance while, Karanas, meravanas, movements and pictures, were shown rerely some dancing on poles, some on ropes like birds, some staging shadow plays the stories of Bharata etc. behind the screens through pictures some staging puppet play by making the pictures play in a most astonishing manner by ropes through pillars, some signing and dancing, and some dancing exhibiting great enthusiansm and dressed in disguises.[68]

Somanatha describes[69] a complete and regular dance performance staged at Srisailam on the Sivaratri day. With flowers on head, ears, neck, arms, hair knot and legs, with karavikas to the eyes with ashes applied and colour (pachchena) painted on it, with small bells, and anklets, with sirenges with lines set with gems on them, dressed in white clothes with tongallu, earing chauris of ivory and garlands of flowers, the actors entered the hall - asthana - in the most surprising manner, while the audiance applauded, and their entrance was announced by the play of appropriate combination of several musical insturments. Slowly they came out of the screens, and to the astonishment of all without acting, without looking, by movements - anhinaya - making signs indicating pride and delay, standing in tribhangi pasture, pretending to be tired, looked at the audience, smiling a little, walking making every part of their bodies move slightly, making their eye brows dance, in high spirits, thus appeared glad, kind, healthy, nodded their heads, tapped their fingers, and danced the following dances - lagu, vajalam, dhalam vali, tiruvu, bagu, vahini, sali, bayagati, sugati, bahaugati, gati and so forth. The music and dance concerts were in strict adherence to the Bharata's natya sastra. Somanatha mentions the dances - Kolatam, patragondli, perni, kilika, joka, and their performances in Basavapurana.[70] Kolatamu is the dance with sticks in hands patragandli is a particular kind of gondli - dance performed in a circular fashion, perani is the dance performed over a pot-bhanda, Kalika is probably pole dance. He mentions the dance all bow, and perani in Samashtra style - perhaps, same as the Kumabha dance in the north. In his story of Sangayya, in worshipping Siva, Somanatha takes occasion to describe a fine dance performance by dancing women to the accompaniment of music. The arrangements is Akka ama hadevi was to play on drum Basava pramathavva to play Kahala, sakalavva and sangalvar to stand at ease, Balarudrama to play on flute, Guddavva to keep time with cymbals, Sivadevi to dance, Bangudarama, mahesvari, and Virabhadra Lingavva to perform kolikas, Purantamma to wear silk cloth, bodice, and another cloth tightly round the waist, and yet ready to dance and all to be ready to keep time with cymbals. Thus after being announced, the dancer came out of the curtain and danced exhibiting sentiment in face, health sweetness, ideas, other kali, jhankali, theva, vibharama, and rekha, when worship to Siva was made to the accompaniment of auspicious musical sound.[71] The Tandava nritya of natya namittandi in keeping with the jatigitas, and complete dramatic performances (natakamu) are mentioned[72] by Somantha.

Vina - the Indian lute - is ancient finding mention in the Ramayana, for Valmiki, in the words of Ravana, compares fighting in the battlefield with playing on Vina - Somanatha says that for all the battis ragas, so many vinas, one for each raga were used in playing in praise of Siva. He mentions twelve such raga - Vinas - ravanabastamu, brahmavina, tavanya vina, Kailsavina, akasavina, pinakivina, sarangavina, kurmavina, svayambhuvina, gaurivina, kinnara vina, and janakavina.[73] He enumerates thirty six vinas not found in Bharati's work, which were used in the Sivaratri festival. They are vinottamam, ravana vina, gandharva vina, bana vina, kasyapa vina, bhujangavina, bhojavina, trinarivina, sarvasvativina, mollavina, manoratha vina, sarathigananatha vina, Kanmaravina, ani vani tipiri, sakaneya, vali, vichitraka nata, sagarika, gunbhika, vipanchika, saravina, varavadivina, mallari, golashti, svaramandalam, ghoshavti, yandambari, tantrisagaramu, ambiya vina, gitamugamu and so forth.[74] besides the twelvementioned above. On the whole forty four kinds of vina are mentioned. Modern gottu vadhyam was also known as sthalavina or mahavina.[75]

The wires named karavinikas, ravanangas, samahastamu, bandhamu, prabandhamu, vadya chda etc,the talas-chenchuputa, seven prathama talas, twenty seven suddha talas, bhanga, abhanga etc. talas 22 gatis, 7 alapanas, 49 kinds of hamsandas, 22 srutis, 22 ganakas, seven particular gamakas, ragabhadas, songa, raganga, bhishanga, kriyanga, sangotopangasanjanitaragas, parivachakas, anuvachakas, twelve firunolu, eleven vahani bhedas, visuddhathayas, 15 salagatala gatis, 20 angaharas, 22 danakas, chettisudvashi chanhahasti bastas, battisu charulu, 108 karanamulu, 100 alankaras, thirteen sirobhedas, thirty-two dadanas and further 'variations'[76] in this days were displayed in music - vocal and instrumental and dance during this festival. In describing the festival, Somanatha rendered the entire Bharatanatya sastra into Telugu. He dealt with the same subject briefly in Basavapurana, as displayed in playing on vina accompanied by song in the presence of Siva. In this connection, he mention some new tmayas and ragas.[77]

Bharata was the earliest author or Indian dance, music and stages. Though the name Natyasastra suggests that it was a work on theatrics, in which eight chapters were allotted to music proper Bharata enumerates several compositions used for dance of which the simplest is the giti of which there are four kinds - magadhi, ardhamagadhi, sambharita and pruthula. He defines music - sangita - as a combination of voice instrument and dance. This definition applied to temple music in Velanandu times for frequently grants were made for Gita, vadya, nritya in the presence of the god.

As for war music, the Pithapur pillar inscription says[78] that Gonka II's starting on expeditions was announced by sounds of huge drums.

**The Kona Haihayas of Kona Mandala**

Little is known about the progress of arts. Kona Bhima (AD 1168) is mentioned as budhanidhi - a treasure for scholars.[79] Soma of the engravers and inscribers of records are known - kirtiraja's inscription at Draksharama was written by Marapachari and that of Kona Mummadi (AD 1079) there by Peddanacharya, obviously identical with Dakaremi Peddanacharya, the inscriber of Kona Rajendra choda's record. The records of Sattiraju, Malleparaju and one of the three Kona records at Drakasharama dated 1150, were written by Peddamacharya, The other two records of the year were written by Surapa charya. [80] The pillar record at Pithapur was written by Kantachari. Satya's Palakol inscription was written by Saranoju. In AD 1254, Annamalla's record at Drakashama was written by peddan charya, probably a descendant of Dakarami Peddanacharya. The Palakol record of the sons of Kona Ramanatha (AD 1318) was written by Nagoju, son of Sarajnoju.

Music and dance received royal attention. The Kona insignia includes a protidhakka. Mallideva and manmasatya in AD 1195 provided for festivals, and singing, dancing and music - gitavadyanittadivividha bhoja of Kimkimadhava at Pithapur.[81]

**The Haihayas of Panchadharala**

From the Panchadharala pillar inscription of Choda III (AD 1403) one verse has been verbally borrowed into the record of Visvesvara of the Chalukyas, at Panchadarala, dated AD 1407. As the style is similar in both the records, probably both originated from the same poet.[82]

**The Gonas of Vardhamanapura**

Scholars and authors themselves, the Gonas encouraged poets, arhitects, musicians and dancers in their courts and rewarded them duly. They gave the Andhra, the complete Ramayana - purva and Uattara - popularly known as Ranganatha Ramayana. Some even opine that portions of Bhaskara Ramayana were done by a member of the Gona family. Temple music and dance progressed under the Gonas and the Malayala family.

**Literature**: According to the Raichur inscription, Ganna at Vardhamanapura and his rajya rekshamani [83] Vithala at Raichur were amusing themselve in the courts in the company of learned men listening to good stories. According to Buddha, the court of Vithala had experts in puras, sastras kavyas, natakas, besides minister, priests and friends.[84] Malayala Gunda's Court included jesters, readers of Panygyaries actors, dancers humarists, speakers, voice entertowers, persons proficient in gestures, expressing emotions, musicians, debators, orators humarists, poets and connoisseurs.

Gona Buddha and his sons- Kacha and Vithala were writer of the Ranganatha Ramayana. The authorship of this Ramayana especially the purvakanda is a matter of controversy and plenty of literature has grown round it. Tradition says that Hulakki Bhaskara was writing Ramayana with the help of his friends, his patron being asked Ranganatha a relative of his to write Ramayana. Bhaskara did it as Champu were as Ranganatha wrote in couplet metre. The story goes that when the works were taken to the king, he extended his right hand to Ranganatha and the left to Bhaskara. Some opine[85] that Ranganatha Ramayana was written by Ranganatha in the name of Buddha, and so was known by the author's name e.g. Valmiki Ramayana, Bhaskara Ramayana. For if Buddha was the author it would have been known as Buddharaju Ramayana.[86] The only point in favour of Ranganatha's authorship, who according to some was a poet of Buddha, and according to others a relative in charge of Dupadu pargana, is that he finds mention in the work of the laksalikas, and was praised with other poets in the beginning of works of later poets. But evidence for Buddha's authorship of the work is overwhelming. [87] None of the authors who praiase Ranganatha mention his work as Ramayana, and if Ranganatha was the author, Buddha would not have allowed its propagation in his name. Internal evidence is clear that the author was Buddha who did it in the name of his father King Vithala.[88] As is probable, Vithala was called Panduranga Vithalanatha or Vithala Ranganatha, and so Buddha called his work Ranganatha Ramayana either after the god or his father. Perhaps later poets mustook Ranganatha to have been the author. Buddha's not finding a place in Kavistutis, was due to that he was not a Brahmin and Appa kavi has said that none other than Brahmins should be poets, and men of higher castes should not praise those of lower orders.[89]

Buddha wrote the work in the middle of the 13th century AD. Ranganatha Ramayana is the first and most popular of the Ramayanas in Telugu. It is like Vidhipurana for people about Nellore, It is well-known in the western Andhra hilly regions than in eastern Andhra-coastal - districts - where Bhaskara Ramayana took its palce. Written in desikavita which flourished in western Andhra as marga literature in the eastern, this Ramayana, like Valmiki Ramayana was, the text says, sweet, meant to be read as Kavya and sung as a song.[90] So it was like by scholars and masses "Usually desi kavita by nature is gejakavita; dvipada kavyas protect giyabhava. Therefore among these are not as widespread as the padyakavyas." So written in couplet metre, Ranganatha Ramayana was more apt to be sung unlike other Ramayana in Telugu. It is a prayana in western Andhra. Women sing a few chapters from the Ramayana, as songs and during puppet shows, this Ramayana was sung by men explaining the play. [91]

Easy, beautiful and faultless in style, Ranganatha Ramayana is the best of work in couplet metre. Buddha in the beginning of the work says that he would narrate Srirama charitra in the way told by adikavi Valmiki to the liking and pleasure of deserving persons. [92] But he was the first among Telugu poets to have made major changes in the main story while rendering Sanskrit works into Telugu and deviated from the original. He introduced some new stories, not found in the original, but found perhaps in Padma Purana, Navavidha Ramayanas and so forth, and sung as songs and ballads by people. Buddha selected a few stories from the folk songs, and put them in his work, thus giving it desilakshana, - indigenous appearance and adding its greatness. Almost every Kanadahasa new story hot found in Valmiki Ramayana. In Balakanda, he narrated how Ahalya in the form of a stone came back to life by the touch of Rama's feet. [93] The story has close resemblance to the popular song in Telugu with the same burden. Atrivrittanta which is at the end of Ayodhakanda in the Valmiki and Bhaskara Ramayanas, is in the beginning of Aranyakanda in this work. The story of Jambu mali in Aranyakanda is not found in Valmiki Ramayana but is in Bhaskara Ramayana. The stories of Kalanemi, Sulochana, Kaikai, the display of splendour by Ravana in the battlefield the conversation between Kumbhakarana and Vibhisna in the battle in the battlefield and the laughter of Saimitri - all in Yuddha kavita are not found in other Ramayanas and add to the beauty and importance of the work. The laughter of Lakshmana —Sanmitranavvu is borrowed from the song Lakshmana devaranavvu, which with the songs faint of Lakshmana,sleep of Urmila, Lamkayaga and so forth were in vogue prior to the Andhra Ramayanas. The major difference between the Ramayanas of Valmiki and Ranganatha is that the latter gives a true picture of the Panchastya family, and the good parts and greatness of some of its members Ravana, Kumbhakarana etc.

Buddha is compared with Brahma in Andhrabhasha, karved in itihas and puranas and as suggested by Dr. C.R. Reddi, introduced Dravidian outlook in his picture of Ravana's family.[94] Buddha, thus, was mahakavi and a poet of the people, for he selected as his theme the popular version of the Ramayana,and presented it in local garb suitable to popular taste. Between Buddha desikavita - pure desi style, with subject, language and prosody - all indigenous with giti as its life blood, and pure marge style - suddha marga kavita; Buddha struck the medium - taking some lakshanas from desikavita and following marge style for the rest. This formed a special feature about the writers of doipala kavyas.

Buddha begins the work with adoration to Adinarayana, Sarada, Valmiki, author of Ramayana, Parasarasanu, author of Bharatmajari and his son Sukayoji. The occasion for his writing the work is thus - one day while in Vithala's court, while scholars were discussing Bharata and Ramayana, the king asked "who is fittest in the world to do Ramayana in Telugu in Kavya style." The sabha replied that his son Buddha - sarvajna, Kavi sarvalahanma, kavilokabhaja, expert in sabha, artha and style and the intricacies of the Ramayana. Then he sent for Buddha, and asked him to tell Ramayana in Andhra bhasha in purana marge, in his name to the satisfaction of poets and scholars and spread it in the world - Buddha says that his work is unsurpassed in pada, artha bhava, gati,s style, meanings, yati, rasas, gurubhavas, prasa and alankara etc. and mentions[95] that Valmiki Ramayana has 24,000 slokas. 500 sargas in six kandas and the rest in the story in Uttarakanda. [96] A fairly long phalaruti generally found at the end of a work, is appended to every kanda in this work.

Ranganatha Ramayana - Uttarakanda - on the basis of name, the authorship of this work too is attributed to Ranganatha,[97] But internal evidence is positive that it was the work of Kach and Vithala dedicated to Buddha and current in the name of their grandfather Ranganatha Vithala alias Ganna Reddi. In style the work resembles Purva Ramayana written in couplet metre. Both the Ramayanas together form Sampurna Ramayana. Written under Buddha's command, Uttarakanda belongs to the same period as the Purva Ramayana. The style is faultless, sweet, flowing and continuous. The text says that Buddha himself wanted to write the complete life of Ramachandra, and acquire fame, prosperity, and praise from people. When he adored his favourite deities, Vishnu appeared before him and said thus "I am pleased with your devotion your sons possess capacities to satisfy your desires: ask them; they would respond to your call with due respect."[98] So Buddha sent for his sons and praised them as royal poets like kavi Bhoja, possessing knowledge in many puranas, and arts, lights of his lineage and asked them to write the katha which he wanted to write for the satisfaction of all.

In the work, in the beginning, the authors adored Vishnu, Gananatha, Valmiki, Sarasvati, and say that as Ramavatara is the most beautiful of all incarnations, Valmiki did it in devabhasha and following him they would render Uttarakanda in Andhra Bhasha in dvipada kavya in grand style rich in diction.[99] This Uttara Ramayana differs from Tikkana's Uttara Ramayana in some respects. The narration of some evil saying by a Rakshasa woman to Sita, and the story from Yadhajit to the end of rama in this work are not found in Tikkana's work.

Bhaskara Ramayana like Andhra Bharata was written by many poets in parts at varying periods. Sahini Mara, the patron of the work is mentioned as the son of Kachamamba and Buddhaya. If this Buddha is identical with Buddha, the author of Ranganatha Ramayana, Mara becomes a brother of Kacha and Vithala.[100] But this Books improbable on chronological grounds.[101]

Isvara Bhattopadhyaya[102] a poet entitled sabdavidhyavisaradas, and a scholar in Yajurveda composed the Bothpur records of Malyala Gunda.

**Music and Dance**: The existence of musicians and dancers in the courts of the Gonas and Malyalas, is attested by records. Buddha mentions that music and dance concerts were held in most auspicious fashion, while bhari mridanga, muraja and couch were sounded and to the accompaniment of many musical instruments. In his Ramayana, Buddha describes a dance performance. Dressed in golden sarees, women grouped together to sing and play. While Tumburu and Narada were singing songs about Raghava, they in the presence of Bharata, showing their expert knowledge in Bharatasastras, and in strict adherence to the specified talas, played kolatas, performed perani dances, and danced in gola, charini, sindhu, gujjari and desi style in different goups, Buddha refers to dancing girls, experts in music and dance who could dance in suddha marga singing samagana, and to dance by some women according to talagati, while their anklets, bracelets and beels produced fitting sounds and while some played mridanga and some sang while other played on vina.[103] The vourt of rama is said to ahve included musicians - vocal and instrumental, dancers, poets, jesters, experts in arts, puranas, sastras, and vedas and dancing girls with sweet faces, playing on musical instruments and singing pleasant songs. The instrument nissana [104] was used to announced the beginning of war.

**Learning and Architecture**: References to learning, painting and sculpture are many in the Ramayana. The buldings in Lanka are said to have been well sculptured and set with gold and gems. Bharata ordered the delineation of the stories of Setubandha etc. in the court of Rama[105]

**The Haihayas of Poland**

Arts were at their best under these Haihayas. The period produced best results in literature, music, dance, architecture and sculpture. Even after the fall of the kingdoms, its history provided ample material for writting works and raising temples.

**Literature**: The courts at Gurizala and Macherla had many poets and scholars besides musicians and dancers. Srinatha gives a fine description of Nalagama's court and its activities. Some of the rulers and minister were scholars of merit and patronised learning. A brahmin of Kamanur, who had studied the padapatha is mentioned in a record of Beta. Pedda Kodamangadla was perhaps a centre of learning for Haihaya kama provided for the continuance of mendicants and students there. [106] Kullaya Sahini, a subordinate of the Haihayas, was a patron of scholars. His Amaravati epigraph was written by Nallacharya.

Palnativiracharitra, was the theme of several poems in the 14th and 15th centuries. No single poem is complete, and each poet took up a particular aspect of the story and dealt it in a poem. The battle of Paland is compared with Bharat and Viracharitra is known as Palnativira Bhagavata.[107] Mack MSS have several copies of the work - all incomplete each having some portion. The earliest work is that of Srinatha in couplet metre sung by village bards to this day in Palnad dealing with the story of Balachandra, the hero of the battle compared with Abhimanya in Bharata. After Srinatha, Mallaya, Kondaya, Mudiganda Virabhadrakavi and Balarama dealt with Palnativiracharitra. In Mack MS in an incomplete copy of the work in 3 skandas in dvipada metre. [108] The remainder is in another MS and was the composition of Balarama. In one MS, the altter part of the account - a modern composition differing from the original is found. The verification is much polished, the poet saying that he has copied it from a version of Srintha nevertheless had lengthened it by adding new episodes.[109] The battle of Kannamaraju is attributed to Srinatna.[110] The portion narrating cock fight was the work of Mallaya, son of Ramanamantri and grandson of Ganranamatya of Kamudinyasa gotra. Kandaya, the author of the portion dealing with the battle of Manmaraja, was the son of Ramisetti Sarvanarya, devotee of chajarla chennarya, and an expert in literature, music and dance. Virabhadra's work in verse, written in AD 1862 is the latest. For the story of Balanagamma - Nayaluralu, Panuyal was the birth place.[111] Palnativira charitra was concerned like epic modelled. The Mahadbharata. Either the poets did differant parts of the work or only parts remained though they wrote complete works.

**Art and Architecture**: The engravers of the records of Haihaya Beta at Macherla were Kannada persons and wrote their name at the end of the records in Kannada. Most of the architecture of Palnad, which has received the attention of scholars was executed probably in this period or a little later. At Macherla are three temples dedicated to the Heroes - the Virapapurushulu mentioned thus is a record of AD 1315 on a pillar in front of the images[112]. On the surrounding walls of the celebrated stone temple are a series of sculptures representing sciences from Mahabharata and Bhagavata.[113] In an ancient temple there, the Ramayana is delineated in sculptures and onesculpturesof light red coloured stone by slight touch produces particular sound.[114] reminding us of the pillars in the Singita mandapa in the Vithal temple at Hampi, producing seven svaras by mere touch.[115] On the towers of the temple are respresented in sculptures the sixty four bandhis in Kamasastra.[116] The sculptures who built the local Adityesvaratemple were eulogised in a record of Haihaya Beta. The record says that Visvakarama, son of Brahma was the proginator of the achitects and father-in-law of the sun Visvakarama is stated to have converted the rays of the sun, his son-in-law into devine weapons e.g. discus of Vishnu. Some well-known acharyas of the Visvakarma family are mentioned as "experts incutting lingas (of Siva) in preparing images; in understanding the proper place of the latter (in Indian cononograph) in building the four kinds of mansions (prasada) and their innumerable subdivisions, in grasping the geometry (Kshatra) involved in the study of Vastu (sastra) (architecture) and in gracefully handling the implements of their profession." The epigraphist adds "in the southern temples too, the term Tachchcha riyakkani so often met with, means an endowment set apart exclusively for the architects who were to look after repairs in the temple. A record from Coimbatore district states that the duties of these architects, consisted in ten kinds of repairs (dasakriyai) which are not enumerated." [117]

In the temples at Bugga, Sankarapuram, Gamalapadu, Kavalapolle and Pedlagarlapadu, are several sculptures. At Melvagu, both Vishnu and Siva temples are sculptured. In the former, each of the bracket capitals supported by the pillars in madhyaranga and kalvana mantapas, has on its rounded front a serpant head, hood and nect, represented as if the animal was rising from inside the pillar where the shaft joins the bracket.[118] And outside on the main walls of the temple are sculputres of fishes. On a stone was the siva temple is sculptured figure having four arms carrying the sword, double drum, and discus, but the head is very broad and thick at the chin and the head dress is either a metal helmets or surrounded with a kingdom and decorated with plumes or a Doth burbam with heavy folds falling on the shoulder with plumes of Kathers round it. At Ranpicharla of the many Naga one had the body of a woman with the seven hooded shake as each by a canopy over her. At Karempudi is the temple of Heroes, where in the 100 heroes as represented each by a smoth stone of the stream ranged round the temple. Thus temple is same as the curious Mandapa called, Nayudu Mandapa in the middle of Karempudi. The roof of the manadapa has fine flower sculptures. A slab there has two figures 1. Hanuman standing in front of a figure riding on horseback. 2 The panel bemath this represents two women sitting with a pot between them. The mandapam at the northern gate way has pillars standing on high raised platform of large slabs. On each side of the entrace, the wall below the platform is sculptured with designs of elephants, horses and a series of large star shaped ornaments. On one of the pillars are two female figures, one standing and one sitting. They bear no names, but it said that they possibly represent Silambika or Nayukaurula.[119] Another pillar has the figure of a king on a horse back with the words "Peddala Balaravutu" i.e. perhaps Balachandra. A slab has the design of four feet impressions surrounded by a snake holding its tail in its mouth. Another slab has a row of figures like soldiers each holding a trident in one hand, an umbrella in the other with carnice work underneath representing a series of conventional bulls.[120] Against the eastern wall is a Saraswathi in a sitting posture with arms three destroyed the fourth holding a club. Beneath is a hamsa (swan). Nearby is the figure of a Bhairava standing, with four arms, the two right destroyed, the left upper arm holds a trident, the lower one a human head at which a dog jumps to bite it. Portion of a frieze consisting of a series of female figures liews near the Ganesa temple. In the old temple at Karempudi, a stone bears the figure of a four handed female deity holding trisulam, damarukam, and a sword in the three hands and the fourth is destroyed. A standing horse is facing the deity and people call it Durga.[121] In the Siva temple against the well stands a stone representing Siva and Parvati sitting on his thigh. In the Nayudu mandapa on the architrave are some thinly cut figures representing scenes from Palnativiracharitra.

Near Singarutla agrahara is a stone carved with the figure of Durga, sitting on the conquested Maushura - bull. There are several figures, broken all headless. People call them Alwars i.e. Vaishnava aposties. In the case of one figure larger than the others, the head of the largest of these figures has been found and replaced, had a broad face with thick lips and long ear lobes. In all the figures, the hands are raised, the left hand supporting the right arm and the right hand raised as of teaching.[122] Sewell says that the other figures of alwas, he had seen, have the hands clasped on the breast as if in prayer and that "Pandit Natesa Sastri thinks it certain from the description that the figures are Saiva figures representing Dakshinamturi."[123] But as Viravaishnavism prevailed under the Haihayas, it is possible that the figures are alwars than Siva. A slab has a human standing with hands in the attitude of worship or adoration with a five headed cobra hood over the head, and with couch and discuss on each side. At Oppicheria, the temple has a stone bearing four foot impressions surrounded by a serpent with the tail in its mouth. Two slabs represent the sculptures of a persons on horse, and another a Durga slaying Mahishasura with a spear. Another stone has the figure of a man in the attitude of walking and shooting an arrow from a bow.[124] The temple at Obalesvarapalle has stones with figures two of Alwars and another with Rama, Sita and Lakshmana.[125] At Durgi, near a mandapam in the temple is the lower half of the figure of Sarasvati on a swan. In the Durga shrine is a slab showing Durga sitting on the bull with weapons in her numerous hands. On two slabs which are portions of a frieze carved with a number of deities each with his appropriate vashana. On one are the goddesses and on the other the gods. Only three gods Ganesa, India and Vishnu on a boar, are seen now. Of the goddesses, Rati, wife of Kamadeva is recognised by her parnot, Parvati, by her bull, Sarasvati by her swan, Sachi, wife of Indra by elephant, Lakshmi by Garuda, and underneath is another on a horse. [126] At Veludurti, a virakas has an armed soldier advancing to the attack with sword and shield in defence of a woman. Another virakas represents a huntsman on horse back with a stay, boar and a dog under his horse. A slab represents an elaborate battle scene. Six horsemen accompianed by three soldiers are seen rushing to the attack. [127] At Gottipadla, a slab has a male figure probably representing some prince or celebrated person. Another has a Durga with six arms in standing posture. One stone represents a husband and wife with arms around each others' necks Another has Siva and Parvati on the bull with Paravati sitting on Siva's knee.[128] A man in a squatting position, another a four armed Durga slaying the bull - mahishasura with a spear, a four armed goddess with an elephant goad in one hand, setti with chank, discuss sword and shield in hands and standing on a lion, a man cutting off his own head and offering it to the sacred lingam, while above sits Siva with two attendants having their hands clasped over his head Siva with two attendants having their hands clasped over his head are all figured on slabs.

Dachapalle has some very interesting sculptures. In the Nagesvaraswami temple is a stone representing a male figure four armed having a spear in one hand and a fighting cock in another. The temple in the fort has finely executed and graceful sculptures on the walls and beautiful stroll work. In a nicha on the southern side is a scatel goddess with two attendants. To the left of it on the north at the foot of the scroll work in form of a tree is a woman with uplifted hand holding the branches. The grace and symmetry of the figure are striking.[129] On the conical roofs on the top are groups of conventional parrots. There is the figure of a Bhairava with sword trident, damaru and a cup in his hands and serpents by the side of his legs. In the Siva temple - the mukha or Sannidhi mandapa has a raised paltform with a hall in the middle with its roofs resting on pillars. The slabs forming the sides of the platform bear sculptures in a superficial lineary style representing scenes from the Ramayana.[130] One represents Rama's army of monkeys. Another has the monkeys building the bridge to Lanka, and the fighting between Sugriva's monkey army and the rakshasas. Another slab Lakshmana sitting on the monkey - Angada's shoulders fighting with Indrajit on his flying chariot, while Hanuman siezes rakshasa by the hair. On another portion of the same slab is the scene of Ravana conversing with Hanuman. Below this is the monkey army following Rama who was fighting in his chariot with Ravana who was also in a chariot and was followed by his Rakshasa army. The Rakshasas are represented in wild and grotesque shapes.[131] In side the mandapa, on one slab is seen Ravana ten headed, aided by a Rakdhasa, fighting against Hanuman. A similar battle scene, and a man killing a monster who is transfixed with an arrow from the former's bow are represented on two slabs. The monster has the body(?) and the head, arms and body of man. At the base of the outer wall of teh group of garbhalaya buildings, is a frieze of elephants varied by star shaped ornaments in a diaper pattern. The doorway of the ante chamber of the garbhalaya is .ldecorated with lions at intervals and sculptured pilasters. Star shaped ornaments in a diaper pattern. Star shaped ornaments and elephants are carved on the inner wall of the platform of the pradakshinamandapa. A group of men and women fighting with bows and arrows is represented in one place.

The sculpture in the Nayakuralu temple are fresh even now. One sculpture represents a queen, probably Nayakuralu, with attendants worshipping the lingam. Another shows a king and queen - probably Narasimha and Nayakuralu accroding to Sewell embracing. [132] But Nayakuralu was the minister and not queen. One stone has the churning of the milk ocean. Nearly lies a beautiful black granite sculpture of Durga. Bhairava holding in his four hands, a damaruka a erosked sword, a trisula and a human head at which a dog jumps up and licks, is represented on a stone. Over his head hangs a serpent whose is neck is twisted round his legs, the hood expanded, and head erect in front. Over his head is a cobra hood of many heads. Another stone has a Durga with Mahishasura. She has eight arms, and holds the chowk, scaptre, sword, spear, discus, bow, shield and the keil of the buffalor monster whose body hands loosely, the forehead resting on the ground. She has killed them with the trident shaped spear. There are two figures of ascetics with their hands clasped before him. Another slab has the figure of a Ganesa at the end of a row of six females seated crosslegged and holding lotus buds in their right hands.[133] In many of the temples in Palnad are representations of Gajalakshami on the door ways.

Some sculptures outside palnad bear close resemblance to those in Paland in subject and style. Of the four sculptured stones near the Cutcheri in Bapatla, three represent three women one with a hao around the head and the path, a circle formed by a serpent with its tail on its mouth and two pairs of foot prints in it; and four standing persons in striking attitudes. People call them Palnativiralu[134] i.e. heroes of Palnad. Whether there is any connection between these sculptures and the temple of Heroes at Karempudi is not known. A stone in the enclosure of the Agastisvara temple at Guntur resembles the one at Bapatla. On the top are two pairs of foot prints and some figures standing on one side.

Srinatha speaks of a temple of Heroes at Warangal in the region of Prataparudra in which the figures of the Heroes were painted on slabs.[135] The celebrated temple of Visalakshi on the banks of the tank at Tripurantakam, is mentioned in Palnati vira charitra. For it was visited by Vira (Brahma neyadu) during his stay there.[136]

Painting was practised in this period. Srinatha says that many pictures showing the stories of Sri Rama and Sri Krishna were hung on the walls of the court of Nalagama, multicoloured canopy above, and five coloured carpets below.[137] In the temple of Macherla, the walls in the hall were adorned with huge pictures, a canopy above and a chavike below; and upstairs with many pictures. [138]

**Music, dance and drama**: The growth of these arts is attested by records, sculptures in temples and Srinatha's descriptions. In AD 1103 at Satrasala, Mandodi Revinayaka provided for the angarangabhoga of the deity. At Durgi, a stone bears the figures of Gopalaswami holding a vinu (flute) in two of his hands and in the other two a chank and a chekra.[139] Besides him, are two female figures his two wives Rukmani and Satyabhama. At Veludurti in the temple of Durga is the representation of a group of players, two on drums, one flute, and a monkey on the bagpipe. [140] In slab in the Siva temple at Dachepalle shows a group of musicians playing musical instruments[141] and between the temple and the small shrine outside it lies on the ground a large slab sculpture showing a procession of gods in the upper entablature and a group with Siva dancing in the middle in the lower. The god with matted locks dances to the sound of musical instruments played by ganas at the head of whom are Brahma and three legged Bhringi. The upper portion of the slab shows the procession headed by a band of music behind which is a camel and its rider. Behind him comes Bhringi dancing.[142] Then comes Siva with Parvati riding their bull, Vishnu on the Garuda; Brahma with three heads visible on his swan, Kumarasvaswami on his peacock, Indra on his elephant, yama on buffalo, vayu on antelope, another god on horse and still another god.

By the time of Prataparudra, Palnati vira charitra, written as a prabandha in couplet metre was popular all over the Telugu land Kridebhirama describes [143] the abhinaya dance performed by men and women at Warangal, showing the valour of the heroes, while the prabhandha is sung i.e. music. Beating time fast with symbols producing the natural sounds of dhum dhum kitatkara, a woman sang beautifully the story of the heroes specially set for the purpose, as dvipada prabandha. While the princes i.e. persons dressed like heroes were enamoured. Shouting aloud one person beat his thighs with a stick - virasambetakola, another standing with his right leg spread to the front like a bowman, danced with a spear Kuntabhinaya;another with excited looks, shouting aloud, sang performing dola dance, one drives in open yard the horse so that it moved in bhanjali i.e. he curves like a snake, one makes jump Kudumu in the court, while woman was singing about the heroes of Palnad. The Vira kumarakoti applied yellow sandal paste to their bodies, wore wooden anklets, garlands of red flowers, dressed their hair in knots, held a stick - Virasamveta having tassels were new waiste cloths, and jewels set with emerales. Such was their equipment dressed like old warriors armed with long spears, daggers, long sharp swords and shields giving a dance presentation of the song. [144] Thus the ballad of the heroes of Palnad was the subject of dance performances in the 13th century AD to the accompaniment of music vocal and instrumental - to the delight of the vast audiences.

The importance attached to music and dance int he courts of Nalagama and Mallideva at Gurizala and Macherla is seen from Palnati Viracharitra. Music and dance by women to the accompaniment of music in Nalagama's court. Srinatha describes a music and dance concert that took place in the court of Nalagama thus[145] the vocal musicians in a striking fashion took the vinas, tightened the wires, tuned them and palyed in such a marvellous way the svara saptakas, the different arohanas and avarohanas, several ragas, samchari and samsthasi and pleasant ideas of the vigorous almkaras with their movements, and muchansas etc. prominent qualities (dharma), accompanied by vocal music so that even withered trees could sprout new leaves. Then Nalagama's Court resembled that of India. At that stage, a party of learned dancers arrived there, bowed to the king, stood aside when the king smiled at them and ordered them to give a dance performance. Then the expert player on mridanga stood to the right, the players on symbols to the left, the dexterous player mukhavina, with the two women who do alapana of the ragas behind - all awaiting in eager expectations when the great dancer named Kanjalochana, majestic in gait, sweet in speech, learned in the several ragas suited to Bharatasastra, came and stood while the audience were describing her and looking at her. She bowed to the Vetrapani-dance master took the finglring bells (gajjas) give by him, tied them to her feet with devotion, tied tightly the kasa of five colours, repeating sacred hymns, and stood in the centre. With side glances at the king, taking the initial step with her feet - samapada - bowed to the gods with all attention, gave pushpanjali and began the dance to the musical accompaniments whose sounds filled the court. In highly technical style, she danced kaikolu and vidudala i.e. receiving and releasing (with her arms) and shared by her gestures - Kaimudi and Katna (used for keeping time). Next she performed the bhuchari dance of nine kinds, a kasa chavi dance of sixteen kinds and the angahara of nine kinds, and then showed gaticahri differences. After these, she demonstrated pani bhadas differences by clever and expert gestures; by combing, sthanka, samchaya and samyukta. She danced wonderfully the sapta tandavas prerani, desini, prenkhana, suddha, dandika kundali and bahuchari to the great astonishment of the assembly. Then with several women assistants on both sides she performed - samyuta, asamyuta, chalna - manifesting santuchita - intricate and several gestures of arms expressive of thoughts - nanardha karamulu and natyahastamulu postures of hands appropriate in a dance. Then making use of the eighteen angas - the six angas, six upangas, and pratiangas - namely head, eyes, cheeks, eyebrows, teeth, lips, neck, Chin, facila expression, chest and so forth, they danced the several gitas in Andhra and Sanskrit in praise of god Macherla Chenna demonstrating most effectively, the meaning of those and similar songs. All were astonished (at this grand performance) including Rambha as others who bowed their heads feeling ashamed. The king presented them with several cloths and ornaments. Thus first music performance, then dance by a single individual, followed by group dance took place. The bhuchari and akaschari dances and their sub-divisions as suggested by their names, probably delineate the movements of life on earth and heavens; and angach and gatichari and their divisions perhaps represent the movement of the different parts of the body itself and the progressive changes in life. Panibhadas, nanarthakaras, and natyahastas, are probably same as mudras in natyasastra. Of the supta tandavas, Kundaki is the dance performed in a circular form; Kaimudi is a kind of musical instrument used for keeping time.[146]

Several musical instruments are mentioned by Srinatha. When Mallideva stared for war the following instruments were sounded damayi, muraja, bura, bheri, potudhara, kahala, vankini, kalikanmu, couch, sannyijollu, murali, mukhavina, naraga, tappeta, dollu, tammatammu, viranamu, heavy runja, Kamakatappeta, cheyanta and cheruganta.[147] Ranbheri, dhakka, dhamamika, dangura, patcha, were.[148] also sounded at times of war. Of these damangi is a leather instrument Potudhara means huge couch, dangura and Viranu are identical.

## The Chagis

The high standard of Sanskrit and Telugu in Chagi records attest the flourishing condition of poets and literature in the kingdom. Ramavilasa by Enugu Lakshmana kavi, the only work about the Chagis is of a later period. The kings and queens patronised poets. Rajamba, queen of Chagi Pota granted plenty to scholars. The Ammanchipalli inscription [149] of Manma Ganapati mentions a family of schoalrs. Bhaskara Somaiaji was the son of Annimanchi Kumaravivan, and grandson of Chevalindrayajvban of Srivatsa gotra who had performed jyotishtoma and other sacrifices.

Chagi Pota's Amaravati inscription was written by Nallacharya. In the region of Doranaya in AD 1240 at Chintapalle, the merchants made a grant for the angarangabhoga of the deity. At Animanchipalle in AD 1270, Chagi Manma provided for the angarangabhoga of the deity. In AD 1477 at Vinukonda, Sage Gannamanayadu built a finely sculptured mandapam. The record attesting this has a fine figure of Gandabherunda.[150]

**The Kondapadumatis**

No literary works of the period are known. But the flourishing condition of literature, architecture, music, dance, and drama is attested by Kondapadumati inscription.

Buddhavarman, is mentioned as an armour to good poets. The epithets - Iaviavindoa i.e. delighter in poertry sukavi kirasujana janadhra i.e. mango tree to parrots i.e. excellent poets speak for the general interest of the rulers in literature. King Buddha gave plenty to his favourites, pupils and scholars. His son Manda is compared with a Mandara tree to Vandi brinda i.e. group of bards. King Malla was a favourite of scholars.

Mantri Somana of the time of Manda, hailed from a family of scholars. His ancestor Vennayabhatta Somayaji is said to have been a scholar and conversationalist in the court of Trinayamapallava. Entitled Mahavadimadebhasinha, he vanquished in argument Gandhbhatta and pleased his patron by his learning and obtained Irralur from him.[151] In AD 1149 Manmamanda made a grant to Vidyamantulu i.e. learned men.

The main duty of bards in kings courts was to praise kings and compose prasastis. Some of the Kondapadumati records are long in high blown Sanskrit. Some of the Telugu records are good poems. But in no case the name of the composer is recorded. Manda's record at Draksharama was written by Peddancharya.

King Choda made grant to temples for services, music, dance and so forth. He granted a Ghanta and Khala to the deity at Nudendla. A record there, gives a list of the dances and specifies their shares and duties - to pauranikas 4 kha, dance, master kha 6, drummer, vamsakara (flutist), couch blower, and some shares to four singers - 16 kha at the rate of four puttis for each.[152] Manma Manda made a grant similar to this, among the dances figuring the pauranikas, avajindu dadepoju Baine, Virimaddaliya Mande, vivimaddaliyaketa, padi deme,

Vendipaḍivani, dadapoju maraka, sankudhraṣ Kanne, dadapoju rajehagopa, and the shares vary from three kha to four kha.[153] Sankudhara is same as Sabbedhara of the previous records meaning couch blowing, virimadaliya is perhaps a special kind of drum, and women with padi prefixed to their names were singers. Manma Manda made a further grant to temple servants-sanis, priests etc. The Gudipudi record dated AD 1140 enumerates persons forming the singing and dancing party to play before the god. The names of dancing girls attached to the local Rajarajesvara temple are given in the Pedda Kuduru[154] record of AD 1173.

**The Kotas**

The title - Kavigalamogada Kaibedu varigiva kaigandaraganda in the prasasti of the Kotas attests to their patronage of schoalars the language of the title - kannada - speaks for its influence over Telugu and the place of Kannada poets in Koda court. King Kota I was a scholar. His daughter-in-law Subbama patronised poets. Keta II was a patron of scholars, Bayyaladevi, a scholar herself is compared, with the sun to the lotus tank i.e. scholars.

Some of the poets [155] of the period were Ubhayakavi Narasimha, and Varakavi Gunda both of the reign of Ganpati and Narasimha bhettopadhyaya, the composer of the Yenamadala inscription of Ganapamba.

**Architecture, music, dance and drama**: The epigraph of fKing Choda at Draksharama was weitten by Peddana - charya. The lofty Buddhist chaitya well decorated with many sculptures at Dhanyakataka, was in good condition under the Kota aegis. Kota built some buildings at Amaravati which were denoted in AD 1665 by Sabnavis Timmagipandita.[156]

The Kotas provided for temple, music and dance. At Paddakonduru in AD 1209, King Kota provided for the Kamabhoga of Bhimesvara. The donees were Mogali Surama, putra Kama, avajamu Dase, modyala Devaya, Guruva, Prolama, Potana, Anyama, Pina Anyama, sankhu Brammana, who received each 1 Kha. Provision was also made for Ghanta and beri.[157] Putra is a dancer. Among the bhogastris of Kota II, Kasavanadevi, Chodamadevi, Gundamadevi, Suramadevi, Amarana, Ketama, made a grant to the temple at Velpur. Ganapamadevi, caused to be performed festivals and concerts in honour of Siva, daily and enjoy them.[158] In AD 1248 she granted lands to dancers. Some of the professions of the donees were vasé, mukhari, patra, tagaram, savari, bhagavata and shavasi. The records at Velpur show that Velpur had sani 300 attached to it who in AD 1216 formed parley along with priests for an agreement between Bhima and Rudra. In AD 1254, Bayyala and Ganapati presented Akkamadevi as Sani, and gave land and house site for her maintenance. [159]

Atitle of Doddabhima was Kondiyabhatanatana-matikasutradhara - the man behind the scenes to the dance drama of Kondiyabhata, which speaks for his interest in dance and drama. Probably Kondiyabhata was an expert dancer and Bhima directed the performances.

**The Natavadis**

One of the poets of the Natavadi court was Balabharati kavi, the composer of the Kundavaram inscription and the donee of a grant from Kundambika. The record says that his sayings shone like pearls.

**The Parichchodis**

King Chikkabhima bore the epithet-sishteshta chintamani. Bhimaya Panda was a scholar well versed in arts, He could compose poems like ancients which could in sweetness and movement were modelled after desi and marga types of literature.[160] His ideas, words and their meanings could equal descriptions in suktis.

The Parichchedi recirds at Draksharama were written by Peddanacharya. King Panda is described as Vilasavidyadhara and Bhogapu randara. In AD 1158 he granted Gudipadi to the sanis, manis, dancing masters, drummers, flutists, artisans, couch blowers, and other servants of the Agastisvara temple.[161] The titles - vibudha-santarpana, and vilasavidhadhara borne by Alladanatha show his patronage of scholars, musicians and dancers.

**The Malayas**

In AD 1248 Malayamu Ganapati provided for angarangabhoga of Gajjaramu Mahadeva.[162] Bantaraja's record at Draksharama was written by Peddanacharya.

**The Kandravadis**

Kona Kandravadi choda was mentioned as vidvadjanamanombhoja saptasva i.e. sun to the lotuses i.e. scholars. His son Tyagi Pota was an expert in sastras and logic. The title Vinoda Vidhyadhara in the Kona Kandravadi prasasti indicates the patronage afforded to music, dance and drama. In AD 1137 at Nukakki, Bhima granted lands to dancing women attached to the Saktisvara temple. The Kona Kandravadi records at Draksharama were written by Peddanacharya. The record at Dharanikota bears the signature of Ketelu Surepreggada Moda at the end.

**The Saronathas**

Kolani Kesava was the protector of scholars. A title in his prasasti is sukavi jana manorathartha pradudu i.e. satisfier of the desires of good poets. This title was borne by Kolani Somayo also. Kesava is compared with Vishnu to the faces of scholars and a Brahma to lotus i.e. language. Kolani Pota was a poet and was interested in writing sweet prose.[163] Pallacharya was the composer of the c.p. grant of Ketamana yaku.

The Kolamu records at Draksharama were written by Peddanacharya. The records of Kesava at Paslakol and Ellore were written by Annachari. Samaya's Ganapesvaram inscription was written by Kesava charya and the Ganapesvaram records by Erramacharya. Erayaya's record at Guttiga, and Bhimanapreggada's record at Palakol were engraved by Annachari.

King Katamanayaka was interested in music. For a record say that he was pleased by the music of songs.[164]

**The Second Kolamu Dynasty**

The literary and artistic activities of the Induluri family are known from Sivayagasara by Kolani Adiganapatideva a later incumber of the family who lived in the 14th century AD.

Sivayogasara has more than four cantos dealing with Virasaivism and the introductory of about a hudnred verses speaks about the ancestry of the author and that of Nukanaradhya to whom it is dedicated. Soma, sun of Pedavalla was learned in vedas and sastras. Kolani Rudra was a schoalr, learned in agamas, Saiva and Vaishnava sidhantas, and darsanas and was praised as Vyakarana brahma by people. [165] Kasikavritti vyakhjana, a work on grammar is written by him. In the work the author is mentioned .as Rajarudra, whose identification with prataparudra of the kakatiyas is wrong. For the colophon is another copy of the work says, that the work was by the son of Gannaya, the seal bearer of Prataparudra. [166] Obviously Manma Gannaya of Sivayogasara was Ganaya of the new work, Rudra of the former is Rajarudra of the latter, and hiscomposition of this work justifies his title. Vyakarana brahma. Ganapati, Anbala and Admula were learned in Veas and sastras. Nukaya of the lineage of Nukamardya was a sarvajna possessing a knowledge of the vedas, puranas, and sastras. Nukaradhya was the author of Saivayogasastrasara amuchohaya alias Sivajnanpustakaslokam in sanskrit.[167] Adiganapati was an expert in writing new poetry i.e. Desi Tenugu in which he wrote many kavyas and dramas about siva to the applause of people.[168] Nukanaradhya is said to have asked Adiganapati to reveal the truth contained in the work in the form of slokas, by taking mercy on the masses and acquire merit. Thus he commanded Adiganapati to write Sivayogasara in Telugu with his work as the model.

Adiganapati begins his work adorations to Nukayadesika, Ganapati, sodasiva, adideva, parvati, Virbhadra, Pramathas, Saiva devotees, and saiva poets. Next he praises Sanskrit poets -Vyasa, Kalidasa, Sivabhadra, Bhatta bana, Bharavi, Magha, Valmiki, Mayura, Bana and the Telugu poets - Nannya bhatta, the originator of Andhra Kevyas, Tikkana celebrated as Ubhayakavimitra and Errana.[169] Then the poet praises Palkuriti Somanatha, and blesses the Vedas, sivasamhitas and Yogi. The object of the author is the propagation of Virasaivism. So he says that mahakavyas describing forts, hills, oceans, tanks, women and kings by proved poets are of no value for they do not show the path to salvation. A kvaya according to him, must be ever beautiful, appealing to scholars, lively, capable of removing pains of humanity, pssessing higher meaning, advising the masses, and to the satisfaction of experts in purnans, sastras and agamas. He was determined to write a kavya, consisting of the essence of agamas, and purnans and forms amodel for life and would give salvation.[170]

**The Chalukyas of Pithapur**

King Vijayaditya III was a patron of poets and scholars. He wrote the commentary - Bharatakyava;[171] not extent. Some records like the pathapur pillar inscription were in good Sanskrit. The Two Draksharama epigraphs of Vishnu vardhana, engraved by Potanacharya and Virarajendra Acharya and the Pithapur Pillar by Kanta charya. King Udaya Chandra provided for sani, mani nibandhas etc. devabhogas in the Rajanarayana temple at Bezvada.

**The Chalukyas of Elamanchili**

There are greater signs of progress of literature and arts under those rulers than under the Pithapur Chalukyas. King Upendra III was a cholar and patron of scholars. In his court flourished a poet, the author of a work on agriculture. Upendra IV was learned in arts and science. The Panchodharala pillar inscription says.[172] that none could equal him in the knowledge of the Vedas, tradition and the eternal Siva doctrine. A versatile scholar and poet, he could write kavyas, and being a critique could decide the merits of a work. He apreciated good works and laughed at poets writing the gramya style. Visvesvara and scholars patronised by him were ever contented and happy. Visveswarais compared with Bhoja and was ever in the company of good poets. He used to give sandal, alum, musk, servant maid and articles signifying prosperity and victory, in charity.[173]

The poet of Upendra III's court, in the introduction to his work speaks about the rulers and their achievements. The work in Telugu verse, [174] is interesting and important, being one of the few of its kind, a treatise on agriculture. It has several chapters and of great practical value, giving plenty of hints to the cultivator. It speaks about the rains, their importance, variety in them, their utility for tilling different kinds of soils for raising particular crops, their appropriateness at particular seasons etc. The variety of crops, methods of raising them and so forth.

Vinnakota Peddana was of Kausika gotra, son of Govinda notya, devotee of Siva obedient to scholars and praised by them. He begins the work invoking the blessings of Lakshmi and Saraswati to Visvesvara, and says that Visvesvara who studied the secret implications of the vedas, sastras, grammar, astrology, medicine, learned in literature and music, wanted to group in one place the kavyagamas, which are scattered for the convenience of good poets.[175] So he sent for Peddana, and asked him to write a work dealing with bhava, rhetoric, prosody, language and forth. Peddana says that with visvesvara's permission as the book, he secured precious gems of the kavyas, from the rasa i.e. ratnakara (ocean). The work is known as Kavyalankara chudamani, being a work on almkara lakshana and also as alamkarasastra. [176] It consists of none cantos - ullasas - the first dealing with bhava, the second with sringara, and the eight sentiments, the third with nayaka and nayaki differences, and the supportersof each, the prabandhalakshana and the seven kinds of poets, the fourth with kavya bhadas, and their merits, the fifth with arthalankaras, the sixth with sabdalankaras, he seventh with defects in sentences, their meanings etc, the eighth with prosody and the ninth with grammar.

Kavyalankara chudamani is the oldest of the Telugu works on alamakaras i.e. sahitya sastra, the second being Narasa bhupaliya by Bhattumurti in the 16th century AD.[177] It is summary of the works an alamkara in Sanskrit with some additions Peddana followed Prataparudra Yasobhushana in his cantos, four and five, except the sections on Gunalamkaras, and Dandin's Kavyadarsa in the portions on gunariti and almkaras in cantos four and five. Gunadasaka, alamkaralakshanas, and enumeration of defects on an almukara just below it, and the order of alamkaras similar in the works of Peddana and Dandin. Like Dandi Peddana did ritilakshana following Vamansutra. In latikariti, the differences between dhira and adhiranayakas, nrisimhas ankaram etc, Peddana followed Sahitya darpana and similar works, as they are not found in Kavyadarsa and Prataparudriya. In his Prabandharaja Venkatesvaravilasa, Ganapavarapu venkatakavi mentions the lakshanajnata of Peddana.

Virvesvara's Panchadharala pillar inscription was the composition of the poet [178] who was the author of the pillar record of Kona choda III there. The style is similar in both and one verse from the Kona record (AD 1403) was borrowed into this (AD 1407). In the Panchadharala pillar inscription of Nagendra Chakravarti (AD 1417) the five verses - pancharantnas- were composed by Chenna preggada Kesavaraja in praise of Dharmalinga. [179]

**Engraving, music and dance:** Upendra I's Draksharama inscription was written by Suracharya. His palakol inscription was engraved by Tarpaku chiddama charya, and Narassimha's panchadharala inscription by Hosan Gangu.[180]

Visvesvara, himself a good musician encouraged dance and music in his court. Peddana says that a woman in Visvesvara's court, was admired and praised by scholars for capacities in Sangita and sahitya. A dancer, singing, suggesting beautiful meanings by gestures of hands, expressing idea by looks, and keeping time by the play of feet, danced in the presence of Visvesvara. Peddana mentions that dance accompanied by the play of various musical insturments and songs expressing the nine sentiments.[181] In the technique of dance, the dancer of visvesvara's court are said to have excelled Rambha etc. dancers.

At Panchadharala, in AD 1437, Buddesani and Nunkasani, daughters of Virakka, the Vengastri of king Narasimha, Tallasani, daughter of dancing master (nattuvan Golavada potu and Pola Gangasani made grants for the angarangabhoga of the deity.[182]

**The Chalukyas of Srikurmam**

A record of these Chalukyas mentions that Rajaraja I together with scholars, translated into Andhra the history of Bharata race. One of the court poets was Narasimha kavi the composer of the Srikurmam pillar inscription of Purushottamma[183] and the record of Rajaraja.

**The Chalukyas of Nidadavole**

A family of ministers in the service of the Chalukyas [184] patronised arts. Nandamiya of Karenchedu was learned in the

Veda, sastras and their intricacies. His son Narayana was like Mamadhanu to poets. Narayana's son was Bella and daughter-in-law Nagamba was praised by poets. Bella's son was Ananta who had three sons. Of them Bella was a treasure to scholars, and Vengi was learned in the Saivagamas - its philisophy, logic and inner meaning. He was learned in the puranas like Bona was devoted to Siva and was a minister of Venga, son of Mahadeva.

**Engraving, dance and music:** Vengi Malla's record at Draksharama was written by Peddanacharya; Ayyapa's record at Tadikalapudi by Nagacharya, and that of Gonka at Ganapesvaram by Pakachari. Mahadeva's Palakol epigraph was written by Saranoju that of Gonka at Draksharama by Suracharya, son of Peddanacharya and Rajanarayasa's Palakal inscription by Saranoju Nagoju, son of Saranoju. Minister Venga was an expert in architecture and music. At Telikicherla Narayana, minister of Ayyapa, provided for gitavadyanritta - in the temple and arranged for the employ of vocal musicians, dancers, flutists and drummers.[185]

**Other Chalukyas:** The Peddakallepalle record of Bella (1154 AD), was writen by Kunchacharya. The Rumathirtha inscription of Mummadi Bhima is in Kannada prose and verse. The name of the composer is not known.

Attached to the temple at Peddakallepalle were sani 300 dancing girls in whose charge some grants were made. At Burugugadda, Ammajiyya Ganapaddena provided for rangesa and angarangabhoga of the deity.[186]

**The Pallavas of Guntur**

Among the rulers Keta and Tammubangi were learned in arts. Boddana patronised scholars and Tammubhima made all the gifts including vidyastana. Among ministers, Prolaya, Baddana Bhima's minister was praised by scholars, Kuchenapreggada protected many good poets and Dettana Soma did the sapta Santanas including a good prabandha. Some of the records of those rulers were in good Sanskrit and

Telugu. The Bezavada record is long in prose and poetry in Telugu. Soma's record at Guntur was written by Peddana - charya.

**The Pallavas of Nellore**

Literature and arts progressed. Murya, son of Devaya and servant of Nadivarma was the composer of the Yadadevi inscription[187] of Doraparaja (AD 1102). Most of Vijayagandagopala's records are in Tamil and grantha. Some in Sanskrit and very few in Telugu. His conjeevaram e.p. charter in Sanskrti verse in Grantha characters, except the donor's signature in Tamil. The charater is said to have been written by the king in his own land. [188]

Vijayagandagopala encouraged education, learning and poetry by making grants. He granted Ambikapura to the great personage who resides in teh malla to the west of Hastisaida. This teacher explains to his pupils the hidden meaning of the Vedanta and pleases the eternal (atman) and the Brahmins daily by his gifts. Gundur Singapperumati alias Abhinava Bhatta Bana of Velichcheri, figuring in a record of the 21st year of Vijayagandagopala [189] must have been as suggested by his second name an excellent prose writer in Sanskrit, a precursor of Vamana Bhatta Bana of the Reddi age, the 14th century AD.

**Engraving, music and dance.** Tikkaraju alias Tikkarasur Visaiyadevan, A Tyagasamudra petti and officer of Vijayagandagopala was the writer of Sriperumbudru inscription of Solagangadeva, a subordinate of Vijayagandagopala. [190]

Inumadideva at Nagalavaram granted a dhupaghanta, single couch (divya dhara), for continuous blowing during service times, and for angarangabhoga of the deity. [191] Vijayagandagopala provided for Tirumoloppadin "the padi or offering intended to be made when tiurmoli is sung" on each day from the second day of the Vaikasi festival of Govinda Perumal at Tirumala.[192]

Kamenayaka and Devinayaka, subordinates of Vijayagandagopala granted four pattus of paddy field besides many other lands to dancing girls for performance of dance in the Mallikarjuna temple at Chiramana. The record specifies that if the dancing girls lease out the lands, the kapus who rule the village, with treat them as a sarva manya; 1/2 na (tum) paddy field is given to the conunblower. Dance is given special importance in this case, for the purpose of the grant is specified solely as ranga bhoga.[193] At Kanchi, a dancing girl of the temple of Tiruvegambam Udaiya Nayanar made gifts to the deity at padi. Pidainaru Sivadiyar, a dancing girl of the temple at Tiruppalaivanam gifted a golden necklace to the God in the 8th year and a silver plated four sided procession car to the temple in the 15th year of Vijayagandagopala at Tiruppukkuli, a dancing car processions. In the region of Viragandagopala at Tiruppukkuli a dancing girl was granted a santana chamam to the temple. At Vippada, Allada pemmayadeva granted Jalamur to the sanis for the ranǵa bhoga of the deity.

**The Dynasties in South Kalinga - The Maksyas of Oddadi**

Among the subsidiary dynasties in South Kalinga, the Maksyas stand first in their encouragement of arts. Some of the kings and ministers were good scholars. Virarajaganta was learned in arts. Arjuna I granted Dibbida as agrahara to Twenty brahmins the details of which are as follows - the teachers of the Rigveda were Merabrahman and Viddana of Barita gotra, Namana of Kannadinya gotra, Vennkakata of Salavata gotra, Potasarman of Vadhulagotra, Ramana of Mandgalya gotra, and Dommana of Bharadraja gotra. The students of Rigveda were Vennakuta of Harita gotra, Manavarman of salavatagotra, Yajnamurtarya of Kanudinya gotra. The teachers of Yajurveda were Akondi of Vatsa gotra, Bhimasvararya of Bharadvaja gotra, Srirangarya of Kavundinya gotra, Lokanatha of Kasyapa gotra, and the students of Yajurveda were - Raghava of Mandgalya gotra, and Purushottama of Gautama gotra. The student of Kanvasakha (Yajurveda) was. Madhavarya of Jatakarana gotra. Mankanarya of Harita gotra was a student of Sribhagavata (purana).[194] Thus Arjuna provided for the teaching and study of Rig and Yajur vedas, Kanvasakha and Bhagavata and encouraged scholarship. Oddadi Bhimanapreggada, in AD 1365 provided for the repetition of Sahasranama daily during day time two persons, Narasimha Kavacham by one person and for once circumchibalation in the Simhachalam, temple and also for vidiya sahasranama by one person Narasimha Kavacham by another and for cicumambulations there.[195]

**Engraving, music and dance:** The Matsya e.p. grant bears a seal which bears two fish in relief on an elleptical surface about 1" by 1/8".[196] A record of the Maksyas at Draksharama was written by Peddanacharya. Varadana preggada of the reign of Arjuna II was a musician of repute entitled sangitaratnakara. The importance attached to dance is seen from the mention of dance masters and dancing girls in inscriptions. In AD 1377, Arjuna made grants[197] to Mansani, Narasimha natavu (dance master), Purucrasani, mankari mtagu veda, dancing girl tappasani, daughter of Narasimha, Natava kuna, madasani, majkhari, purasani, daughter of Arjunadeva. Varadana preggada made grants to Kunusani, Pratasani, Anyasani and Varadasani for holding charis in the temple at Simhachalam. In AD 1467, in the reign of Pratapa Vallabha, a grant was made to the dancing girl, dance master and Srivaishnavas in the temple at Duttada.

**The Pallavas of Virakuta**

A title in the Pallava prasasti is Kaduvaya pareghoshana-kuduvayapure is the drum included in the Pallava regalia. In AD 1420 at Simhachalam Saubhagyadeva made a grant to Purushasrutram Singinayaka. Obvious by Purushasutram is a mistake for Purushasutram singinayaka, and probably singinayaka's duty was to repeat it in the temple.[198] The Pallava records at Draksharama were written by Peddanacharya.

**The Gangas of Jantarnadu**

The Gangas learned in arts patronised them. Viraganga (AD 1368) was specially good at music and provided for chamera Kolupulu - to fan the duty with churis - by making grants to sani redi Aryasani, and Gangasani, daughter of Arjuna Reddi Chingupatunayadu, for one Chamara for each.

**The Silas of Nandapura**

Madaya, father of poet Mallaya who wrote Rajasekhara charitra, wrote Mairaranacharitra. A verse in it says that Poet Madaya was honoured by Nanda purisu i.e. lord of Nandapura with lustrous gold jewels and so forth. This king of Nandapura had been identified with Bhairavadeva[199] (AD 1510-1527 or 1540).

King Bayyaraja in 1427 AD made a grant to dancing girls to be in the service of the deity both in the mornings and the evenings. The dances of Jereddi Brammasani, a Khandamare and Ambikasani were to carry on chamara Kolupulu according to the prevailing cistern.

**Other Dynamics:** The inscription of Ganesvara chamunatha at Simhachalam was composed by chitsukhacharya. Mumara Anantajiyana of chikuti, provided for two Purushasuktagodavulu- repetition of Purushasukta - twice daily in Simhachalam temple.[200] Nrisimha bhattopadyaya and Merumadhavarya, learned in the agamas figure in two inscriptions at Srikurmam and Boni. Astrologer Visvesvarabhatta is mentioned in a record at Panchadharala. Singaraja Mahapatra was well versed in Natyaveda[201] - the science of dance. At Srikurman Palakonda Sarvajnadeva (AD 1471) presented to teh temple - Sutasani sanrasani, two men to hold four chamaras one each and be in the service of the god in the mornings and the evenings Konda Kamati Pratapa singa provided for the holding of the chamara by Nagadeva Gangasani and bhudi Singa sani during both times of worshipping the temple at Simhachalam. In AD 1312 at Sri kurmam provision was made for singing and playing on Vina in the presence of the deity.[202]

### The Yadavas of Addanki

King Sarngadhara II made gifts to Brahmins, thoroughly versed in the Vedas and the Vedangas, and devoted to the study and teaching (of the Vedas) and versed in commentaries, logic and ethics. [203] King Madadideva is compared with Bhoja, and his fame is sung by soldiers and ministers. Minister Mayideva preggada was a patron of scholars. Visvesvara Pandita and his sons - Appana, Manchana, Bayyana, figure in Vaijegadeva's inscription. Tara Pandit and his brother figure in a record of Madhava.

**Engraving, dance and music:** Madhava's irecord at Nagulappalapadu was written by Karanam Dasi raju and that of sarngapani by Karunam Jakaraja. Singala's chandalur epigraph was written by Kase Damoju. At Nagulappalapadu in AD 1239 Madhava nayaka made grant - 200 kuntas to the writer of the record, 200 kuntas to the dancing girls of the deity and drummers.[204] At Chandalur, Singadeva made a grant for the angarangabhoga of the deity. Queen Mallanadevi at Tammalur in AD 1269 provided to the dancing girls for angarangabhoga of the deity.

**The Yadavas of Panugal**

Sarngadhara's Panugal record dated AD 1267 is in quite ordinary sanskrit. The name of composer is not known. "The opening verse of the boar in carnation of Vishnu speaks for his fertility in imagination and capacities" and shows that he "could infuse a spirit of ramance and beauty even to an oft repeated and stale old mythological story."[205] Sarnapani provided for the angarangabhoga of the deity.

The temple of Chaya Somesvara at Panugal presents many peculiarities of architecture. It is like a shadow to the sluice of Udayasamudra tank near Panugal, and faces east. There is a Kolamu in the front and a strong Prakara wall with three gates round the temple. A long it other temples joining three of which is a fine mukhamandapa. In the temple facing east the linga is inside water - Waist deep. There seems to be some connection between this water in the innermost shrine garbhalaya and the Kolanu opposite the temple. The water is flowing, but it is not visible where it goes. Another peculiar point is this. Just opposite to the Chayasananatha temple is another temple; and between the two is some space-antarola. Due to some speciality of silpa architecuture, a long black shadow next to the linga in the garbhalaya is seen throughout the day, steady at the place without moving. Because of the shadow, the god came to be known as chayasomesvara temple.[206] Local persons say that several Europena architects and physicians who visited the place could not get at the cause of the shadow.

Sarnagadeva, the author of Sangitaratnakara, was patronised by the yadavas of Devagiri and was contemporary with Sarngadeva of Panugal. Son of Sodhala patronised by Singhana of the Yadavas (AD 1210-1247) grandson of Bhaskara Sarngadeva was accountant general of the king. He speaks about his learning in detail and styles himself as anavadhavidhavinoda Sri Karanadhipatinissanka Sri Sarnagadeva. [207] The best and most scientific of medieval writers on music - he divided the entire musical system into marga and desi-bygone and popular studied the problems of musicians, details the lakshya and lakshna of Sangita - in use and out of vogue. he gives an account of the four gitas, saptatalagitas, and deals with many new composition, not dealt with already. He shows with examples " how the time measure is manipulated to be exhibited in dance in various ways." [208]

**The Yadavas of Alavulapadu and Erragaddapadu**

Though little is known about the encouragement accorded to arts by the Yadavas, their history formed the theme of poems, ballads and songs of a later day. The Gundlapalem record was engraved by Ramaya, son of Kondayya. Katamaraju Katha or Erragaddapoti potlata was the subject matter of many interesting poems and ballads in Telugu. There are many versions of it in Mack Mss. The story is supposed to have sung by contemporary bards. It is most popular in Marellasima, where are seen to this day the statues of Katamaraju,[209] who is worshipped as a deity by persons possessing plenty of cattle, for he won in a fight concerning cattle.

During the festival of Ganga at Alavulapadu several nights are taken up in singing Bhatturaya baramu, Yerragaddapatipotlata and Kakamu raju katha. In the festival of Panchalingalakonda, men of cobbler caste called Kammuvalu i.e. trumpeters, and piolivallu, a sect among shepherd caste, sing the ballads about Katamaraju. But in accordance with the prevalent custom, the pililis should not raise their Gudaru (tent) before the Kommus raised theirs. [210] Tradition says that Katamaraju gave permission to kammus to propagate his tale and they are responsible for the existence of the ballads to this day. The pikilis are chiefly found in Muppalla (Kanigiri taluq) and in all the festivals of the local deities held in Kandukur taluq, they go to sing the songs about katamaraju and enjoy special grants, vrittis - allotted for the purpose. [211]

**The Nagas**

In AD 1395, king Asvadeva is said to have been listening to good stories and witnessing amusements: Bajuni voju the vojulu (artisan) who constructed the Pratapa Gopinatha temple was given a grant by Asnadeva.[212] At Peddakondur, Nagadeva provided for dance performance in the temple.

**The Banas**

One of the titles in the Bana praśasti is paisachikapatupatahaghoshavale one who beats the clear sounding drum named Paisachika. [213] As the Banas claim descent from Mahabali Bana, the Rakshasa, it is appropriate that their drum is styled Paisachika, as that of the Pallavas was Kaduvayapari.

**The Saluvas**

Information is meagre. In the reign of Salva Kampa, son of Anbalayya (AD 1422) seems to have lived Manumanchibhattu, the composer of Hayalakshnasara in Telugu. In AD 1446 at Talluru, Kasavayadeva made a grant of land to vedic scholars (srotriyas), Narasimhadeva, son of Ravu Pinnama and a subodinate of Saluva Narasimha acquired the title Sarvajan by his great intellectual capacities. He was a clever speaker (Brahma), learned man (Buddha), a gem among the learned (Indra), a poet (Sukra), and intelligent (sani).[214] His glory is praised in seven verses in Sanskrit at the beginning of one record. His brother Kasavaya is praised in five Sanskrit slokas at the beginning of the record (AD 1475).

**The Kayasthas**

The Kayasthas encouraged learning by making substantial grants to religious teachers and maths. The title Brahmanaveda in the Gunnavaram epigraph of AD 1254, of the reign of Ganapati, probably suggest that the bearer was learned in Brahmanaveda. In a record figures Isanagurudeva (AD 1257), probably identical with the author of Isanagurudevapaddhati. Santasiva of Golaki matha was the spiritual preceptor of Jannigadeva, to whom in AD 1260 Janniga granted Porandalur, to enable him to teach adhyana in the Vidyamantapa, and to worship Brahmins, guests and visitors. Ambadeva in AD 1298 made a grant to Tripuranataka Siva, the people of Agharasiva.

**The Telugu Cholas**

In their contribution to literature and other arts, the Telugu chodas are second to none among the subsidiary dynasties. Some of the most important works in the entire range of Telugu literature were produced under their patronage. Kings Nannichoda deva and Baddena, poets, and Tikkana Somayaji, the foremost of the poets of any age, rendered the major part of the Mahabharata into Telugu.

**Konidena Cholas**

Nannichoda of the Konidena Cholas, was the author of Kumara Sambhava. Like all Saiva poets, he gives few details of biagraphical interest in his work. He calls himself Ravikulasekhara, Kavirajasikhamani, and Sakkaviraja, [215] dedicated Kumarasambhava to Gurujangama Mallikarjuna deva by whose mercy he learnt to good poetry and refers to him as God also. Lord Siva and this guru are described as identical persons in the verses at the beginning of the work, beginning and ending of each canto, and in adorations to deities in narrating the story in the middle of the work. The identity of this guru, among the several Mallikarjunas of Srisailamath, who were royal preceptors is not known. Mallikarjuna was an expert in nyayas, vaisashika etc. six tarkas, vedas shadangas, sastras, puranas, Itihasas, agamas and all sciences.[216] He could teach to scholars, the essence of vedas and sastras.

Kumarasambhava of Nannichoda is a champa kavya in Telugu, consisting of twelve cantos, Nannichoda followed the eight sargas of Kumarasambhava and alamkarasastra, of Udbhata. Linguistic, prosodical and other familiaritis of his work may be traced to : religious influcence-Virasaivism prevalent in the Telugu and Kannada lands in the 12th century AD. The work shows Nannichoda's scholarship in the sixty-four arts. Somanatha says in it are unique and the figures of speech are modelled after the slokas in Kvayalankara of Udbhata. In some respects, the poet followed Kalidasa's Sakuntala and Dandin's Kavyadarsa. Some opine that Nannichoda was the best of all poets including even the Kavitreya. His style is flowing, words convey deep thoughts, and descriptions of nature are superfine.

The work is called mahakavya. Udbhata (AD 778-813) the Vidyadhipati of the court of Jayapida of Kashmir, is distinct from his name sake figuring in the works of Somanatha, and author of Kavyalankarasamgraha in Sanskrit. Nanni choda's changes in the narration and translation of the work, attest his original capacities. The story is found in many puranas. In Ramayana, in Balakanda, Visvamitra narrated Kumara Sambhava to Rama. With this as the source, Kalidasa referred to the birth of Sati, her sacrifice of life, and destruction of Daksha's sacrifice in a single sloka, and confined himself to Kamadahana, parvatiparinaya, Kumara sambhava. He omitted Kumara's fight with Uttara and later stories [217] Nannichoda praises Udhata saying that he did Kumara-sambhava and pleased Siva. [218] In spite of the resemblances between Nannichoda's work and Tikkana's Nirvachanottara Ramayana, Bharata, works of Ketana and Somanatha, to say that he studied those works is improper on chronological grounds. On the other hand it is likely that they studied and followed Nannichoda's work. Several of Nannichoda's verses were converted into dvipadas by Somanatha in Basavapurana. [219] Nannichoda followed Nannaya's Bharata in usage of words, descriptions etc.

Nannichoda begins with a mangala sloka in Telugu praises the gods, adores Valmiki, Vedavyasa, Kalidasa, Bharavi, Udbhoa, Bana etc. Sanskrit poets and says that when Marga kavita was already extent in the country, the chalukyas revived desikavita. It is opined that this chalukya who kept alive Telugu by reviving desikavita was Rajaraja I narendra. The verse says while marga kavita (Sanskrit poetry) was already extent in the country (desa), several kings beginning with chalukyaraju, created and brought about the birth of desikavita (i.e. Telugu poetry i.e. writing of works) and thus kept Telugu in Andhravishaya. [220] It is opined that the version of M.R. Kavi that it was the work of Satyasaraya etc. chalukya is unauthorised by evidence. [221] Marga and desi thus according to some mean Sanskrit and Telugu, where as some others opine that the terms were borrowed from Bharati's Natyasastra, the first implying the indication of bhava by abhinaya of facial or other gestures, while the second indicates the expression of bhava in clear terms and so the terms when applied to literature signify ballad literature and works of poetric art, and accordingly the verse means while Telugu ballad literature including music was in existence before, the chalukyas from Satyasraya witnessed the birth of Telugu poetry.[222] But this cannot be accepted in the light of the explanation of the verse given above.

Nannichoda praises ancient poets, good poets who write in best marga style and desi poets. But he does not mention the Telugu poets. He abused dead poets thus - they follow faulty methods. He cannot distinguish between merits and demerits in a work and so calls merits demerits. He is satisfied with bad works and is not moved by good works. Good poetry is understood by scholars, but not ordinary man. Then the author praises good poets thus-a good poet respects other good poets, and with the blessings of scholars and guru, and like an astrologer instals his works on a good day.[223] Vowels and consonants are saktis to scholars. A poet must possess clear thoughts, write in easy language, and the work must possess sweet sayings, descriptions, desi figures of speech, and live in the world permanently like an image. Possessing witty sayings, figures of speech of all kinds, thoughts and emotions, good combinations of words, sounds, qualities, a good kavya, like an arrow paosses through the heart, and pleases man and roams in the world like a mast elephant. Further he says except for good poets who possess good control over sixty-four arts, is not possible to write works.[224] Nannichoda calls his a prabandha and has indicated the eighteen descriptions-a prabandha lakshana.

After the praise of Gangana Mallikarjuna, Nannichoda begins the story. In a single verse[225] he summarises the entire story - birth of Sati and Ganesa, destruction of Daksha's sacrifice, birth of Paravati, Siva's penance, marraige of Uma and Siva, their enjoyment, birth of Kumara, his fight and victory over Tarakasura. Kumarasambhava besides enlighten descriptions has forty-five dasa-pranas, nine rasas, and thirty-six alamkaras. Nanni choda wrote Kalavilasa which is not extant, except a few verses quoted in the lakshana granthas.[226]

Kavaliya Gundimada Anna was a scholar and Rudrapandita and Kama pandita were well versed in Saivagamas.

**Music, dance and drama**: Elaborate temple grants and descriptions in Kumarasambhava attest the encouragement given to music and dance. In a grant of Tribhuvanamalla Pottapi Choda (AD 1142) among the donees figure, avajakadu, drummer, kasyavaru, Mukhari Tippaka, Kamaka, Bhumaka, Mariyaka, bairaka, kapaka, dance master mallaya, Mataketaka, nattavuchokkaka, Machcheka, Eriyaka and Kamaka.[227] It is worth noting that in this instance mankari and dancing master (Nattavaji) are women. In AD 1147, 1148 Tribhuvana Malla C.M. and P.Kama made a grant to nattuvula Sanke.

Manni choda mentions the musical instruments - pataka, panava, bhumbha, uttunubha, mridanga, sankha, Kabala, Karya, Venu, tatata-Vipanchika, Ghanasushira.[228] (big wind instrument).[229] He refers to the play on vina producing Chaturvaras which equal samagana, and maids playing flute, and singing in praise of Brahma. He refers to the Subara women singing many ragas while pounding rice, girls singing while plucking flowers and today tappers singing while tapping today.[230]

Parvati is said to have learnt dancing while in the presence of Hara with great devotion, the differences in gitas and their vitis, while singing songs in the form of prasastis in praise of Siva and all arts with Siva as guru. Nannichoda says that women danced singing sweet songs, to the accompaniment of harmonious instruments, under the direction of a dance master and dance misterss on the pitha on a highly set stage. Rambha danced expressing her thoughts and the nine sentiments with her angas, while Narada and Tumburu were singing, on playing on their instruments. He refers to war music when saying that while bards were singing auspicious songs, some singing and playing on vina, and other instruments, songs in the form of prasasti, the viramaddalas of soldiers made noise. [231] Nannichoda refers to Salamanjaram - a purusharaga and Somanatha refers to many purusha and strirugas in his Basavapurana.

Nanni choda described the arts of image making, sculpture and painting of pictures. He refers to the methods of drawing of the picture, doll making and pressing models. By drawing of the picture of Siva, Parvati learnt the art of drawing . She learnt patrachachedas, cutting of leaves to make dolls, and Kusumbavdhas - typing of flowers, while worshipping siva in different ways. [232] She painted the picture of Mara and Sringara

Lakshmi. Nanni choda refers to the lifelessness of Kama in a picture, the representation of forest in another, the dolls made of sand and image making by passing model, and burning it in liquid metal.[233] According to Nannichoda, Parvati took the necessary paraphernalia and proceeded thus. [234] - she fixed the plank (palaka) made it shining and smooth, prepared the background and by adopting the line rijvagata in chitrasastra, shudras patraka binduka, ups and downs, side looks, mana and unmana, pointed it in the specified method, applied colour and finished it. The picture is lifelike, and she removed the curtain covering it, Siva appeared to be laughing aloud, opening his eyes, moving eye brows, looking at her with desire, extending his hands to embrace her and as though standing and dancing in her presence. The description shows that the picture was that of Nataraja. Nanni choda says that a golden image is washed well to lose its bitterness i.e. perhaps dirt, and mentions that the pigeons in the sculptured panels on the mansions are so life like, that cats took them to be real pigeons, approached them in anger but found them voiceless. [235] He refers to vjralapa-the application of paste mixed with vajre i.e. diamond, to paste two separate articles, and alatikeeping of time etc. and upangas in connection with mukhavina. Suyana also mentioned as suchiyana, one of the sixty-four arts means embroidery - stitching swan etc. figures with neeles thread, on the borders of sarees, shawls etc. [236] fine drawing oil painting and printing are mentioned. Nanni choda used chitrakavita suggesting pictures in arohana andavarohana. The varieties in chitra kavita are Kandagarbhavitta, chaturvidhamandas, nagabandha, murajabandha, and chakrabandha. Nanni choda wrote all these beautifully.

### The Pottapi cholas

Among the Pattapi cholas, opilisiddhi (1224 AD) was the protector of pupils, favourite, relatives, poets and Brahmins. Mallideva C.M. lord of Kundukur; was learned in puranas, nyaya, mimasasa, agamas, vedas, dharmasastras etc. 18 sciences.[237] In AD 1224, the ruler made a grant for the angarangabhoga of the deity.

**The Nellore cholas**

The capacities of some of the Telugu cholas of Nellore in literature were remarkable. King Tammasiddha in Kavali in AD 1207 summoned Brahmins, Bandari Tripuraya, and others well versed in the vedas, masters of all sciences, six Karmas and made a grant to them. [238] Ketana mentions Tikka as Abhinavabhoja.[239] Obviously Tikka was a scholar and patron of scholars. Manmasiddha III, according to Tikkana, achieved mastery in several sciences, as a result of indefetigable industry, and was a writer of fine works. [240] He was a protector of scholars. His son chola Tikka alias Tikkas I was fond of poets, evident from his title - pathakaputra. He studied all the sciences and acquired the title - kavisarvabhanma. His son Manmasiddha III was a scholar, could enjoy poetry thoroughly. He was a protector, Patra and friend of poets bards and scholars. Allutikka was found of scholars, and is said to have been enjoying in his court listening to good stories.

The rajyapratipalaka of Errasiddha (AD 1217) is described as a panditapundarika spandamartanda i.e. sun to the host of lotuses i.e. learned men.[241] In the home of general Ranatikkana, at Nellore a chatu verse says, discussions were held aloud among heroes and vedas were recited aloud day and night. [242]

**Some of the important poets of the period were thus:** I Tikkanasomayaji - Tikkana Somayaji of the region of Manumasiddhi III was one of the best generals of the age and the greatest poet in the entire literature of the Andhras. Entitled Ubhayakavimitra, Tikkana was the first Telugu poet to whom a work was dedicated. For ketana dedicated his Desakumaracharitra to Tikkana. The poets merits, intelligence, learning, interest in scholars, munificence, and handsome personality are delineatedin Ketana's work. Tikkana was brilliant, selfless, and expert in polity, a genius in all sciences, possessed great capacities for all work. He patronised poets, is compared with Mayura etc. poets, and is mentioned as kavijanaraja Kira Sahakara[243] i.e. a sweet mango tree to the best of parrots i.e. poets.

**Ancestry and early life:** Tikkana descended from a family of scholars. Mavenarya was learned in the agamas. Ketana, second son of Bhaskara was interested in the welfare of scholars and was learned in literature (sahityanidya)[244] ketana Mallana, Siddhana and Kanmana are compared with the four faces Brahma in their knowledge of many arts and with four arms of Vishnu in protecting scholars, Ketana wrote poetry having nine sentiments in it. Kottaruvu ketana, younger brother of Kumma was a versatile scholar. Nallasiddha, younger brother of Gundena was learned in many subjects. His sons Ketana and Mallaya were learned in several arts. Mallana was a great orator and was praised in courts by scholars. His son Manmasiddhi was praised by poets. General siddhi is compared with Brahma in learning. Of his sons, Pinabhaskara and mantri Bhaskara patronised poets. Polama Malla was well versed in many sastras, Kottaruvu Kamma was the youngest son of Bhaskara mantir, who was learned in the Vedas[245] and wrote Bhaskara Ramayana in Telugu. Tikkanasomayaji was the son of Kamma.

The descendants of Tikkana are found to this day at Indukurpet in Nellore, and at Patur, 46 miles from Nellore and three miles to the west of Kovur, on the Penna. Tikkana's son was Kamma, the karanam of Patur. His son was Harihara, whose son was Kommana. Kommana's sons were Remana and Tippana. Ramana's son was Sana. His son was Marana. Marana's son was Soma linga and Chitivira. Soma's son was Papana mantri. His son was Virana, whose sons were Gopalabhadra and Narasimha mantri. Narasimha's sons were Sarabha, Bhaskara, and Narasimha, Surabha's son was Vira. His son was Sarabha, the karanam of Patur.[246]

A verse in Mack MS says that in saka year 1210 - Kalayukti, Bhadrapati Tikka yajva, the precious ornament of the sky reached heaven. The saka date agrees with Tikkana's chronology.[247] It is popular belief that Tikkana lived for a hundred years. So he must have lived up to AD 1300 at least for eighty years from AD 1290. His early ancestors lived at Vellatur (Kistna district). His grandfather shifted to Guntur. So Tikkana must have spent his early years at Guntur. Next enjoying Manmasiddhai's patronage, Tikkana shifted with his family to Nellore and lived in ahouse built for him by the king near the Harihara temple, where the present Rangannayaka temple stands. After Manmasiddhi Tikkana's family lost the patronage of Telugu cholas.

Tikkana is of Gautama gotra and Apastamaba sutra. His mother Annamamba was a native of Nellore. So Kanma during his visits to Nellore must have made his acquaintance with Manmasiddhi. Tikkana praises the capacities of his grandfather Bhaskara in his father and grandfather lived. But Ketana prefixes Kottaruvu to the name of Kanmana, father of Tikkana. So Tikkana's family name was Kottaruvu. After Tikkana, it changed into Patur, as his son was Paturi Kanmana and remained thus to this day.

**His learning and capacities:** Tikkana was an expert both in Sanskrit and Telugu and was praised by his title - Ubhayakavimitra.[248] He could write all kinds of Mavyas in both languages. He was praisedin court of Manmasiddhi II. Ketana says that of all poets only Tikkana was fit to write and receive works. Tikkana wrote a variety of works, patronised poets, received works, was the poet and minister of Manmasiddhi and after writing Bharata used frequently the title Ubhavakavimitra. He was learned in the Vedas and satisfied the desires of scholars. He knew several arts, studied all the sciences, and was a critique of several subjects. By his poetry, rare in words,and meaning and beautiful, he disproved the saying "Banochachishtam jagatsarvam."[249]. Tikkana could equal Brahma and Ravana in his knowledge was a great orator, and could write kavyas of three kinds beginning with padyakavya, obviously the other two being champu and gadya. His mastery in Vedanta, sankhya yoga, purva and uttara mimamsa, is revealed in his writing slike Bharata, and conversations with gains during his visit to the court of Ganapati of the Kakatiyas. He advised Ganapati to administer the kingdom with the permission of his great minister Sivadevayya.[250]. Tikkana was known as Chaturvana for having transleated Bharata. He was held in great esteem by contemporary kings. He says that as Manmasiddhi used to call him mama and so that it may prove relevant, he asked him to give a work i.e. Bharatikanya to him.

When he decided to write Uttara Ramayana as Nirvachana-all verse, he said that it is good to write a work entirely in poetry with the theme fitted in easy but good verses. Tikkana was well versed in the tenets of Buddhism and Jainism for Somadevarajiya says that he successfully argued with the Jains and Buddhists at Hanumakonda who were invited for the purpose by Ganapati.[251] Tikkana style himself a great schoalar and an expert in the writing both kinds of Kavyas.[252]

**His works**: Tikkana's works are not many. But Bharata secured him permanent fame and greatness. This wonderful scholar possessed a fascinating personality as attested by evidence and his influence was so market that not a single poet of merit contemporary and later except the Virasava poets, in the world of the literature of the Andhras wrote his work or works without paying homage to this great poet. Tikkana remains unsurpassed in every respect, by any other poet and his fame in the field of Sanskrit literature is not insignificant.

1. Nirvachanara Ramayana is the earliest of Tikkana's works known so far. Tikkana wrote this before he performed the yajna. Valmiki Ramayana consists of seven kandas. The reason for Tikkana's selection of Uttara Kanda as the theme for his already rendered into Telugu by his grandfather Bhaskara and was popular on Bhaskara Ramayana. Tikkana did the work is nirvachana and omitted Sriamaniryana.

While translating works. generally poets followed the main trend of the story in the original, followed their own way in the order of narration of events and descriptions and made additions. Tikkana took the story in the Uttara Ramayana as the basis and exhibited much originality in his work. He summarised his own descriptions. His Uttara Ramayana comprises tne cantos, style is natural and resembles that of Bharata, though not so dignified. In respect of style, perfection etc. Tikkana's Ramayana Tikkana calls himself Ubhayakavimitra, Budhajanaradhanavidheya and son of Kanmanamatya. Two verses from this work, Tikkana included in his Bharata. Later poets followed him in this respect e.g. Srinatha. Tikkana some Telugu sayings not used by Nannaya, in the work.[254]

Following Nannaya, Tikkana began the work with mangala charana in a Sanskrit sloka, and adored Haihara and Vishnu. Next he says that king Manma sent for him and asked him summarily without mentioning their names. He says that a work must be good, and works make the world laugh and bad poets are like innoral men.[255] He describes bad Telugu poetry and good poetry which scholars like. His estimate of a good poem is as follows any poet likes his own work, and a good kavya is one liked by other good poets. Next Tikkana speaks about poetry interposed with prose passages, traces Manmasiddha's genealogy and begins the story. Tikkana did not use shsthayanta. The Kritipali is not addressed in the verses at the end of each canto. Instead Tikkana started a new "method."[256] Manmasiddhi si described in the same vibhakti (case of the noun) as the one with which the last verse of a canto eblonging to thes tory ends or that of the first verse of the next canto belonging to the story of the previous canto. Besides, in the verses at the end of each canto, the meaning applies both to Manmasiddhi and the hero of the story.

The statement that Uttara Ramayana was the last of Tikkana's works and that Tikkana wrote it, was lost is baseless.[257] Tikkana purposely left the work incomplete because of his dislike to say Ramaniryana which was written in recent yearsby Jayanti Ramabhattu and Kamkanti paparaja. In Ramayana which the six kandas form the first part the second part - Uttarakanda- speaks about Ramarajya—birth of Lava and Kusa, performance of Asvamedha sacrifice and Rama's ascendancy to heaven. Tikkana's was the first Uttara Ramayana in Telugu i.e. rhyming letter of each verse) rhyming syllables), parsa (the second latter i.e. rhyming letter of each verse) and their offshooks (tadbhavas). For completing the last canto left off Tikkana, Jayanti Rambhattu gives the reason as follows.[258] - Tikkana Samayoji who did Uttarakanda left off one, so I do it that it might appear like placing of a golden poet on a nice temple. He dedicated it to Bhadaradri Rama, The poet was the son of Jaynti Krishnabhattaraka and Subhadramba and belonged to Gargeyara gotra. Ramabhattu learnt to write poetry by the grace of Bhadradri Rama. The colophgon says that in Ramayana- uttarakanda - in the portion omitted by Rama, performance of a hundred sncrifices beginning with Atirata, Panudarika, vajapeya, and so forth and finnaly Rama is Narayana entering Vaikuntha. Kankanti Paparaju addresses scholars not to criticise for writing this prabandha which Uttara Ramayana has been done as nirvachana kavya by Tikkana, for the history of Raghavesvara deserves to be written by any number of poets, in many ways.[259]

2. Mahabharata: Tikkana did the major part of Mahabharata-the last fifteen parvas beginning with Virata parva and dedicated it to god Hariharanatha. Probably because Nannaya's death was attributed to his writing Bharata, Tikkana to expatiate himself from the sin of writing Bharata, did yajna and then began the work. As Somadevarajiya says that Tikkana held discourses with Jains etc. disbelievers in the vedas (nastikas) it has been suggested that Tikkana wrote Bharata to please orthodox brahmins and revive varnadharmas.[260] Tikkana was the first to use Shasthayantas.[261] He begins Virata parva with adorations to Hariharanatha, all deities - sakalabrahma, krishnadvaipayana, author of Bharatakaya amanya and Nannaya bhatta andhrakavitvavisarada, who did three kritis beginning with Adiparva. Then he says that he would do the fourth, Virata and udyoga etc. 15 parvas in Telugu as desired by people for the pleasure of scholars; and calls the work a Prabhandhamandali.[262] The Kavyas between Nannaya and Srinatha are not many compared with those after Srinatha; and with the translation of Bharata by Nannaya, began the movement of the revival of Brahminism as against Buddaism and Jainism whose works were translated in large numbers in Telugu. The other parvas are - udyoga, Bhishma, Drona, Karna, Salya, Sanptika, Stri, santa, Anusasanikya, asvamadha, asramabase, mansala, mahaprasathanika, and svargarohana.

Many stories are current about Tikkana's writing of Bharata. According to one version.[263] Nannaya is said to have refused to continue Bharata after hearing the death of Atharvana and suggested a device to the king for its completion. He took a verse from Sabhaparva, and sent it to all countries saying that whoever writes a verse equal to it deserve to continue Bharata. The soldiers went to Benares and shown the verse to Tikkana, when he was returning from a prostitute's house. Tikkana wrote the same verse, applied a colour to it, mentioned his name and went away. The soldiers returned and Nannaya said that Tikkana was the fittest person to continue Bharata. There at Kasi, Harharanatha with Kommana by his side appeared in his dream, and said that he was to write Bharata. Tikkana proceeded to Rajahmundry did yajna to purify himself and did Bharata. According to another version.[264] Rajaraja asked

Manmasiddhi to send him Tikkana, the king refused and then Tikkana did yajna. A third version.[265] is that after Nannaya's death, Rajanarendra, was anxious to finish Bharata, had shown it to many scholars but in vain. Then he circulated a verse from Sabhaparva, to all courts asking for an equivalent verse. Then Tikkana in the court of Manmasiddhi, wrote the same verse, painted it and sent it. Rajarajanarendra understood that it means that his poetry would be like that of Nannaya but different form it. Another story[266] is that Tikkana did yajna consequent on his refusal to go to Rajahmundry at the instance of Manmasiddhi. He was angry with Manumasiddhi and so dedicated the work instead of him of God Hariharanatha. On chronological grounds little from these versions can be accepted. For Tikkana and Manmasiddhi lived more than a century and a half later than Nannaya and Rajarajanarendra and it is impossible that they were contemporaries.

As Tikkana began with Virataparva either Aranyaparva was complete by that time or Tikkana did not finish it out of fear. It has been said that just as he left off Srirama miryana in Uttara Hamayana, he omitted the remaining portion of Aranyaparva, probably thinking of finishing it, after completion of the work and did not do so for want of time and health.[267] But as Tikkana says that the three parvas were done by the great scholar Nannaya in expert fashion and he was beginning with the fourth,[268]. we may, until overwhelming evidence to the contrary is available, take the poet at his word which means that the three parvas were complete and so he began the fourth. So part of Aranya parva was lost after Tikkana, and prior to Errna. Tikkana had Kummara Gurunatha his natural son, according to one version, a marvelously quick writer to write Bharata while he composed it.[269] Tradition has it that Tikkana bowed while writing Bharata that he would say only once and will not repeat it. But in a verse in canto I of Salyaparva, he said half, could not proceed and said "what shall I say Gurunatha."[270] which Gurunatha wrote down and it fitted in the verse perfectly meanings as though Sanjaya addressed Kurunatha. Another version.[271] is that at Tikkana's request, Rajaraja secured Gurunatha, a soilder from Nellore to write while he said.

The adoration of Dharmaraja to Isvara in Bharata applies to Hariharanatha also. Tikkana explained the purpose of writing Bharata at the beginning of Virataparva in three verses.[272] He was the first among the Telugu poets to have believed and recorded dreams dreams in his works.[273] The fifteen parvas consist of forty cantos, having a total of 20,000 verses. At the beginning and end of every canto, Tikkana adored vyasa along with Hariharanatha. He worshiped Harihara besides in shasthyantas in three verses just before beginning the story addressing him to listen to the work.[274] His knowledge in Vedanta and sankhya is seen from Santa and Anusasasitaparvas and parts of other parvas. He must have taken six to seven years to complete the work. Of his vocabulary, 1/4 are Sanskrit words and the rest are Telugu words. His style was of the best and highest type. One or two verses from his early cantos Tikkana put on totem under similar circumstances in later parvas. His Virata parva is larger than the original but in his other parvas he had summarised the story. He dealt in five verse and prose pieces Somatkumaropadesa (Somatsujata's adhyatmatatva to Dhrutarashtra) which is fairly long in the original.[275] Tikkana dealt in fifty three verses and prose passages, giving the essence of Bhagavadgita which comprises eighteen chapters in the original in Bhishmaparva, and omitted Uttaragitas and refers to Upanishads in a single prose passage.[276]

While Tikkana was engaged in thanking as to the fittest person to receive his work - prabandhamandali - his father appeared to him in his dream and introduced Hariharanatha who came with him and also appeared before Tikkana. Tikkana prostrated at the god who praised him for his conduct in accordance with Vadika marga nishta and devotion to him, praised Bharata as Panchanaveda, addressed the poet as Tikkasarma and asked to dedicates his work to him.[277] God conferred on him the capacity to be away from birth, death etc. sins resulting from samsara, when asked by Tikkana to be relieved from future births. So Tikkana says that it is adoration itself (avadhana visesha) to praise a sacred prabandha in the presence of god and thus begins to write Bharata. Thinking of Vyasa, with intent (steady) after receiving mahakavitvadiksha-vidhi he would write works in prose and verse, so that the andhras (Andhravali) may listen to Bharatamritra and feel happy.[278] Tikkana says that the purpose of his life is served when he could write Bharatasamhita with paramesvara as Kritinatha and made him lord of patta of kindness - a pratimakarunikatra mahaviboti, and to give Bharata to devadeva is like joining new pearl and gold; and he would describe for the pleasure of devotees - bhaktakoti.[279]

Virataparva is the first work of Tikkana in Bharata and is the best parva in the entire Bharata. It has five cantos.

Though the first verse in it - Hariharastava - is in Telugu, Tikkana introduced a sloka on. The theme in this parva is great and the nine sentiments had their full display in it, Tikkana did it as a Kavya, and it has the mahakavyalakshanas and most of the eighteen descriptions of the Kavyas. Vira is the main sentiment. Tikkana showed his great capacities in this parva and it differs in many places from the original. This and Udyogaparva may be called almost the independent works of Tikkana.[280] Tikkana added at the beginning of Virata parva the portion which is towards the end Aranyapavva the portion is towards the end of Aranyaparva in the Mahabharata in Sanskrit. He says that the story in Virataparva is interesting and pleasing to heart and gives rise to all sentiments, prosperity and pleasure.[281] Tikkana omitted the Durgastava by Dharamaraja in the original; his Dharmaraja is a sanyasi, whereas in the original is a Brahmin named Kanka. Tikkana's Brihanala pariksha by Vrata is one of the subjects differing from the original, and the translation surpasses the original in its narration and propriety.[282] His descriptions of Sringara rasa are perfect, faultless and inimitable.[283] Nilakantha, the author of Bharatabhavidpika, a commentary on vyasa bharata, did an elaborate treatise on Udhyogaparva.[284] Tikkana omitted Vedantasasfras and summarily dealt with the composition. In other parvas, he left off the tale of sweta, sanatsujatiyam, etc. several stories found in Bhishma parva of the original. But he did Sanatsujatasupadesa of tatva to Narada in Anasasanita parva in twenty-six verses and prose passages and conversation of Sanatkumara with Siva.[285] Tikkana's Bhishma parva has three cantos, Drona five cantos, Karna three cantos, Salya two cantos, Sanptika two, Anusasanika five, Asvamadha four, Asramavara 2, Mansala, mahaprasthnika and Svargarohana - one each. In striparva, which has two cantos, Tikkana used some new kind of vritis - tarala, vasanta tilaka, mattakokila, in drarajra, atruvoja, totaka, utsaha, Kavirajavirajitamu, dodka, manjubhashini, upajati, rugmavati, todeka, bhujanga prayata, manini, manimala, svagata, ranamayura, narkuta, bundhura, drutavilambita, suddhavirati, layavibhati, upendravajra, upendravajra, sravini, pranava, jaladhara, medini, kraunchapada, amburuha, praharana kalita, sikharini, malini, maniganankaramalayagrahi, mangalamahasri, sarasija, bhaskaravilasita, layvibhati, mandakrantamu. Before concluding the work, in Svargoarohanaparva, Tikkana gives the phalasruti in nine verses in the last of which he asked Hariharanatha to be ever merciful to him so that Bharata sambita which could give paramapada - salvation, to the happiness of Sannuka etc. Brahmins.and those who read and listen would fell happy.[286]

Like Nannaya, Tikkana was an expert in using similes. In his Viduraniti he followed the Rajaniti of Kanika, in style and so forth; and also in his description of Dranupadi speaking about her insult to Krishna.[287]

3. Kavivagbandhamanu is the lakshanagrantha written by Tikkana Somayaji. It has not got any special details of interest. The last verse in it says that while people praised. and scholars permitted, Tikkana somayaji did a work on prosody called Kavivagbandhamu.[288] 4. Vijayasenamu of Tikkana is not extant. Verses from it are cited in later works - Appakaviya, Prabandharatnakara and so forth.[289] 5. Krishnasatakam seems to have been composed by Tikkana as compensation for his having said Krishna's and in Bharata. The work is not extant and venkatarangakavi quoted a single verse from it.[290]

Tikkana had many pupils and was praised by contemporary and later poets in their works. Mulaghatika Ketana, who dedicated his Dasakumaracharitra to Tikkana, was a contemporary and probably a pupil of Tikkana Marana, the author of Markomdeyapurana, dedicated to Nagaya Canna a general of Drataparudra, at the end of the 13th century AD, was the son of Tikkana matya and a pupil of Tikkana Somayaji. In the Colophon the poet call himself-Udbhyakavimitra Tikkana Somayajiprasadalakdha sarasvati patra. At the beginning of the work, he praises Tikkana as an expert poet in two languages performer of sacrifices a relative of scholars, possessing good qualities, and author of Bharatasamitikatha a modern (vyasa), and praised in the three worlds.[291] Potana in Virabhadravijaya refers to Tikkana as Sri Somayaji.[292] Jakkana in Vikramarkacharitra praised him as Tikkakavi who secured heaven by the condesection of Hariharanatha who appeared to him when he did bharata - the Panchamaveda in Andhra bhasha.[293] Nissahkuni Kanmana refers to Tikkana Somayaji in Vira maheshvaram. Kakumani Gangadhara in Balabharata devoted a verse to the praise of Tikkana. Andhra Kavi Ramayya in Vishnu Kanchimahatmya praised him as the great writer in two languages.[294] Pedapati Somaya in Arunachalapurana, mentions Tikkana as the poet in tow languages, and the protector of maharajya and refers to his great capacities in writing poetry in Andhra.[295] Duggana in Nasiketopakhyana, and Dubagunta Narayana kavi in Panchatantra praise. Tikkana.[296] Ganapavaram Venkatakavi in Prabandharaja Venketesvaravilasamu - a lakshya lakshangrantha refers to the sweet easy style of ubhayakavi.[297]

Singana, the translator of Ganavasishta into Telugu says that he was related to Tikkana Somayaji. His grandfather Allada mantri, married Chittambika, daughter of Gauturi Kanmana, grandson of Tikkana. Here probably grandson is a mistake for son, for Tikkana had a son Kommana Singana was the ruler of Ravela agrahara in Kotabhumi and scholars differ as to whether his family name was Madiki or Ramagiri. In Sringara naishadha, Srinatha adores Tikkayajava. In Bhimakanda, he says that he raises his hands in adoration to Tikkana Somayaji, the famous poet who equalled Brahma and wrote Bharatasamhita - the Panchamuveda in Andhra bhasha - fifteen paravas. In kasi Khanda, he says that at times he writes poetry like Tikkayajva, verses full of life and sentiment, Bayyana mantri, great grandfather of Anantamatya, author of Bhojavajiya received the title Bhavyabharati from Tikkana somayaji[298] Nachana Somanatha closely followed Tikkana's embassy of Samjoya in Bharata in his embassy of Janardana in Uttaraharivamsa and in writing many verses with easy words but with depth of meaning; and the poem is dedicated to Hariharanatha to whom Tikkana dedicated Bharata. He refers to Tikkana and his Bharata with the utmost veneration in the colophons of the work.[299]

Gangadevi, wife of Virakampana of Vijayanagar (14th century AD) in her Madhuravijayama mentions the ancient poets - Valmiki, Vyasa, Kalidasa, Bhattabana, Bhavavi and Dandin, pays homage to later poets a Karnamritakavi (Libasuka), Tikkaya, Agastya, Gangadhara and Visvanatha.[300] Here Tikkaya is Tikkana Somayaji, mentioned as kavi-Sarvabhauma by Errapreggada in Harivamsa. Allasani Peddana praised Kavitraya as the authors of Bharatmnaya in Andhrabhsha.[301]

Tikkana was praised by Kannada writers also. "Under Krishnarya's patronage, Timmana rendered Mahabharata into Kanarese in Shatpadi metre. The translation was made not directly from Sanskrit but from the Telugu version of Tikkana whose terse and classical style must have excited the admiration of even the Kanarese scholars."[302] Mahabharata ashtaparvavu alias Karnata Krishnaraya Bharata Katha majari consists of the last eight parvas beginning with striparva. This Kannada mahabharata alias Uttarabharata, also known as Krishnaraja bharata is written in Bhamini Shatpadi metre and consists of forty sandhis and 3736 verses.[303] This Timmana kavi (AD 1510) styles himself as Karnata Kavikalasarvabhanma. Timmana Kavindra - a devotee of Gadaguviranarayana.[304]

From the artistic point of view, Tikkana's bharata in some parts is more polished than the original. Some scholars opine that Tikkana had the greatest dramatic genius[305] which is revealed in his works. Mack MS says that during the visit to Ganapati's court, Tikkana was greatly honoured by the king and scholars of his court. He explained to the king the essence of the Vedic learning, sastras and the Mahabharata. In serious disputation with the Jains and Buddhists, Tikkana denounced the enemies of the vedas - who consequently were driven out of the country and put to death. He gave instructions to the king in politics and philosophy and praised the Saiva Philosopher Sivadevayya, a minister of Ganapati.[306] The wooden cover of the instrument with which poet Tikkana wrote works on a kadjan leaf is preserved in the house of the poet's descendant living at Indukurpet (Nellore taluq). A draw well in the outskirts of Paturu is said to have been constructed by the poet and is held sacred.[307] Ketana says that Tikkana pleased his relatives, possessed a critical knowledge of agamas, could discuss them, was a Ravana in knowledge and could not write expression to nine sentiments and performed the rites prescribed in the Vedas.

**Katana** : One of the well known poets in Telugu literature, Ketana entitled Abhinava dandi was the first to do lakshana for Telugu and render dharmasastras into Andhra. He was of Koundinyagotra and his family name was Kulghatika.[308] His parents were Mranava (Maraya) and Sankamamba also mentioned as Gangama. He was the brother-in-law of Bhandaru Ketana and lord of Ventirala. agrahara in Vengidesa. About his poetical capacities, Ketana says.[309] where as it is rare even for Brahma to please Ubhyakavimitra by writing poetry, he pleased him by his Dasakumara charitra and so he need not praise himself any more. His style if flowing, faultless, lively and good. Younger brother of Prolanarya, poet Ketana was a general, a moon to the Nulaghatika lineage, famous, and could write poetry in Sanskrit, and other languages. But none of his works, in languages other than Telugu are known so far. His poetry though not so good as Tikkana's could be enjoyed by that great poet. In his Andhra bhasha phushana, written after Dasakumaracharitra, Ketana wrote that he was an expert in all the sciences praised by scholars, as Abhinavadandi, and was well known in the world by that name. Ketana was truthful and a friend of poets. As he was a contemporary of Ganapati, Tikkana and Manmasiddhi, he lived in the 13th century AD - approximately from AD 1200 to 1280.

**His works** : 1. Dasakumaracharitra is the earliest and the major work of Ketana. It is the Telugu rendering of Dasakumaracharitra in Sanskrit by Mahakavi Dandin in the first half of the 7th century AD. Ketana's is not a literal translation. He exhibited originality in narration, effected changes in many places, added new descriptions, and thus enhanced the beauty of the work. In the narration of some stories and descriptions Ketana is briefer than Dandin; and in some interesting portions, he is more elaborate than Dandin. In Canto XII of the work, Ketana's narration differs from the original in many places. His omission of Uttarapithika is perhaps due to that it was not the work of Pandin. He compressed the story of the dancing girl in the story of sleeping angle.[310] In the rest of the work, prominence is given to the main story with addition of several parenthetical stories. The rajaniti in the story Visruta is clearly depicted. Ketana fitted in the ideas of Dandyacharya with slight changes. He used plenty of words of common usage in Telugu in this work. Some of his original verses are beautiful. Later poets followed him in his descriptions of theft, cock fight, gambling, rice pounding duties of abhisarika, sunrise, hardship in hell etc. As Ketana did vyakarana - lakshanagrantha in Telugu, Dasakumaracharitra may be called lakshyagrantha to it. Dasakumaracharitra is the treasure for the fame of Tikkana Somayaji and one of the best kavyas in perfection. Softness and sweetness in Telugu.

Ketana did not mention any works of Tikkana the reason for which is not clear. Tikkana wrote Uttara Ramayana and did Yajna by this time and was probably writing Bharata, when Ketana dedicated his work to him.

Andhrabhashabhushana of Ketana is the earliest work on Grammar in Telugu language. It is throughout in verse. He begins with adoration to Saraswati, Siva, Vignesa, sun scholars and modern poets. He says as none did lakshana for Telugu so far, he would do it with the kindness of Nannaya to the satisfaction of scholars.[311]. As poets in the past did lakshana for sanskrit and Prakrit, their not saying Lakshana for Telugu is not due to their incapacity but so that he may be fortunate to do it. He calls it sabdasastra and did it to the satisfaction of grammarians - who may feel that it equals Shanmukha and Panini.[312] He begs poets to praise if there is any good in the work, know and correct the bad mistakes if any, but not say bad is good and good is bad. He implores them not to criticise and dislike him for his new adventure. For as even Kalidasa and Mayura were not free from faults other people have faults and kindness of poets is their prosperity. He says that he would show a path to Andhra bhasha. The common endings of the verses are nutagunabhirma, nutanadandi, and kavijanamitra. In the colophon the author bore the title - Abhinavadandi.

The words in Telugu are divided into two divisions. Sanskrit and Telugu. The Telugu words are of five kinds - Katsama, tadbhava, Tenugu, desya, and gramya. Gramya is permissible only in abusing others.[313] He distinguishes between pure Telugu and desya and two kinds in the former and a division of one of the two being gramya.[314]

3 Vijnanaesvaram of Ketana is a treatise on Hindu law in Telugu also in verse. Ketana, at the beginning of the work says[315] that he would say in Telugu for all people what Vijnanesvara said after listening to sakaladharmas. Yajnavalkya taught dharmas to the sages. The work is a translation of yajnavalkva's dharmasastras in Telugu. 4. Kadambar - some opine Ketana did Kadambari in Telugu as a Padya Kavya. In Prabandharatnakara Mranayaketa, is mentioned as the author of Kadambari.[316]

**Marana** : Poet Marana dedicated his Markandeyapuram to Nagaya Gunna a minister of Pratapa Rudra, and a scholar and patron of scholars. Markandeyapurana is the seventh among the eighteen puranas. The poet left off some portions found in the original and added some descriptions of his own. He omitted the stories of Arishyanka, and his son Damuda. He did the story of Svarichicha Manu in one hundred and fifty verses which is complete in the original and was developed into about eight hundred verses by Peddana in Manucharitra. Pedana followed Marana closely using the words of the latter in large numbers. The identity of Marana's father Tikkana with the learned scholar the Tikkana and the last son of younger paternal uncle of Bayyana ancestor of Anantamatya has been suggested.

**Peddaya** : Peddaya, grandfather of Jakkana author of Vikramarka charitra, was a poet of remarkable capacities and was in the court of king Tirukala of Nellore. This Tirukala has been identified with Immadi Tirukalati who came to the Telugu chola throne in AD 1277 lost it soon after, and was restored to the throne in AD 1297 by Recharla Errachacha, a general of Prataparudra,[317] who vanquished his enemies and this is attested by his titles. Nellurivirakshatra no bharati kamalla and Tirukala rajyastha-pancharya. Tirukala ruled up to 1310 AD and so his court poet Peddaya lived towards the close of the 13th and the beginning of the 14th century AD. The identification of Tirukala with Tikka I (AD 1209-1248) is untenable on chronological grounds. Peddaya's capacities are as follows :- in Sanskrit, prakrit, Sauraseni etc. languages he could say a sataka a hundred verses in a ghatika (24 minutes) with expert capacities in prakasana, prakarana, bhana etc. several kinds of dramas, he could write many minor kavyas, such as chakra, chaturbhadra, chaturuttaradhika etc.[318] In Telugu poetry, it is not worth writing a prabanda to the satisfaction of the people where as he could write in any riti (style) with any dhatus (grammatical roots), give descriptions in any sentiment, he could read aloud, and very fast in ekasandha, dvisandha and trisandha (i.e. by listening once, twice and thrice). If anybody knew any avadhana, Peddaya could do it better than him, he could say the best of garbhakavyas, with Urittakanda, Kandavritta, chetushkanda etc. could write new prabandhas in new styles, and write aksharachyutakam, matrachayataka, bandhachyutakam, numagopyam etc. in goshtis (sabhas) could read pady (verse), gitika and arbhatika. He knew the implications of all sciences, exhibited his learning in literature (sashitya) in the presence of king Timkala of Nellore and is mentioned as Peddayamatyasukavi.[319]

Annaya, son of Peddaya, was a great poet. A verse about him says that he does not dance like Mayura hurt the minds like Bana and was well known for his oratory in the world. He was praised by all poets in the courts of kings as one who could give lively discourse and compose poetry while conversing.[320] He was praised by all poets in the courts, of kings, Gakkana in Vikramarkacharitra followed Srinath's writings in many places.

The lineage of the family of Vennalakanti Siddhana mantri, the minister to whom Jakkana dedicated Vikramarak charitra is as follows—[321] Sage Harita was born in Brahmakula, born from the feet of Brahmins who was born from the Nobel lotus of Vishnu. In the lineage of Harita, whose greatness is described by Jakkana, in the thirty - second generation was born Surana Samayaji. Surana was a scholar in vedas, sastras and puranas and received agraharas from Peddanapudi Rajendra Choda, [322] and the regal insignia of a golden staff palanquin, paras Ms, chowris etc. His son was Siddhana mantri, a capable minister whose sons by Surambika the daughter of Perayannarya, were mantri Bhaskara, and Jannamantri of Devaraya. Jannaya by Akkambika had sons were Tippa, Jannaya and Bhairava.

Vennalakanti Surana was the elder paternal uncle of Siddhana. Siddhana mantri was the minister and treasurer of Devaraya I (AD 1404-1422) and Davaraya II (1423-1447) and Jakkana was the court poet of the same kings. Siddhana's ancestors belonged to Nellore district.

**Ketanapreggada** : Ketana, son of Bhaskara was the author of Kadambari according to Prayogaratnakara. [323] Evidently he is different from Mranaya Ketana, author of Dasakumara charitra. Dasa Kumaracharitra mentions Ketana, an uncle of Tikkana Somayaji and son of Bhaskara. The reference shows that Ketana mantri was a poet. The face that the work is not mentioned is not surprising for Ketana when he did not mention Tikkana's works would not have bothered to mention these of his uncle. Perhaps because the more interesting work Kadambari was already done by his time, that Ketana did Dasakumara charitra. So the author of Kadambari may be identified with Tikkana's uncle Kuvalayasva charitra was written by Ketana preggada whoes identity is not yet established. Mulaghotika Ketana, in a verse Andhrabhastabhushana, not found either in the text or MS copies prostrates to good poets and implores them to praise a work when it deserves, not to praise when it does not please their minds, but when praising not to swallow it and not to say that they praised it when they really do not do so in mind.

**Mantri Bhaskara** : Bhaskara was the grand father of Tikkana Somayaji. His great poetical capacities are attested by Tikkana and Ketana in their works. He is different form Kalakki Bhaskara with whom he is often confused and identified by some scholars. But both are associated with the authorship of Ramayana and yet it is uncertain to which of the work, Bhaskara Ramayana owes its name. But most probably after Mantri Bhaskara who either did the complete work, or at least begun it. It has been conjectured that becuase his grandfather did Ramayana, that Tikkana did Uttarakanda. [324] Mallikarjunabhatta who did parts of Bhaskara Ramayana has been identified with Mallama, the second among the four sons of Bhaskara, Mallikarjuna styles himself ashtabhashakavimitra in the colophon. In the work some portions were written by Ayyalarya, pupil and friend of

Bhaskara and some by Kumara Rudradeva. Balakanda war was composed by Mallikarjunabhatta, Ayodhyakanda by Kumarakudradeva, son of Maraya and dedicated to the son of Buddhaya and Rachamamba. He styles himself sakalavisarda. Kulappi kavi Bhaskara did Arayanakanda and dedicated it to Sahini Mara. Mallikarjunabhatta wrote also Kishkindhakanda and Sundarakanda and dedicated them to Sahni Mara. Ayyalarya did Juddhakanda, which gives the genealogy of Rudra, son of Sahini Mara and grandson of Buddhraja. [325]

There is popular belief that when portions of Ramayana written by Mantri Bhaskara were lost, Chimmapudi Amaresvara of the 14th century AD completed them. From the fact that unlike other Kandas Aranyakanda consists of asvasas, and the style in it which is superb in the entire work, the work may be attributed to Mantri Bhaskara. But its dedication to Sahini Mara of the 13th and 14th and centuries AD seems to suggest that it was probably the work of Hulekki Bhaskara. A palm by MS says that Ayyalarya did Yuddhakanda at the request of Vedagirinayaka. Mallikarjuna was the son of Hulakki Bhaskara and Sahini Mara was the son of Buddha, who if identical with Buddha of Ranganatha Ramayana, Ranganatha Ramayana must have been written twenty or thirty years earlier than Bhaskara Ramayana.[326] But the two Buddhas are different. [327] Maraya's son Kumara Rudradeva did Ayodhyakanda. Thus in the Ramayana, Mantri Bhaskara did Aranyakanda, which appears to have been written earlier that the rest of the work, Hulakki Bhaskara did part of Yuddhakanda, Mailikarjuna did Bala and Kishkindha kandas, Kumara Rudra did Ayodhyakand, and Ayyalarya did the latter part of Yuddhakanda.

As for chronology of the poets of Bhaskara Ramayana, a gap of not less than a century intervened between Mantri Bhaskara and Hulakki Bhaskara. The former belonged to the time of grandfather Buddha and latter to that of grandson Buddha. Except Mantri Bhaskara, all other poets lived in the time of Prataparudra of the Kakatiyas. As Andhra Bharata was completed in three hundred years by three poets, Andhra Bhaskara Ramayana was completed in a period of over a hundred years by not less than six authors. Consequently the work has several styles. In volume consisting of 15,000 verses and prose passges it is much less than Valmiki Ramayana which has 24,000 slokas. In some parts, the translation is more voluminous than the original. In Uddakanda, the seventh sarga, in Magha's Kavya is rendered into Telugu. [328] On the whole style in Bhaskara Ramayana is good Several copies of the work in the MS library have several colophons all differing from one another. Praising the capacities of Mantri Bhaskara, Tikkana says that if not far intrinsic merit, at least because of the great poetical capacities of Bhaskara, the work would be popular in the world. Errapreggada's Ramayana belongs to Reddi age and the author of Bhavadipika, the author of Sri Ramakavi says that Hulakki Bhaskara wrote the Ramayana called Dasagatis in Telugu and dedicated it to Maraya Sahini.[329]

Pratapacharitra etc. works mention on Bhaskara along with Sahini Mara who probably was Hulakki Bhaskara. Except Mantri Bhaskara, other writers of the Ramayana, belonging to the Kakatiya kingdom, probably lived in the neighbourhood of Warangal. Sahini Mara figures in a record of AD 1311 recorded a grant by Machaya Sahini, adhikari of Palnati Sima for the merit of Gajasahini, Gundayasahini and Maraya Sahini. [330] It is opined that even Ayydarya was not of the time of Maraya, as he does not mention himself a friend of Bhaskara, and addressed not Mara but Siva at the end of Uddakanda and the verses in praise of Siva were interpolations; and even Mallikarjuna was not contemporary with Mara and so most of the work was written Mara's time. [331] It is argued that Mallikarjuna was not the son of Bhaskara. [332]

**Engraving, architecture and sculpture** : One of the arts learnt by the princes in Dasakumaracharitra is alekhya - the art of writing. Tikkana refers to many sculptures in the mansions at Ayodhya. Some records including the Nandalur epigraph.[333] are in Tamil granthascript and language. Either Tamilians were imported for the purpose or Andhras learnt the language and imposed and inscribed them. The sculptures in the first storey of the vimana of the parasuramisvara temple at Attirala are a rarity in the Telugu country surrounding Cuddapah. [334]

**Music, dance and painting** : In the reign of Tikka I at Palicheriapadu, Daminayaka and his wife Potasani, made a grant of land to dancers, drummers, couch blower, patra (dancing girl) and lavadandu (musician).[335] In AD 1297 at Narasaraopet, Manma gandagopala made a grant in charge of three men and Kottari in favour of Kesavadasi and Kotikesavadasi. They were to celebrate Gandgopala tirunallu in chitramasa. [336]

The princes in Dasakumaracharitra are described to have learnt to play on vina etc. musical instruments and vocal music among other arts. Tikkana says that the dancing women at Ayodhya were beautiful like sculptures as though made by melting of Manmatha.[337] Sangitakalayas i.e. homes of music and pretty homes with painted and coloured pictures on them and built by the community of dancers. At Rama's asvamedha, are said to have been present vocal musicians,' players on vina, flute etc. Among the arts taught by Rama to his sons were included Bharatasastra, Vatsayana sutras, flute, vina etc. Tikkana mentions the dances - dandalasaka, kundali, prekkanam (i.e. prenkanam), and Peranami (prerani) and their performance to the accompaniment of music - vocal and instrumental giving expression to though by abhinaya. [338] He refers to dance master (nattu vojja) dance hall - rangagara, nartanasala or nattanamandapa. Arjuna's fight with Chitrangada is compared with music with Gandiva as Vina, vavindlavaru as ottukaru and gunadhrani as tantrinada. [339] He mention poets, bards, vocal musicians, flutists, players on vina, pretty sculptures in palaces paintings on walls and pretty dances to the accompaniment of music vocal and instrumental, and mandapas in heaven in which discussions in sradhyaya, literature and music are held. [340]

Tikkana mentions the war musical instruments - Sankha, bheri, mridanga, dundubhi, nissana, panava, kahala, chindamu, gomukha, damara, qhenta and so forth. He says that in the camps, during nights, the immates spent their time in enjoying fine sangitas - dance, music, drama (concerts) and pleasants, literary discourses. Bhishma, after his fall was entertained by actors who were experts in gitavadyanritta - music and dance.[341]

Manmasiddha III was a patron of architects. In his court were jesters, vocal musicians and buffoons. At Kambhampadu in AD 1254 in the reign of Tikka, Potayadevachola made a grant for the ranga bhoga of the god. General education was the work of temples. At chepalapalle in the 25th year of Kulottunga, Nilama Kattaiyan provided for the reading of Bhagavata on the sacred temple door way of the Yadava narayana perumal temple.[342] At Murikipudi in AD 1296 Manmagandagopala provided for the angarangabhoga of the god. A record of Nallasiddhi at Chandur (AD 1232) recording adoration of Bollijiyya written by Bhuparasa, son of Bollajiyya.[343] The word Kandarise meaning inscribing or incising on stone is Kannada, the Telugu form of which is gandarinchu from which word comes gandarinchubomma i.e. a figure carved out of stone. At Tikkanapadu, on the Pinakini to the east of Pottapuravi is a stone with the sculpture of a soldier on horse-horseman. People say that it was the image of Ranatikkana and this finds mention in local records.[344] In Katamarajukatha, a few verses describing the part played be Ranantikkana are supposed to have been sung by contemoporary bards.[345] On both sides of the mandapa in front of the Somesvara temple at Somasila alias Somesvaram on the Penna, are two stone statues sculptured on two black stones - two feet in height and width. A hero on a horse with a raised sword in the right hand, and holding the bridle by his left hand, riding fast, perhaps to the battle is represented. The rider and the horse had plenty of moments on their persons. The rider's face looks disfigured with several cracks. There is a popular belief that the statue is that of Khadgatikkana going to fight katmaraju.[346]

**Others cholas** : Some of the Chola made substantial grants in the fields of literature, architecture, dance, music and so forth. Baddena was the author of Sumatisataka and Nitisastramuktavali. His style is soft, easy and beautiful. Sumatisataka is one of the best and most popular works in the sataka literature of the Andhras. It is his earlier work, as he refers to in one of the his verses in Nitisastramuktavali. The title - kavibrahma attest Buddean's poetical capacities - Nittasastramukatavali is also mentioned as Baddenanituala.[347] several verse in the work resemble these of Nitisara inSanskrit by Rudras of the Kakatiyas.

The c.p. grant of Mummadi Cholas Bhima (AD 1077) was, composed by Muhayabhatta and engraved by Pattala.[348]

The Peddamudiyam inscription of Bhimadeva chola mentions a ghatikashthana i.e. a seminary at Konkanur.[349] At Katrayapadu (AD 1309) king Tiruvengadanatha made a grant to Katravaja. Angareni Tiruvengadabhatta, learned in the vedas. At Kalunjuvvalapadu, the record of Tondayaraju was engrawed by Dondaya Molgaji lara Sarvadeva. The builder of the temple was Tammaluri Vankaya Raddodi. The royal issuer of the edict was Tammadhandani.[350] At Kolimigundla Vankana C.M.'s record (AD 1234) was written by Hevaraja and engraved by Bommoju. The chodur record of AD 1192 was written by Senabova Macharasa and engraved by Bomboju.

Of the cholas of Kandur, Mailamba is compared with Sarasvati in her knowledge. Among the temple servants at Panugal to whom she and her sons Udayaditya, Bhima and Gokarna made a grant, figure sutradhari Brammoju, Bhaskara bhatta, somesvarabhattopadhyaya, and Appanabhattu. In the portion set apart for the deity some grant was made for angabhoga and some to the vrittikaras for gita, vadya, nritya, Gankudhara etc. The word Kelasamu - Kannada for work is used in this record.[351] Sutradhari is either temple carpenter artisan, or the man behind the suaesic principal actor in a drama. Probably here, Sutradhari refers to artisan.

In the vicinity of Nandalur are fourteen stone images, two of them bearing Tamil inscriptions by their sides. Every images has bow, arrows, swords, daggers, spears and bridles and big axes. Their costumes, head dress, etc. suggest that they belonged to the times of the cholas and the pandyas. Inscriptions in the local Sammyanatha swami temple attest the cholas pandya regime in these parts. The architecture of the temple greatly resembles the temples of the cholas in art and sculpture. In the images, king and his subordinates could be distinguished by their costumes and ornaments. People there believe that the images were those of the Makla chiefs who ruled those tracts as the feudatories of the kings of Vijayanagar. But it has been said that the presence of Tamil inscriptions, their dress and pewels seem to contradict the popular notion.[352] But the contradiction falls to ground, for the Matlas claim origin and bear the title cholamaharja suffixed to their names like many of the Telugu cholas.

1. Mahabharata, Ramayana, Bhagvata, Markandeyapurana etc.
2. Basavapurana, Panditaradhyacharitra etc.
3. Palnativiracharitra, Katumaraju Katha etc.
4. Errapreggada had the title - Prabandhaparamesvara.
5. Rajarajasanchika p. 187.
6. The Colas II - I p. 187.
7. 262-A of 1897: S.I.I. VI 234.
8. Basavapurana, Panditaradhyacharitra.
9. Tikkana's Bharata.
10. Panditaradhyacharitra.
11. Sivatatvasara.
12. 151 of 1897: S.I.I. VI 109.
13. e.p. 23 of 1917.
14. M.P. Aradhyachirtra I pp. 508-516.
15. AR 1933 page 61 para 41.
16. Keyurabahucharitra I v 22.
17. AR 1933 page 60 para 13.
18. 443 of 1915.
19. E.I. V. No. 17 p. 146.
20. Keyurabahucharitra I vv 46-47.
21. E.I. IV No. 4.
22. Introduction to Basavapurana pp. 63-64.
23. Karnataka Kavicharitra 1 p. 212.
24. Sivatatvasaram Introduction p.16.
25. Sivatatvasara Introduction p. 201.
26. Sivatatvasara Introduction. p. 21.
27. Panditaradhyachirta I pp. 508-516.

28. Panditaradhyacharitra Introduction pp. 74-75.
29. Panditaradhyacharitra Text I p. 512.
30. v 387.
31. Panditaradhyacharitra Introduction p.13.
32. Sivatatvasara Introduction p. 14.
33. Bharati III No. 3 p.48.
34. Karnataka Kavicharitra I pp.173-174.
35. Nizam's Arch. Series No. 3 p.12. Ins. B (a): 169 of 1913.
36. Basavapu. Intron. p.8.
37. Panditaradhyacharitra Intron. p. 8.
38. Andhra Patrika Annual Dundabhi p. 144, B. Tammayya in Kakatiya Sanchika: Hist. of Andhras V p. 332.
39. J.A.H.R.S. XI p. 132.
40. Basavapurana Intron. p. 27.
41. V.P. Sastri Chatupadyamanimanjari p. 110.
42. J.A.H.R.S. XI P. 131.
43. J.A.H.R.S. XI p. 132.
44. Karnataka Kavicharitra I p. 226 II pp. 133-136.
45. - do - I pp. 291-296: II p. 23.
46. Basavapurana Introduction p. 22.
47. Keyurabahucharitra Introduction p. 25.
48. - do - Text I v 7.
49. 151 of 1899: S.I.I. VI 109.
50. 441 of 1915.
51. S.K. Aiyangar: Hist. of Tirupati I p. 245; Hyd. Arch. Series 13 II p. 208.
52. Proceedings 7th Or. Conf. p.656.
53. 831 of 1922: 439 of 1915.

54. 128 of 1893: S.I.I. IV 945.

55. 443 of 1915.

56. 441 of 1915.

57. 157 of 1913.

58. J.A.H. & C.I. p. 74.

59. 164 of 1893: S.I.I. IV 989.

60. J.A.H.R.S. VII p. 182.

61. E.I. VI No. 17 p. 146 v 13.

62. J.A.H.R.S. VII pp. 182-183.

63. E.I. V No. 17 pp. 145-150.

64. Brown: Tel. Eng. Dictionary.

65. P. Aradhyach. I p. 512.

66. G.V. Ramamurti Pantulu Commemoration Vol. T. 15 at p. 266.

67. Bhramaruma is a particular gesture of hand in dance - sabdaratnakara.

68. Panditaradhyacharitra II p. 434.

69. - do - p. 436.

70. Text pp. 22, 29, 30,

71. Text p. 61-62.

72. - do - 77, 78, 124.

73. - do - 89.

74. P. Aradhyach. II pp. 433-434.

75. Bharati 18 part I p. 651.

76. P. Aradhyach. II pp. 437-465; Basavapurana p. 90.

77. Text pp. 89-90.

78. E.I. IV No. 4.

79. 214 of 1893: S.I.I. IV 1036.

80. 249, 250 of 1893: S.I.I. IV 1102, 1104.

81. E.I. IV No. 17.

82. E.I. XIX No. 25 p. 164.

83. Kakatiya Sanchika App. Inscn. No. 33.

84. R. Ramayana Text pp. 3-4.

85. Lives of Tel. poets I p. 227.

86. Hist. of Andhras V p. 503.

87. G.V. Subayya Bhattumurti Ramarajabhushanuda p. 4.

88. R. Ra. Text p u 1 23.

89. R. Ra. Introduction II p. 2.

90. R. Ra. Text p. 9 1 6.

91. Ra. Ra. Introduction I p. 10.

92. Ra. Ra. Text p. 5 u 3-4.

93. Ra. Ra. Text. pp. 57-58.

94. Ra. Ra Introduction II p. 7.

95. Text pp. 4, and colophons.

96. p.8.

97. Uttara Ra. Introduction.

98. Uttara Ra. Text p.2.

99. Uttara Ra. Text pp. 3-4.

100. Lives of Tel. Poets. I.

101. History of Andhras V pp. 541-548.

102. Telingana inscns. 1 No. 36.

103. Ra. Ra. Text. pp. 12,37.

104. - do - p. 382.

105. - do - p. 641.

106. A.R. 1912 p. 104 para 4.

107. Palnativira ch. Text. p. 21,53.

108. Wilson, Mack. Cant. II p 729.

109. Taylor: Mack. Cat. II p 729.

110. Panditaradhyacharitra Introduction p. 123.

111. Sarda I - No. 2 p. 189.

112. A.R. 1910: II p. 100.

113. Hindu College Magazine Guntur (1943-44).

114. I.A. I P. 155.

115. I have verified this during my visit with my sister late Miss K. Janaki Devi B. Sc.L.T. of the Govt. Secondary School for girls, Bellore, to Hampi on Monday Nov. 26, 1945.

116. Hindu Coll. Mag. p. 52.

117. AR 1910 II p. 107 para 60.

118. Antiquities I App. A p. 12.

119. Antiquities I App. A p. 14.

120. Antiquities I App. A p. 16.

121. Antiquities I App. A p. 16.

122. - do -

123. - do -p. 16 fn 1.

124. - do - App. A p. 18.

125. - do - do - p. 19.

126. Antiquities I App. A. p. 21.

127. - do - p. 22.

128. - do - p. 21.

129. Antiquities I App. A p. 25.

130. - do - 25.

131. - do - 25.

132. Antiquities I App. A p. 26.

133. Antiquities I App. A p. 27.

134. I.A. I. p. 373.

135. Kridabhirama Text p. 40.

136. Bharati I No. 3 p. 132.

137. Palnativiracharitra Text p. 16.

138. Palnativiracharitra Text pp. 71, 75.

139. Antiquities I App. A p. 19.

140. Antiquities I App. A p. 24.

141. Antiquities I App. A p. 25.

142. - do - 26.

143. Text pp. 36-37.

144. J.A.H.R.S. XII p. 43.

145. Palnativiracharitra Text pp. 17.19.

146. Sabdaratnakara: P. Virach. Text p. 18 fn.

147. Palnativiracharitra Text p.4.

148. Palnativiracharitra Text pp. 107-108.

149. 283 of 1924.

150. 528 of 1913.

151. 286 of 1932-33.

152. 215 of 1892: S.I.I. IV. 663.

153. 227 of 1892: S.I.I. IV. 667.

154. 696 of 1920.

155. 141 of 1917, 302 if 1932-33; Mack Ms 15-4-41 Yenmandelaṇika.

156. 302 of 1934-35.

157. 244 of 1897: S.I.I. VI 207.

158. Kistna Dt. Manual p. 14 & 21.

159. 564 of 1925.

160. 146 of 1897: S.I.I. VI 103.

161. Kakatiya Sanchika App. Insn. No. 14.

162. 506 of 1892: S.I.I. V 116.

163. 529 of 1893: S.I.I. V 175.

164. 204 of 1893: S.I.I. IV 1301.

165. Kakatiya Sanchika App. vv 52, 56, 57: Proceedings 7th Or. Conf. p. 589.

166. Proceedings 7th Or. Conf. p. 589.

167. Sivayogasara vv 93, 94.

168. - do - 81,92.

169. Kakatiya Shanchika App. 10-11 v 7.

170. - do - App v 14.

171. 440 of 1893: S.I.I. IV 1373 A.

172. E.I. XIX p. 26 v 18.

173. Kavyalankarachudamani I v 108.

174. Bharati.

175. K. Chudamani I v 108.

176. K. Chaudamani I v 16.

177. Andhra Vajnana Sarvasvam II p. 480.

178. E.I. XIX No. 26. p.164.

179. 209 of 1899: S.I.I. III 656.

180. 214 of 1899: S.I.I. VI 662.

181. K.Chudamani III v 65.

182. K.Chudamani V v 106, IV v 95.

183. E.I. V No. 4 D.

184. 113-A of 1893: S.I.I. VII 737.

185. 275 of 1930.

186. Telingana inscn. Hyd. Arch. Series 13 II No. 21.

187. Nell. Ins. III U 6.

188. E.I. XIII No. 16.

189. 405 of 1919.

190. 464 of 1905.

191. Nell. Ins. in Kanigiri 24.

192. Tirupati insic. I No. 61 (127 G.T.).

193. Nell. Ins. I AR 25.

194. E.I. V Np. 14.

195. 284 - P. of 1899: S.I.I. VI 839.

196. E.I. V No. 14 of 107.

197. 248-A of 1899: S.I.J. VI 876.

198. 343-J of 1899: S.I.I. VI 1101.

199. Kalingadesacharitra p. 423.

200. 250 F of 1899: S.I.I. VI 712.

201. 213 " " 661.

202. 340 of 1896: S.I.I. V 1222.

203. Nell. Ins I c.p. 17.

204. Nell. Ins III O 88.

205. Hyd. Arch. Series 13 Telingana insns. I p.12.

206. Sarada 2nd year Vol. II No. 2 pp.186-189.

207. Sarangadeva Sangita Vatukara I (1943) Edited by P.S. Sastri Text p. 10, Introduction p. 10, Text p. 11 vv 10-14, Introduction p. 21, Part II - adhyayas 2-4.

208. J. Mad. University XI p.233.

209. Bharati V - II p. 799. Mack Ms 15-4-9 p. 1-5.

210. Bharati V - II p. 799.

211. Bharati V - II p. 799.

212. Nell. Ins. Darsi 13.

213. 174 of 1899: S.I.I. VI 640.

214. Tirupati insns. II No. 58 (347 TT) and gave 59 (574 TT).

215. Ku. Sa. I v 59, also colophon.

216. Critique on Ku. Sambhava p. 16.

217. Bharati XI - I p. 361.

218. Ku. Sa. Texi I - Canto I v 21.

219. Sarda VI 2nd year Vol. I No. 5 pp. 543 - 545.

220. Rajarajasanchika p. 202.

221. C.R. Reddi Presidential Speech (Rajarajasanchika p. 202).

222. J.A.H.R.S. I p. 146.

223. Ku. Sa. Text I v 34.

224. Ku. Sa. Text I v 42.

225. Ku. Sa. Text I - I v 6.

226. Prabandharatnavali vv 184-187.

227. 179 of 1899: S.I.I. VI 624.

228. Ku. Sa. Text X - II v 144.

229. Brown: Tel. Eng. Dictionary.

230. Ku. Sa. Text I - II v 325 VI v 705.

231. Ku. Sa. Text II - XI v 620.

232. Ku. Sa., Text I - III v 281.

233. Ku. Sa. Text I - III v 317; vv 482, 488, 516, 578.

234. Ku. Sa. Text I. V. vv 597, 598.

235. Ku. Sa. Text I - VI v 912, 947.

236. Critique on Ku. Sa. p. 172.

237. 183 of 1899: S.I.I. VI 628.

238. Nell. Ins. II Kavali 39.

239. Dasaka ch. I v 16.

240. Nirvachana Ra. Text I v 4.

241. Nell. Ins. I A.R. 38.

242. Chatupadyamanimanjair p. 23.

243. Dasakumacharitra I v 8.

244. - do - Iv. 32.

245. Mahabharata II Virataparva I v 10.

246. Lives of Tel. Poets I p 117: N. Ramayana Introduction p.4.

247. Mack MS cited in Lives of Tel. Poets I p. 87: L.R. III p. 389: Wilson: Mack. Cat.

248. Dasa Ku. Ch. I v 129.

249. Dasa Ku. Ch. I v 90.

250. Ekasilanagaravrittanatamu, Andhra Patrika - Weekly Vol. 37 No. 17 31-12-44 p. 2.

251. Mack MS 15-4-5 Ms p 45: 14-2-5 Siddhesvaracharitra citation in lives of Tel. poets.

252. N. Ramayana I v 13.

253. N. Ramayana Introduction p.6.

254. - do - I v 6 Rajarajasanchika p. 64.

255. N. Ramayana I v 6.

256. Andhravijnana Saravasamu I p. 64.

257. Lives of Telugu poets I p. 132.

258. Citation on p. 155 of Biographies of Tel. Poets.

259. Citation on p. 156 of Biographies of Tel. Poets.

260. Rajarajasanchika p. 204.

261. Bharata III Virataparva I vv 32 - 36.

262. Bharata III Virataparva I vv 1, 2, 3, 5, 7.

263. Biographies of Andhra poets p. 57.

264. Biographies of Andhra poet p. 57.

265. Lives of Tel. Poets I p. 132.
266. Lives of Tel. Poets I p. 137.
267. J. Tel. AC II p. 29.
268. Bharata III Virata I vv 6,7.
269. Lives of Tel. Poets I p. 138.
270. Bharata V Salyaparva I v 451.
271. Biographics Andhra poets p. 57.
272. Bharata III virata I vv 27-30.
273. - do - vv 9.25.
274. - do - vv 38-40.
275. Bharata III Udyoga II. vv 102-106.
276. Bharata IV Udyoga II vv 102-106.
277. Bharata III vv 23, 21, 15, 17.
278. Bharata III Virata I v 30.
279. Bharata III Virata I vv 27, 28.
280. Bharati III No. 10 p. 11.
281. Bharati III Virata I v 7.
282. Bharata III - Virata I vv 234, 254: Bharati V - II pp. 860-864.
283. C.R. Reddi: Kavitattvicharamu pp. 287-307.
284. Bharati IX - I p. 28.
285. Bharata VII Amisasanika I vv 319 - 345; IV vv 169-282.
286. J. Tel. AC II p. 33 Citation Text.
287. Rajarajasanchika pp. 205, 210-211.
288. Lives of Tel. Poets I p. 148.
289. Lives of Tel. Poets I p. 148 Prabandharatnavali vv 152-160.
290. Lives of Tel. Poets I p. 148.
291. Markandeyapurana I v 10.
292. I v 9.

293. I v 13.

294. Prabandharatnavali vv 413-423.

295. Prabandharatnavali vv 491, 111, 119.

296. I vv 8, 9.

297. The verse is cited on p. 92 of Bhattumurti Ramarajabhashanduda: by C.V. Brahmayya.

298. Anantamatya: Bhojarajiya I v 24.

299. Canto I - Colophon p. 40.

300. J.H.Q. VII pp. 338-339.

301. Manucharitra Pithika v 48.

302. T.T. Devasthanam Report p. 185.

303. Karnataka Kavicharitra II pp. 189-90.

304. Mahabharata Ashtaparvavu Text Ed. 1928 Bangalore, Kannada.

305. Bharati VI - II p. 183.

306. Mack MS 15-4-5 p. 45.

307. Nellore district Gazetteer p. 342.

308. Andhrabhashabhushana v 2.

309. Andhrabhashabhushana v 4.

310. Dasakumaracharitra: Introduction.

311. vv 5,6.

312. v.7.

313. v 18.

314. Andhravijnana Sarvasvamu 1 p. 287.

315. v 5.

316. Prabandharatnavali p. 7.

317. Bharati XII - 1 pp. 692-693.

318. Vikramarchairta I v 20.

319. Vikramarkachritra I v 20.

320. Vikramarkacharitra I vv 21, 22.

321. - do -vv 30-62.

322. Eddanapudi (Nararaopet taluk) This ruler is different from Velnati choda II and Rajendra III of the cholas Bharati XII - I p. 693.

323. Prabandha ratnavali pp7, about Bhaskarauni Ketana Preggada vv 96-97.

324. Biographies of Andhra poets p. 130.

325. This is the view of the opposition - Hist. of Andh. V pp. 543-544.

326. Lives of Tel. Poets I p. 303.

327. Hist. of Andhras V pp. 541-548.

328. Lives of Tel. Poets I p. 312.

329. Hist. of Andhras V p. 540.

330. AR 1910 para 48.

331. Hist of Andhras V pp. 540, 546.

332. Hist of Andhras V pp. 547, 577.

333. 580 of 1907.

334. AR 1912 p. 2 para 5.

335. Nell. Ins. III Rapur 47.

336. 213 of 1892: S.I.I. IV 661.

337. N.U. Ramayana I v 55.

338. Bharata III - I vv 240, 241, II 330, III 243.

339. Bharata V 73.

340. Bharata III Udyoga III 232, 154, Drone II 227, V Salya II 157, VII Anusanika II v 318, Mansala I v 38.

341. Bharata III Bhishma III v 426 II 343.

342. Nell. Ins III v 14.

343. Mack MS 15-3-32.

344. Bharati VI I p. 405 - Chatupadyamanimanjari p. 28.

345. Mack MS 15-4-9 pp 1-15.

346. Somasila is 45 miles to the west from Nellore and on the border of Cuddapah and Nellore Dts.

347. Two vv from the work are dited on p. 166 of Andh. Patrika Annual (Sadharana).

348. AR. 1921 p. 97 para 5.

349. AR 1935-36 p. 67 para 24.

350. Nel. Ins. III Podile 22.

351. Telingana v 12 I Misc. No. 18. Hyd. Arch. Series 13 I No. 36.

352. Bharati VI - 1 pp. 437, 438.

# 3

# The Social Life

**General Introduction:** A survey of the political conditions in medieval Andhradesa shows that society in its General trend of life was unaffected by military expeditions and conquests. The fourfold Hindu castesystem, despite occasional attacks on it by Virasaivism and allid sects in Saivism Viravaishnavism, Buddhism, and Jainism, was strong fostered by Advaitism of Sankara and the new cult of Harihara, the great gift of the age. Virasaivism and Viravaishnavism enjoyed regal patronage, aimed at discarding the caste system, created plenty of commotion in the ranks of the society and for a while shock it to its foundations, though failed in their ultimate object, due to difference among the major propagators e.g. Basava and Pandita, and the inherent strength of the caste system. Consequently they came to be absorbed into Hinduism and continue as its sub-sects to this day. Buddhism and Jainism wanted to supplant Hinduism and the former was the court religion of some dynasties in Andhradesa till the 13th century AD. Buddhist preceptors are heard of and public controversies between than and virasaivites were held. Temples of Buddha existed. Comparatively Jainism was lesspopular.Buddha and Jainism had much in common and Hindusim overcame their opposition by taking the former into its fold. As though in return for the substantial services of Buddhism to Hinduism for in Professor Sastri's words "Lacking Vedic sanction almost entirely, the practice of worshipping images may have grown up under the stimulus of Buddhism which while it attacked Vedic places and objects are holy and countenanced the use of images."[1] Buddhavatara came to be included as the 9th among the ten incarnations of Vishnu by the middle of the 11th century AD (AD 1066).[2] The concept of Harihara steadily gathered momentum as attested by the records and literature of the period and by the 13th century AD temples were raised to the god and works dedicated. It was the one unifying force in Hinduism preaching toleration and oneness of Vishnu and Siva, as against narrow sectarianism, exercised great influence over the minds of the people, achieved tangible results, though Virasaivas exploited this concept to strengthen their view point. Hara is superior to Hari.

"The temple gave typical expression to the life and culture of the Southern India for several centuries in the middle ages."[3]

It is the highest manifestation of Hindu thought. The innate qualities of mankind, humanitarianism, devotion and service found expression in the temples building and promotion for worship and festivities of the god. The attention of society in general and of villagers in particular centred round the temple and its activities. Though "worship in temples however, never attained the importance in Hinduism that church services attained in christianity,it is on the secular side and as a social institution that the temple is seen to have filled in the past a considerable place in the economy of national life."[4] The role of temple in the medieval Andhradesa was important though not so marketdas the temple in South under the Cholas. Several temples in the land, many of them disolated, some renovated, some with names distorted and changed, still indicate the glory of the bygone ages. Temples were built in honour of and as memorials to kings, princess, queens, princesses,ministers, generals, religious teachers, persons of importance, and anybody dear to the donor, or builder and were named after them, a practice followed by the chalukyas of Vengi and the Chalukya cholas. Raising of temples to God Hari Hara, and the heroes of Palnad, as in the case of the heroes of the Ramayana and Mahabharata, in places of their birth, activity and distant places like Warangal and the prevalence of Hero worship carried on in them even to this day from the two distinguishing features of the period. With the exception of the temples of Heroes, in all other temples the god is either Siva or Vishnu, in some aspect or another and to the name of the particular deity Isvara or Narayana is addes e.g. Gonkesvara, Chodanarayana, Rajarajesvara and so forth.

As pointed out by Professor Sastri,[5] dana is preferred to yaga in this period which applies to the Telugu country as well; and despite occasional references to the performance of the yajanas, the general bent of all was in the direction of making grants to temples. The position of Brahmins in the caste system remained supreme. all knowledge - secular and sacredotal, was their privileged treasure and fostered and protected by the temples and religious maths. Women were honoured in this age. Some of them rose to great heights in every field. The ideal of womenhood was grihalakshmi and ardhangi. Her aim was service and devotion to god and husband and propitiating the former for the bestowal of happiness, health on her family and herself. The history of the period reveals ideal wives. mothers, lady ministers, generals, administrators and benefactors. Some princesses and private ladies undertook works of public utility, built temples and endowed them with rich gifts, and some women learned in arts, performed religious austerities and festivities paying to minute details. Generally their time was taken up in domestic work. Some women went through the hardest penances and did many difficult vratas promoted by religious motives.

Dancing women, learned in music and dance were attached to temples in large numbers. Their settlements consisting of usually three hundred or five hundred persons, located around important temples e.g. Draksharama, Bhimavaram, Palakol, Srikakulam, Chebrol, Velpur and so forth. Incidentally it may be noted the settlements of temples priests - manis - comprised same number as the sani settlements. The sanis are devadasis-servants of the god and their lives were dedicated in the service of temple. Bhogasteris or preyasis of kings enjoyed company and support. They were benefactors of society extending their charity to temples and scholars. They figure along with kings, queens etc in records and were far from the trickey and treachery of the vesyas who aim at the acquisition of wealth promoted by their cunning mothers to the detriment of the seeksers of their company. Nanni choda refers[6] to men prostitutes in this period.

As for private life of the people, monogamy was the rule. But its hold on kings and men of the royal family was elastic. More often them not that a king had more than a single wife and the number varied from one to five. Some kings had bhogastris besides queens. Indulgence in poligamy was the result of actions of political diplomacy. For generally each queen was a princess of the Royal family and bonds of unity were created and strengthened by marriage allinaces. King's household was a big affair. royal palace, servants, variety in food, personal attendants, men for bathing, maids for massaging feet[7] etc. are heard of from inscriptions. Members of royal families were dressed gorgeously and indulged in a variety of amusements, e.g. hunting, swimming, cock fight, ram fights etc. Princess took pleasure in swimming and boys delighted in flying kites, playing tops etc.

People generally were engaged in tilling of the soil or writting of books. Conditions of housing, living, food and clothing were good, hygienic and simple. All classes of people wore jewels the higher classes gold and the poorer classes of lesser metals. Rich jewellery was worn by royal personages and deities. The popular amusements were dice, cock and ram fights, play of ball etc. Even like medieval Britain which was not free from indulgence in cock fights, the local dynasties in Andhradesa delighted in cock fights. Every home had its cattle pen. Jingling bells and tinklets tied to the necks of domestic animals announced their movements when addressed by their sweet names. The cow - kanadherru - was considered in Hindu-homes which is clear from invocations at the end of inscriptions.

Diseases and their cures were many. Ayurveda was a favoured sciences. Diseases pertaining to the eye - a Kshiroga are enumerated by Somanatha.[8] Families of hereditary physicians living on rich royal donations are heard of vaterinary science was cared for. Three generations of a Brahmin family of experts in Asvavadiyasastra are heard of from inscription at Palakol.[9]

## The Velanandu Chodas

Under the Velanandu rule, society in Andhradesa resembled that in contemporary Tamil land under the Cholas. The name of kings, temples, services in them, donations etc.. reveal the impereptable influence of the Cholas in the kingdom. The four fold caste system with eighteen subcastes prevailed and people adhered to the caste code for occupations and so forth. There were strong religious upheavals under leaders like Mallikarjuna Pandita and Brahmanayadu throughout the country, disturbing though lightly the even tena of life for a time. The Velanandus built temples and endowed them richly for their requirements, gay life, and festive appearance. Some ministers, generals, rich men and women vied with the rulers in raising temples and making donations to them. Rest houses, chaultries, water houses were maintained in the vicinity of temples and places of pilgrimage and on the paths leading to those places for the benefit of travellers and pilgrims. The sacrosanct position of Brahmins is clear from the term. bhudeva applied to them, Life in the villages was simpler and quiter than life in towns and cities.

**Religion:** Though Buddhism and Jainism did command a few select votaries from the princes and the masses. Hinduism predominated in the kingdom. Generally in records; the birth of the four castes is attributed to the different parts of the body of purana purusha - Vishnu or Brahma. The main purpose of the division was the allocation of occupations, rights and duties of each caste, avoiding friction, jealousy and overlapping among people, for birth almost determined one's position in society to which he had to reconcile himself and live a contented life. Maintenance of Varnasramadharama was one of the incumbeu duties of the king. Mancham says that in the capital

Tsandavole, Brahmins equalled Atri, Kshatriyas Arjuna, Vaisyas Kubera and Sudra Vidura. [16] At times when the kings favoured Buddhism, the caste system must have felt the blow, overcome it, assimilated it and converted it into a source of strength. The caste system, probably consequent on the support of Advatism which was widespread won a permanent victory over Virasalvism. For even a great personage like Mallikarjuna Pandita when asked by Basava to give up caste remove sacred thread and join him could not shake off the shackles of caste and is said to have replied. I cannot give up my love to devotion (bhakti) and attachment to Brahminism".[11]Thesepersons who rebelled against caste distinctions turned to be its devotees.

**Saivism:** Saivism was widespread in the Telugu country. It was propagated by Sankara in Advaita form. The Saivaites adore lord Siva and Vishnu, extend their patronage and charity to both the religionists, raise temples to those and other gods of the Hindu pantheon and make grants to them. The catholicity of worship sense of toleration and goodwill were responsible for the popularity and widespread nature of Saivism. The Union of Hari and Hara into one god, and Gauri and Lakshmi marks a step further in Advaitism, perhaps a measure to level the extremists e.g. Virasaivas and Viravaishnavas.

The Velanandu chodas were tolerant towards other religions, Mallavarma installed a Sivalinga at Tsandavole.[12] Dhandapura - Gonka I was an ardent devotee of Siva i.e. a Samkara Kimkara. Choda I made donations to Siva tempels. Gonka II is described as the medikator at the lotus feet of Sankara and very incarnation of Siva.[13] His prasasti has the epithet - Siva padasekhara - borne by the cholas emperors. In inscriptions choda II is described as the worshipper of the lotusfeet of Siva though Somanatha mentions that while all his predecessors were saivaites, he accepted Buddhism.[14]

Of the persons in the service of the rulers, ministers Kommanamatya, and Prola, Danadaproli chodinayaka, treasurer Erramenayaka Nanduri Gundamentri, Narayana I and Jaya of the Ayya family, were all devotees of Siva.

**Virasaivism** : The need of the Saivaites to protect themselved from the attacks of Buddhists, Jains, brought into prominence great religious leaders e.g. Basava in Kannadadesa and the Panditatraya in the Telugu land. Basava assisted by Ekambara Ramayana, Padmarasa, casting off sectarian differences based on varnasramadharma, revived a new Saivism called Virasaivism, acceptable to all saivaites. This invigorated religion ended fights among different sects of saivaites and spread fast among people using for like Islam for propagation. thus Virasaivism was the work of Basava about AD 1150. So to trace Virasaivism to prehistoric times[15] is wrong. A Virasaiva should give up caste, vedic rites, sacred thread and eating with non-virasaivaites. Lingadharma is essential for virasaivsm. A Virasaiva is called Viramahesvara, and his vrata is called Viravsata. Virasaivas accept Isvaradwita and not sarvadvaita. Piduparti Somanatha's dikshabodha in Telugu describes the nature of Virasaivism.

Virasaivism in Andhradesa was not a replica of Karnata Virasaivism and came to be known as Aradhya religion. The Pandita traya, great admirers of Basava, propagators of Virasaivism in Andhra, drifted apart from their master, which speaks for their courage originality and constructive genius. Virasaivism in Andhra met with strong opposition from the masses and persecution from the rulers. Sripati Pandita alias Prachinadesika, a great saivacharya preached Saivagamas. He preached that Siva is the only god, devotees of Siva possess good caste, Viamantra is one for life, and things offered to Siva are the best to be eaten.[16] His vrata was not to follow caste differences and cited the works of Jabala and Satarudraya approving his actions. Sivalanka Manchana Pandita asserted that Isvara is the only god and Viramahesvara padam is the best.[17] In the presence of the followers of others religions who assembled in the Gadadharesvara temple at Benares, Manchana in said to have asked Vishnu to come out of his Virumuttam and bow to Siva which he did. The bearers of the family name Sivalanka, were probably the descendants of Manchana Pandita. Mallikarjuna Pandita proclaimed to the world that devotees of Siva were superior to the divine sages. In Choda II's sabha he vowed that he would offer his head to prove that Siva was the greatest god and he would kick the person saying that there is a god greater than Siva. He declined the invitation of Basava to join him because of his affinity to Brahminism. Because of diffences between Basava and Pandita as vital points, their religions drifted apart. The Lingayats of Kanadadesa observed no caste where as the Aradhyas of Andhradesa held fast to Brahminism. But the religion of the Pandita traya awas also known as Virasaivism which according to them was identical with Brahminsm.

The Panditaraya accepted Vedic rules and Varnasrama dharma Mallikarjuna Pandita was displeased with Basava's discandence of Brahminism and Vedic rites. He believed in Vedas and was devoted to Brahmins, and discredited Advaitism in his Sivatatvasara. He wanted to stabilise saivism by reviving ancient customs in Vedic methods. He destroyed Buddhism and Jainism at Tsandavole and spared Pasupata Saivism. Sivatatvasara, Andharavasira upanisha and Sri Kanthabhashya give the essentials of Pasupatam. Brahma pranava pancha shari prasada etc. mantras, differentiation of pasu, pati and pasu application of ashes, tripundradharana, rudrakshadhrama and lingarchana are necessary for Pasupata Vrata pasupatas hate advaitism, and differentiate between Jina Insvara. Pasas lives by the kindness of pati - rudra attain freedom from pasa and get moksha - Salvation. Pasupatas Pillar Visishtadvata[18] M. Pandita in Sivatatvasara says that the books abusing Siva should be burnt, and their authors killed. One gets salvation if he kills an abuser of Siva or dies in that effort. Many Saiva saints, whose lives are narrated in Somanatha's works lost their lives in spreading virasaivism by violent methods and secured salvation. For a person who dies for Siva, no sraddha ceremonies need be performed, his dealth should be celebrated. Mallikarjuna explained that Sivaniramalya should be eaten only by Sivadikshitas.[19] and not others. To worship Siva without worshipping Saivaite devotees is uselsess. There was no salvation without devotion.

Among Pandita's pupils were Donamayya, and Karasthali Somanathayya. The Saivite devotee Telugu Janmayya was a contemporary of Pandita. The Ardhyas of Andhradesa follow the tenets promul gated by M. Pandita and theirs is called Pandita Sampradaya. Unlike-Vira-Saivaites they follow Brahmin rites and theirs is chinmayadiksha. About AD 1500, sixty-six Brahmins families went to Srisailam and received lingadharchadiksha. Some of them remained there as Virasaivas where as other follow Vedic rites.[20] So we find Linghdaris and no-lingadharis among Aradhya Brahmins.

Panditaradhya hated ascetics, and he never became one. Somanatha says that after Pandita's end, Donamayya enthroned Kedarayya the oldest son of Panditaradhya to lokaradhyapettam and himself ruled bhaktirajya - kingdom of god. Kedarayya had four sons. His and Donamayya's descendants spread the tenets of M. Pandita. Theirs was grihsathapitha[21] and Panditamalla was not gangamamatha. Pandita's sons and pupils were contemporaneous with Palkuriki Somanatha.

In spreading their religion, the Virasaivas for mass appeal, collected the stories of Saiva devotees and saints from ancient times who distinguished themselves in Tamil, Kannada and Telugu lands. Aruvattumuvara alias Nayanaras - the sixty three saints famous in Tamil land were known in Telugu as nainars and nayanars. Several of them are praised in Basava purana and Panditaradhya charitra. They are enumerated in Sahasragana nama Samakhyana in the latter. The names of some saints vary sin Sanskrit Kannada and Tamil works and some referred to in Tamil and Kannada works are not found in Telugu wroks. There are variations in the stories and their narration and the total number is increased. Sundaranayanar is also known as Nanbinanar and Odayanambi. A great poet in Tamil he composed a saivastora. Tiruttondar Toghai. Somanatha partly transalated this work in Basavapurana. Odayanambivilasa in Telugu deals with the life of this saint. Udumuri Kannappa is Kannappan of Kalahasti whose story is celebrated in Kalahasti mahatmya in Telugu. Tirunavu Karasu alias Appar was a poet in Tamil. Chitutonda was also known as Seriyala and Dobrabhakta. His wife was Tiruvengani and son was Siraludu. Chitutondanambi's story is dealt with by Srinatha in Haravilasa. The lives and stories of the Nainars reached the people through Somantha's works in easy Telugu. Some of them were presented in local garb by later poets in their works. Udbata is praised in Sivatatvasara and Udbhakaradhyacharitra is rendered into Telugu by Tenali Ramaingakavi.

Srisailam was the seat of Andhra and Karnata Saivacharyas. In the Virasiromantapa there, Saivaite devotees are supposed to cut their tongues and heads in their religious fervour and get them back. The Virasaiva movement in Andhra was continued by Somantha by his works dealing with the lives of the celebrated masters, their teachings and innumerable saints from ancient times to his day. Somanatha is considered as the incarnation of Bhringi and is said to have been taken to Kailasa by Siva. Somana read out his Basavapurana to Palkuriki Surnamatya, the brother-in-law of the author. Palkuriki Surayya is mentioned as the minister of Prataparudra of the Kakatiyas in the Kaifiyat of Warangal.[22] Just as Prataparudra is a mistake for Rudra I, Palkurti is a mistake for Palkuriki. Incidentally of both Suras may be suggested, and on his advice Prataparudra is said to have listened to Aradhyacharitra etc. Saivaite stories of Somanatha in the temple of Sambhu at Warngal. This Suranamatya was a Brahmin and Palkuriki Somesvarapurana definitely says that Somantha was a Brahmin and a descendant of Balidevi Vemanaradhya and many Telugu and Kannada poets refer to as Aradhya Somanaradhya. Somanatha says that he was the son of Basava, of Basavagotra and pupil of Gurulingarya, grandson of Balidevi Vemanaradhya. His dikshaguru was Gurulingaryya and Karasthali Visvanathayya and Kettakuri Potidevara[23] were his two other preceptors. Somanatha dedicated his Anubhavasara to Tripurari Somana, and read out his Basavapurana to Sanganamatya, lord of Gobbur. His works deal with religion. His chaturvedasara deals with Sivaparamya, Anubhavasara with Saivadhramas, chennamthasisamulu with Shatsthalavibhava, and his vrishdhip-asataka has several verses in Sanskrit, Tamil, Malayala, Karnata, and Maharastra language. His Basavapurana discusses elaborately the meaning of Harihara, its significance from the view point of a Virasaiva. The idea that Harihara is one is due to ignorance of the meaning of the word, namely by stealing Hari, he became Hara and so was known as Harihara and greater than Hari. This is an indirect indication that the cult of Harihara as one god was widespread in the country and formed a formidable rival to Virasaivism. Basavapurana has been literally translated into Kannada in Shatpadi met by Bhimakavi and in verse by Rughavanka kavi and was rendered into Tamil also.

**Vaishnavism** : The Velanandu chodas were not sectarian. Some of them were devotees of Vishnu - Choda I, Gonka I and Gonka II and Choda II were devoted to Vishnu. Gonka III and Prithvisvara were devotees of Kuntimadhava of Pithapur Nanduri Kommanamatya, Bhimayagunda, Ponda and Jaya were devoted to Vishnu.

**Buddhism** ; With Srisailam as centre, the Buddhists and Jains spread their religions. Choda II was a Buddhist according to Somanatha. His court religion was Buddhism and his teacher was Buddha padapada charya. Challenging M. Panditaradhya, the Banotha Guru says that it remains to be seen whether Bauddha darsanapattabhadra was the guru or vaidikasaivabaddha was the guru; and if Buddha is Prabuddha of the three worlds, if Bauddham i.e. Buddhism is the only way to salvation he must be considered lokaradhya and be called Pandita. On the other hand if rudra is daiva, saivism is mokshasadhana, and Pandita Lokaradhya, he wants a discourse Panditaradhya condemns that a Bauddha is a Vaishnava and Buddhism is against smritis. It is attached to havi, have and pasa.[24]

Gokavaram appears to have been a centre of Buddhism. It was originally called Gonkavaram, probably built by Gonka. The Velanandus made gifts to the Buddhist monastery at Errabalem.

**Jainism** : Signs of Janism are few. Somantha mentions gains among the audience in Choda II's Court on the occasion of Saiva Buddhist controversy. Pancharatras chavakas, adhyatmikas, ashtamurtavadas and to kayatas were also present in the sabha.[25]

**The Temples** : The temples, their number, size and among donations to them speak for the glory of the kingdom and the people - Almost every big temple had its establishment.[26] Gonka I founded the Sankara temple at Tsandavole and called it Pandisvara after his younger brother Panda.[27] He kept a golden pinnacle on the top of the shrine at Pulivarru and donated five jagamadas for Uramala - necklace tokumara deva at Chebrole, Choda II presented horses and elephants - spoils of conquests to Bhimesvara at Draksharama.[28] On the top of the shrine of

Bhimanatha at Draksharama, Gonka II placed a golden pinnacle of sold gold: built a manchara mandapa to the god, a kshtagara for the annual davanotsava of the God, another mandapa, Gangiyarayamandapa, and a prasada, all to Bhimesvara. He provided for Kshirabhisheka, and presented a davanavanam, Kanakavalyam - bracelet in the name of Virapadrajau, metal mirror, gold plate, gold kolagam, gold vessels and a suvarni vidvijam to the god. Gonka made grants to the temples of Nagesvara Mahadeva at Kumudavalli, Prithvisvara. Mallikarjuna and Ganapesvara. Probably Prithvisvara and Ganapesvara are after two wel l- known rulers who preceeded Gonka II and not Velanandu Prithvisvara and Kakatiya Ganapati who were posterior to Gonka II. Gonka II kept golden pots on the tops of the temples at Sripurashottamam, Sriparvata and victory pillars at conquered palces; and on all temples of Vishnu i.e. Krishna in the entire Andhramandala. He built many temples of Siva and Vishnu all over the kingdom and richly endowed them. Choda II made vauable presents to the temple of Kantimadhava is Pithapur. He covered with gold the image of Vishnu i.e. Narasimha at Simhachalam. He gave a thick covering of gold to Bhimanatha at Draksharama, placed him on a padestal of pure gold and presented golden utensils for worship, a golden aurcola (prabha), set with gems, an ornamental arch i.e. matara korana of soilied gold and horses, elephants, cons, gems to Bhimesvara. Jayambika, queen of Gonka III rebuilt the temple of Sripithapura and covered with gold the image of Vishnu at Simhagiri. Minister Kommana installed Vishnu at Srikurmam, Kurudurti, Krottacherla, Tripurantakam, Kottidona, Boggaram, Elamanchili, in Kalinga rashtra at thirty two places. The present Gopalaswami temple of the hill at Pelamandurti is probably the Vishnu temple built by Kanma.[29] At Davulur, Kanma built the temple of Gonkesvara mentioned him in a record but now called Gokesvara, and is now known as Gokarnesvara. This is one of the many instances in which historic names of temples have been in course of time superseded by puranic names given to them with puranic stories attached thereto.[30] At Mrontukur, Surama Nayaka built chodesvara temple after his maternal uncle who may be idenfied with general choda son of Maraya Panda. Uncle of Gonka II. At present the temple is called Ramachodesvara which "name might have been given on account of a later restoration of it, by the chief Ramachoda who flourished in this part of the country in the 12th century AD."[31] Errananayaka erected Sabbesvara temple at Kadaminjalur, and at Srikakulam built a Srivimana in the Bhimesvara temple and provided for Bhoga-service to the God. Gonka's uncle Panda, built a Siva temple at Nidubrole, and that of Gokisvara mahadeva and shrines to several deities at Cherukupalli. At Kondena the Suresvara temple and the Gokesvara temple at Karempudi were built by minister Tsanapreggada, and that of Ballisvara by an officer of Gonka II. At Timmapuram, Saramaya, brother-in-law of Gonka II installed Sarvajana as Gonkisvara at Chevaram and the deities-Mallikarjuna Mulasthanadeva and Narayanadeva there and provided for worship. At Appikatle, on the banks of the tungabhadra, Narayanayaka built the Visvesvara temple.[32] In AD 1170 and 1173 Mallideva of Kandruvu, Kanda, lord of Kandruvu and his son Rama made grants to Rajarajesvara temple at Padamata Vipparru.[33] Tradition has it that this temple was built by chola rajarajanarendra. Possibly it was built by the chola emperor Rajaraja I the great, the builder of the great temple - Rajarajesvara at Tanjore; or by a legal subordiante of his in the Telugu land. At present it is called Rajesvara temple.

Several temples in the kingdom said to have been built by Cholarajas or under Cholas regime, were probably built by the velanandu chodas under cholas ageis. The temple of the Bhavanaryana at Ponnur i.e. Svarna in Sanskrit, was built by the cholas. Ponnur is obviously the name given by them, and a legent about the place refers to the time probably when the local tungabhadra appeared or reappeared because of a flood in the Kistna.[34] Two temples at Kakaraparru, one at Tetali and three at Padameta Vipparnu are believed to have been built by Rajarajanarendra and a temple at Turuvipparru by Rajaraja choda. At Pulivarru, according to the Kaifiyat of the village, Rajanarendra, Mallavarma, Kulottunga chola anointed in AD 1117 (probably a mistake for Vikrama chola) built temples and carried on worship.[35] The Sangamesvara temple at Gudali is said to have been built by chola tondaman. The oldest Siva temple at Gandavaram was founded by a chola king. According to popular belief, the design of the temple admits the falling of the rays of the rising sun on the deity named

Udayalesvaraswami i.e. Isvara of the morning time.[36] At Mudivarati, a corruption of Muni varti i.e. wandering place of sages, the Tarakesvara temple is said to have been built by the cholas.[37] At Dimile is the temple dedicated to Siva in the most unvommon form of Nagnesvara. The story goes that sago Agastya felt grieved at his absence in the marriage of Siva and Parvati and Siva promised to appear before him with his bride whenever he wished. Agastya expressed the wish when they had no clothes on and they appeared before him as they were Nagnesvara temple was built to commemorate the event.[38] The temple of Kalahastisvara Kurichedu was built under chola regime.

The Chodesvara and Bhimesvara temples at Divi Vishnu and Karavalabhairava at Buduladivi,[39] Bhimesvara temple at Vadlakurru were built by Narayana I of the Ayya family. General Jaya provided Sankara at Tsancavole, with a fresh pedastal, as the old had been stolen, placed golden pinnacles on the temple, and gave vessels for worship; built the Ganapesvara temple after king Ganapati, at Ganapesvaram and consecrated it in AD 1231.[40] The Ganapesvara temple survives to this day, In AD 1213, at Chebrole i.e. Tamrupura, the city of Shanmukha or Kumaraswami Jaya repaired all the temples, whitewashed them, and placed golden pinnacles on their tops. He covered with gold the image of Tarakavati i.e. Kumarasvami, supplied gold, silver, copper and brass for the worship of the gold. He presented another image of Kumaraswami and two consorts - valli and Devasena made of a base metal (loha) and meant to be carried about in procession during festivals, built an enclosure, a Mandapa of Sani (Saturn) and a gopura of three storeys. He built another mandapa for the resting of the god after the sport of the hunt on every Makara Sankranti, a painting which represents the gods who assembled for the occasion witnessing the representation of battles between the gods and demons.[41] He set up the linga in the Mulasthana temple and the Kaduvettisvara linga which had been destroyed by the robbers. To Kumaraswami, Anantesvara at Kollur, Chodabhimesvara and Vasudeva, Jaya presented many villages with their bands indicated by peacock pillars. In AD 1235, he set up god chodesvara after his father and the Ayyakulatilaka temple after the title of his.[42]

Of these temples, Chodesvara survives by that name, being one of the many temples to the north east of Chebrole, all facing east and chodabhimesvara is the Bhimesvara temple, one of the three standing on the top of a mound. " Like the celebrated Saivaite temples of Amaravati and Draksharama, this is a storeyed building with the grand floor walled up on all sides and the sanction built on the first floor." The temple has traces of Pallava architecture. The Vasudeva temple is probably the pretty temple of Vishnu of today. The Kumaraswami temple does not exist now. The Kaifiyat of chebrole [43] mentions that Tribhuvana malla Vikramaditya VI built a temple for Kumaraswami at Chebrole. As Abavamalla also made grants to this temple, it was of earlier origin and obviously Vikramaditya made improvements to it; further improvements were made by Ganapati of the Kakatiyas, Rudra I of the kakatiyas is said to have built eleven temple and did sahasralinga pratishta at Chebrole. In one linga were cut 998 linga two were installed on the northern and southern directions in the temple.[44] The Kumaraswami temple was in a flourishing condition till the 13th century AD. Fragments of black granite blocks, pillars, and a fine idol identified as Kumaraswami are found at Chebrole on the basis of which it has been said that "in the open yard situated between the Bhimesvara and Vishnu temples, there is a high mantapa containing a large side Nandi facing the east".. and that it must have constituted the temple of Kumaraswami.[45]

At Pavalur, in AD 1132 Kammanayaka constructed a temple of Gonkesvara. To the Armugaswami temple at Tiruttani, the surrounding wall was built by king Timvengalanatha of Velanandu. [46] To the temple of Kalyanakesvadeva at Kranza i.e. 1154 AD a queen of Choda II made grants. At Avanigadda was the temple of Dhanadaprole choda deva - Jaya's chebrole record gives a list of villages and shares which were the property of the temples and the names of donors, which was compiled from the records of the temple at the order of Jaya, after he received chebrole from Ganapati. [47] At Nannepadu was Somesvara temple, Vindhyavasini temple at Penugudurupadu, Amritesvara temple at Amritalur, Sri Kantha temple at Kandakanch, Bhogisvaradeva temple at Bhattiprolu Chodesvara at Sriramapuram, god Amaresvara at Peddamakkena,

Nerendrasvara and Kesava at Royali, Madanagopala at Kovur, the Chodesvara temple at Ilindaparru, Dandesvara and Venugopala temples out Prattipadu, Papesvara at Chavali, Chodesvara at Moparru, temple of Traipurushashthanam at Veliveru, Komaragirisvurmin at Viswathunikhandrike, were some of the temples of the period.

In inscriptions whether the differing number of Brahmapuris in each case has any real significance - religious or puranic, and depended on the resources of the donor is not certain. In a record dated AD 1145 the Brahmapuri land given on the occasion of the consecretation of the Siva temple was distributed among eight Brahmins. [48] Here probably eight members represent the ashtamurtis. The eleven Brahmins in the record of 1151 AD chosen and devarabrahmapurudu probably have some bearing on the eleven Rudras on Sivas. [49] Provision for camphor lamps before god is not so common as oil or ghee lamps.

**Temple festivals** : Besides daily worship, every temple has weekly, fortnightly, monthly and annual festivals, which were celebrated with due care, pomp, and mirth. Annual festivals, or tirunallu of any temple attract larger crowds from outside. Srikakulam on the left bank of the Krishna was a great centre of pilgrimage in the Telugu country from early days. It was the home of Vishnu i.e. Srikakulaswami, famous in Telugu literature as Andhra Vishnu, andhrasvarar Teluguraya. It had a settlement of three hundred dancing girls attached to it. The legent about Srikakulam and the god speaks for the lax morals of the priests. [50] In velanandu and later times, the tirunallu were celebrated on a grand scale. Bhimayagunda is said to have given plenty in charity during tirumallu. [51] Men and women mingle freely make merry and set aside the usual moral code. Srinatha gives a beautiful and realistic description of Sri kakula tirunallu in the 14th century AD in his Kridabhirama and few chotu verses in Telugu.

Located almost in the centre of Andhradesa, Srisailam was a place of remote sanctity. It finds mention in Mahabharata. Tevaram - a Dravida Kanya describes Sri Sai lanchatinya. [52]

Brahmins made it on important Siva Kshetra where self born linga was worshipped as Lingachakravarti and Sakti as Maddhavi, Bichavamba of a later day. The festivities of Sivara trimahotsava, attracting pilgrims in large numbers from all over India are vividly described by Somanatha.[53] Festivities to the god and goddess are celebrated separately from February to May. On account of the great devotion of the Chenchus to the god, Mullikarjuna is also known as chenchumallayya. On the sivaratriday all Hindus could enter the innermost shrine of the temple, after bathing in the Patalaganga. Of the several maths on Sri Sailam, Siddhabikshavritta matha was the most important and Bikshavrittis called chakravartis administered Sri Sailarajya Santasiva and Vira stationed themselves in the Virabhadradurgam, Sri Sailam is also mentioned as Srikailasa.[54]

In this period, the marriage celebrations of Bhimesa at raksharama as attested by Somanatha attracted crowds of pilgrims from all over the country. Draksharama or Daksharama, also known as Dakshataporana or Dakshamati, was one of the most important centres of pilgrimage in India, and Andhradesà in particular. It is considered that Daksha did the Yjana here-daksha yaga, and gave his name to it. Chalukya Bhima I installed god Bhimsvara at Draksharama. Records mention the place as Dakaremi, Peddadakaremi, Dakaremi are mentioned, together, obviously referring to different parts of the kshetra. The importance and sanctity of Draksharama may be guaged by the grandeur of the temple innumerable records in its walls of many dynasties some ruling in and over Andhradesa and the works to Srinatha. Bhimesvarapurana and Kasi-khandam. Almost all the rules who led expeditions of conquest either from the north or the south took particular care to visit Draksharama, propitiate god bhimesvara and made presents to him. Rulers and people of Andhra never failed in pleasing Bhimesvara by their gifts. The marriage celebrations of god at Penumetta, the jatra i.e. festival at Goddavapuram used to be largely attended. Pilgrims flock to Vijayapuram i.e. probably Vijayasvaram to pray to Virasomesvara, and pilgrims starting for Simhabrihaspati go to the Godavari and to Tripurantakam for Kartika Punnama.[55]

Tripurantakam is considered the foot of Srisailam and its eastern gate is also known as Taruhachalam alias Kumarasoila or Kumaragiri. Its sanctity is described in Sriparvata purana by Seshanaradhya.[56] The Tripurantaka temple was built in AD 1254-55 under the orders of Ganapati of the kakatiyas. The Tripurasundari shrine was built in the bed of a tank, and like Jambukesvara, the goddess is ever floating in the water.[57] Several records there speak of human sacrifices and the Golakimath, its teachers and influence.

**Private life:** An epithet of Choda II is devabrahmanapadaradhaka. Each king had more than one queen and a few concumbines. Generally the rulers had good appearance were dressed in rich cloths and fine jewels, highly educated and cultured and lead lives of good conduct and discipline, and not of self indulgence and licence. We have few details about palace servants their duties and emoluments. Angandi who used to massage the feet of Choda I, his daughter Leyyama and granddaughter Periyandi, the mistres of Kona Rajendra Choda.[58] are mentioned in a Draksharama inscription. A record of Gonka II there mentions his mudiseli talayanka Muddanayaka, an expert in giving head bath to the king.

According to Manchana, it was the janma vrata of Kanma to feed daily one thousand Brahmins with milk food. He built houses on in banks of the Krishna and kept Brahmins in them. He celebrated the Upanajuna and marriage of several Brahmins.[59] The prosperity of Tsandavole is described by Manchana saying that the people were not used to ticker cots, cottages, cotton sarees, and gold ornaments. A record mentions Kamma Vaisyas. According to Sammothi, towards the close of the reign of Choda II, mari spread in the country and Choda I, was treated by the Jains, Buddhists and physicians for his boil on the chest though not with any success.

**Women :** Some of the queens were cultured and undertook utilitarian activities. Subbama, queen of Gonka made gifts to the temple at Nadendla. Gundambika wife of Choda I was beautiful, virtuous and faithful. Sabbambika, queen of Gonka II was beautiful virtuous and did many good deeds. Jayamba devi, queen of Gonka III, is described the incarnation of the best among noble women. Devoted to Vishnu, she built an asthana mandapa, a prakara, and gopuras to the Kuntimadhava temple at Pithapur, set up Lakshmi with due rites, and propitiated Achyuta with Lakshmi and provided for service-bhoga. Her covering with gold the image of Narasimha at Simhachalam is described poetically thus "she made manifest to men the name Hemanaga of the highest being which has assumed the shape of the lord of Sri Simhagiri in order to remove the distrust of his devotees."[60] At Jannalagadda. Valyasani, wife of Surya preggada built a temple of Vallabhesvara.

Manchana says that if a woman is alone in the house without anybody of her husband's family, if she stays always at her mother's residence, if she goes alone to pilgrimages and festivals, if she goes to neighbours houses often, if she talks frequently with men and makes friends with bad women, if the husband is away in foreign lands or old or defective in limbs, if she likes bad men she will get bad. Under no circumstances she should be given great freedom for then she spoils caste life, money etc. M. Pandita says that when the husband was not devoted to Siva, wife could leave him and Anasuya and Nilayani, wives of great sages in the past did thus and secured boons from Siva.[61]

Dancing women had a palce in Hindu society as devadasis. They were called sanis and their duty was to be in the service of God - to dance and sing and they had permanent emoluments. Manchana says that Tsandavole had beautiful dancing girls.[62] and gives a typical description of a Vesya.

**Amusements:** While kings and princes delighted in painting ordinary people indulged in cock fights Manchana refers to cok fights.

**The Haihayas of Konamandala**

These Haihayas were devotees of Siva, specially of Bhimesvara at Draksharama. The name Bhima of kings, queens and princes was perhaps after Bhimesvara. Their patronage was extended to vaishnavism as well. There appear no signs of Jainism, Buddhism and so forth.

**The temples:** Kona Rajendra Choda I built the mandapa called Gandavendadeva in the temple of Bhimanatha, furnished it with two wings.[63] and an enclosure. Mallideva III and Manmasatya II provided for the daily worship, offerings, oblations, monthly and annual festivals of Kuntimadhava at Pithapur.[64] In AD 1276 in reign of Kona Ganadhipa Mallinayaka presented doorway and bell metal doors to the natyamandapa of Kshiravamsisvaradeva.[65] The temples of Rajesvara deva and Vindhyavasini at Palakol find mention in two kona records.

**Festivals**: Temple festivals were conducted with due care and facilities were made for pilgrims. In AD 1150 provision was made for the residence of paradesi - ascetics in the western chaultry of the Bhimesvara temple at Draksharama, during the celebrations of Simha brahsapati Vishnu Sankranti. In AD 1153 Kona Bhima at Draksharama made arrangements for the stay and food of tiruvidhi ascetics in tituvidhimatham during the course of the marriage celebrations of Bhimesvara[66] Provision was also made for a choultry, maintenance of desantara ascetics, in the chodaganga Vairagi andari matham, the devabhoga of Bhimesvara and Vishnudeva of Boyivelumpale, devatarchana kata to the north-east of arpakanagari, and for the choultry in front of Bhimesvara donated by chodaganga vairagi antaru. Manmamallideva in AD 1218 granted Kandi kuppa constituting a portion of the village Pallamkuriti to chodesvaradeva and some land to Bhairavaswami.[67] The chodesvara swami temple was a vidyadhana in this period.

**Private life**: Though dual kingship prevailed, it is not clear whether both kings lived in a single palace, or each king had a separate palace and establishment. The kings usually had and two or three wives and some concumbines. At Palakol in AD 1318, the sons of Kona Ramanatha provided for Udakadana free supply of fresh water at all times in the presence of the deity.[68] A grant of land was made to the Brahmins, chandrasekhara who supplied water daily for Salivendra (water house).

**Women**: The Kona queens distinguishes themselved by their acts of charity. Padumavati, wife of Bhima, possessed lotus like eyes, was devoted to Bhimanatha at Draksharama, provided for amutupadi to the god, and built a temple to Kamakoti. Bhimaladevi queen of Venuaya choda, presented a huge lustrous mirror to Bhimesvara. The temple of Ishtakamesvara at Gajjaram was important. Surapa Reddi made a grant to Ramesvara for atonement of the sin of previous birth. [69]

**The Haihayas of Panchadharala**

The Haihayas of Panchadharala, were devoted to Bhimesvara at Draksharama and Dharmalingesvara at Panchadharala.[70] The Panchadharala pillar inscription says that king Choda's idol was Bhimesa linga at Draksharama and his bathing place was the Godavari the banks of which were beset with sacrificial stakes choda erected a gopura in the eastern entrance of the Dharmesvara temple for the repose of the god in AD 1403. The gopura was like a new pleasure hill for damsels in heaven to witness from there the festivals in the temple - Dharmasvara. God Rajarajesvara was always surrounded by 500 lingas and devils on mount Nagudra. He was known as Varasiddhalinga as he granted successes to his devotees. Tradition has it that later on the god became Dharmesvara as he was kind to the faithful pandavas. The name Panchadharala is derived from five jets of water fad by a natural perennial spring, and are found in a paved enclosure to the south of the temple. Close by there is a lingam on which are carved 1020 lingams in twelve rows of eighty-five each. It is known as Kotilingam i.e. were of lingas. [71]

**The Gonas of Vardhmanapura**

The Gonas maintained Varnasramadharama and favoured Vaishnavism. Buddha Reddi begins Ranganatha Ramayana with a long description of Vishnu as nitya chidanandu, sarvalokasraya, purnasvarupa, adideva, madeva, and adinarayana and the god who protects him and his family. In the next wherever possible.[72] Buddha gives descriptions of Vishnu. He described the eight incarnations of Vishnu, calls him Tribhuvanadhisvara and drives into the mind of the reader that Rama was Vishnu and Sitalakshmi, Kacha and Vithala give a beautiful description of Vishnu at the beginning of the Uttara Ramayana. They refer to the birth of the four castes from the person of Vishnu in the words of Bali to Ravana. [73]

Saivism also enjoyed rega patronage. Yona Rudra was a devotee of God Rudra Buddha's Ramayana speaks about Siva's greatness on several occasions e.g. Bhagirath's penance, breaking of Siva's bow, Rama's praise of Hamma and so forth. The Malyala family were devoted to Siva. The Conas were aware of the union of Hari and Hara as one and their inseparability-the culmination of Advaitism Buddha refers to Rama as the combination of the three mantris and the one above the three as adipurushottama and as both Hara and Vishnu.

There appear no signs of Buddhism and Jsinism, unless the name Buddha born by some of the rulers imply any attachment to Buddhism. Buddha speaks about atheism as taught by Japali to Rama. Kuppama in AD 1276 built a temple at Budapur for the merit of her deseased husband Gunda, installed Gundesvaralinga after him.

**Private life:** The Gonas strictly adhered to monogamy. Vithala was virtuous and kind. Buddha was orthodox, of good condutc and charitable.[74] Kacha and Vithala led pure and virtuous lives. It is due to the genius of Buddha that we get a fine picture of Ravana's family free from the barbarity as dineanated in other Ramayanas. Buddha's Ravana was aware of the strength of the enemy. He recognised Rama as Guru in archery and praised his supreme capacities in that sphere - thus indicating his own capacities in the use of bow and arrow. Ravana was conscious that Rama was an incarnation of Vishnu and took Sita not out of lust but to get killed Rama and acquire salvation-Vishnu Sayujya after death. [75] Thus "the poet who could see godliness in beastliness elevated Ravana from the world of Rakshasa to that of Adhyatmika." and his work forms the basis for the mentary that Ravana was a yogi and that merely a Rakshasa.[76] But the usual estimate of Rama in Ravana's mind was that he was human being - weak and slender and his friends were monkege still worthless. So being the conqueror of gods, he thinks that he should not care for men and finds it impossible to reconcile himself to bow to Rama and save himself but was ever ready to fight even at the expense of his kingdom, race and himself. [77] Buddha's Kumbhakarna was a follower of dharma, devotee of gods, was kind and learned. He advised Ravana to fight Rama, and though aware of that dharma wises sacrificed his life for the sake of his brother. His forsight is clear in his conversation with Vibhishana in the battlefield advising him not, to get killed. so that Bakshasas lineage may continue.[78] Almost all the important warriors on Ravana's side were aware that Rama was god and advised Ravana not to fight but none could induce him to bow to the man incarnation of Vishnu.

**Women:** Kuppambika did many vratas - Lakshminaryaana, Jalasayana, asunyasayana, anataarundhati, sukla, krishnadvadasai, and others mentioned in Kalpa texts. [79] She did the vrata of giving away land every day during chaturmasya. In the Ramayana, unlike Rakshasa men and women excepting Tataka, Lankini etc. were endowed with commonsense, good qualities and intelligence. Buddha's fine pictures of women of Ravana's family might have served as models for contemporary women Kaikasi, conscious of the danger threatening her sons' existence, went to Ravana's court thinking that she could convince Ravana in public conversations, but in vain. Mandodari time and again attempted to dissuade Ravana from wordly pleasants and take to penance. She wanted Ravana to live.[80] for she was a chiranjivi. She was every ready to prevent Ravana from doing the worst e.g. killing of Sita etc. She enumerated seven faults on Ravana's past. She was heroic and courageous for when Ravana fled from the battlefield, she sent him back saying "Won't people laught if you do not conquer Ramachandra" Buddha's picture of Mandodari, though comprehensive is based on Valmiki's which is one of the best and most beautiful in the entire Ramayana. [81] Sulochana, as has been suggested already, stands comparison with Sita in all repects. Then Lakshmana killed Indrajit and presented the head to Rama Sulochana was determined to perform Sattee, started from Kumbhinasapura, her father's residence, went Ravana's Court and asked him to get Indrajit's head. When he said that he would get it after winning Rama, Mandodri spoke to her about the impossibility of Ravana's Victory, and advised her to get it from Rama himself. Sulochana boldly went ot the battelfield,[82] was honoured by Rama and Lakshmana, secured the different parts of the body from the battlefield, exhibited her chastity as Sita was to do. Later on and returned home with Indrajit's body, to the surprise of Ravana.

Buddha described the qualities of a pativarata in the advice tendered by Mandodri to Sulochana.[83] He speaks about the importance of sahagamana self immolation in the words of Sulochana to Ravana. She said that a woman without her husband was worthless, arthangi could not be separated from nathanga, a woman should never lose her husband for the earth could never bear a widow and so there is no salvation for women except to go with her husband.[84] Sulochana's sahagamana is said to have been witnessed by Rama and Lakshamana.

Princess in the family were taught riding e.g. Sulochana from Kumbainarayana to Lanka, and there to the battlefield, rode on a horse. Pearl necklaces, gem studded girdle, toe, rings, anklets, maddikayala (a kind of earrings), wet with fine diamonds (gonabuvajrala) and a few pearls, raisreka (head ornament worn by children and women) necklace with puligoru i.e. tiger's claw pendant, set with diamonds, necklace (addiga) of emeralds, nose ring, Kattanibogadas gold ornament set with pearls worn on the upper part of the ear, baviras of rubies, ear ornament in circualr form worn from the tip of the ear), anklets of emeralds, ruby studded girdles, anklets, (andiya) studded with topaz - are the jewels mentiond by Buddha.[85] Some of the these were peculiar to the Andhras.

Ladvamula (sweet meats), atirasamalu (sweet cakes made of rice meal and sugar fried in ghee), mandagalu, sara resamulu, kalamannam (finest sort of rice), Kalavantakamulu (a hotelu potch, disu containing a number of ingredients), pickles, amballu (porridge), rice pudding, jidugupalu, butter, sugar, (chinichakkera), rasayanamulu (sweet preparations), supamulu (split peas, cooked in water), apupamulu cakes), curds, nanavalu (new rice soaked in water or milk), juntiteniyalu (virgin honey) sikharulu or siganilu (butter milk seasoned with spices), tiyya charu (sweet soup), panakamu (sweet drink), chutneys, cheese, dried vegetables, cakes of black gram dried or eaten as pickle, were the items of food mentioned by Buddha Reddi.

**Amusements:** Buddha mentions the tricks of a hunter and the implements cage, net, ropes etc, to catch and kill crud animals in which he is justified.[86] Brahmahatya was considered the greatest sin and even Rakshasa women e.g. Kaikasi abhored it. [87] Sandal, musk, fine silks, benzoin, sapphires, ruby, alum, guja-rati kampulu (Raja's from Gujarat) and apa raji gold find mention in connection with decoration of Kalyanavedi.[88] Nalugu (fragrant paste used as soap) of Kemkuma, ox-gall, civet, oil of gold flower waters mixed with camphor and surabhi thick cloths (jilugu), red coloured shirts, and their cloths with ends full with fine gold, (jaluva)[89] and lace of gold, paste of crude comphor, raw scent, jackets embroidered with gold lace, and fine gold armlets of a wavy shape (kangula) find mention in connection of dressing up of Sita and her sisters - as brides.

**The Haihayas as Palnad**

Viravaishnavism prevalent in Palnad aimed at the unity of castes but with ephemeral success, resulting in the Hero cult. Buddihismand Jainism also prevailed. New temples were built and novel festivals instituted. Srinatha refers to the birth of the four castes from Brahma and duties assigned to each - Brahmins to study the Vedas, Kshatriyas to fight, Vaisyas to trade and sudras to serve the first three castes. Varnasrama dharma as ordained by Manu, and taught by Krishna to Arjuna prevailed as seen from the conversation of Balachandra to his mother.[90] Either this tone of Balchandra shows that Viravishnavism was not strong enough or Srinatha writing in the 15th century AD pictured contemporary Palnad and not Haihaya Palnad.

Saivism was popular and Virasaivism was widespread. Balamallideva, Anugu, Narasimga, were saivaites. Kamaraja and his son Alaraja were Virasaivas. Alaraja Worshipped linga with double jasmine, sacred ashes, and leaves used as on offering before dining and prior to his start as to Nalagama's court and put sacred ashes on his forehead. This attachment of Alaraja to Virasaivism, show that it was tolerated by Brahmanayodu.[91] Nalagama also was a Virasaiva. For on Alaraja's death, Nalaganma's daughter waited to perform Sati, at the invitation of Nalagama came punyajangalu holding golden vessels, padamata jangamas in tens and sixties, and elders came.[92] The armies of the grandfather of Alaraja are said to have included vodiyajangams -four thousand wearing black robes, and eight thousand wearing red robes. Some of them were -

Medayya, Padamatimeti Basavayya, Bodaisvaya, Dobbado Buggayya, Karakantha lingayya, Kalana Basuva. A kayya Kukkayya, Adimallayya, nijalinga chikkayya, Nilakanthayya - all with lingas shining on their chests and rosaries in necks.[93] There were ninety thousand Virasaiva mendicants who were expert soldiers also - Probably black and red robes distinguish two sects among Virasaivas. Lingapuja prevailed and Jangams- not necessarily all non-brahmins - existed in large numbers.[94] The names of oxen like Andala Basavanna, Karinandi Basavanna, etc. attest to the popularity of Virasaivism. By the time of Prataparudra of the kakatiyas, the worship of Bhairava, Mailaradeva became widespread. Probably Pasupeta and other creeds prevailed for a record of the 19th century AD quotes another of AD 1513 mentioning the ancestor of the donor as Mantramuriguru who had after death became a Sivalinga in the temple of Uttaresvara at Pedda Kodamagandla.[95] Another record mentions a teacher of Pasupata creed who had become a sivalinga in the temple.

Brahmarayadu and his followers followed liberalism and toleration in religion. They all prayed to Siva Tripurantaka and Mallikarjuna at Srisailam Balachandra was devoted to Siva. He says that in one of his past lives he won Siriyala.[96] The family gods of Anapota were Sriyarilinga of Sri Sailam and chennakesava of Macherla.

Viraraishnavism: Not so narrow as Virasaivism in its tenets, practices and austerities, viravaishnavmis, was not spread at the point of wood. It aimed at the abrogation of castes. But caste system had its roots deep and even Balachandra could not follow his father's tenets. To escape the probability of Brahmahatiya Balachandra, sent his Brahma in friend Anapotu, away from him, on the advice of his wife Manchala.[97] But Anapots says that it is no sin if a Brahmins dies in the battlefield fighting the enemy in the battlefield according to dharma sastras and cites instances of Kripa Drona and Anaththama.[98]

Brahmanyadu converted low caste persons into Vaishnavas. Kannamandayadu, was of Mala caste and bore mudras on his arms. Among Balachandra's friends were men of all castes, Brahmanayadu was regarded as the incarnation of Vishnu, a

Krishna with four arms. By mingling of all caste he created a new caste order - the padmanayakakula i.e. the caste of heroes. In his religious activity, Brahma had the support of the Macherla Haihayas. The names of oxen - ambudhisayana, Garutamanta, goverdhanachala, Gopaladeva, Vaikuntha vasa, Vasudeva indicate the widespreed nature of Viravaishnavism.

**Hero worship:** The hero cult is the essence of the Viravaishnavism. It originated in the administration of the people for the great deeds of Brahma and the heroes. So they were regarded as gods or their incarnations, temples were raised, worship and festivals were conducted. Some of the heroes were Vaishnavaites some saivites, and these and others worshipped all gods. So the hero cult is the adoration of heroes irrespective of their caste and religion. This unifying feature was perhaps responsible for the oneness of devotees of all castes in celebrating festivals e.g. the Hindus and the Muslims. "The origin of this strange cult of heroes is not traceable in inscriptions at Karempudi." Karempudi is the seat of a Brahmin preceptor, the president of a section of the Brahmin community which worships the heroes. According to Virabhendra, the heroes and Nayakurala beeame gods after death. Brahma Vishnu, Alugu, Indra, Dodda, Brahaspati, Baludu, Brahma, Sankara, Damanayada varma, Kanmaraja Bhiringi, Alaraja Nandikesvara, nayakuralu yogamaya and so forth. " The heroes were credited with the possession of the knowledge of their past lives.

**Buddhism and Jainism:** Doddanayadu and parivade counterpersecuted Buddhism and Jainism, fought their upholders, and won substantial victories, thus strengthening the hold of Hinduism. During their tour of pilgrimage with Alugu, Dodda and perinadu while bathing in the Krishna near Amaravati, met a man with no caste mark on his forehead, asking for alms. Questions by them, he replied that he lived at Tsandavole where the king possessed some sparrows. Disguised as Brahmins, Dodda and Peri went to the king's court as Tsandavole. The sparrows came but were driven off. Then followed combat between them and the king's guards followed by their fight with the king's armies Dodda and peri were victorious, and Dhavalasankha's daughter was given in marriage to Alugu. "Thus the Velanandus persecuted Hindus and Brahmins and spread Buddhism by violent means. Thus the opposition to Hinduism was faced by Dodda whose son Brahma founded Viravaishnavism."

**The temples:** Many temples to Vishnu, Siva and the heroes were raised in this period and after. A temple at surizala is said to have been built by Nalagamaraja Narasimharaja. [100] Alugu built temples of Vishnu and Siva hero. At Macherla Brahmanayadu raised temples to Vidhnu and Siva one of them being the chennakesva temple, Srinatha describes chennakesva as Kanakambara, reclement on milk ocean, protector of Brahmins, in carnation due to the spear of Alaraja, wearer of the Pendara (anklet) with 101 figures on his left leg, fold of parrots, and the giver of victory to chandaragiri Ranga and Venkatadri. In the temple, the shrine of the god is to the west of minosa suma tree which a small plant when Brahma visited the place was tended by him which people say that the tree existed till 1900 AD and signs of its past existence till recently.[101] Brahma built a temple of chennaraya at Markapuram and the Rupalamamagudi, standing in a tank bed at a distance of 1 1/2 miles from Gottipodla. The Rupalamma temple is interasting and remarkable "being decidedly northern or original in style. Its character is totally different from that of numerous shrines scattered over this country. The gopura bulges out at sides and is crowned by characteristic amlasila or point shaped knot as in Orissa or Bengal."[102] At Tengeda three old temples are said to have been built by the Nayadu heroes of Palnad. [103] At Karempudi on the river bank on the west is a Vishnu temple. It was originally built by the Heroes themselves and rebuilt in AD 1547. It is fine solid and good and the garbhalaya has its walls resting on carved stones much older than those of which it is built. [104] Half a mile to the west of Sambhu temple at Ubbapalle on the opposite bank of Nagileru is the temple of Nayakuralu erected by her dedicated to self. It consists of the garbhalaya, antaralika, and mukhamandapa. The first two are surmounted by a low but well proportioned and remarkably well carved gopura. [105] These were the temples built by the Haihaya kings their ministers and heroes.

Mandadi Ravinayaka, in AD 1103 at Satrasala consecreted the images of Bijjavara, Mughdhesvara and Revesvara named after the donor with the attendant deities. [106] At Garizala is an ancient mantapa with regular arches cut in stone. In AD 1139 a Brahma from Kamanur founded the temple of Hindu trinity-

Brahma, Vishnu and Siva at Gurizala. In Macherla, on the banks of the chandravanka are three small temples dedicated to the heroes i.e. Virapurushaulu. As in AD 1315, Devarnyadu made grants to them, it is clear that the hero cult came into existence by the time of Prataparudra and also spread in to the heart of the kakatiya kingdom for in the capital warangal was a temple of heroes. Karempudi has a temple dedicated to the heroes. A record in it dated AD 1424, during the reign of Anuguraja, a merchant built a temple for vira Koti. [107] The novel tower in the middle of Karempudi was erected by Jivaraksha Timmana, son of Macherla chennudu, on the spot where chilamanagadu planted his spear. The Suresvara temple there probably means Isvara of the Surasi of the heroes. Tradition that says the temple of Heroes on Nagileru was originally a small one built in their honour. Later on a muslim resident of Karempudi an admirer of Brahmanayadu, warned by Ganesa in a dream, raised a fine temple now ruins. The Muslim and his brother after death were buried in the temple premises and two graves were raised in the vicinity of the principal hall of the temple. The temple is enclosed in a strong wall with two gate ways. To the south of the temple is a mandapa now in ruins nearer the temple is a mandapa of twleve pillars. The northern gateway of the mandapa of twleve pillars was built by Muslims. The main central portion of the temple consists of a hall supported by four pillars. It was built in 1333 AD. The shrine of Kannamada is on the eastern side of the temple. Round this shrine is a mandapa with a tower, bearing an inscription of AD1324 recording some building activities. [108] To the south of the main hall is the Pakasala i.e. cooking manadapa. In other parts of Karempudi are mandapas named after the other heroes. The Suresvara temple has a vimana, mukha or sannidhi mandapa. In Viracharitra and a record of the 19th century AD, Kersmpudi is called Uddandaviratirupati, [109] i.e. Vaishnava temple of the great heroes. Srinatha mentions it as Sriviratirupati. [110]

One of the many temple at Dachepalle, was dedicated to the heroes. At Gamalapadu was a temple of Nayakuralu. At Gundlapalem is a Sivakesva Temple. At Balamachapuram are temples of chennaraya and Mallikarjuna. The fine Vishnu temple at Melvagu consists of three parts - garbhalaya with a gopura and a mandapa. Adjoining this is the Kalyanamandapa i.e.

madhyaranga. At Chintapalle is a temple of Doddamallesvara. In Singaretla agrahara are a few figures of alwars. The Venkatesvar temple at Durgi was built in the reign of Ganapati. At Uppalapadu is a temple of Durga Mallesvara, at Gottipedla are Siddapagullu, one of which was Siddhesvaraswami temple. At Ubbepalle is a Sambhu temple. In this sannidhi mandapa has a raised platform. "The raised wall is a characteristic of northern than southern temples and found invariably in Orissa and Bengal and seldom purely in Dravidian styles."[111]

**Temple festivals:** Festivals at Karempudi were celebrated with great pomp. Towards the close of the 14th century AD the natives and the badagalavaru quarelled about participation in the temple festivals. Badaga means a no-ner, and Badagas in large numbers immigrated into Palnad and so were looked upon as foreigners by native Vaishnavas.[112] From a record, it is inferred that the Badagas were probably shepherds of Yadava race. The Kannada and Telugu shepherds of Cuddapah district are called Vedugas.[113] Prior to AD 1396, 113 the Badagalu, representing themselves as the natives of Palnad secured a bull from the acharya sanctioning the right to splash Kumkumavasanta, during festivities like others. The natives objected; the case was presented to Nallangachinda Chakravarti who made an enquiry into the case. Kallipadu is the fifth day, and offering of rice mixed with blood as ranabali by persons with no clothes on the midnight of the eighth day are conducted.[116] All this is conducted by a pithadhipati called Brahmanayanimudrakarta. It appears that when all people promise present to the heroes and fulfil their promises on recovery. During marriages and festive occasions, the symbols of heroes are worshipped in some families. [117]

During the festival of Palnad heroes, to the temples at Sannigandla, and the stone called Potarajau, some ceremonies are performed. [118] The Virapujas were celebrated in many places. Like kerempudi, Macherla was a centre for the festivities.

Alugu accompanied by Dodda and Perinedu went on pilgrimage to all sacred places. After his marriage with the princess of Tsandavole, he worshipped Kotisvara at Ellamanda.[119] At the close of the battle, Brahmanayadu, is said to have brought back to life the dead heroes by means of certain herbs and drugs and recitation of solemn incantation.s He erected temples on the east of Nagileru and appointed Brahmins priests to carry worship in them. People show to this day on the banks of the Sarpa (Nagileru) the lingas installed by the heroes. The bhutaratsthambha installed at Karempudi had eight faces - with the representations of Trimurthis on one side, siddhas on the other, sages on the third, ganga, durga, kalabhairava, verndevi and gandharvapati on the rest. [120]

Private life: Monogamy was the general rule, though Alugaraja was a exception. Nalagama before going to his court,[121] bathed in scented waters, wore clean clothes, sat on a chitrasana, put on caste mark looking into the full sized mirror, did prayer and had his food. Then he applied to his body, sandal mixed with civet, and musk were a golden coat, tied a turban, wore a necklace, ear rings, ornaments and talismen on arms, bracelets and chains on hands, rings on fingers, waist belt set with gems, gandapendara anklet and covered himself with a golden shawl. The decoration of the court was as follows ;- the floor was washed with musk water rangavallis with pearls were drawn, water mixed with camphor and greengram was splashed in the front portion, huge multi coloured canapoied with pearls in lines and cahins hanging were tied, large mirrors were kept on them, woven cloths were spread on the floor and coloured cloths on them and give coloured carpets on them.

Brahmanayadu had four brother - Peddanayadu Perinadu, Surinidi and Mallindu. His son Balchandra was born under unlucky stars, and was entrusted by Brahma to Mannamadas to be killed who instead entrusted him to Perindaud, where Bala with his six mates was brought up. For a second time, Brahma ordered Kannama to kill Balachandra, when he was brought into the court as spouse for Manchala, daughter of Gandukannamanadu. This time by god's grace, Bala escaped death. Brahma took him into his household. When he was fourteen he was married and enamoured of a vesya named Syamangi. He was chided by his parents and his friends for his spendthrift habits. On seeing his wife for the first time, Bala repented for his past conduct. He was learned and loved by his friends.

The customs of dowry, pankuva or oli prevailed. Oli is the money that the bridegroom gives to the parents of the bride. The king of Tsandavole gave Palnad five desas as dowry to his daughter Mailama, on the occasion of her marriage. He also gave multi-coloured silk canopies, jewels, cows, horses, and elephants in large numbers when giving away the bride.[122] Balachandra gave oli to his maternal uncle on the occasion of his marriage with his daughter Manchala Palnativiracharitra.[123] narrates the details of Balachandra's marraige. when Itamma asked for Manchala, her father retorted saying that unless she gave one tumful of madas, which should be of proper type. and the most valuable selected from the presents given by many kings. She brought the money, poured it as a mound asked her brother to measure and take. He is said to have built a step, stood on it, winnowed the money, measured with a big tum greater quantity than the sheduled, took the money found in the place of measuring and that which is scattered for himself and carried away in bundles. In the description the words used for light and improper coins, for separating them from better ones and the place where they are measured are- talu (grain with no corn in it), pollu (grain in which the corn is too small), turpara (i.e. sifting chaft), and kallam (place where grain is measured respectively). Thus oli was observed rigorously in this period.

Food was good and cheap for people, where as the rich had a large variety in it. Pastry or cakes, ghee, sugar, candy, sweetyams chutneys, are mentioned among articles presented to the devine pillar at Tripurantakam. Musk, camphor, saffron, Indian blettium, benzoin gumgual and sandal paste, were the articles of perfumery used in decorating the pillar. [124]

Brahmanayadu aimed at scrapping away caste distinctions by making people of all castes eat together. Vira charitra[125] attest to his discardance of caste distinctions, conversion of even low caste person into Vaishnavas, honouring them in courts, and eating with them - Sahapanktibhojanamu. He looked upon Kannama, as his eldest son. In the party given to Brahanayadu, by Madugula Brahma Reddi was partaken by Kannama, besides persons of shepherd castes. In another context Viracharitra says that Brahma sat in the midst of low caste people and ate with him. Brahma says that Madhavakula was the best among all castes. [126] The sixty six heroes were drawn from all castes and communities. In the Karempudi camp, says Srinatha all set in a line, the cooks served food, and were about to serve ghee when they were disturbed by the arrival of Madachi. This community eating of all soldiers observing no caste distinctions was to create bonds of unity among fighters to enable them to fight with greater vigour. The battle is called Kulamporu in Viracharitra. The chapakudu, had diplomacy of Nayakurala i.e. Aruvelli Nayinari and Kodiporu are mentioned as three principal causes for the war of Palnad. Some of the generals and officers on the side of Brahma were drawn from pariah and cobbler castes. Viracharitra suggests that even Brahmins became padmanayaks. For Anapotu, the Brahmin friend of Balachandra, when sent back by a trick by Bala, before committing, suicide said that he had become fool before the Velamas, joined them not for want of wealth or inferiority of caste; but had come away form his parents relatives trusting Bala's friendship's so became an enemy to his people.[127]

This Anapota's family name was Oddi and his father Mallaparaja was a writer near king Mallideva. Unable to bear separation from Balachandra, he committed suicide by cutting his head after praying to his parents, family deities - Srigirilinga and Chennakesva, and Brahmanna.

Cattle formed an essential part of home establishment. They were petted with sweet names,[128] being those of gods or great personages or reflecting on thier colour or characteristic features e.g. Nagavasayya, gogula bayyanna, perumallu, Karinandi, adinatha, Kanchivarada, Balchandra, nilavarna, jayakanthanada, Indrunivarama, Ippagirinatha, gogubhairava-murti, Govindaraja, Chenchula yobayya, chennamallayya, kanchi Ekambara, Kalikanatha madhura puripriya, Nandinatha, Kama, Soma, Kamajavara, Rama, Bhima, etc. Oxen possessing plenty of blood in their horns, those with many bulges in tail, black and white spots, those completely black, those with humps, with smooth and spotted foreheads, those all while and appearing intelligent and with yellow spots were considered auspicious. In popular Telugu songs sung by women, Sri Krishna is represented as addressing the cows one by one by their names to milk them.[129]

The homes of the rich were decorated well. The upstairs of Manchala's house had pictures, parrots repeating words, pleasure park, many gold images which could be made to play, and one room specially arranged with pictures was called chittarvumeda. The mansion of Syamangai was decorated with pictures and mirrors. [130]

Balachandra was dressed well. He wore ornaments -waist belt, anklet etc. applied sandal to his body, and wore gold cloths.

**Women**: Virambika alias Ratnala Peramma wife of Alarachamalla performed Satee. Anapota's wife also committed satee on the funeral pyre of her husband. Satee or Sahagamana seems to have been common in Palnad though evidences of its prevalence in other parts of contemporary Telugu land are not heard of. Manchala says to her mother-in-law that her son had been enjoying, chewing and eating in harlot's house, and she was destined to die with him whereas the harlot enjoys. Manchala's view was confirmed by Syamangi; when she did told Bala that only his wife was entitled to give him happiness in the other words. [131] When Peddana went away riding on a horse, by a trick of his father-in-law and brother-in-law, his wife was ready to kill herself when Peddana came and saved her.

Mothers and wives of great persons were honoured. Chirala was built after Silamba, mother of Brahmanna. Nagamma, was a dominant personality of her times. Tradition has it that Nayakurali-Kanama originated thus - while Balachandra was going to Karempudi for Viramadapai, Nayakuralu stood across with feet apart. Bala thinking it improper to fight a women, cut on one side of the hill with his sword, made a way reached Karempudi. Since then it is known as Nayakurali pass.

Women wanting children underwent the hardest penances and greatest hardships. With no son to save from the hell-punnama, [132] the riches of man and life of women were considered futile. Itamma says that there is no love equivalent to putramoha. She did several vows, performed duties and made gifts. She prepared many betael nuts with small presents (money), stole them and left, stole the oxen of oil mills, worked in Kummararamas (potter's work place), celebrated the marriages of many poor Brahmins, restored worship in deserted temples, established choultries with free provision of food was made, at every eight or ten miles, kept water house for pilgrims in big parks, presented huge copper bowls used by ascetics, and beggar's bowls to saivaite devotees going to Srigiri, gave gold and silver pumpkin fruits with presents and offering to Sai-Sailapati and Brahmaramba. She did the vratas of Gauri Mahesvara sikhari, of Elesvaram, after descent form Tilaparvata, of Vishnu Kanta, sandhyavarti, jagajyoti, of Ekabanamu (single bone) with five women as supporters, of Manmatha with ten women, she gave pulagam (dish made of rice biled with green gram), improved the rows of asvaththa (holy fog) trees on the path to Srisailam, tied round the trees threads of gold and silver, celebrated marriages of animals, did the varta in dark room, raised her hand and bowed to every limbless person that she had seen, and saluted with raised hand to Katredu.[133] i.e. the king of the cemetatry. Finally she did the bone of big lime (gajanimma), which was favoured be god vishnu. It should be performed for one year, and the performers should bathe in chandrabhugha, flowing close to the chennakesava temple, facing the north - wear silk saree with gold laced borders, wear a vermillion mark and turmeric, apply sandal paste to the bow, proceed to the chennakesava temple, worship him, give offerings and lamps go to the lime tree in the part - vaikuntha sringaravan (atteched to the temple), clean and purify it, draw rangavallis invite the presence of the garden deities, fetch water from Palakalabavi, pour it in the watered earth round the tree, do the requisite services, give all articles of food to Brahmins, should eat less food and more fruits which were ripe towards the close of the season, they should be offered to God chenna. Itamma did the vrata for a year, and on the last day, after daily worship, she sent for the wives of the Brahmins, received them, holding the plate having the fruits in both hands accompanied by her mates, music and dance and bards singing songs, she went to the temple, when she was to present the fruits to the God, he turned to the west;[134] to the astonishment of all. Itamma prayed to the god saying that everything of theirs was this, praised his deeds in the incarnations of Rama and Krishna, and with her mates unsheathed their sword and were about to kill themselves, when chenna, turned towards them. When the fruits were offered one fruit from the plate fell in Itamma's hands which she gave to the Brahmin woman to be distributed among eight of them. She did accordingly and at Itamma's request ate first. Then all bowed to the god after washing their hands and feet, the priest gave them tirtha prasada and kept padapitha over their heads and they walked backwards and came out of the temple. Then all the eight women became pregnant and Balachandra and his seven mates were born to them. The unsheathing of swords shows that women hid them in their clothes and the Brahmin woman dividing and eating the first attests the existence of caste system despite Brahmanna's efforts to scrap it.

Manchala was an ideal wife and daughter-in-law. When Itamma with her comrades visited her, her mother received them warmly. Manchala applied aguru (superior kind of sandal) mixed with musk, civet, to Itamma and those who accompanied her, presented them chekatlu, anklets, ruby studded jewels, prophasied the cause of the visit of her mother-in-law correctly, told her that they were married while children and she would accompany him to heaven if he died in the battlefields. Asked by Itamma, she promised to prevent Balachandra from going to the battle and the harlot, Itamma gave her gold lace border, gold ornaments, and gold jewels. She gave bala coins; jewels, sandal mixed with camphor, to be given to Brahmins, bards, songsters, dancers, maids, mother-in-law[135] and so forth.

The description of Manchala[139] getting ready to receive her husband, gives the names of some rare jewels. Gold flower oil to Manchala's head, sandal as atakali (a stuff used to rub on the head to clean the hair) were appplied. She was bathed in rose water. Her hair was combed put into a knot on which were tied round in lines flowers of god, tilaka with gold and pearls was kept at the parting, sun and moon on both sides of it, vermilion mark on the forehead, a mark of musk in the midst of eyebrows, nose ring set with pearls, makaritas with musk on cheeks were drawn, gold earrings set with nine kinds of gems, and pearls on ears, tarsels, bhavirelu (ornament worn from the tip of the ear), Kantendlu (large ear rings) tied a pair of pearl tassels to the hair, and sandal mixed with camphor, musk and saffron was applied to the body. She wore a silk jacket, with gold flowers on it, necklaces of pearls, gems, pendants, corals, bhannasavaralu, pearl necklace (patteda) apanlets set with nine kinds of gems on both arms, bracelets, double talismans, bangles of Sapphires, emeralds, chemelakadiyas on hands, were chekatlu, jewels, rings on all fingers. Her saree was full with gold with a treble border, a belt with small bells hanging, wore anklets and gold chains on legs, gold toe-rings. After the reception, she wore another saree having figures all over and sets of pearls int he front portion, and jewels of pearls, anklets and tassels of pearls. She looked so pretty, that Balachandra says that behaving like an animal, he lost good name in this world, and chances of happiness in the other by being away from her in the past.[137]

A true picture of dancing girls is seen from Srinatha's Syamangi alias Sabbayi and ehr mothers.[138] On reaching Syamangi's house, Bala was told that she was having a headache., but when he sent word saying that he was going necklaces of nine kinds of gems, gold bangles, pearl tassels, and received him. Her mother described as old and ugly,came at her daughter's instance to receive Oli or Unkava from Bala as Syama was to accompany him to the battle-field and heaven before Machala. Bala gave her 12000 cash together with a silk sareee. Afterwards Anapota retorted Bala for giving Oli to harlot.

Women want about in palanquins e.g. Madachi from Medapi to Karempudi, Itamma to Manchala's house went in palanquins. They were interested in witnessing games. Almost all young ladies of Macherla and his mates.

**Amusements:** King, princes etc. took pleasure in hunting. Peddanayaka and Teppalinayadu went on an hunting expedition to Narlakonda.[139] All people evinced keen interest in cock fights. During Brahma's visit to Gurizala, Nayakuralu arranged fights betweeen several pairs of cocks, and every time she called the coinner Nayakaralu, and the vanquished Brahmanayadu. Brahmanadyadu saw and blamed her for this conduct. Then a vanquished cock dubbed Brahmanayadu, revived and conquered its late conquerors, and other cocks. Nayakuralu challenged battle terms and bought away all cocks, so that none were left to Brahma to be purchased. Then received by Peddana, Brahma got the miraculous cock from Panugallu, Balagopanna alias Muvvala Gopanna, a friend of Brahma was appointed the judge. In the presence of distinguished audience including the king, courtiers and people, Brahma's cock crowed. At once all the cock of Nagamma fell down dead. Because of the spell thrown by sorcerers at the instance of Nayakuralu Brahma's cock fell down dead. Balagopanna killed all the cocks of Nayakuralu and was beheaded by Muvvala Bhima at his own desire. Brahma is said to have restored all the cocks and Balagopanna to life. [140]

Sewell says cock fighting is a recreation which the inhabitants of the peninsula are passionately found of and large sums of money change hands, amongst the spectators, large by comparison in many cases, for those most interested are often miserably poor. Still they do not hazard to stake the result what to them seems a fortune; Brahmanayadu and Nayakaralu doing with higher interests depending on the issue.[141] As the heroes indulged in cock fighting, the people of Karempudi are interested in keeping this custom. "So once a year Karempudi becomes a scene of cock fighting festival to which people throng from far, near and large sums of money change hands." On the way to Gurizala, 14 miles east-north-east in a barron piece of rocky land are two big cairns formed of a large quality of big stones. Tradition has it that these mark the place where the great cock fight between Brahma and Nayakuralu took place. [142] In the Negesvara temple at Dachepalle, is a sculpture of a man holding a fighting cock in one of his four hands. Probably it represents Brahmanyadu who as Vishnu is described to have possessed four hands.

Balachandra with his mates played many games such as pumpkins, wager of sugar cane, pokalata, pearl balls, kuntam and won all indoor games, rukala kuppalu (heaps of coins), game of keeping cruel animals in temple, releasing and witnessing their fight. He wanted to play tops. They first worshipped gold, kept on furnace huge crucible of gold. The colour remained steady though latter the gold developed into balls. [143] Viracharitra says that 42000 tops were made with 1000 madas - evidently an exaggerated number.

Bala and his mates dressed themselve in multicoloured silk clothes and wanned by mother not to play in crowded streets, bazars and near houses of scholars but to go out of Medapi and play under Mallaravi tree near Choluravi tree, riding on rams decorated with silks and gold saddles, started out. Implements of play like bags, containing fruits of a throny plant (gachchakayalu) fine poles, backgammon or dice play, the pieces or pawns used in dice play, balls, birds, cages, bares, bulbul, parrots, sarikes were taken by servants with them. Standing on multicoloured carpets under the tree, they started the play. Many women without taking the permission of their elders assembled there to witness the game. Among them were a Brahmin woman and a vaisya, who with water vessels on their heads came and stood in the play ground.[144] Anapotu drew a circle, kept a gold tankadinara in it and asked Bala to begin. Bala ordered silence which was carried on by men with sticks in hands, and humbly requesting women to witness from a distance and played a top. It touched the stone called Sanyamisa, pierced through Komati Annamma's foot and reached the ground. The women fainted, others crowded round her, put clothes in ears, applied camphor on feet, and sandal with musk on hands. She recovered consciousness and cursed Bala. Anapotu was angry and began to drive all women with a silk rope in hand and begged Annamma to forgive Balachandra. They applied medicine to the foot and tied a bondage with green silk cloth and gave 500 madas for use till recovery. Thus the play of tops was dangerous, [145] and as in modern days, the players carried medicines with them. These are references to riding on rams, e.g. Balanayadu's ram could a cross a canal while the horse of Alavachamalla could not on his mission to Gurizala.

At Karempudi, in the street near the Siva temple, there is a curious water worn hole in the rock forming the road way, which people say that it was made by the hool of Balachandra's horse. A sign on the bank of Nagileru is supposed to have been made by the horse of Balachandra. Tradition derives the name Nagileru from that a hill broke as a result of the Paleti thunder, killed the snake i.e. naga and passed through its midst and came to be known as Nagileru. Of the villages named after the Haihayas Alugurajapalle is named after the king Anuguraja. Rachemallapadu after Alarachamalla, Jenettipalem after Jhattiruaju. Mallavaram after Malladeva Perula after Perinedu, and Nayanipalle after Doddanayadu. [146] People believe that in the past Macherla was ruled by Maricha, Karempudi by Khara, and Durgi by Dushna. Srinatha praised Karempudi Pettana comparing it to Benares. He says that there the heroes were sacred lingas, Nagadu, Vishnu, Kalipotaraj Bhirava and Gangadhramaduga Manikayaka. [147] The Palakalabavi to the north east Chennekesava temple at Macherla is said to have been dug in the time of Brahmanayadu. People believe that there was another well within it which probably was covered with stone plants to avoid danger and so came to be known as Palakalabavi. In the midst of chandra banks people say, was a Talupulabavi. [118] Elders in the villages in Palnad, to this day, point out the placer of historical importance, where the feudatory chiefs intent on war ate chapakudu, the place where Nayakuralu though over her plans, where Bilasani walked over Nippula yeru i.e. fire, to clean herself, the place where the fings - step brethern of shepherd caste with earth i.e. kingdom as ager and the place where the seven heroes fell down in the battle.[149]

### The Chagis

The Chagis maintained varnasramadharma. Chagi Pota styled himself Narasimhavardhana and was devoted to Yogananda Narisimha. Dora was devoted to Yagananda Nrisimha. Potta II bore the epithets Narasimhavardhana Sriyogananda nrisimha devaradivyasripadapadmaradhka, Mallahamatya was devoted to Vasudeva.

An epithet of Pota is Sivabhaktaparayana. The son of Dora was devotee of Amaresvara of Amaravati. Saivism was encouraged by the kings.

**Temples:** Yogananda Nrisimha is the famous god in Vedadri hill not far off from chintapalle. It was the Tutelary god of the chagis-Potta II set up golden pinnacles on the temples of Rajanaryana Mallesvara and chodanarayana at Bezvsada, the temples of Tripurantaka, Kasmira Mallesvara, Visvanatha, and consecreted the image of god Nandikesvara before

Mallikarjuna at Srisailam. He built the Mukkisvara temple at Muktyala and presented a gem studded crown to the god. He made a grant to the Narendrasvara temple at Kona Kanchi probably one of 108 temples built by chalukya Narendra Mrigaraja Vijayaditya II. He installed Siva at Gudimalla Manmaganapati granted a village on the Krishna to Vedari Nrisimha, and to the temple of Chagi Manmaganapesvara built by Somyaji Bhaskara. Manmachogi built a siva temple at Anumachipalle. [150] and made a grant to Bhimesvara at Manaledapalle. Dora installed Ellesvara to Punaganchiprolu. The Visvesvara temple at Gudimetta was built by pota I and rebuilt or improved by Manmapota. [151]

Mallinayka of Vipparala family [152] built the Sankara temple at Rampicherla in Dora's reign, dug a tank and provided for worship. Pedamallinayaka grand father of Mallinayaka built the Mallikarjuna temple of Konakanchi. At Kotappakonda was the temple of Trikotisvara Mahadeva. In AD 1477 Sagi Gannama built the temple of Lakshmi Nrismha at Vinykonda,[153] installed the pinnacle and built a Maamantapa alias Bhogamantapa in front of it. In the same yar he built the local Raghunatha swami temple.[154] He built many other temples, laid out parks and gardens, built tanks and celebrated the marriage of Brahmins.

**The Konlapadumatis**

Hindusim was predominant though Buddhism had influence over the king's court and the country for a while. The Kondapadumatis favoured Saivism and Virasaivism. One of the epithets in their prasasti is Virmahesvara. Pronbably they were Buddhists till Pandita's time and became his followers later on. This gains support from the fact that they did not make any grants to Vishnu temples in this period. They raised temples to Siva. According to the Kaifiyat of Tsandavole. [155] M. Pandita stayed in the mukhamandapa of the Pandisvara temple and vanquished the Buddhist guru of king Buddha for religious controversy. When the nakshatra harati essential for Pandita's worship of Siva, was stolen by the Buddhists, it was replaced by his pupils Pandita after bath sandhya and amushtana, according to the method prescribed in the sastras, performed puja sat in front of flingodhbhava, with all devotion pulled out his eyes and kept them in the presence of the god and got back his sight. By royal order, poison was put in his eyes and pandita cursing Tsandavole, presented the four eyes pulled out in the king's presence to Lingodhbhava left for Gokarnavarma in the south and got his sight in the presence of Gokarnesvara.[156]

The name Buddharaja borne by some of the kings was probably due to Buddhistic influence. The preceptor of king Buddha was a Buddhist from Buddhism, He was jealous of M. Pandita. In the controversy with Pandita, the Jains and the chervakas were also defeated which attests to the prevalence of these sects in the kingdom. Before leaving Tsandavole, Pandita cursed that Buddhism shall never prosper in Tsandavole.[157] About this time Buddhism prevailed in Andhradesa, especially about Guantur and Tsandavole. Amaravati and Tsandavole were centres of Buddhism from ancient times. Buddhavada formerly the home of Buddhists was in the neighbourhood of Tsandavole.

**Temples:** Several temples were built in this period. Manmamanda built a temple of Siva at Nadenadla and provided for offerings to Sakalesvara consecreted on the hill on the south west of Nadendla-Somanapreggada built the Somesvara temple with a mandapa at Itlapadu. At Lingamgunta and Itlapadu, his son Mandena built two temples of Siva. At Vaddavalle, kondapanayadu consecreted the image of Mallikarjuna. At Palagugu, Proli Reddi constructed the temples of Bhimesvara.

King Manda in AD 1171 made grants to Pandisvara at Tsandavole and Goddess Karnamoti (i.e. chamuda). King choda presented ornaments, a bell, a trumpet, and a couch to Mulestham Mahadeva at Nadendla. A subordinate of Manda, in AD 1118 made grants to Kumaraswami at Chebrole and king Mallaraja under gifts to Kesava at Nadendla. Tradition has it that when Pandita presented four eyes to Lingadhava at Tsandavole, the god wore the three years on his three eyes, and the fourth on one foot to make a pair with the eyes on the other foot presented to him already by Vishnu.

King Buddha was high minded a Jayanta to the eyes of woman and found of musk (Kasturikamoda).[158] At Nadendla he provided for a feeding house for Brahmins. Some queens and women distinguishes themselved by large donations. Gadiyamadevi presented ornaments made of couch shell silken parasol, chauris and flags to the goddess at Nadendla.

**The Kotas**

The Kota epithets - dvijagaurudevatatparya tatparulu, and Brahma Kshetriya Vaisyasudradiakhilavarnasrayadharma partipalitulu, meaning devotees of Brahmins and preceptors, and the maintaners of Dharma of the four castes, how that they maintained varnasramadhrama the mention of adi after sudra in the title suggests the existence of lessor castes also. The Kotas favoured Saivism. Their family god was Amaresvara of Amaravati. An epithet in the kota prasasti is Amaresvaradwadivyasripadapadmaradhaka Bhima I was a worshipper of Siva and Kota was devoted to Tripurantaka and Amaresvara, Ganapama was devoted to Siva. The age saw the revival of Saivism and Brahminism. Vaishnavism also prevailed. Beta, Dodlakota, Vellebha and Ganapathi were devotees of Vishnu.

Amaravati, the great Buddhistic centre was within the limits of Kota kingdom and worship of Buddhadeva was maintained. Keta II and his two queens, Bayyala queen of Manmageta, made grants to Buddha at Amaravati. [159] The god is referred to as the preceptor of all men, lord Sugata and who is pleased to reside at Sridhanyaghati (i.e. Amaravati). In this period, we see the last traces of Jainism. The Jains and Buddhists are often confused in local records. The Kotas was wrongly mentioned as the Jain kinglets of Dharanikota. Kakatiya Ganapati is believed to have presecuted jains throughout his dominions from Divi to Nellore and crushed them in oil mills. [160] The worship over Amaravati was obviously reponsible for the Kotas being called Jain Kinglets indicating the substantial favour shown to the Jains. According to legends Amaravati was the scene of a grand dispute between the Jains and the Brahmins, in which their Brahmins overcame the Jains by magic and the Jains were ruthlessly destroyed and crushed in oil mills Hindus. Many relics of Jainism are found in the vicinity of Amaravati.

**Temples:** At Velpur Kota II built a temple of Ramesvara. The mandapa built by him of Kollur and other mandapas of the Ramesvara temple were renovated in 1665 AD by Sabnavis Timmaji Pandits. King Beta founded the tmeple of Vasudeva Gopinatha at Yenamadala in AD 1250. In AD 1260 he installed Krishna. His wife queen Ganapana built a temple with a prakara to Betesvaralinga, after her husband at Dhanyakotaka, kept golden pinnacles on its top and gave Bonadevi for its maintenance. [161] She consecreted Ganapesvara temple, granted Chintalapad for its maintencance. She placed golden pinnacles on the top of the Amaresvara temple at Amaravati. Queen Pandambika at Tadikonda raised a Siva tmeple for her husband's merit. Prolinayaka built the temples of Ramesvara, Ganesa and Kumaraswami. At Pedaganagam, [162] Padasappa repaired the dilapidated temple, and reinstalled the god as Pinnisvara after his father Pinasappa in AD 1270. Now Pinnisvara is called Visvesvara. In AD 1081 at Vengipuram a temple was built for the merit of king Gandharaja. The temple of Kotesvara mahadeva was built by Mahadevi Setti at Uvvamdona. At Betapuram, Uddanda Prolinayaka built temples of Ramesvara, Ganesvara and Kuramraswami at Pulipadu. His brother Dasinayaka built shrines of Kesavadeva and Kuppavinayaka. Vellabhapreggada founded the temple, of Anantagopinatha at Rampicherla. At Yenanddala. Prola, son of Keta, constructed Gopala temple.

At Tadikonda is a temple said to have been built by the Buddhists of Jains and contains Jain and Buddhist figures. [163] A small edifice near the Krishna Midway between Dharanikota and Amaravati looks like a jain temple. At chejerla is the Kapotisvara temple, built in memory of Sibi, who at that spot is believed to have savrificed his flesh to redeem the life of a hunted pigeon by hawk. [164] The place is believed to contain 1000,001 lingas at one time. Records of the period mention chejerla Kapotisvara shining in the midst of 4444 lingams. The Amaresvara temple at Amaravati is probably a thousand years old. Inscriptions show that Amaravati was one of the Pacharamas and Panchatirthas, and Pancharamatirthas in Andhradesa. The temple is built on a huge building, covered fully on four sides and the top perhaps it was originally a jain basti, and the saivas occupying it built the temple on it. Thus the under most floor of the temple is closed completely and some historians opine that the Amaresvara linga was originally a Jain or

Buddhistic image, converted into a linga later or by the Brahmins. This is confirmed by several Jain images in the vicinity of the temple of the temple and the resemblance of the temple in some aspects to a Buddhist stupa. As the linga is very high, one must climb a few steps to do abhisheka to the god. The lofty chaitya of god Buddha close to the Amare:: ·· temple, constructed about the beginning of the christian era was in excellent condition in this period. Its remains are in Madras Museum and British Museum and it was finally destroyed by a local raja in the 18th century AD.

**Festivals:** Amaresvara at Amaravati is said to have been worshipped by lord Indra. Ganapama provided for a marriage festival to the god. At Pedda Cherukuru, in AD 1219 Keta provided for the Kama bhoga of Mamara Bhimesvara. At Yenamadala, the merchants provided for angeranagabhoga of Gannisvara mahalingam i.e. Gomesvara mahadeva. At Manumaka was a temple of Amaresvara. Keta II provided for lamps to Buddha at Kranteru and granted Kranteru, Medikanduru and Donki Karum Lord Buddha. Bayyale provided for worship of Buddha at Amaravati. Gasavi Surama and Prolama made gifts to the same god.

**Private life:** Keta II had five queens and seven bhogastris. Some of the rulers were religious minded. Ganapama by her grants procured for her husband Beta, the festival of everlasting and joyful residence in the world of Siva. Kota Ganapati patronised the pontiffs of Golaki math of Tripurantakam e.g. Rajagurudeva.

**Women:** Queen Ganapama was an embodiment of purity, and equalled Gari and Lakshmi by her virtus. Many of the queens and bhogastris made gifts to Amaresvara at Amaravati. It has been suggested.[165] that Surama and Sabbama donors to Buddhadeva at Amaravati "may have been Buddhist upasikas and induced him (Keta II) to join them in making donations to their own god."

**The Parichchedis**

Viramahesvara was an epithet in the prasasti of the Parichchedis. The rulers favoured Virasaivism, the religion of their overlords, the Chalukyas of Kalyani. Many temples were built and grants were made to them. Pandraja built a temple for Agastyasvara with a mandapa subsidiary shrines, prakara gopura, at Guntur in AD 1158.[166] In AD 1222 at Prattipadu, Kusumaraja founded the temple of Gandesvara mahadeva. In AD 1240 in Bhima's region, the temple of Gopaladeva at Pottur was founded by Surama setti.

Chikkabhima made grants to Mulasthama Somanathadeva at Ellore Ganda, son of Panda made gifts to the temple of Brahmadeva at Peraveli. The rulers were devotees of god Srivallabha of Srikakulam,[167] to whom they made many grants.

**The Netavadis**

The Netavadis built temples of Siva Mailalamahadevi in AD 1219 constructed the temple of Melambikesvara after herself, near the Tripurantakesvara temple at Tripurantakam.[168] Queen Muppambika installed god Muppesvara, at Tripurantakam.[169] and her husband Dugga provided for worship. Muppama was virtuous and Ketabharani is compared with Rambha, Rati and Tilottama.

**The Malayas**

The Brahmin Predominance in the kingdom is seen from records. The titles borne by Brahmins in the c.p. grant and Natakki inscription show that they were special devotees of (an image of Hanuman given to them by Rama himself and established in the agrahara of Mashapuri. Vengipura Brahmaghoshanasraya.[170] probably meaning the loud recitation of the Vedas by the Brahmins, borne by the early malaya kings, attested their patronage of Brahmins.

In AD 1235 the Somesvara temple at Tilatirtha in Suryanarayanapuram was built. At Rajahmundry in AD 1178, king Surapa provided for special works in the Virabhadresvara temple and plates to the god. In AD 1237 Mahadeva made grants to Ishtakamisvara at Pattisam and in AD 1248, Ganapati installed Mahadevesvara at Gajjaram.[171] In AD 1240 Lokami devi, wife of Ganapati provided for mantrabhoga-service of sacred incarnations of Velpura Ishtakamesvaradeva. [172] This service is not mentioned in other records of the period.

### The Kandravadis

The rulers made many grants to temples. In AD 1140 Muppama made grants to Mallesvara at Bezwada. In AD 1207 Kesava gave lamps to Muktisvara Mahadeva at Muktyala in AD 1215 to Mulasthan Mallikarjunadeva at Anignadlapadu. At Atmakur in AD 1238, Palakolanikotinayaka founded the temple of Lakshmi nrisimhadeva. [173] in the name of his father Kakati Lakshmanna.

### The Saronathas

Katamanayaka in AD 1135 set up a Nandi pillar on front of the temple of Mahadeva at Yetikaru (i.e. Elurpadu). Somaya Kumara built a temple to Duttika Sriramesvara mahadeva and white washed it. [174]

Okkattuganda provided by giving gold in charge of sani 300 for a lamp in the temple of Vasuki Ravi Somesvara at Duttika. Padachchodi nayaka gave a camphor lamp stand, weighing 300 palams of metal to Bhimesvara. Two records at Palakol dated AD 1212 and 1269, record gifts of Prola and Bhima for sandhyadipa - twilight lamps to kolami Somesvara and Kolami Prasannadevara. [175] The former gift was intended to express the donor's satisfaction in the happiness of this world and thinking of his parents and mother-in-law. In AD 1195, Kolami Somaya made grants to Swarnesvaradeva at Padminipura.[176]

### The Second Kolamu Dynasty

The Induluri chiefs were Virasaivas. Induluri Anna was regarded as an incarnation of sage. The details of his birth were as follow :- when Pedaganna and Gaurama were desiring sons, a sage came to their house, was duly honoured and told Gaurama that he was a king for twenty years, became an ascetic, would go to Manthana and Kalesvara, die there be reborn to her. [177] He told her some signs for identification after rebirth. Thus he was reborn for a set purpose and was considered an incarnation of Visvesvara Sivadesika. His descendant Adimula was a pupil of Pattisapu Virabhodra. His son Adiganapati was a pupil of Nukanaradhya. Nagayaganna, of the family of the Kritapati of Sivayoga sarsa was a follower of Saivaite customs. His son Nakuraya was a follower of Pasupata virta. [178] His son Nukayya was a follower of Yajurvedaguru (Sri guru). A devotee of Siva and a Philosopher, he wondered about the places of pilgrimage like Benares. He was well known as Chennasadasivayogi.

**The Chalukyas of Pithapur**

These Chalukyas had learnings towards Vaishnavism. In AD 1123 Udayachandradeva Chakravarti made grants to Rajanarayanadeva at Bhima varam and provided for sani and mani unbandhas. In AD 1177 chalukyanarendra and Mallapadeva provided for offerings to Rajanarayandeva Mallapa in AD 1202 made a grant to a local temple at Kenmur.

Kuntimadhava is described as the imperishable lord and the glorifier of the heart of Kunti. Coronation ceremonies of the rulers took place in the presence of the god, e.g. Mallapa III. In AD 1257, Rajamaraju, Eralaksharaja, Vengisvara and Pinalakshmaraja granted an arecanut garden to the temple of asanti Ramisvara at Achanta. [179] Presented to his father by the king on the occasion of his marriage with Mailaradevi Chandaladevi queen of Mallapa III is described as charming, clever, accomplished, auspicious, noble, faithful, inteligent, virtuous and lucky. [180] Tenuku according to popular belief, in the days of Nannaya, was called Tarakapua where Tarakasura is said to have ruled. And Velpur in its vicinity is believed to have been the place where heavenly beings made a halt and that Devadanavapumta is the marga - way through which devas (gods) and danavas (demon) walked through. [181]

**The Chalukyas of Elamanchili**

The Chalukyas of Elamanchili favoured Saivism. King Manumopendra was unequalled in Siva doctrine. The Panchadharla pillar inscription says that "the fire which in the worship of Siva performed by upendra, assuemd the form of many lamps and which was satisfied by plenty of good vessels with good oil, cared but little for the sacrificial offerings of priests. From the fact that the five nectarian substances dropped on the hoods (of sesha) from Siva's head, be sprinkled by him (Upendra), it is concluded that the serpent Sesha became pure through he has two tongues (and) carries poision in his mouth. Already in this life Bhava (siva) gave to king Upendra the state of being rajasekhara, sarvajna and Sankara. Uppendra who was the receptable of the condition of assimilation to deity. The famous king Uppendra got, by feasts, in which there were a hundred of sivadikshas union with sambhu (siva) very difficult to get even by nob hundred of vedic sacrifices".[182] His son Visvesvara was a follower of sivatantra

Some of their rulers made grants to Nrisimha at Simhachalam and bore the name Nrishimha chakravarti. The Panchdharla pillar inscription ends with salutation to Hari, Hara and Hranyagarbha. [183] The rulers built temples and made grants to them and others. Dharmalingeswara of Panchodharla was the tutelary deity of the kingdom. The town-nangara - sarvasiddhi (Elamanchili taluq), was built by Juyasimhavallabha I (633-666 AD) after his title - sarvasiddhi i.e. satisfaction of all his desires. [184] It later on was a provincial capital. Visvesvara built a large mandapa with four halls for the annual Kalyana mahotsva of Dharmesvara with Parvati. The Mandapa was magnificent and grand as though built by lord of Himavat and praised by Kubera. Visvesvara installed the image of Vishnu with a shrine in Upendravara agrahara, laid out by him as a pleasure ground for gods. [185] In AD 1428 Nrisimha built a mandapa to Dharmesa at the western gate of temple. His preyasi (love) Viramba gave kitchen (mahamasagriham) to the god. [186] In AD 1432 Kumara Errama built antaralamandapa to Dharmesvara.

King Upendra, devoted to the feet of Mahasena donated a garland to sri Simhachalesvara. In AD 1377 Visvesvara granted a tirumala and one potful of tirumanjanam daily for nights. In AD 1401 he presented twently sasukanotankas to Sribhendura for the iron pillar - garaddarohanakambham for the festivals of Simhadrinatha. [187] In AD 1390 Elamanchili chola gangu provided for six garlands for decoration and Singayyangaru to hold tiruvalikakola to Nrishimhanatha at Simhachalam. In AD 1422 Nrisimha presented a lamp and a five faced covering (panchaktrakohali) in gold to Dharmalingesvara at Panchadharala. In AD 1437 provision was made for angarangabhoga and amritamani upakarmadravyamulu on rice to Nrisimha by king Nrisimha [188] and his concubines. Ambikadevi provided for a garland during night offerings to Simhachalesvara. The daughter of Kumara Errama provided for lamp before Gundesvarlingamu at Peddapuram. In AD 1494 Singaraja mahapatra provided for a bhoga to Uma mahesvara i.e. Dharmalinga.

**Private life:** According to Peddana, visvesvara was handsome, some of the queens and concumbines made grants to Dharmalinga at Panchaharla, Garlands, Sirisha flowers lodharajamu, sandal past, kasmira rasa, aguru, and majishtapa were used by women in decorating themselves.

**The Chalukyas of Srikurmam**

Those rulers were devotees of Srikurma at Srickurmam. The temple Srikurmam was a very important one dedicated to Kurmavatara of Vishnu and the image is in the shape of a tortoise. In records the god is referred to as the great lord of Kurma, Mura's enemy Vishnu who has the form of a tortoise lord of Kurmapuri and lord Nrihari who is pleased to reside at Srikurmam [189] generally the records in the temple end with the invocation i.e. Srivaishnavaraksha i.e. the charity is placed under the protection of all the vaishnavas.

Vijayaditya and Purushottama in AD 1273 and 1277 made grants to the god at Srikurmam. Sometime prior to AD 1305, Visvanatha built a dharamandapa (abhisheka), in the temple and in that year made a grant to Narasimha for its repairs every year. Four years hence he provided for the sringarabhoga called visvanatha bhoga, after the donor of Kurmesavara by granting forty nishtas and a gold necklace.[190]

**The Chalukyas of Nidadavole**

Vengi Mahadeva was a devotee of Srimallesvara of Bezvada. A title in the prasasti of Vengi Goka is Sri manmallevsvaradevadivya - Sripadapadmaradhaka. [191] His titles-bhayalobhasamkarana, and satya harishchandra speak for his good conduct. Bhimavaram, the abode of god Bhimoovara was formerly known as Kumararama, Skanda Rama

Chalukyabhimesvarapura, chalukya Bhimanagiri and chalukya bhimapura. Mallapa's Pithapur pillar inscription [192] refers to the founding of the Bhimesvara-temple by chlukya Bhima I. Because of the rich presents made by Bhima I, it came to be called chalukya Bhimesvara and was already existing by his time. The Vengi chalukyas of Nidedavole made grants to this temple. Narayana, minister of Manmagonka, built a temple of Siva called Narayanesa at Telikicheruvu i.e. Telikicherla with a gopura, madapa, kept golden shed and decorated the temple and granted land to kesava preddingaru, the prasasti acharya, of Narayanesvaramahadeva. [193] At Dendulur, manteri, Vengisvara built a prasada (temple) with a mandapa and installed vengisvaralinga in it and also a nandi mandapa to the west of Dendalur. Appasani, wife of Anantapreggada and brother of Vengisvara provided for daily worship to samasta bhuvandhisvara Denduluri Vengisvara mahadeva. God Vengisvara was named after minister Vengisvara. Building sites for sani and mani nibandhakara, sribalidevara pratima with viru prabha gold girdle, 2 plates, addena kilapukora, Chettugam, chimpa manta, white couches, dhupaghanta, jaughanta, dhupapatra, dipa patra, four pairs of bell metal ambols another pair of cymbols, big couches, Kondlakaru, and a mandi of bell metal [194] were all presented to the God. In 1208 Mahadeva presented lamp to Harunisvara temple at Tadikalapudi and Vishnuvardhana Srivallabha to Agastyaesvara there. King Goka provided for a lamp before Svarnishvaradeva at Pasdmihipura. [195] Indusekhara granted a[196] kuncham set with sapphires to Bhimesvara at Draksharama. His servant prolinayaka [197] provided for offerings during the three sandhyas and oil for lamps in the morning and evening to Somanatha and Vighnesvara at Kolamupaka.

Women distinguished themselves by making rich donations to temples. In AD 1266 Chalukya Udayamba gave a lamp to Kshiraramisvara. Pina Odayambadevi daughter of Vengi Mahadeva provided for the maintenance of a thousand lamps for dipavali mahotsava and Sivaratri festival for 1000 Brahmins, tempattas of land rice for offerings, three curries curds and arecanuts to Ramesvara at Palakol.[198]

**Other Chalukyas:** Somana Manadinatha Annadevaraja in AD 1133, provided for celebrations of annula festival of goddess Durgabhavani at Ramatirtham. [199] Ballahachakravarti. presented a bell and bhadram to Koppanatha at Palivela. His queens Kamaplarani and Somaladevi made grants to Bhujangamesa i.e. Nagesvara at Kadalupalli i.e. Pedda Kallepalle.[200] At Burugugadda, Ammajiyya Ganapaddeva granted chennagópinatha a upahara plate, adyana, kaduka and provided for lamps and offerings.[201] Vishnuvarshana chakravarti and Rudradeva in AD 1299 provided for worship of Agastyasvara at Pasavamula. In AD 1145 Prolisetti of Penugonda made a grant to Virabhadresvara at Pattisam. At Ramathirtham in the reign of Mummadi Bhima the Jain teacher Trikalayog Siddhanathadeva of Desigama and teacher of Vimaladitya is said to have constructed Rama konda. [202] At Kammarapudi, Chalukyamarayana Velampati Triumalarajadeva maharaja performed service to Vedadri Srinarasimhadeva.

### The Telugu Pallavas of Guntur

These Pallavas maintained Varnasramadharma as an epithet in their prasasti is patdevagurudvya bhaktulu i.e. devotees of lord, god, preceptor and Brahmins. The rulers and their ministers and subordinates made many grants to temples of Siva and Buddha all over the kingdom. Somana preggada built many temples at Guntur and lighted perpetual lamps in the temples at Draksharama etc. Pancharama tirthas. His records dated AD 1147 at Yenanmadala and Bapatla show that he provided for perpetual lamps in the temples of Mahadeva at Bhimavaram, Dakareni, Valkolanu, Drachyaramapuri, Srimadanaradalu - the Panchalramas in Andhradharani and Buddhadevasra in then, Mahasena at Chebrole Hunkarasankari at Bidapuram, and Srinathesvara at Bezvada and to gods at Cudipudi, Virabhadreswaram, Bhavapattana, Ghantasala, Cotaram, Elesvaram, vegisvaram, undaville, Velpur, Guntur and kadalpalle. [203] In AD 1159 he made a grant to Virabhadresvara mahadeva at Pattisam. Of the places, chebrole is also mentioned as Tamrapura, Bidapura as Bijapura Bezvada as Vijayavataka; Bhimavaram is chalukya is Bhimavaram, Dakaremi is Peddadakaremi, Velkolanu is palakol i.e. Kshirarama borne of god Ramisvara, Drachyaramapuri is Draksharama and Amaradalu i.e. Amararama i.e. Amaravati. Somana donated the lamps for Mahadeva and Buddhadeva in each of the

Pancharama tirthas, enumerated in the records at the rate of two gods in each place. Thus in the 12th century AD in Andhra desa, the pancharamatirthas were celebrated centres of Saivism and Buddhism, and Siva and Buddha were worshipped side by side either in the same shrine or different shrines in the same temple or in separate temples of which there is no evidence. And not only few Buddhists but nultitudes of Hindus adoring siva at Panchatirthas paidtheir adorations to Buddhadeva as well in the Pancharamas. Probably tirtha in the Hindu terminilogy is name as aramas ie. perhaps vihara in the termonology of the buddhists. And both are combined in the name pancharama tirthas. Thus Buddhism and Jainism lost their rivalry and Buddhism was taken into fold of Hinduism.

Tammubhima built chaultires and water houses. About AD 1138, Bejvada was'known as Dakshina varanasi, Sivayogi Mallaya, a devotte of Mallesvara lived on Indrakiladri, and provided for worship to the god. [204] Another Sivayogi Madayadeva who was doing penance on Indrakilaparvata without taking food in AD 1232 celebrated the marriage of the god and goddess at Bezvada. [205]

**The Pallavas of Nellore**

The Pallavas of Nellore wre Saivaitas, though they did not persecute Vaishnavism. Their prasasti has the titles - paramesvara, Paramavamsodhbhava, lalitardhachandradhara, Kamakotyambikada, Khotnangudhvaja and Vrishabhadanchana, indicating their devotion to siva and goddess Kamakotyambika of Kanchi. Some rulers had Vaishnavite leanings too. King Abhideva Malideva is described as the abode of the grace of Kamakotyambika and Varadaraja of Kanchi. [206] Some rulers were devotees of Vankatanatha of Tirupati.

The temples: In raising temples, these Pallavas imitated the imperial Pallavas. In AD 1102 Yammaraja built two temples. At Somavarapadu in AD 1238 built a temple at Viddara Kambarapuram and installed Mallikarjuna in it. At Nagalavaram, Inumadedeva set up chennakesava and performed the ceremony of infusing life into it. At Gandavaram, allutikka made a grant to Udayakalavatisvaradeva and constructed a mandapa in the name of his mother Kattadi Prolamma. [207] In the 7th year of Vijayagandagopala, to the temple was given an image of goddess Tirukkamakottam. At Padi, a dancing girl of the temple of Tiruvegambam Udaiya nayanar at Kanchi consecreted the image of the goddess Tiruvidinachchiyar in the temple. At Kolattur Irulapperumal alias Rajaraja Vilupparaiyan constructed a shrine to the Goddess. In the 5th year of Vijayagandagopala, Sivakkolandudaiyanayanar was built.

**Temple festivals and grants**: Generally in Andhradesa of this period, religious charities were in the form of provision lamp in the presence of the god or elsewhere in temples and worship. But a change came over under the Pallava aegis. For institution of services and offerings of holy food to deities were made. The rulers and their subordinates besides making huge grants, provided for the conduct of special services. To Chennkesava alias Lakshminaryana at Nagalavaram Inumadideva appointed Perumadinambi, a devotee of Tiruvengadanatha to perform worship and provide for amritapadi, decorations kariyamodu (food with vegetables), and two flower gardens. [208] For rice to be distributed among travellers of different countires, for sandal to god, a big plate for keeping the light was given by Namana Appana. A gong was presented by Mallika kamana, a bell used at the time of incence, single couches, for abhishaka with milk and thirteen cows were given by the royal family, Rajendra chola Mummadi Vaidumba Maharaja provided for a lamp in the Ennayira paraiyurputteri and for the celebration of a festival during, tiruvadirai in the month of Margali to nayanar at Suralun.[209] (Sulurpet). Tanikkuttukandal, consort of Tammadidevan provided for a leamp in the Rirunagisvara temple at Suralur and for timmargali festival. In the 24th year of vijayagandagopala a grant was made to Tirunagesvara to carry the god in procession on the new moon day. the place is mentioned as Singalatapuram alias Suralur. [210] To the temple of Alaganathaperuam at Parlapalle some grants were made.

These Pallavas made many grants to Venkatanatha of Tirupati. Princes Devarasiyar, queen of Vijayagandagopal granted three cows for three lamps in the temple of

Tiruvenkatamudaiyan. eleven measures of rise, ghee, sandal and other articles for offering during the vaikasi festival of Srigovindaperumal at Tiumala, from the second day of the festival of Tirumoloppad.[211] The Kaikkalur (temple servants) granted sixteen vatti of rice for the daily service and four vatti during chittirai festival at Tirumala. Amaraka provided for a camphor lamp and nandavilakku during the festival on Puruttasi this year and two madas for supply of camphor from forest and for three lamps of ghee provision was made for offerings to the god during the morning sandhi and force tirunandavilakku. the saliyas of Vikramadevipuram provided for one timpponakam for the festival of Tiruvenkatamudlyan, when the deity is seated in the mandapam, grants were made for a halt of the deity during chitrai and puruttasi festivals rice for tiruppavippadi, during the festival oil for lamps and other articles, sandal plastc and expenses.[212] In the fifth year of Vijayagandagopala, Purattasi, daughter of .....Talliraichchar constructed tiruppu mandapam (pushyamandapa) at Timmala. Apapadix was to be offered to the god on certain occasions[213] and provision was made for certain food services during the festival of Govindaraja on Tirumala. At padi, a temple woman from Conjeevaram presented many jewels and vassels i.e. a gold fillet (paltam) weighing 3/4 Kalanju, one crescent (Kiruvilampirai) weighing 1 Kalanu, 1 Tirumangai weighing 1 Kalanju a pearl neck lace containing eight superior pearls, 528 second class pearls two gold beads. Thirteen long corals, forty round corals, altogether weighing 10 1/2. Kalanju a dish a plate for washing lights, a cup.[214] and so forth.

The temple of Tirumalasai Emberuman (Jagannatha) at Panchanadvanchaturvedimangalam, was also known as Panchanadivana vinnagar and "it is not unlikely that the Vaishnavaite settlement and the temple of Tirumali sai came into existene by the time of Nilaganga raiyur i.e. the latter half of the 13th century AD and were vastly improved by him."[215] A mandapa in this temple was set apart for the worship of Tirumalisa alvar, a Vaishnava saint, for Tirumalisai is popularly known as his birth place. Nilagangaraiyar, in vijayagandagopala's reign made gifts to this temple. At avilala was the temple of Kavaligovara mudaiyanaganar and a record refers to

Sivalingachalana i.e. probably the loosening of the linga in the sanction. Another record refers the temple of Tirukkalatti mudadyananar and the mankapa of Tirukkannappadevar at Tirukkavanam, perhaps at Kalahasti. In the temple of Tiruppalaivana mudaiyanayanar at Tiruppalaivanam, panguni and Uttiram festivals were celebrate. Alappirandan Sambuvaraya made arrangements for the revival of the festival in the month of tigasi to Brahmapurisvara at Perunagar,[216] which was instituted by Vijayagandagopala and discontinued subsequently. The Brahmins of Punganur in the 13th year of Vijayagandandagopala. [217] granted 300 kali of land in Alagiya pallava C.M. to the temple of Tiruvuragattu ninrarulina paramasvamin in Kanchaipura for expansion Sankramana day. Virasolanallur in Rajadhiraja valanadu was granted to the temple of Svetaranyesvaru at Tiruvenkadu for the service - Adaiyavalayandan Sandi. [218] A grant was made to Sokkaperumal in the temple of Rajendrasola vinnagar Emberuman at Uttaramerur alias Gandagopala cheburvedimangalam. Pallava Nallasidharasa provided for the contact of the service - Rahuttarayan sandi, called after the donor at little Conjeevaram.[219] At Mẹlur provison was made for the worship and offerings to god Tiruppalaivana mudaiya nayana and for offerings to Tirukkamakkotta madiya Tiruvudainanchchiyar in the temple of Tirumanga Araiyanayanar Grants were made to the temple of Karavisvara at Lepaka. To the temple of Tirumanikkemgaiudaiyanayanar at Kalahasti. Toyasamudrapattai Nallasiddharasa made grants. This temple is probably the same as Mani Kanthesvara, which along with the shrine of Kasivisvesvara, lies adjacent to the sourthern side of the big temple - Kalahastisvara. The Kalahastisvara temple extends to the west of the Kannappa hill and contains the vayulinga. On the Kannappa hill is a temple of Brahma. [220] Kalahasti i.e. Tirukalatti or Srikalahasti is picturesquely located between two steep hills the northern having the temple of Durgamba and the southern that of Kannappesvara.

Grants were made to the temple of Alagiyaperumal at Kaveripakkam. M.P.C. made over the proceed of same taxes to the Masilamanisvara temple for celebrating the festival. Vijayagandagopalasandi at Tirumallaivayil. [221] Vijayagandagopala made grants to the temple of Tirukkavapura mudaiyanayanar at Tirupparkadal and that of Nirvannaperumal at Tiruniranch. Provision was made for the conduct of early morning sandi and the service in the Vallesvara temple at Tiruppachchur. At Big Conjeevaram provision was made for lamps Instituted by Kannudaipperumal Sambuvarayar, Nachchandeviyar, wife of chalamartignada Nallasiddharasar, in the temple of Turkay disvaram Udaiyanayanar and for offerings to the deity in the temple of Kandavinnagar Emberuman at Kunnattur.[222] At Atti, to the temple of Edirilisolavinnagar Emeruman provision for repairs were made by Rajaraja Sambuvaraya at Periyanallur. To the temple of Ponmalai Udaiyanayanar at Pulipakkam, grants were made and provision for a twilight lamp before the image of Durga set up in the temple.[223] In the 18th year of Vijayagandagopala Alappirandan Samburaraya made grants to the shrine of Vannaikudiya rulina pillai (Krishna) founded by Amaiyanchchi alias Palarril venran in the temple of Edirili Solavinnagar emberuman. At Annakkavur, provision was made for four twilight lamps during his time of worship for fifteen days to god Hanumiruramudaiyanayanar.[224] At Big Conjeevaram provision was made for offerings to God Tirukachchalai Udaiyanayanar and for a watershore. At Tirukachachaiyur[225] was the temple of Visvesvara and Senban Kudaiyan Saran Avaiyandi of Tirukachchaiyur alisas Nittavinodanallur gave a flower garden called Tirujanana Sambandan Tirunanadavanam for the temple and money for prabha of the god. At Little Conjeevaram, Paraiyur was granted for festivals in the months of Adi and Purattadi and the service called Gandagopalasandi.[226] To Sekkaperumal at Uttiramerur, Madhusudana Pallava made grants. For Madhusudana's merits some festivals and services were instituted in the temple at Takkolem. A record of the period refers to the Mukkoti Ekadasi Pradakshina mantapa in the Venkatesvara temple at Tirupati. To the temple of Ganapti Prasanndeva at Motupalle, grants were made.[227]

Some of these Pallavas were devoted to Mallesvara at Bezwada. A record of theirs gives the origin of Mallesvara. Agastya named the god Jaysena and Arjuna called him Mallesvara. Arjuna is supposed to have fought Siva at the foot of the Indrakiladri before obtaining from him Pasupatastra. A record of the 9th century in the temple records the building of the temple of Kumaraswami by Yuddhamallu alias Nriperudra in the name of his grandfather Mallapa. So "How a temple dedicated to Kumara (skanda) generally worshipped in form of an image came to be the shrine of a formless linga"[228] is not clear. But this must have been due to the Saivacharyas were bent on establishing the superiority of Saivism to all other creeds. By the time of M. Pandita's visit to Bezvada in the 12th century AD, Karttikaya was converted to Mallesvara.

Vijayagandagopala's records in the Vishnu temple e.g. at Tirumala, invoke the protection of the Srivaishnavas to the donations made as his records in Siva temples place the charities under the protection of the Mahesvaras e.g. Sulurpet. Being devotees of Srivenkatanatha, to Telugu Pallavas, the Yadavarayas, Sambuvarayas provided for nityadipam and nityanaivedyam, daily lighting and food offerings and festivals to temple at Tirumala and Tirupati. In this period camphor was provided for lamps and offering Vijayagandagopala's inscriptions "illustrate the procedure regarding arrangements for the service of lamp lighting through donations of gold and silver coin or through gift of cows."[229] In this period, the number of temple festivals multiplied for in addition to the Brahmotsavams - Tirukoditirunal celebrated in the months of Purattasi and margali, similar festivals were established in the months of Adi at Tirumala for Srivenkatesvara and Ani in Tirupati for Srigovindaraja besides the usual festival held in Tirupati.[230]

**Religious preceptors and maths:** Srisankaracharya or Sankarayogi of the math at Conjeevaram finds mention in the c.p. grant of Vijayagandagopala. [231] This Sankara si probably indintical with the occupant of the Kamakotipitha in the matter at Conjeevaram which tradition says was founded by the great Sankaracharya. The Kamakotipitha possesses some lands here even now and the math is to the west of the abode of Lord of Hastisaila. Golakimath on Srisailam was presided over by Rajaguru. His desciple Santasiva is heard of from a Tripurantakam inscription of Vijayagandagopala.[232] At Tiruvorriyur was the math of Nedikesvra alias Ariyavratanakonda Mudaliyar. Kidara Haraiyan made a grant to the mathateacher and pupils. Tirujnanasambhandhamatha was at Tiruvorriyur and at Timkachachaiyur attached to the temple was Tyagavindomatha within the precincts of the temple.[233]

**Private Life:** King Inumadi is compared to Bhairava in firmness of character and to Kanarapa in appearance. Vijayagandagopala and Alladapammayar were devotees of Komakotyambika. Devarasiyar alias Perumandi Arasiyar was the queen of Vijayagandagopala. Pirainaru Siradiyar a dancing girl made substantial gifts to the temple at Tiruppalaivanam and was conferred hereditorily the right to wave chamara to the god during car processions.[234]

**Other Pallavas:** Vijayaditya of Pentrala, in AD 1261 provided for celebrating amavasya utsava i.e. new moon festivals amutupadi, and satupallu to Marganaragana Perumal at Pentrula.[235] King Ahobalesvara built the shrine of god Tirkutesvara inside the prakara of the Vaidyanatha temple. In AD 1254 Khanderaya installed an image of Sivain the temple and Machelambu, sister of Ahabalesvara made gifts to the temple.[236] In AD 1182 Childdanadeva provided for the service of the god Indresvaradeva of Pushpagiri, after washing the feet of Palaya Mallya, son of Sankaradeva.[237] In AD 1264 Allada Pemmaya provided for the rangabhoga of Mallesvara at Nipparla i.e. Pedavipparru.

**The Dynasties in South Kalinga:The Matoyas of Oddadi.** The Matoyas were Vanishnavaites and upholders of varnasramadharma. Among the subjects in thefourthcaste figure Pedamunnuti and Kondamunnuti of Pedamunnuti Vijaya's daughter,[238] Surama was the queen of Arjuna and Bmimala was the queen of Annayachoda of the Kona Haihayas. The Matsyas made many to the temples of Vishnu. Lakshminarasimha at Simhachalam, one of the most celebrated Vaishnavaite centres was the protecting deity of the Matsya kingdom. Saivism was not neglected as soon from the Matsya grants at Draksharama Madhava religion was on the ascendant and some of the acharyas had influence over the Matsya kings.

On the basis of some important donations, the rulers assumed epithets indicative of their religion. Arjuna was a Narasimhavardana, Annama a Sopalavadha, Mankaditya a Srirangavardhana and so forth. One record says that Arjuna's prosperity was the result of his service to Gopinatha. In the Dibbida grant of Arjuna too shares were set apart for god Hari and Hara. The Matsya queens made grants to Bhimesvara at Oddadi. Purushottamatirtha, Naraharitirtha and Anadatirtha figure in a record from Srikurmam dated AD 1281. [239] Naraharitirtha was the pupil of Anandatirtha, himself a pupil of Purushottama - tirtha made donations to the temple at Simhachalam and induced Jayanta to make grants to Nrisimha. Several records of Naraharitirtha dated between AD 1264 and 1294 were at Simhachalam and Srikurmam. As Mandalika of king Nrisimha of Kalinga he protected Srikurmam when the Sabara tribes invaded it and in AD 1281 built the shrine of Yoganandu Nrisimha, just opposite the Karmalaya. [240] In AD 1186 he made grants for the Srijayanti mahotsava of Srikurmanatha. [241]

**Temples and festivals:** The Matsyas made elaborate grants institued new festivals and services in temples especially of Vishnu. The many details in grants to temples of Vishnu e.g. Simhachalam are in striking contrast to the comparatively few details in grants to Siva temples, e.g. Draksharama. Pleasures of life - bath, food, dress, decoration, sleep, etc. persons attendant on the god were all essential for Lakshminrisimha, accorded by his devotees where worshippers of Bhimesvara propitiated him by providing for lamps in the presene of the god.

At Gudivada, 6 miles of south of Sringavarapukota stands a temple of Brahmlinga. Some of the festivals of Bhimesvara of Draksharama came to light from the Matsya inscriptions. In AD 1252 Surama, queen of Arjuna gave Sankubhimapuram in Alikattandu, to Bhimesvara of Draksharama for the celebration of Gaurivrata in Sreshtamasa punnama i.e. full moon day in the month of Jyestha. [242] Arjuna granted Maruvada in Oddadi in AD 1275 to Bhimesvara for the celebrations of dolotsava on Davanapunnama, for havirbaliarchana on that day and the name of his wife Akkasani. In AD 1285 Akkamba regranted Muruvada for Havirbaliarchana on chaitra davana pauranami dolotsava of Bhimesvara and presented a crown studded with gems to Parvati and gold car rings for her body.[243] In AD 1293 Naraharitirtha set up the images of Rama, Sita and Lakshmana in the Srikurmesvara temple at Srikurmam.[244] In AD 1292 Jayanta, pupil of Narahari granted flower garden for deity worship, gold Uttarajandhyelu and a silver plate to Nrisimha. His wife Bhimidevi provided for the daily presentation of a tirumala of five cubits to the god and supply one potful of water for tirumajanam time. In AD 1364 Arjuna provided for six tirumalas to the God and in AD 1377 provided for Appalabhogam in Ankapalle, which should be taken into sibhandara and this prasada to be taken after night serviceavasara - pudimarapuja, provision for bhoga parikoha, nambyalu, servants, pulamundapa garu kali, kalu, Srikaryamgodava, apamu, vidiyamum and alavattam. Arjuna for god's milk during Vijja avasara ceremony before sleep as Arjunabhoga gave 300 cows, provided for sugar candy into it, and vessels for bringing milk. In AD 1369 he gave 836 cows for milk to got during daily night dhupa avasara (service), 236 cows and 5 plates to be taken with milk as Arjunabhoga and for eight lamps. [245]

Sriyadevi, sister of Prataparjuna provided Patrigunipala kalasalu daily during Dhupaavasara to the god. In AD 1412 Prataparjuna provided for triguna anupamula, atikalu; and in AD 1416 he appointed Narisana for bringing tirumanjanam garaya, during the avasara for tirumanjana. Nrisana used to bring it and appointed one tambhanalu for the same purpose.[246] In AD 1420 Prataparjuna presented a patakam (pendant) to the god; and in AD 1421, he presented fifteen jewels for the daily use of the god, namely doshasamsthi sikila, pearl necklace comprising 182 pearls and a gold pendant.[247] In AD 1415 Annumaraju gave a lamp, lamp stand, fifty cows, garland, curds, kalasa, for smritamarai. Virarajuna gratned bangara sasu kani vadi 100 (gold and silver) for sribhujas, vali, two tambagariyas for daily tirumanjana of the God and ten silver tankas as Padmanidhi in Sribhandara. It is ordained in the record that enjoying the grants daily five bhatas and the son of Jyotisha Varadanayudu were to bring tirumanjana garayalu. For drink to god during this avasaravurds 4 kunchalu, cows 100 for it, curds 2 kunchalu, during tirumajjana avasara, were gratned. Prataparjuna in AD 1421 granted 510 cows, curds for patuvaulu, and trigunipalakalasalu for amrita mani to Nrisimha Matha. In AD 1402 Prataparjunapuram in Oddadi was granted for god's bhogamu. Minister Narasimhapreggada granted a tirumala of six cubits, daily padi appalu, and two betal nuts. Pradhani Mallapreggeda in AD 1383 kept a dipa pratima in the presence of Simhadri Appar.[248] Varadanapreggada granted a tanubhagaraya for tirumajjana for bringing one tirumajjanamugarya. Surapreggada in AD 1382 gave a chauri with a gold handle to be held during ubhayadhupas of Narasimhanatha. Bhimana preggada presented a garland to the god for use on Krishna ashtami day [249] and a pretty gold and gem studded vanamalika called Vaijayanti and Sithana gabburahavu (head ornament), two silver poets, eight silver petals for ashta mangalalu during dhupa avasara for bringing milk and one silver pot for drinking milk and presented a golden sahasradhara for tirumajjana avasara. [250] Kept sixty padmanidhi gandam solas in sribhandara for an karpura vidiya for got after milk provided by him during daily night, dhupa avasara, daily one vidiyam and six arecanuts pachcha karpura of weight of 1/4 patika and kalasa for dhupa avasara. Pradhani Surapreggada in AD 1409 provided for holding alavattam, godavu, and bringing tirumajjanagara for repeti dhupaavasara. King Singa in AD 1471 granted Duttada to Vallabharaya of choda varan., Valleyapadelu mahapatra provided for the celebration of the pitha bhoga of Vallabharya. [251] (god).

Oddadi was formerly the capital of Virata, and Madugula that of Drupada Viratakonda in the vicinity of which Abhimanyu and Uttara are said to have been married in the vicinity of Srigavarapukota. The coins found there are considered to be the talambralu of Uttara and Abhimanyu. Jami and Alamanda- in the neighbourhood of Sringavarapukota are called Samipura because of the sami tree on which Pandavas kept their weapons and Virata's herd of cattle were kept. People believe that the whole of Mahabharata took place there. [252]

Private life: The ruler generally followed monogamy. The Dibbida plated mention the family priest of Arjuna named Vamadeva and also the village artisans, carpenter, goldsmith, barber, blacksmith, potter and sesamum grinder. A tank called the tank of low caste poeple was set apart for the use of the classes.[253] The name Jayanta of some of rulers perhaps reflects on their appearance.

**The Pallavas of Virakuta**

These Pallavas made grants to Nrisimha of Simhavhalam, Kurmesvara of Srikurmam, and Bhimesvara of Draksharama. The title Tiruvengadanatha in their prasasti speaks for their devotion to Venkatesvara of Tirupati. King Bayya in AD 1226 provided for naivedya, sandal, karpuravidiyala, ghee, sugar candy gurru pepper, oil for lamps and similar articles for monthly sukla ekadasi festival.[254] In AD 1348 king Nrisimha presented a pushpavati for daily tirumala to the god. Sabhagyadeva in AD 1420 for daily amutupadi to the god gave rice, silver plate for eating, silver tamba, imadevi silver pots, tambagaraya, two men to hold two alavattam, and achanagarayanibandhamu. He presented a plate for use for offerings to Bhimesvara. Bayyaraja gave gold plate of 500 gadyas and silver plate (chatta) of 133 gadyas. [255]

Queen Kommamadevi, presented a Kanakavalaya of 108 gold Bhimesvara. In AD 1157 on the occasion of Kalyanotsava of in Phalguna queen Lakshmidevi presented a lamp to Bhimesvara. Lakshmidevi queen of Narasimha in AD 1357, presented lamp stands to Bhimesvara and Simhadrinatha.

**The Gangas of Jatarnadu**

Jantarnadu is a tract of land and not a place. Consequently its identifications[256] with Jalantra and Dantalada in the vicinity of Vijayagar are off the mark. In AD 1285 Ganganrapa granted a Pushpavatika - for giving daily one flower garland to the god. In AD 1461 Pratapasinga provided for five services with tiruvalika kolas during ubhayadhupa kalalu[257] i.e. two times of dhupa. In the same year Pratapakarama provided for amritamani prasadam to be eaten during times of leisure in day time, and four Orayalu. In 1399 Sangama provided for milk, trigunipalu, three potful for thrisadhya avasara. Queen Sumitradevi in AD 1346 gave twenty five cows for a lamp and a lamp stand. [258] Satyamahadevi provided for a tirutomala to the god during daily night dhupa service.

**The Silas of Nandapura**

Nandapura has the shrine of Sarvesvara in it. The silas were devotee of Nrisimhanatha of Simhachalam. King Singaraja gave a lamp with lamp stand, trigunipolekalasa and a Kalasa of curds. In AD 1406 Buchchaladevi, daughter of Bayyaraja, presented a lamp with a stand and a pendant set with gems, and pearls for daily wear to Nrisimha.

**Other dynasties:** Prolubupa of Chikali presented to Murmesvara at Srikurmam milk canopy with a moon on it, majatera, Sribastam, Srihastam, silk rope, chonam paddiplate majitidara vimanam, tambadunda, big padamulu 40 sapphires, pearls 58, a pair of ear rings, 24 gadyas of the weight of ganda with gold, emeralds gutamu Sribhallivimanam godavulu 82. In AD 1300 he made grants to Siddhanathdeva and Viradurgadevi at Srikurmam[259] In AD, 1274, Chikati Kumara Anantajiyana provided for the apalu, 20 betelnuts pepper, camphor incense and two villages for havirabli achana for daily avasara naivedya of garudanarayna Narasimhandatha. Palakonda Sarvajnadeva granted silver sahasradhara, weighing 114, dandtama, Sindalamu and bindalamu for a vaist - all of gold to Sri Kurmesvara.[260] The Ponnada chief Kurma in AD 1502 built a timuchattumala between the central shrine and Gopala temple in the Bhavanarayana temple at Sapavaram.[261] By the princes of Eastern Ganga descent, many grants were made to Nilakanthasvara temple alias Nilisvaradeva at Narayanapuram alias Nirunjerua. Bottu Sriramabhadra, Lord of Koravi devoted to Gopaladeva and grants to Srikakulesvara at Srikakulam.[262]

In AD 1494 in the region of Mallaya Mahapatra, the Panchananavaru made grants to Kamakesvaradevara at Dharanikota, for 16 services. They claim descent from Visvakarama bore the epithets - Samastadevata nistaraka, tribhuvana bhunanirmitadhara, Sriparvata lamkara, and Sarvajanapurusha prayakutala.[263] The Panlunavemvaru consisted of a plate of Amaravaram and golden hill. To Bhimesvara at Draksharama, Nandapuram Mallikarjuna presented an ivory, padanquin, parasol, Chanri with a golden handle, and pagalu, Satodabehara Mahapatra Mukunda bhupati performed samvriddhibhoga to god and provided for Mukundabhoga and other services.[264] The record mentioning this is in the mukhamandapa of the temple of Varahanarayanana Vaibhogaraya at Chodavara, where Mallya installed the image of Gurutra i.e. Garaturanta for the attainment of longevity.[265] In AD 1452 a dolemandapa was erected in the Srikurmesvara temple. The Zakkireddipalle record of the time of Ganadeva mentions provision for the worship and bhogaranga in the temples of Papavinasadeva and Rudrapada at Bezvada and two choultries for Brahmins and jangams.[266] At Gopalapatnam were the shrines of Kuntimadhava and Siva and the village is called Kuntinagara. People believe that while Pandavas were spending the 13th year in exile at Voddadi i.e. Viratnagara of Bharata Sahadeva with cattle went up the hill, and saw a beautiful idol in the mound, revealed by the sain which he called Kuntimadhaya to perpetuate the names of his mother and Krishna.[267] Itasani, wife of Kupari Upendra provided in AD 1263 for angaranga bhoga and taditokotsava - festival in the palngrove - to Bhimesvara of Draksharama. A record in the Nrisimha temple to Guntur dated 1485 AD records the grant of cows by Tirumaladaus Mahapatra to Mulasthana Malikarjunadeva. It specifies that the cows were to be milked drring night time, so that the milk fell on the madhyaranga, and milk during day time to be offered to the god and then enjoyed by the tammalas. The imprecutions at the end of the record say that if the tammalas do not carry this, trisula of Isvara would break on their breasts. And if king - Vedde, kurka, and Telugu and their subordinates steal the cows, they incur the sin of killing a Brahmin.[268]

**The Yedavas of Addanki**

They built some temples and made many grants to them. In AD 1249 Madhavanayaka Mallesvara in the temple at Nagulappalapadu and made grants to priests, Brahminshiyogi and Vaidiki, servants, barbers and so forth.[269] At Yendluru to the Madhavaraya temples grants were made by Singadeva M and Sarngapani. In AD 1253 Sarangapani consecreted Srigopaladeva naming him Srichakranarayana Madhava Gopinatha of Nagulappalapadu and provided of daily worship and occasional festivals to the god.[270] In the same year at Chandalur Mayideva preggada made a grant to the local Chenna Mallinatha temple. In AD 1268 king Singa made a grant to

Kandavidu Kumaraswamideva at Ongole [271] for worship, offerings etc. The record is in the Amaresvara temple at Alluru. The name of the temple - Kondevidu Kumaraswami perhaps shows that there was another temple of Kumara at Kondavidu. King Madhava M set up the image of Gopisvara, caused the prisnacle of the temple to be erected and provided for worship and enjoyments. [272] In this period at Ongole was the temple Vaijegarayadeva. At Molakalapundla on the hill i.e. Siddalayya konda is an old cave temple with idols - navakotisiddhulu, navanatha siddhulu and Sarngadhara. The legend says that the first two were great sages doing penance on the hill, were as king Sarnagadhara was a devotee of theirs. On account of their greatness idols were set up to be worshipped.[273] Obviously Sarnagadhara is the king of the Chakranarayana line and this speaks for his popularity. Tradition has it that in AD 1179 Ramachandrajosyulu visited the court of Gajapati Sri Ramadeva at the capital Addanki and obtained his favour by showing his learning. This ruler is neither a Gajapati nor a Yadava of Devagiri but is identical with Sarngapanideva as the date and the Capital support the identification. The king and Josyulu visited Mokshagundam (cumbum taluq) and the former provided for worship to the God and gave land to Jusyulu recording it in c.p. charter. Ad Josyulu built the village and lived there his. descendants acquired the family name Mokshagundamvaru.

### The Yadavas of Alavulapadu

A little in the prasasti of the kings is Chaturvarnasharmadharmarakashana. [274] When the Yadava armies perished in the presence of Somesvara to set at nought the fears of the Yadavas Trirumurtis it is believed, told Yogamaya that being the daughter of Nanda and vasudeva, she would prosper and be honoured by all, praised by her eighteen names and offerings and sacrifice would be made to her. Of the eighteen incarnations in eighteen shrines, she is Romakrifi at Pithapur, Bhagirathi on both the banks of Paleru and so forth. Alavulapadu was the holy place of Bhagirathi Durga. [275]

**Festival:** At Sangamesvaram, which is in the meeting place of Makeru and Paleru, the Sivaratri festival is celebrated grandly to this day in the Sangamesvara temple. [276] In the vicinity of Panchalingalakonda, near Alavulapadu, Ganga tirumallu are held every year fore vatsakha purnima. It attracts people from Konigiri and Kandukur tracts. On the other side of the shrine is the temple of Ganga. [277] The people worship Ganga and Katanaraju, desiring the safety of their cattle. Even now while taking out cattle to jungles, shepherds promise presents to Kalakatamaraju, on the safe return of the cattle, and do accordingly. These are many temples of Ketamaraju, in which the images of Gangas are found.

### The Nagas

King Gonka claims to have bathed in the ganges and was handsome. King Asnadeva in AD 1375 constructed the temple of Pratapagopinatha at Darsi. [278]

### The Banas

King Aggapa in AD 1043 granted Srannamur to the local Agastisvara temple. [279] A bull and linga are carved at the top of the secred.

### The Saluvas

Teluguraya of Podile granted Sunkarachannagrahara to Amudalapalle Basivamma, She renamed it Sivapura, provided for the daily rites of the devotees of Siva. [280] Sambuvaraya constructed a temple of Andhra Runalingesvara at Kuchapudi in AD 1426. [281] Teluguraya of Guntur in AD 1428 made gifts to chnnakesava at Santaravur Tradition has sit that he visited Markapuram provided for worship and festivals to the god, built additional structures round the temple e.g. Mukhamandapa and Arthamandapa. [282] His subordinate Chennayya of Kavur in AD 1444 built the surrounding wall of the temple. In AD 1445 Dachchiboyani Telunguredu installed the image of Gopayya (i.e. krishna) Kasavayadeva in AD 1446 made grants to temple of Gopinatha and Hanuman at Tallur. Tirumalagadeva granted lands to the temples of Gopinatha and Chohayamallikarjuna and Visvesvara at Nutulapadu in AD 1543. In AD 1449 Dalavayi

Mallinenigaru constructed the temple of Kesava and a mandapa at Daggabadu[283] Paravataraya built a mandapa at Tirupati, built two chaultries on Srisailam, and provided for offerings of Mallikarjuna.

**The Kayaslthas**

The Kayasthas favoured Saivism. They built many temples and made grants to them. Some of them were Virasaivas. Kamaladevi, wife of Gangaya Sahini built a temple to Pushpesvara at Pushpagiri in AD 1257. Gangaya's minister Namayapandita, built the temple of Vankesvara, in the name of his father at Dugyapattana in AD 1251. [284] In Janniga's regime, by AD 1264, the gopura, the prakara, and mandapa to the temple of Suresvara at Karempudi were built. In AD 1261 Janniga consecreted Bhimayalingam in the temple at Annalur. In AD 1269 Karanam Namaya consecreted Gopinatha in the temple at Durgi.

Atliral is considered a place of Sanctity where by the purity of the waters of Cheyyaru, parasurma was freed from the sins of natricide. The temple of Parasuramesvara date back to an early time. Peddinayaka built an enclosed verandah and mandapa to the temple, in the reign of Ambadeva. The residents of Pottapindu mention the Chitramalimandapa to raise money to built an embankment to from the Cheyyaru to the temple mentioned as Parasuramesvara mudaiyanayanar. [285] Chodaraya constructed the inner prakara and mandapa in the temple, planted a coconut garden round it, and built feeding houses to the temples of Bhairava and Ramanatha. [286] According to the tradition, the Parasuramesvara temple was built by the Veddes i.e. the Kayasthas by Godderaya, who no doubt made substantial additions to the temple. The temples of Tractesvara and other shrines were renovated by the Kayasthas. Parasuramesvara was also known as Godadharesvara. [287] At Peddanapadu, the Kayasthas made additions to temples. Tradition has it that there was a temple of Siva and a shrine of Madangopala, built by a Chola king. then Ambadeva, during his halt there with his army, on the coax to Ramesvaram, commanded by God Chennakesava of Martapur in his dream, built a temple and sit up the idol which was unearthes there.[288] He repaired other temples. At Tripurantakam in AD 1294 general Adidemma presented a golden image of goddess. Trailokayasundari and married her to Tripurantaka, provided for procession and festivals of the god and goddess. [289] At Joti in AD 1247 chenti Raminayadu built the constructed a temple for Irugalasani at Takaprolu. At Lepaka, a subordinate of Ambadeva built a temple of Kesava perumal. [290]

**Festival:** Tripurantaka provided for daily worship, sandal, musk, saffron, camphor and milk to god Sri Tirupurantakadeva at Potlapadi[291] and made a grant to Siddhesvara at Siddhavatam. A Kayastha made a grant to Vaidyanatha at Pushpagiri. [292] Janniga made grants to the temples of Mallesvara at Virapalle and Lankamallesvara at Tankatur, provided for festivals and margali utsavams in the temple of Sanmyanathaswami at Nandalur. [297] Choderaya provided for a annasatra and worship Ramaiesvara at Attirala. Ambadeva provided for margali festivals of Chennakesva at Lepaka, temple of Lakshminaryana at Gudlur, Karavisvara mudaiyanayanar at Lepaka, Mulasthana Naganatha at Kamala and Svayambhu Srimahadeva at Satrasala.

**Religious preceptors and maths:** A Golakimatha was situated in the locality of Pushpagiri and Gangavaram. Isangafurudeva was a Saivacharya probably of this math. Santasiva Desika was the guru of Janniga and belonged to Basavagolakimatha of Srisailam. Sadasivaguru is perhaps a mistake for Santapurvasivadesika. Tryambaka Siva was probably the preceptor of Tripurantaka. [293] The statement that Tripurnataka was the pupil of aghorasiva, of the math in Cuddappah district is mistaken. [294] Aghorasiva's pupil was Tripurantakasiva. To both the preceptors and pupil grants were made by Tripurantaka, son of Ambadeva, and pupil of Aghorasiva. [295] Ambadeva was also a pupil of Aghorasiva. Srigurudeva is heard of from a record at Gangavaram. Nandasiva was a pupil of Tryambakasiva led a deputation of Amabadeva, and in return got Gangavaram, near Penukonda from Tryambakasiva, Santisiva, disciple of Rajagurudeva, is head of from a record at Darsi. [296]

Monogamy was the rule. Porandalur is said to have been founded by one of the Chola kings in the name of Purandaravithala.

**The Telugu Cholas of Konidena**

These cholas maintained Varnasramadharma. They favoured Virasaivism. Some of the rulers e.g. Nannichoda were virasaivas. Virasaiva preceptors e.g. Mallikarjuna, are head of. Balliya chola worshipped sahesa - guhesa at Attirala. Ballichoda and Tribhuvana malla C.M. were devoted to Siva. Several temple were built and many donations were made in this period. The hill in Konidena is called Abhinava Vaivatakadri.[297] and the three temples - Ballisvara Konisvara and Tribhuvana mallsrikesvadeva at Konidena were built after the name of kings. Choda ballya choda, Kama and Tribhuvanamalla. No traces of Ballesvara and Kamisvara temples are seen now where as that of Tribhuvanamalla is located on the hill. The temple of Bhimesvara with attendant deities was built and consecreted in AD 1148 at Konidena, by Bairya, a subordinate of Tribhuvanamalla C.M. Tradition says that Kakatiya Ganapati kept his elephantry at Konidena and the traces of the place - Enuguladiddi, and Enugala inetagadi are seen to this day. And people call Konidena as "Kotienugula Kondiganapatapatta" i.e. the town of Kondi Ganapati, the possessor of the crore of elephants. [298] Here Kondi is a stortened form of Hanumakonda mentioned as Kondipattana in some records. Kamachoda built cholaballesvara temple after his brother chodaballi, at Chanduri. [299] In AD 1237, Chodadeva C.M. Malladevaraja and Chikkiraju constructed a front hall, and kitchen in the temple of Nilakanthesvara at Cudlur.[300] In AD 1137 minister Mara built a temple for god Somesvara at Kopparam, and Mallikarjuna of Palur was placed in charge of the temple. [301] A Siva temple was built in AD 1148 at Kanamarlapudi. At Konidena in AD 1171 Kosanaya setti dug a tank and built Somesvara temple on its bund. [302] At Nadendla his son Kamisetti built the Viresvara temple. Gundimeda Anna many Siva and Vishnu temples and provided for nityotsava and trikalapuja.

**Festival:** Ballichoda in AD 1145 provided for sacrifices, worship, offerings, lighting and decorations-angarangabhoga of Mallesvara at Mannapalle. Kannara in C.V. 46 provided for the ceremony of Khandaspattia to God Bhimesvara at Draksharama. In AD 1119, Chodadeva C.M.granted villages for Vaisakha tirunallu, archana and bhoga of Bhavanarayana at Ponnur in whose presence several marriages of Brahmins were celebrated.[303] In AD 1149 Anna made grants to the temples of Bhavanaryana at Prempalli, Kesavadeva at Konidena, Bhavanaryana in Kammachadu, Bhimanatha at Draksharama, Haimavati vallabha at Dannola, Tripurantakesvar.[304] etc. He lighted lamps in the temples of Mallikarjuna at Srisailam, at Tripurantakam, Ramesvaram at Setu, Somesvara in Saurashtra, Bhimesvara at Draksharama, Amaresvara at Dhanyavati, Mahadeva at Gundimada, Madhava at Prayaga, Purushottama and Narasimha at Jiharigiri in Oddadesa, Bhavanaryana at Prempalli, Bhavanaryana at Ganjam, Trivikarama at Cherukur, Sankara and Kesava at Konidena, Mallsena at Tamrapura, Kumara at Svamimala, and Maribhattakhya at Maddrevula.[305] In AD 1137, Koma choda, Sriyadeva and Tribhuvanamalla made grants to Ballisvara, Kamisvara and Tribhuvanamalla Kesava at Konidena.[306] Mara in AD 1115 built Somesvara temple at Tangedumalli. To the temple of Tribhuvanamalla Mallikarjunadeva at Degaramudi. At Katepalli was the temple of Komesvara.

**Religious preceptors and math** : Svetesvara Bhatara, the donee of a grant from Balliyachoda was probably an ascetic of the Pushpagiri math. Guru Mallikarjuna was the preceptor of king Nannichoda. He is regarded as the incarnation of Mallikarjuna of Srisailam and an equivalent of Vishnu, Brahma and Paramesvara. A Paramayogi with mind above thoughts of grief, death, free from family life, resembling paranjoti, he was a purushottama as the satisfied the purusharthas. He was a grihastha who became an ascetic.[307] A sarvajna, brahmarshi, handsome and fair, Mallikarjuna is described as Virasaivadikshaprasandra, and was interested in talking matters concerning dharma. Mallikarjuna of Pulur, the follower of Kalamukhavrata who received Somesvara sthana from king Kannara in AD 1115 was probably a pupil of Mallikarjuna, the preceptor of Nanni choda. The Kalamukhas originally lived at Srisailam and Alampuram. The worshipped Sakti and were ever bachelors.[308] Nannichoda refers to the worship of Srichakra and resort to drink - the customs of the Kalamukhas whose teachings were widespread in this period. The other divisions among Saiva ascetics were suddha saivas, Pasupatas, and mahavratins. According to the Suddhasaivas the five acts of creation, continuance, destination and so forth were accomplished by Siva, where as some believe that Siva creates only with the help of Parvati. [309] The mahavaratins are the same as the Kapalikas and Nannichoda in the context of Rati addressing Manmatha not to disturb Siva, says that Siva was engaged in the Mahavratha. Bhairava tamtra was in vogue as seen from the building of temples of Bhairava and Vondhayavasini Nannichoda has much about Saivism in his work which mirrors the contemporary religious condition. He says that a fool could not understand the difference between Siva and Sakti, and mentions the Paramamahesvara building huge temples of Ganesa. He praised Siva in two verses having Nagabandhu and muraja bandha and described Nilakantha appearing as an incarnation of love to Parvati. [310] Potana in the 15th century AD mentions that Nilakantha as shown by the four vedas was the greatest of the gods and has Nilakantha star in a few verses. [311] Nannichoda struck the highest note in the standard of Srinagara while picturing the mental and physical completion or union of Siva and Parvati in the form of Arthanarisvara.

**Private life**: Some of the kings had more than one wife. Tribhuvanamalla C.M. had three queens, Machala and Tribhuvana. Some of the amusements of girls were playing with dolls, and swimming. Nannichoda refers to woman arranging chilka dolls, ivory dolls, best glass bannarulu and so forth in rows, build doll houses, cook doll food, and celebrate the marriages of dolls. [312] Women used to swim lying falt on their backs with head upwards in water. [313] Nannichoda says that Parvati drew rangavalla with Kasmira, mánjishta, garuda, sapphires and pearls and bathed in scented luke warm water. Daragriha set with arrangement for shower bath was used by her. [314] Play of women in water is described by Nannichoda. They throw water on one another with sirenges filled with kashmira waters; with Karayantra etc. playing, they press water on one another. [315] Pressing water through sirenges, each holding the other and ducking in waters and pressing jaladharas. Nannichoda gives a fine description of Manmatha *316* and drugs out the wisdom of Rati. When Mankata was to go to distract Siva from penance, as ordered by Brahma, Rati tells him that he would not be able to bear the fire of the third eye of Siva and Brahma jealous of his as he was liked by women, planned to kill him this way. [317] But Manmatha felt confident of his powers and said that Siva was no exception to the bond of love inherent in humanity.

Poytala i.e. false head was one of the implements on burglars. For passing through holes into houses, to see whether the inmates were awake or asleep, they used to push the false head through the holes. An expert in rasavadasastra, Nannichoda refers to the turning of baser metals into gold by dhumavedi and sabdavedhi. In one place he says that non could get at the truth of women's minds, [318] reminding us of similar description of Srinatha in Sringaranaishadha. He also refers to Magalanjiyalu i.e. men prostitutes who dressing themselves attractively by artificial means deceived woman. Four kinds of Vitasbhadra panchala, dattaka, and Kuchimara, [319] Kanyavidulu - men who trade in getting girls for marriages and take money and dhatuva dulu who change shapes and colours are mentioned by Nannichoda.

**The Pottapi Cholas**

Some of the kings donated gifts to Sanmyanathaswami temple called Srikulottunga cholavinnagar Alwar in Srikulottunga chaturvedimangalam. [320] The goppru of the temple was built by Somisvara, son of Vimaladitya. In AD 1139 at Pushpagiri, Trilokyamalla Mallideva C.M. made grants to the Santana Mallesvara temple. A stone mandapa for a bull in the Siva temple called Mobbu Devalam at Upparapalle was built in AD 1259. [321] A record of AD 1260 at Chintalaputtur mentions the temples of Kaludasankara, Vijanath, rudrapada, Durgidevi, Pushpesvara, Mallinathadeva and Siddhavata. A later record of AD 1294 mentions the five temples of Pushpagiri - Vaidynatha Mamalasankara, Durgadevi, Rudrapada and Ramesvara.[322] Poli had the temple of Kariyamanikka perumal. At gundlur are three temples. Natives believe that once in every five years the lingam in the Siva temple was bathed with waters from the Ganges which falls from the roof, [323] while Mallideva C.M.

was ruling from Vallur in AD 1149 the consecretion of god Kesava on the southern side of Rudrapada temple took place at Pushpagiri.

**The Nellore Chodas**

These cholas distinguished themselves most in the sphere of social among all the contemporary dynasties in Andhradesa. In the words of Professor Sastri "It is one of the most remarkable achievements of medieval Hinduism to have harnessed the religious emotions of man in the effective service of society. The temple and the math together with the agrahara, the chaturvedimangalam of Choda of South Indian religion."[324] These Nellore Cholas did much to foster these in the Telugu land. They maintained Varnasrama dharma.

Nellore had good Brahmins. Ketana refers to brahmins who giving up studies caste, homes went to jungles, became one with boyas and took to high way robbery.[325] Vijnanesvara specifies the sixteen karmas for all with the difference that in the case of Brahmins they are performed with sacred incarnations.[326] Tikkana in vijayasenamu refers to the prosperous condition of the vaisysa. They could purchase even Kamstubha at a heavy cost if sold, sell gold and supply any article at any time for any body.[327]

Manmasiddhi III was interested in protecting the fourfold caste system and spreding Varnasramadharma.[328] Tikkana's works give five descriptions of the Brahmins, their superior position in the caste system, the other three castes, their rights, duties and so forth. He used the term Komati in Andhra Bharata for Vaisya in the Sanskrit work. Innumerable records show that the Komatisettis from important towns e.g. Tsandavole, dharmapuri, ghautasole, Penugud, Dendulur etc. in Andhradesa of the period show that they call themselves vaisysas, aryas and of Kubera lineage.

**Saivism.** Generally the rulers were Saivaites and "as saivism like many other manifestations of latter day Hinduism, required its followers to obtain its initiation from aguru" royal preceptors are heard of. Neither the rulers nor the ruled were narrow sectarinas to avoid the worship one god in preference to that of another. None were exclusively devoted to either Siva or Vishnu, but to both barring the few adherents of Virasaivism and Viravaishnavism Sankara's advaitism was the basis for this religious toleration. The people must have felt the need for one god symbolising both Vishnu and Siva in the revival of the concept of Hariharnatha, which is ancient. for there are fine imaged of god Harihara belonging from the fifth to the eighth century AD in greater India e.g. Java, Malaya etc. Besides modern Venkatesvara at Tirupati was originally Harihara. For Peyalvar of the end of the fourth and the beginning of the 5th century AD "describes how the kindly god of Tirumalai unites in himself the town forms of Siva and Vishnu." [329] Some time early in his life, Tikkana rediscovered this for in his Ramayana he refers to it indirectly. The worship of Harihara was very popular and widespread and Tikkana propagated and gave it permanent form in his Mahabarata. The most sacred and best work in the entire range of Telugu literature of the Andhras, from religious - being the Panchamaveda and literary point of view, Tikkana's Bharata is dedicated to God Hariharanatha. In the work the first verse and the last three in every canto, besides the shasthyantas[330]) were in praise of Hariharanatha. In side, almost in every place where he had to speak about Siva and Vishnu, [331] Tikkana introduced the descriptions of Hariharanatha. Almost every verse in praise of Hariharanatha is well balanced from the point of view of Vaishnavaites and Saivaites in two even halves as in the concept of Ardhanarisvara and his first verse in the beginning of Virataparva and the Sanskrit sloka [332] both in adoration of Hariharare superb. It has been said that his worship of Haraharanatha "a deity neither exclusively Vaishanava nor exclusively Saiva but both at the same time" speaks for his broad religious outlook. Some opine that Tikkana by Hariharanatha does not refer to the god in the temple at Nellore but savayanirgunabrahma, the lord of both Hari and Hara worshipped by Advaitins and that the advaita sampradaya is seen in the verses towards the end of each canto. Thus Tikkana was the first to preach advaitism in Telugu. But this need not deny Tikkana referring to the god worshipped in the Harihara temple at Nellore. As a matter of fact Tikkana refers to god Harihara archavatara and not mere concept for he says that god Hariharanatha accompanied by

Kammana; appeared to him in his dream and spoke to him. Tikkana describes him as Sarvesvara Jagannatha and Lakshmisvara. And the Harihara temple in his time was built. "In the stress of the conflict with periodical rivals who denied the sanctity of the Veda and questioned the existence of the deity, there arose with in Hinduism a tendency to close up its ranks and foster a religious synchretism which found room in the fold of its orthodoxy for all forms of theistic belief. This synchretism was bases on the conception of Trimurti - the tree fold manifestation of the same god head."[333] The concept of Hariharanatha is an approach towards to the same goal. In the propagation of his cult, Tikkana enjoyed regal patronage. For King Manmasiddhi III was devoted to Sripati, Gauripati, Vanipati, and worshipped sun, Siva and Vishnu[334] Tikkana's description of Ganesa taking water from the head of Siva and pouring it on Sahasrakasha at the base of the pitha and taking lotuses as though to worship Siva[335] is unique. He speaks about Sivamahimaand Sivanama.

**Vaishnavism:** Some of the rulers favoured Vaishnavism and ware avowed devotees of Vradaraja of Kanchipura. Tikka I"s devotion to Varadaraja is seen from his declaration of faith " the person who worships the pair of feet of god Varadaraja is my mother, father, great treasure, son, preceptor andfriend."[335]Allutikka was also a devotee of Varadara. [336] Rajagandagopala devoted to Arulalaperumal Varadaraj calls himself at the end of some records the servant who bears the stamp of the feet of the blessed Arulalanatha - Sri arulalanatha padalanchenasya or Alladanatha in place of his signature. Tikka's favourite god was Danavamurari Perumandideva i.e. Vishnu. Probably he called himself Danavamurari Bantara of Vididsa" as it is the custom among Srivaishnavas to name themselves as the servant or dasa of their favourite deity"[337] and some of his coins bear the legend - Danavamurari Bantari - Tikkana speaks about Vaishnavadharma, Vishnujanasvarupa, and Vishnunama prabhava in Bharata. [338]

Buddhism and Jainism also prevailed Tradition records that when Tikkana Somayaji visited Ganapati at Warangal, he invited controversy with the Buddhists and Jains, vanquished them and brought about the stoppage of worship in thirty-six jain bastas and their prosecution of Jains and Buddhists by Ganapati, some killed, some driven out.[339] etc. For want of inscriptional data, and in the light of the life of the poet and the spirit of his message, this is regarded as baseless. The statement that Tikkana was a true advaitin with the breadth of vision that all religions are so many ways leading to the supreme reality, the Brahman cannot be true wholly for Tikkana's advaitism [340] would not have extended to Buddhism and Jainism though to Hinduism in all its divisions. He also speaks about Siva and Pasupatavarata.

**Temples:** "The temple and the math were the two great gifts of medieval Hindusim to Southern India. It was under the cholas that these institutions entered on a process of gradual expansion and adopation which attracted the imagination of the populace and the benefactions of the rich." In raising temples the Telugu cholas followed the great cholas and "several temples of the period and also cheif leons in them were called after the ruling kings who established them."[341] Similarly ministers, officials, and rich persons named after themselves or those dear to them. Services named after the donors or others were instituted in temples. Conversely many kings, princes and people were named after their favourite gods, e.g. Tikka was named after Srikalahasti. After the name Manmasiddha, common too in the royal family were raised many temples to Siva in the kingdom. The names and titles of the rulers show that they were great devotees of Tikka of Kalahasti and Varadaraja of Kanchi.

Tammusiddhi in AD 1205 erected portions of the temple of Arulala Perumal i.e. Varadaraja at Kanchpura. In AD 1240 Allutikka consecreted Danavamurari Perumandideva at Sri Atukur and built a mandapa to the god. Manumasiddha Tikka Gandagopala provided for repairs in the temple of Arulālaperumla; and in the temple of Kalamagha perumal temple in kandaravirapettai alias Gandagopala Chaturvedimangalam in Kanch. [342] At Babbepalle, Tirukalideva C.M. built a temple for Tirukalisa Mahadeva in the name of his father. At Kanch Allutikka donated 35000 kuli of land, house sites for construction of a temple and the compound walls. [343]

In AD 1207 Gollapudi Bommanayaka built a mandapa to the local chennakesava temple. In the reign of Errasiddhi at Navur Siddhanathadeva was consereted and provision for worship and enjoyment was made. In the 26th year of Kulottunga at Kistnapatam a temple to Vishnu with a gopura was built. In AD 1279 at Kistnapatam, the merchants are embled at Tirukkavanam and made a grant for building the temple of Manumasiddhisvara. [344] Sripatanayaka in AD 1198 set up Prasannakesava .at Chintagunta and built Koravadeva temple at Katrayapadu. In AD 1302, provision was made for repairs to the temple of Chittiramelivinnagar at Tirupparakadal in Nellore. In the same temple, Periasiddappanayaka set up the image of Viddharasa Siddharasa. [345] At Kompadu, Konangi Siddappanayaka built three temples and three mandapas found consecreted Ishtakamisvara, Nagesavara and Mallikarjuna and also the Chennakesava temple to the north near them. [346] Takkinayaka set up Kesava at Takkulam. At Pulicherlapadu in AD 1219 was built the temple of Srimathbajabalamallikarjuna mahadeva. The temple and sacred place for karumanikka perumal at Tumbaiyur (i.e. Tummur) was the charity of Tyagasamudra pattai Vimarasan. [347] At Chapalapalle Narumidan Pirraiyandan set up the image of M.P.C. Sidallarasa. Tantrapala Peddinayaka constructed the gopura to the temple at Siddhavatam in AD 1233. At Motupali also known as Mukutapura and Kailasagiri Siddhaya choda, governor of Ganapati of the Kakatiyas constructed the inner prakara and mukhamandapas for the temples now at the west of the village consecreted gods for the merit of his parents and Ganapati. [348] In Nellore was the temple of Sriranganatha on southern bank of the Pennar, same as the modern Ranganayaka temple in ranganayakulapet. Constructed on a rocky ground, this temple though not mentioned by Telugu poets, is mentioned in many records as Pallikandaperumal, or chittiramalivinnagar. The Mulasthamasvara temple also known as Dharmaraja temple was an ancient one. At Tiruvorriyur in the 28th year of Kulottunga Durgaiyandinayakan built vyakarana danavyakhyama mandapa in the temple. [349] At Villivalem, the temple of Gongai Kondacholisvara Mudaiyanayanar was built by Vilvalam Pallavaraiyan Tulaiyaluselvan and Tirujnamas ambandan in the reign of Virgandagopala. [350] To the temple of

Hariharanatha at Nellore Tikkan dedicated Bharata. Nachanasanana dedicated his Uttara Harivamsa and Baicharaju Venkatanatha his Panchatantra to this god. Venkatanatha of the 16th century AD says that Tikka Yajva, Somanatha and himself were devoted to Hariharanatha. The conclusion that Harihara of Somana and Venkatanatha was not of Nellore on the ground that the poets were not natives of the place [351] is wrong, for without being natives they could have been devotees of that god.

**Festivals**: These Cholas instituted many services in the Vishnu Varadaraja temple at Little conjeevaram commonly known as Tiruvottiyur or Attiiyur, he being the Tamil for Sanskrit Hastin. Allutikka established the permanent service called Gardagopalasandi in the temple in AD 1231 and Rajagandagopala provided the service - Rajagandagopalasandi after his own name. Manumasidharasa in the 15th year of Rajaraja III granted Uludamangalam for conducting festivals, in the months of Adi and Purattadi and Gandagopalasandi to Arulalaperumal.[352] Tikkagandagopala granted Vayalaiyanur of the festivals just mentoned. [353] Mannumasiddha granted Mavandur for Gandagopala sandi and other festivals.[354] The villages Pudur, Kondiyarrur Padaipparru, Amedinallur, Akkaramerpakkam, lands in Karavai were granted for the same festivals mentioned above. To the temple of Ulagiyaninraperumal at Kadethallai i.e. Mahabalipuram. Allutikka made a grant. To the temple of Satarayesvara at Tiruvalangadu, Vachisvara at Tirupparur, and Adhipurisvara at Trruvorriyar, Tammusiddhi made gifts. Nalasiddhanadeva M provided for obletain to Yajnesvara at Khundapudi, probably Akkampeta. The merchants of Kollitturai alias Gandagopala pattana, assembled in the garden of Desnayaka attached to the temple of chandirattirai pillaiyar and made a grant to Manumasiddhisvara at Kishtnapatam. Urudaiyan Madapaiswami provided for sacred food to Tirupallirai Nachchiyar i.e. the goddess of the sacred bed room. Rajarapettai Peddarasa made grants to the temples of Subrahmanya at Tiruvambur and also Pandrangabhatta. At Virana Kanupur was the temple of Pillaiyudaiyavarayanperumal, and at Gundlapalem, that of Bhimesesvara, at Pakala, the temple of II Ilangusenu Kuliya and Margamu Palnindi mukkala

Marganarayana perumal, to which grants were made. In AD 1244 at Jaladanki, Peddinayaka, servant of Allutikka, made a grant for sandhyadipa to Chennkesava and provided for lighting evening Innapsin a row in half of the same temple in AD 1264.[355] At Kavali was the temple of Gauvisvara and of Gopala at Masanur. To the god a Timmasamudram in AD 1198 Sripatinayadu provided for offering - daily, weekly, twilight lamps, for observance of Badasidya, and a cow on the day of Uttiranakshtra. [356] Grants were made to Vallisvara, Mahadeva and Udayakalavati at Gandavaram. A record in the Udayakalesvara temple registers provision for festivals to the god Vallisvara at Kanthaparayanapura alias Kulottungasolapura and for feeding ascetics of the math.[357] In AD 1284 at Kodavalur in Manmagandagopalas reign grants were made to the temple of Tirunagisvara and Annapillainayakar arranging for his residence in the building on the banks of the temple pond. At Nellore Gandagaopala made a grant to the god Akkasali.[358] In AD 1194 Rajagandagopala Ranganatha made a grant to god Gopala at Kurucherlapadu. [359] Chittirmallimandapa in Tirupparkadar Chittiramelivinnayar is mentioned in a record of AD 1197. Tikka made a grant to Manumakesvaperumal at Manumakesvapura, a suburb of Nellore. At Poyindampalle (Tetapalli gudur) was the temple of Siddappa. At Koturpalle was a Siva temple. Bhiminayaka, a devotee of this god described in elaborate terms made a grant to Kesayyamgaru, an ascetic. [360] At Manmapolur Allutikka provided for amutapadi foe deity during festivals and he with Allutikka made grants to Siddhanathadeva at Ayyavariplle Tikka and his father made grants to Tiru - Kelesvara. Tripurantaka and Kedaradeva. In AD 1297 at Narasaropet, Manumagandagopala for the merit-anantabhoga of his parents granted land in Manumaganda Siddapuram for the timnallu festival of chnnakesva at Konidena.[361] At Voguru in AD 1265, the rulers provided for a satra to Suresvara at Guvvalenka. At Dongalasani in AD 1159, Kmarapreggada provided for festivals at Srisailam and its four entrances on the occasion of the conquest of Pottapi by his father Ramanapreggada. [362] At Motupalli was the Prasanna-kesava temple and at Voguru Mallinatha temple and at Chanduru Mallinatha temple. At Akepadu was the temple of Videva to which the same village renamed Manmatikkapuram was granted.[363] Allutikka made gifts to Siddhanatha at Seshamambapuram. In AD 1276 at Attirala, deva made a grant to god Bhairava in Ramanatha temple on festival days. At Kalahasti, Allutikka gave gold for a lamp in Timmarikkamgai Udaiyanayanar temple. [364] To Vedapuriswara at Tiruvattur, Masilamanisvara at Tirumallivagil grants were made. Rajagandagopala provided for lampstands and copper pots to the temple of senapati Pillaiyarnayanar at Mallam. [365] To Apaksahayasvara at Tenneri, and Ranganatha at Srirangam grants were made. M.P.C.Gandagopalafor providing unguents to the god at Tiruppalaivanam, a grant was made as Tiruchchanduppattai. [366] He provided for the service - Tiruvòliporappinansandi in the temple of Tirunirmalai Emberuman. [367] Tikkagandagopala provided for worship and offerings to god Alagar[368] at Tirumalirunjolai in Pandimandalam during the service - Gandagoplasandi at Little Conjeevaram. In AD 1239 Manmasiddha made a grant to the temple of (sreshti) Sri Mahesvara at the northern entrance of Sriparvata. M.P, made grant of lands in Kaliyur to the temple of M.P.C. Gandagopal Vinnagar Emberuman Allutikka provided for sacred bath, offerings and Festival on the day of Ardra in the month of Margali to Tiruppalaivanamanayanar at Pulapattur.[369] At Little Conjeevaram were the temples of Tirutonga vilakkoli Emberuman and Alariyar of Tiruvadirakkai. [370] M.P.C. ordered the maintenance of lamps in the temple of Tiruvorriyuru [370] daiyanayanar at Tiruvorriyur. He granted Tukankaḍal for the conduct of Arpasi festival and service Rajagandagopalasandi in Arulalaperumal temple and Attupputtur for Adi festival and Rajagandagopalasandi Rajagandagopala granted Tindurai for worship and offerings to god - Arulalaperumal - during the service called Anaikattina Sankarunaryanasandi [371] - the service named after Sankaranaryana, probably a general. Rajagandagopala made a grant to the Rudramahesvaras of the temple of Senjalainathesvara at Timmalagondakottai. At Tiruppukuli land were granted to Kailasamudaiyanayanar, Vinayapillaiyar pidari and Vijayaraghavaperumal temples. At Kunnattur was the temple of Tiruvalisvaramudaiyanayanar for a lamp to be lighted in the presence of Kuraivaduga pillaiyar, In the same place was the temple of Bhuvanisvaramudaiyanayanar. [372] Nallasiddharayan Vijayadevan made a grant to Vimisuram, Uaiyan Subrahmanyapillaiyar and Vaikuntha Emberuman at Vishar Vijayagandagopala son of Gandagopala Tikka granted lands to Siddhanatha at Siddhavatam. In the reign of Rajagandagopala Muppidi granted 1042 grandgopala madai, 240 of which was for laying a flower garden, and for servants to look after it, 360 madas for daily worship of the god and 382 for building mandapas. [373]

**Religious preceptors and maths:** At Gandavaram, attached to the temple of Udayakalesvara was a math where in provision for feeding ascetics was made. Kesaygangaru, an ascetic lived at Koturupalle. At Tiruppalaivanam was Gandagopalamani Kamatha, [374] and for feeding devotees in it some land in Ponaiyandai was given by Gandagopalamanikkam, the sister of Sittamadeviyar, a dancing girl attached to the temple of Manumasiddhisvara Mudaiyanayanar at Nellore.

**Private Life:** Errasiddha is described as a Jaianta to charming women. [375] Tammasiddhi is described a living necklace of pearls. [376] Manumasiddha III was pure, charitable, and handsome and possessed lotus like eyes. He had four queens - Nunkamadevi, Mailamadevi, Sridevi, and Bachaladevi. Among ministers, Ketana was handsome, Bhaskara was praised by people. Kotana satisfied the purusharthas and navarasas (nine sentiments). Mallana was handsome and Kottaruvu Kamma possessed fine personality. Kottaruvu. Erra was handsome. Ranatikkana was handsome and Bandaruketanantri was truthful and respected by women.

**Women:** Some women made substantial grants to temples and maths e.g. Irumadiasriyadevi, and Nungamadeviyar. Anyamadevi, mother of Tikkana was beautiful. [377] Mother and wife of Ramatikkana possessed strong will and heroism. Tradition records [378] that when Tikkana came back defeated in the battle, his wife arranged for his bath in a corner, where bathe, kept a cot for privacy and a ball of turmeric on it and brought water in a vessel for him. He felt sad and enquired the cause for this strange behaviour, she replied "when you has shown your back to the enemies, they laughed, so we are three women now and why should you feel sorry." After bath when he sat for food, his mother served him curdled milk. When he questioned she retorted thus "the cattle went with you and came back defeated. And so the milk got curdled." Tikkana at once left off eating and went back the battle. His wife was great and tradition has it that her husband was brought back to life by the blessings of Poet Bhima.

Ketana gives a typical description of a harlot and her mother. A harlot should eat little, learn tricks do vows for prosperity and deveive men. Vijnaesvara defines what is prescribes punishments for crimes. Ketana speaks about royal protection to visyas. [379]

**Amusements**: Cockfights and gambling were common. Ketana describes cockfights in Boyappale and mentions two types of cokcs-baka and narikela and gives their characteristic features. Swimming and Jalavihara were enjoyed by men and women. Tikkana mentions jalavihara, and describes dyutaakshavidya - soyatala.[380] He gives a good description of Mallayuddha wrestling between Bhima and Malla in the presence of virata.[381]

**Social Customs**: Both Ketana and Tikkana mention Anuloma and Vilama marriages. Dowry and Oli were in vogue, Burglar's implements were - false head, blue pillow, aches, sword, galachira, selayota, bharmaramu, kolu, mailamandu, stick and nirigrankinarasamulu. [382]

Darpaka and Bhairavi were worshipped the festival Kandukotsavaishna found by Ketana. When somapida prayed to god, he appeared to him and said that every year his daughter should celebrate kandukotisva on his honour. [383] There are no direct references to diseases and medicines. That Tikkana enumerates the diseases of horses and cattle and their cures in his descriptions of Nakula and Sahadeva and physicians who could do salyachikitra.

The prosperity of Nellore is described in many verses. It was the home of good brahmins, agriculturists, dancing girls, wealth corn, money, education, oil, ghee, salt[384], etc. The protecting deity was Mulasthana Vinggaguru. The city compared with Amaravati. It is said to have had 360 temples. A chatu verse says that in no other place except Vikramasimhapura was a diety like Mulasthana paramesvara protecting his devotees, no gods like Pallikondanatha Anantapadmanabha no sacred hill like Vedagiri and the Vemalasetti bavi which is said to have been born by the kindness of Siva. [385]

**Eruva Choals:** Eruvakesava provided for nityosahara to Amaresvara at Amaravati.[386] In AD 1403 Annadeva made grants to Mahendralinga and Nissanka Kamaya the sthanapati of the Siva temple at Mahanandi.[387]

**The Kandur Cholas:** Udaya and his predecessor had leanings towards Jainism. Udaya persecuted Namayya, a follower of M. Pandita. Namaya killed himself and M. Pandita cursed the king and left Pamga.[388] Gokarna, brother of Bhimana was the pupil of Vagindrachudamani, a Jain preceptor, the author of a lakshanagrantha in his name in Telugu and Adipurana. Gokarna himself composed Kavi Janasraya, generally attributed to Vemulvadu Bhima and dedicated it Rechabhupala, a general of Jagadekamalla of the chalukyas. Gokarna who entiled Sravakabharana, and Reche Kavihanasraya. The work has four cantos, speaks about the essential of Jain works and begins with the praise of Sarasvati. [389]

These Cholas were staunch Saivas. Gokana C.M. a viramahaesvara granted on AD 1121 Maduvila with ashtabhoga rights.[390] Further he granted Peddagur for angarangabhoga, dump, incense burning and offerings to god Elesvara at Elesvaram. In AD 1125 Kanduri Pedraya C.M. made a grant to Srimahavisvesvaradeva at Nelakondapalle Odaya C.M. in AD 1152 made a grant to Koduri Svayambhu Somanathadeva and Bhimadeva C.M. in AD 1234 granted Knchanapalle to the temple of Elesvaramahadeva.

**Mailamba:** Says the Panugal inscription - was favour gravious and was considered as Sarasvati by learned men as one who worshipped her lord as god by good women folk, as their family deity by his servants and the Kalpa tree by her supplicants. [391]

**The Hamavati Chola**: Tribhuvanamalla Mallideva C.M. provided for the service of god Desisvara set up by Periyalvarsetti from the chola country in AD 1162 at Hemavati.[392] At Kunkanur, Sekharadeva C.M. erected temples for Ramesvara and Kesava.

Some princes of Telugu Chola descent and other chieftains made substantial grants to temples. At Kurichedu were Kalahastisvara and Divyakirtisvara temples. In AD 1206 Gundapanayadu, lord of Vendlur and his co-son-in-law Erapanayaka installed Tripurantaka on the east of Alagadapa.[393] (Nalgonda district). At Kamireddipadu in AD 1275, Hadapamu Lankaraju, servant of Navedeva C.M. made a grant for offering to Durgaparamesvari on the festival day of Mahalakshmi panduvu on Sunday 11th of bright fortnight, Asviyuja, Yava.[394] In AD 1267, in the reign of Singayadeva Gadideva, Kammanayaka, governor of Tallur made grants to Mallinatha of Pratishtapura and Nagesvaradeva. To Brahmesvara temple at Kondanayanivaram, Viranarayana choda Baddigadeva, son of chola Doraya and grandson of Viranarayana Baddiga, made grants.[395] The temple of Alghanathaswami mentions as Alahapurapadideva at Atutur i.e. Atmakur,[396] in AD 1279 was built by Dhi Bahava M and the Kapus and Karanams of Jilleri. Ghantasala, in the 13th century AD, Avayanisetti, son of choda erected the top structure of the temple of Jaladhisa and gave annually a pair of clothes to the God and the goddess, and set up the image of Bhringimada on the roof of the mandala.[397] In AD 1382 at Kokarur, Bairapanayaka constructed a temple for Virdhyavasi and made grants to Mallikarjuna.[398] Murari Narayani garu in AD 1409 made a grant to Srikantu Ramesvaradeva at Sripatikonda. In AD 1418 in the reign of Madaya Narasimha C.M. Sriramana made grants to chandresvara and Somesvara at Vilichi. In AD 1401 the trading cheifs of many communities including the Nanadesis assembled together in the mandapam of Somesvara at Nadikuduru on the occasion of the Vasanta mahotsva festival of god Nrisimha at Addanti and grated Boggardin (near Muppalla) to Gurrala paramesvari at Boggaran.[399] In AD 1417 the muslim chief Surnkhumalu jenadi Odeya built a fight of steps from the Krishna up to Srirangarajakonda.[400] In AD 1491 Sarvarja, son of Pera maraja constructed a temple with golden pinnacles over it to God

Nagesvaralinga at Nagarajunikonda Singaraja, for the merit of his father made sahasragodana during solar eclipse.[401] In AD 1493 Pedda Ahovela Reddi, a foudatory of Mahamandalesvara Krishnarya ruling at Penukonda built a temple to Ahobala Madihugiri Lakshminarasimha in Sanaghatta in accrodance with the direction given to him at Ahobalam.[402] At Elur in Kali 4890 sambeta Alamandala Kokalanideva C.M. made grants to the temple of chandraprabhanjanesvara,[403] Sidhiraju Timmaraja, a ruler of Nellore, constucted-big asthanamandapa called madhyaranga in the chenna kesava temple at Markapur. M.P. G. Madhura Perumalla raja, son of Kulasekhara Mandaraperumallaraju made grants to Mulasthana Sanagurudeva and Nagesvaradeva at Mahimalur. At Dekankonda, Siddhiraju Timmaraju constructed a bhogamantapa to the temple of Sri chodanaryana.[404] At Pentrala, Gudideva granted a flower garden to Margandaryana Perumal temple . In the Prasanamakalahastisvara temple at Rattanda is a record registering a grant by Pottapi chember to Adirajattideva Tribhuvanayaka having built a temple. The record ends with Salutation to Buddha.[405] Probably there was also a shrine of Buddha in the temple. At Kovidona was the temple of Tribhuvanamallanriharikesavadeva. At Uddyagiri Tirumalanya Vallabha built a bhogamantapa and a flight of Steps to the temple. Mahamadnalesva Mallarasa repaired to the temple of Brahmesvaradeva at Appalapudi at the western door of Sriparvata and provided for worship[406] and angabhoga. Aduva chedirayan at Tirukachchaiyur built a mahamantapa in the Siva temple at Andappur. At Nandalur, king Nirantara is said to have built the shrines for gods Narisimha and Sanmyanatha Samyanatha was very beautiful and was also called chokkanatha.[407] Narayanaraja built the Vijayaragahva perumal temple at Tiruttani Kshanikachola.[408]

### The Yadavarayas

The Yadavarayas were devoted to the lotus feet of Venkatanatha and Srikalahastisvara. In the reign of Sriranganatha Yodavaraya Kalivaya renovated with stone the dilapidated wooden roof of the ardhamandapa in the temple and plastered it with flat tiles.[409] In the 18th year of King Sriranganatha, a grant was made to Desavinayaka temple at Sattirappadi i.e. Satravada and the sects of Senkati Samayakkarar and Virakodiyur were prohibited from it. In the 16th year of the same ruler, provision was made for the special service Kaliyurkilavamasandi in the temple of Adhipurisvara at Tiruvorriyur by a resident of Serrappedu (Chetput).[410]

A family of local chiefs claiming solar lineage and from Madhavavaram of Bezada, ruled in the 15th century AD as the feudaiories of Kings of Vijayangar and contributed much to the social life of the country. Panchatantram and Varahapuranam were rendered into Telugu as Champu kavyas under the patronage of these rulers. Dubagunta Narayanakavi dedicated his Nasiketopakhyana to Anantamatya Gangaya, a minister in the service of these ruler. In AD 1424 at Pillutla, a verandah was constructed for the merit of Temmanagaurngaru, in the temple of Narasimha on the hill. [411] Chegalamarri in AD 1451 singabhupala a feudatory of Mallikarjuna of Vijayanagar built a prakara to the temple.[412] In AD 1460, Tammaraja son of Kondamaraju Vallabhyya of the race of Raghu built the Gopalakrishna temple at Udayagiri alias Kodayapalem and granted 1,000 kunkas for worship. [413] About this temple, the gazetteer says "It belongs to the Pallava type with stupa at the top of Garbhagudi (sanctum sanctorum) with prakaram enclosed by high walls, with entrance gate, tower of an unfinished Kalyanamandapa. The mandapa is a peculiar type of Vijayanagar architecture. The temple proper is an old construction and is a standing evidence of the fact that Udyagiri's graceness dates back to the 11th century AD. The frame work of the stupa is still intact though the images have all disappeared. The remains of the compound walls, entrance gate all of chola type indicate the existence of another temple on which site the present Kalyanamandapa was built."[414] Obviously as the locality formed part of the kingdoms of the Telugu Choals. Telugu Pallavas and the kings of Vijayanagar the temple was built or rebuilt in each period in their styles. The Ranganayaka temple at Udayagiri was also of chola type, with high walled compound with big corridors. Tammaraya built a temple of Kasivisvesvara on the hill of Ddayagiri and granted 2000 kuntas for worship. The eastern gate of the Gopala Krishna temple was begun by

Krishnaray of Vijayanagar and the image was removed to the Ranganayaka temple at Nellore on the decline of Vijayanagar king. The Vallabharaya temple on the hill was named the Yadavarayan Emperuman named after the donor who was a governor under Krishnayaa of Vijayanagar. [415] The Yadavarayana perumal temple at Chopalapalle is same as the Tirunagesvara temple. [416]

Vallabhayyadeva in AD 1468 gave a village to the temple at Tirumala for daily offerings to Srivenkatesa and for construction and repairs of the temple. [417] In AD 1474 and 1477 Tammayadeva C.M. provided for a tirupponakam in his name to Venkatesvara-his share of the prasadam being nali, panakam, pulse, salt, proper, vegetables, and curds.[418] In AD 1502 in the reign of Bhujabla Tammaraya, Penugonda Tammainayaka built the mahamantapa, set up pillars and pinnacles constructed wells, and tanks and provided for celebration of festivals of Rama, Raghava, Narayana and Krishna and the temple of Rajaraja Vinnagar at Bezvada. [419] At Pulivendla in AD 1509, Narasayya, son of Janmaraya, younger brother of Basava made grants. Narasayya is identical with Singarayyadeva Maharaja who claims to have made substantial addition to the temple of Kenakadurga at Bezvada.[420]

The Velamas of Rachkonda and Devarakonda played a significatn role in the social life of the 14th and 15th centuries AD. They offered patronage to literature and some of them were scholars themselves. Sarvajna Singamanidu, a contemporary of Srinatha, wasa etc.celebratedfigure in the literature of the Andhras learned in logic, grammar, music and literature. He wrote Rasarnavasudhekara alias singa bhupaliya (alankara sastra), Sangita ratnakara vyakhya etc. in Sanskrti. Bammava Potana matya lived in his kingdom and his Bhoginidanalakam is supposed, is after a concubine of the king, Singaya Madhava, son of Sarvajna Singa, was also a great poet and wrote Raghaviay a commentary on ramayana in AD 1427 which in attested by inscriptions. [421] Elakuchi Balasaravati, a poet was patronised by king Padamalla of the Velamas and wrote Mallabhupaliyam alias Bhartrihari subheshitam in Telugu Poet Gaurana was connected with the court of Velamas. His father Ayyarlarya was the younger brother of Petaraju, the minister of kind Singaya Madhava. This fact Gaurana mentioned in all his works-Lakshana dipika in Sanskrit, Harischandra and Navanathacharitra both in couplet metro in Telugu. He styled himself sarasasahitya lakashnavi chakshana, chaturasahitya lakshana chekravarti in Harishchandra dvipada[422] and vimalasahitya pravinadhika in Navanathacharitra.[423] Gaurava did Navanatha charitra at the instance of santaraya of Bikshavrittimatha on Sri Sailam, in dedication to god Mallikarjuna.

Beside to many temple in their kingdom the Velamas made donations to the temples at Draksharama, little Conjeevaram and Sr rangam. In AD 1437, at little Conjeevaram, Vasantaraya, son of Anapotanayaka and brother of Singapanayaka presented four dvarapala images - chandica and prachnda at the second and the third gopuras respectively and kept two pinnacles of gold on the Arulala Perumal temple.[424]

Medicine and veterinary science, devoloped in this period. Two records dated AD 1151 and 1154at Bapatla [425] mention Anonatabhatta the son of Physician Suryadevara Pandita and grandson of Perumanambi, a scholar and a native of the village of Brihadankura in Tondamandalam. Ananta's brother was Nagadeva. Obviously the family settled in the Telugu country. Another family of physicians is known form a record dated AD 1430 at Draksharama, Annaya Pandita, the son of Kesavarya, a great physician installed Ganapati at the western gate of the Bhimesvara temple at Draksharama and Devara Pandita granted land to Ganesa. [426] Vasudeva, son of Anantaparya of Atreya Gotra was an expert in Asvayurveda. Anantapandita was also a Asvavadiya. Vasudeva's son was Ananta Peddi. Bhairava, son-in-law of Vasudeva composed the slokas the record at Palakol dated AD 1300. Vadsudeva was devoted to Sankara and made grants to Kshiraramesvara. [427] Gaurana in his Navanathacharitra in the discourse betweeen Goraksha and Minanadha enumerates the names of several cattle diseases Goraksha as seen from this work and Prabhulinga lila claims to have acquire the knowledge of conquring Maya from Allamaprabhu.

Poet Anantamatya of the 15th century AD, in his Bhojarajiya gives us the names of the Vaishnava pravaras Vainateya,

Gajendra, Seshu, pavani, Ambarisha, Dhruva, Bali, Vibhishna, Prehlada, Pandaveya, Pandarika, Vedavyas, Bhishma, Narada, Paratara, Sannaka, Vhrigu, Vidura, Akrura, and Gopala. Ananta's father was a devotee of Vishnu the lord of Srikakulam, His preceptor was Govinda Chekravarti the last of the five sons of Tirumala Nallanuchakravarti the others being Tiruvengala, Alagu, Anbala, and Srideva. Bhojerajiya is dedicated to Abobalanrishimha,[128] the family god of Ananta. Ananta's Rasabharanam is dedicated to the lord of Dhruvapuri i.e. Vishnu. Dhruvapuri is probably Dhulipudi on the banks of the Krishna (Guntur District). Potana in his Virubhadravijaya dedicated to Ivaturi Somanaradhya alias Ivaturi Aradhya chandra, enumerates the Saiva saints - Sriyala, Karikala, cheramuni, Ubhata, Bana, Kesavaraju, Basavaraju, Kannappa, Chennayya, Karayura Chodayya, Kummara, gandayya, Neminatha, Panditaradhya, Bhallana, Neminandi, Mahesa, Madivalu, Mechayya, cheramarajayya, chirukonda no hali, sankhyakonda surichemudu etc. the followers of Viramahesvara, truthful and of good history. Potana adores them. These saints were included in the sixty-three saiva saints - Aruvattumuvar and find mention earlier in Basavapuranam and Panditaradhya charitra by Palkuriki Somanatha.

## REFERENCES

1. The Malaviya Commemoration volume p. 305.
2. A. B. Keith Hist. of Sanskrit literature p. 136 - Kshemendra's Dasavatararacharitra..
3. The Malaviya Commemoration volume p. 305.
4. The Malaviya Commemoration volume pp. 305-306.
5. The colas II - I p 220.
6. Kumarasambhava.
7. 357-B of 1893: S.I.I. IV U 53.
8. Basavapurana pp. 84-85.
9. 514-A of 1893: S.I.I. V 130.
10. Keyurabahucharitra I v 57.

11. A verse cited on p. 35 of introduction to Sivatatvasara.
12. Mack MS 15-4-41.
13. 344 of 1893: S.I.I. IV 804.
14. Nel. Ins.II Ongole 59, 60.
15. S.S. Sastri: Renukavijayam - Intdn of Srivenkatesvara Vol. IV No. 2 p. 197.
16. Verses cited on pp. 64-65 of Introduction No. 6 Basavapurana.
17. Basavapuana Text pp. 197-198.
18. Sivatatvasara vv 21, 30, 31-36.
19. - do - 215-222.
20. Palm leaf MS mentioned in pp. 76-77 of Basavapurana.
21. Sivatatvasara - Introduction p. 40.
22. Andhra Patrika weekly Ed. Vol. 37 No. date 19-2-1945 - Ekasilangara, vrittantamu.
23. AndhraPatrikaweekly Vol. 37 No. 18-8-1 45 p. 2.
24. Panditaradhyacharitra I p. 586..
25. Panditaradhyacharitra I pp. 505, 511.
26. 240 of 1899: E.I. V No. 17.
27. Sarda I No. 1 pp. 3 - 8.
28. 276, 278 of 1893: S.I.I. IV 1140, 1142.
29. Kalingadesacharitra p. 292.
30. 132 of 1917.
31. 655 of 1920.
32. 164 of 1897: S.I.I. VI 125.
33. 696 of 1920.
34. Kistna Dt. Manual p. 204.
35. Mack MS 15-6-44.
36. Nellore Gazetteer p. 331.

37. Nallore Gazetteer, p. 331.
38. Vizagapatam gazetteer p. 309.
39. E.I. III No. 15 p. 91.
40. E.I. V No. 17.
41. E.I. V No. 17 v 26 p. 149.
42. - do -
43. L. R. 19 p. 454 H.
44. Kondariti Samrajyamu pp. 21-22.
45. Proceedings 10th Or. Conf. p. 457.
46. 442 of 1905.
47. E.I. V No. 17 p. 143.
48. 271 of 19 32-33.
49. 317 32-33.
50. Kistna Dt. Manual p. 214.
51. Keyurabahucharitra I vv 44-45.
52. Bharati I 3 p. 129.
53. P. Ardhyacharitra II p. 467.
54. 36 of 1915.
55. P. Aradhyacharitra II p. 413.
56. Bharati I No. 3 p. 132 verse cited.
57. - do -
58. 357-B of 1893: S.I.I. IV 1253.
59. Keyurabahucharitra I vv 26. 44.
60. 253 of 1882: S.I.I. IV 704.
61. Sivatatvasara Text vv 231-234.
62. Keyurabahucharitra I v 18.
63. E.I. IV No. 17 v 17.

64. E.I. IV No. 17 v 17.

65. 523 of 1893: S.I.I. V 157.

66. 246 of 1893: S.I.I. V 1098.

67. Bharati Bahudhanva Jyestha.

68. 513 of 1893: S.I.I. V 128.

69. 517 of 1893: S.I.I. V 139.

70. E.I. XIX No. 16.

71. Vizagapatam Gazetteer p. 310.

72. pp. 267, 335-338, 342, 350, 360, 370, 376, 377, 396, 18.

73. pp. 58, 59, 102-107.

74. Ranganatha Ramayana Text p. 4.

75. Ranganatha Ramayana Text p. 457, 592.

76. R. Ramayana Intdn. II p. 6, I p.17.

77. Text pp. 456-457, 371, 435.

78. Text pp. 472.

79. Hyd. Arch. Series 13 I p. 23; II No. 50, 51, Telingana inscn. I No. 36.

80. R. Ra. Text pp. 490, 592.

81. Bharati I No. 6 p. 26.

82. R. Ramayana Appendix II pp. 800-803.

83. R. Ra. Appendix II p. 788.

84. - do - p. 785-786.

85. R. Ra. Text pp. 22, 84.

86. R. Ra. Text p. 244.

87. Ra. Ra. Text p. 346.

88. R. Ra. Text pp. 81, 82, 102.

89. Jaluva or Jalva "Probably (like Ophir or Potosi), the name of a place, fine gold of Jalva" - Brown Tel. Eng. Dictionary.

90. P. Viracharitra Text p. 60.

91. Citation on p. 28 Intron. to P. Virach. from Alaraju Rayabaramu katha. Palm leaf Ms. Vira katha.
92. Citation on p. 23 Intdn. to P. Viracharitra.
93. Citation on p. 29 Intdn. to P. Viracharitra.
94. P. Viracharitra Text pp. 7-8.
95. 146 of 1913.
96. P. Viracahritra pp. 103-104.
97. - do - 79, 82, 97.
98. - do -
99. Sewell: Antiquties I App. A p. 4.
100. J.A.I. p. 156.
101. P. Viracharitra Text. p. 55.
102. Sewell: Antiquities I App. A.
103. Sewell: Antiquities I p. 62.
104. - do - p. 15.
105. Antiquities I App. A p. 26.
106. 316 of 1931.
107. 557 of 1905.
108. Antiquities I App. A.
109. 551 of 1909.
110. P. Virach. Text p. 12.
111. Antiquities I App. A p. 25.
112. A.R. 1910 II p.99 para 49.
113. AR 1912 II para II.
114. AR 1912 II para 11: 13 of App. A.
115. Antiquities I App. A.
116. His of Andh. V pp. 212-213: Velugotivarivamsacharitra p. 20.
117. Palnativirachairitra Introduction p. 19.

118. Antiquities I p. 62.

119. Antiquities I App. A p. 5.

120. - do - 10.

121. Palnativiravharitra Text p. 16.

122. Verse cited from P. Viracharitra on pp. 45-46 of Introduction to Sri Natha's P. Viracharitra.

123. Palnati Viracharitra Text p. 41.

124. P. Viracharitra Text pp. 7, 15.

125. Hist. of Andhras V p. 211.

126. Hist. of Andhras V p. 211.

127. P. Viracharitra , Hist. of Andh. V pp. 451-452.

128. G.V. Ramamurti Comm. Vol. I Text Sec. p. 260.

129. G.G. Ramamurti Comm. Vol. I Text Sec. p. 260.

130. P. Virach. Text p. 65.

131: P. Virach. Text p. 63, 67.

132. Palnativiracharitra Text p. 52.

133. P. Viracharitra Text p. 53.

134. —do— p. 57.

135. P. Virach. Text p. 64.

136. —do— p. 72-73.

137. Palnati Viracharitra Text p. 76.

138. P. Viracharitra Text pp 67-70; According to one writer either Bala was over fourteen or the introduction of Syamangi is imaginary- Hist. of Andh. V p. 197 fn.

139. Antiquities I App. A p. 5.

140. Antiquities I App. A p. 7.

141. - do - 7 fn 3.

142. Antiquities I App. A p. 25.

143. Palnati Viracharitra Text p. 43.

144. Palnati Viracharitra Text p. 47.

145. Palnati Viracharitra Text p. 58.

146. Palnati Viracharitra Introduction p. 49.

147. P. Virach. Introduction p. 61 The chatu verse cited.

148. - do - Text fn for p. 54.

149. Kridabhirama.

150. 283 of 1924.

151. Citation from Ramavilasa on pp. 405-6 of Hist. of Andhras V.

152. 264 of 1924.

153. Text on pp 2-3 of App. F of Kondavitisamrajyamu.

154. 527 and 528 of 1853: Mack MS 15-6-21.

155. Citation on pp. 23-27 of introduction to Sivatatvasara L.R. 19.

156. Citation on pp. 23-27 of Introduction to Sivatatvasara p.433.

157. Introduction to Sivatatvasara p. 31.

158. E.I. VI No. 26 v 13.

159. E.I. VI No. 15 A and B.

160. Kistna Dt. Manual p.8.

161. E.I. III No. 16.

162. Mack MS 15-6-44.

163. Kistna Dt. Manual p. 188.

164. Antiquities I p. 68.: Kistna Dt. Manual p. 177: Sarda Vol. II (1924) No. 6 pp. 655-665.

165. E.I. VI No. 15 A p. 148.

166. 83 of 1917.

167. 160 of 1893: S.I.I. IV 985.

168. 204 of 1905.

169. Nizam's Arch. Sur. Report pp. 19-21.

170. c.p. I of 1921-22: Rajarajasanchika pp. 187-189.
171. 506 of 1893: S.I.I. V 116.
172. 249 of 1935-36.
173. 63 of 1917.
174. 723 of 1920.
175. 530-D of 1893: S.I.I. v 18.
176. 309 of 1920.
177. Kakatiya Sanch. App. A, Sivayogasara v 33.
178. App. A Sivayogasara V 83.
179. 486 of 1893: S.I.I. V 90.
180. E.I. IV No. 33 v 32.
181. Sarda 2nd year 1924 Vol. I No. 5 p. 547.
182. E.I. XIX No. 26 p. 173.
183. E.I. XIX No. 26 Text p 171 u 108-109.
184. Rajarajasanchika p. 5.
185. 216 of 1899: S.I.I. VI 665.
186. 214 of 1899: S.I.I. VI 662.
187. 296 G. of 1899: S.I.I. VI 919.
188. 218 of 1899: S.I.I. VI 667.
189. E.I. IV No. 4 A.B.C.D.
190. E.I. IV No. 4 D.
191. 280 of 1892: S.I.I. IV 735.
192. E.I. IV No. 32. Also E.I. XIX No. 26 v 6.
193. 275 of 1930-31: 276, 282, 280 of 1930-31.
194. 113 A of 1902: S.I.I. VII 737.
195. 308 of 1920.
196. 386 of 1893: S.I.I. IV 1297.
197. Telingana instsn. I misc. 39.
198. 511 of 1893: S.I.I. V 125.

199. Mack MS 15-6-21.
200. 87 & 88 1899: S.I.I. VI 132, 133.
201. Telingana inscns. I misc. No. 41.
202. 372 of 1905: S.I.I. IX 403,; 831 of 1917.
203. 295 of 1892: S.I.I. IV 749,; 40 of 1912.
204. 293 of 1892: S.I.I. IV 747.
205. 288 of 1892: S.I.I. IB 742.
206. Nell. Ins. I Darasi 69.
207. Nell. Ins. II Nell, 15.
208. Nell. Ins. II Kanigir 24.
209. Nell. Ins. III Sulurpet 8.
210. Nell. Ins. III Sulurpet 3.
211. Tirupati Inscns. I No. 61 (127 G.T.)
212. - do - 74 (652 T.T.)
213. Tirupati Inss. I No. 78 (430 TT).
214. AR 1911 page 63 para 15.
215. - do - 16.
216. 353 of 1923.
217. 38 of 1921.
218. 480 of 1912.
219. 568 of 1919.
220. AR 1893 para 8.
221. 662 of 1904.
222. 179 of 1929-30.
223. 5 & 10 of 1932-33.
224. 434 of 1922.
225. 54 of 1932.
226. 438 of 1919.
227. 264 & 267 of 1921.

228. 536 of 1909: A.R. 1910 para 8.
229. T.T. Report.
230. Tirupati inscns. I p. 89.
231. E.I. XIII No. 16.
232. 272 of 1905.
233. 173 T.T.
234. 210 of 1923.
235. Nell. Ins. II KR 63.
236. Mack MS 15-4-23 MS pp. 88-93.
237. 321 of 1905: S.I.I. IX 275.
238. 211 & 280 of 1893: S.I.I. IV 1043, 1145.
239. 290 of 1896: S.I.I. V 1171.
240. Kalingadesacharitra p. 625.
241. S.I.I. V 1252.
242. 440. 211, of 1893: S.I.I. IV 1353: IV 1353, 1043.
243. 436-A of 1893: S.I.I. IV 1365.
244. 311 of 1899: S.I.I. VI 956: 291 of 1896: S.I.I. V 1172.
245. 288-G of 1899: S.I.I. VI 875.
246. 284 of 1899: VI 825.
247. 284-C of 1899: S.I.I. VI 836.
248. 314-D of 1899: S.I.I. VI 972.
249. 284-T of 1899: S.I.I. VI 843.
250. 284-P of 1899: S.I.I. VI 839.
251. 574 of 1912: Mack MS 15-6-26 No. 64.
252. Bharati X - II p. 755.
253. E.I. No. 14.
254. 365 - XXXVI of 1899: S.I.I. VI 1203.
255. 839 of 1893L: S.I.I. IV 1222.
256. Bharati X - II p. 755.

257. 296-N of 1899: S.I.I. VI 925.

258. 252-a of 1899: S.I.I. VI 715.

259. 335 of 1896: S.I.I. V 1217.

260. 365 and 366 of 1896: S.I.I. V 1247, 1248.

261. 459-C 1893: S.I.I. V No. 25.

262. 141 of 1893: S.I.I. IV 961.

263. 254 of 1897: S.I.I. VI 219.

264. Mack MS 15-6-26 No. 52.

265. Mack MS 15-6-26 No. 63: 54 of 1912.

266. 148 of 1913: Text cited on p. 115 of K. Samrajyamu

267. Mack MS 15-4-14 sect. 11.

268. K. Samrajyamu p. 115 Text cited.

269. Nell. Ins. III O 86, 88.

270. Nell. Ins. III O 89.

271. Nell. Ins. II O 6.

272. Nell. Ins. I D 72.

273. Nell. Ins. Gazetteer, p. 362.

274. Nell. Ins. II KR 26.

275. - do -

276. Bharati V - II p. 795.

277. Bharati V - II p. 799.

278. Nell. Ins. I D 13.

279. Bharati V - II p. 775.

280. Bharati II no. 10 pp. 94-95.

281. Nell. Ins. III Podile 26.

282. Mack MS 15-3-18.

283. 771 of 1992.

284. AR 1910 p. 98 para 46.

285. 406 of 1911.

286. Mack MS 15-3-8 Ms p. 67 No. 2.

287. "15-3-27 MS p. 117.

288. "15-6-2.

289. "15-3-25 No. 12.

290. 423 of 1911.

291. Nell. Ins. I Darasi 57.

292. Mack Ms 15-3-61.

293. Mack Ms 15-3-8 No. 3 p. 11.

294. Nell. Ins. I Darasi 1.

295. Mack MS 15-4-23 Ms pp. 98.

296. Nell. Ins. I D 25.

297. 192, 198 od 1899: S.I.I. VI 638, 644.

298. K. Samarajamu p. 43.

299. 642 of 1920.

300. Ins. Mad. Pres. II NI 293.

301. 327 of 1915.

302. 364 of 1915.

303. 161 of 1897: S.I.I. VI 121.

304. 167 of 1899: S.I.I. 620.

306. 164, 165 adn 199 of 1899: S.I.I. VI 606, 607, 645.

307. Critique on Nannechoda's Kumarasambhava.

308. Basavapurana Introduction p. 73.

309. Srinatha: Kasi Khandan IV v 150.

310. Ku. Sa. Text IX v 225.

311. Virabhadravijam IV v 100.

312. Ku. Sa. Text I - II v 283.

313. Ku. Sa. Text II v 283.

314. Ku. Sa. Text I - II vv 349, 351, V vv 625-627, 638.

315. Ku. Sa. Text II - I vv 250-290.

316. Ku. Sa. Text II vv 390-393.

317. Ku. Sa. Text I - IV vv 417-423.

318. Ku. Sa. Text II - VIII v 169.

319. Ku. Sa. Text II canto VIII v 143: J of Srivenkatesvara Oriental Institute IV - II pp. 42-45.

320. 572 of 1907.

321. 327 of 1905.

322. 413 of 1905.

323. Sewell. Antiquities I p. 131.

324. The Colas II - I p. 220.

325. Dasuku. ch. III vv 9, 11.

326. A Chera kanda vv 11, 12.

327. Prabandharatnavali p. 9 v 156.

328. N. Ra. I v 19 VII v 1.

329. T.T.D: Insns. Report Introd. p. 5.

330. Bharata IV Drona II 339, 361, 378 specially a prose piece (368) speaks about the unity of murahara and purahara. V 407-428: VII Anusanika I 309-385 IV vv 365-380.

332. Bharata III Vrata I 11.

333. The Colas II - p. 172.

334. N. Ramayana X vv 161, 163.

335. Vijayarasamu - coted in Prabandaratnavali.

336. Pro. 3rd Or. Conf. p. 273.

337. - do -

338. Vol. VII Anusasarika I vv 309-385 V 326-335.

339. Andhra Patrika weekly Ed. Vol. 37 No. 17- 31-12-44 p. 2 - Ekasilanagaravvittamtamu.

340. Hyd. Arch. Series 19 I p. 24.

341. The Colas II - I p. 222.

342. 357, 425 of 1919.
343. 407 of 1915.
344. Nell. Ins. Gudur 45.
345. Nell. Ins. II Nell. 60.
346. Nell. Ins. III Rapur 36.
347. Nell. Ins. III Solurpet 12.
348. Mack MS 15-6-44.
349. 201 of 1912.
350. 79 of 1923.
351. Bharati Vol. 18 Part I No. pp. 629-630.
352. 432 of 1919.
353. 434 of 1919.
354. 463 of 1919.
355. Nell. Ins. II Kavali 25, 26.
356. Nell. Ins. II Kavali 51.
357. - do - Nellore 19.
358. - do - Nellore 51.
359. - do - I Gudur 39.
360. Nell. Ins. Rapur 37.
361. 213 of 1892: S.I.I. IV 661.
362. Mack MS 15-4-23.
363. Mack MS 15-3-8 Akwpadu.
364. 201 of 1903: S.I.I. VIII 500.
365. 518 of 1908.
366. 319 of 1912.
367. 514 of 1912.
368. 308 of 1928-29.

369. 562 of 1916.

370. 11 of 1921.

371. 489 of 1919.

372. 224 of 1929-30.

373. E.I. VII No. 18.

374. 330 of 1928-29.

375. Nell. Ins. III Rapur 7.

376. E.I. VII 17 B v 16.

377. Ketana: Desu: Ko. ch. I v 83.

378. Chatupadyamanimanjari pp. 23-27: K. Venkataramanappa. Telugu chatupadyagalu pp. 26-28.

379. Dasa Ku. Ch. vv 10-28.

380. Dasa Ku. Ch. vv 10-28.

381. Bharata III Virata I vv 71-72, V 242, 251, 259. A good technicaldescription of dynasties on pp. 1149-1150 of His. of Tel. Lang. II by Ch. Narayana Rao.

382. Bharata III Virata II pp. 14-20.

383. Dasa Ku. Ch. X v 14.

384. Dasa Ku. Ch. I v II.

385. Chatupadyamanimanjari p. 29.

386. 268 - A of 1897: S.I.I. VI 244.

387. 293 of 1930.

388. Panditaradhyacharitra.

389. Kis. Andhras V p. 266.

390. Hyd. Arch. Series No. 13 II No. 34.

391. C.P. 4 of 1917-18.

392. 15 of 1917: S.I.I. IX 268.

393. Telingana Inscriptions I Miscell. No.7.

394. Nell. Ins. I AR 29.

395. 460 of 1915.

396. Nell. Ins. IAR 11.

397. 850 of 1917.

398. Nell. Ins. II Kavali 33.

399. 205 of 1935 - 36.

400. 306 & 307 of 1924.

401. 390 of 1926.

402. C.P. 19 of 1917 - 1918.

403. 429, 430 of 1915.

404. Nell. Ins. I Darasi. 14.

405. Nell. Ins. I Gudur 106.

406. Telingana Ins. I No. 30.

407. Mack Ms 15-3-27. Ms p. 33.

408. 447 of 1905.

409. 35 of 1911.

410. 242 of 1912.

411. 95 of 1929-30.

412. Ins. Mad. Pres. II Kn 601.

413. 209 of 1892. Nell. Ins. III b 29.

414. Nellore Dt. Gazetteer p. 373.

415. Nell. Dt. Gazetteer p. 374.

416. Nell. Ins. III Venkatagiri II.

417. Tirupati Insn. II No. 60, 35 (159 TT).

418. Tirupati Ins. II 21, 27 (158 TT, 7 TT).

419. 122 & 123 of 1918.

420. 491 of 1906, 329 of 1892.

421. Navanatha charitra Intdn. p. 11 - The insnc. are cited.

422. Text pp. 4, 257.

423. Text p.

424. 634 of 1919.

425. 166, 196 of 1897: S.I.I. VI 127, 156.

426. 441 of 1893: S.I.I. IV 1374.

427. 504-A of 1893: S.I.I. V 130.

428. Canto I pp. 29-30.

## SELECT BIBLIOGRAPHY


I. *Periodicals*

1. Andhrapatrika Annuals, Madras.
2. Andhrapatrika Weekly, Madras.
3. Annals of Bhandarkar Oriental Research Institute Vols. XV (1933-1943).
4. Bharati (Madras) Vols. I-XX.
5. Indian Antiquary-62 Vols.
6. Indian Historical Quarterly Vols. I-XX.
7. Journal of Indian History (Madras) Vols. I-XX.
8. Journal of Telugu Academy (Andhra Sahitya Parishad Patrika).
9. Journal of Andhra History and Culture (Guntur) Vols. I-III.
10. Journal of Andhra Historical Research Society (Rajahmundry), Vols. I-IV.

11. Journal of the Madras University Vols. VI-XV.

12. Journal of the Madras University Vols. VI-XIII.

13. Journal of Srivankatesvara Oriental Institute (Tirupati), Vols. I-VI.

14. Proceedings and Transactions of the All India Oriental Conferences, Vols. I-X.

15. Proceedings of the first Andhra Historical Conference, 1944 (Guntur).

16. Sarada Vols. I and II (Masulipatam).

17. The Hindu College Magazine (Guntur) 1943-1944.

II. *Inscriptions and Reports*

1. Annual Epigraphy Reports, (Madras) 1888-1938.

2. Annual Reports of Archaeological Department of Nizam's Dominions 1915-1940.

3. A list of Inscriptions of Southern India (Epigraphia Indica Vol. VIII Appendix), F. Kiclhorn.

4. A collection of the Inscriptions of Copper plates and stones in the Nellore District, Parts I, II and III—Butterworth and V. Chetty.

5. A Corpus of Inscriptions in the Telingana districts of H.E.H. the Nizam's Dominions (Hyderabad Archaeological Series (No. 13) Parts I and II (1940, 1942).

6. Catalogue Raisonne of Oriental Manuscripts in the Government Library - Taylor Vols. I, II and III.

7. Epigraphia Indica Vols. I to XXVI.

8. Epigraphic Carnatica.

9. Hyderabad Archaeological Series Nos. I-IX.

10. Inscriptions in the e.p. and Berar-Hiralal.

11. Mackenzie Manuscripts (Summaries).

12. South Indian Inscriptions Vols. I-VII.

13. Tirupati Devasthanam Inscriptions Vols. I and II.

14. Telingana Inscriptions Vols. I (Lakshmanarayparisodhaka-mandali Series No. I) Hyderabad (Deccan) 1935.

15. The Topographical list of Inscriptions in the Madras Presidency in 3 volumes - compiled by Rangachari.

16. The report on the Inscriptions of the Devasthana collection (T.T. Devasthanam Epigraphical series) S. Subramania Sastri Madras (1930). The coin of Southern India - Elliot (1886).

17. The Coins of Southern India - Elliot (1886).

18. The Memoirs of Archaeological Survey of India No. 23, (1931).

19. The memoirs of Geological Survey of India Vol. 8.

20. The Historical Inscriptions of Southern India and Outlines of Political History - R. Sewell and S.K. Aiyangar (1932) Madras.

III. *Books*

1. Anantamatya - Bhojarajiyamu (1924) Madras.

2. Anantamatya - Rassabharanamu (1931) Coconada (No. 23. Publication of the Telugu Academy).

3. Aiyangar S.K. - A History of the Holy Shrine of Sri Venkatesvara in Tirupati Vol. I (1940) Madras.

4. Aiyar K.V.S. - Historical Sketches of Ancient Deccan Vol. I.

5. Balasarasvati Yelakuchi - Mallabhupatiyam or Bhartruhari-subhashitamu, (1904).

6. Bannerji - H.D. - The History of Orissa Vol. I.

7. Bhandarkar R.G. - Early History of Deccan.

8. Bhaskara - Bhaskara Ramayanamu.

9. Buddha Reddi Gona - Ranganatha Ramayanamu (Andhra University series No. 29) Edited by V.P. Sastri).

10. Boswell John A.D. - Nellore District Manual (1873) Madras.

11. Briggs - Ferishta's History of the Muslim Power in India Vol. I.

12. Bombay District Gazetteer - Vol. I Part II (1896).

13. Garmichael D.P. - Vizagapatam District Manual (1868) Madras.

14. Con. A.F. - North Arcot District Manual (Revised by M.A. Stewart) Vol. I Madras 1895.

15. Chaudhary, K.B. - The History of the Kammas, Parts I and II.

16. Duggana, Dagguballi - Nasiketopakhyanam (1929).

17. Francis W. - Vizagaptam District Gazetteer, (1907) Madras.

18. G.V. Ramamurti Pandtulu Commemmoration Volume No. 1.

19. Gazetteer of the Nellore District (1942) Madras.

20. Gaurana-Harisohandra Dvipada (1912) Ed. V. Venkatasraya Sastri, Madras.

21. Gaurana-Navanatha Charitra 1937) Madras University Telugu series No. 7.

22. Gurubrahmasarma, M. - Kondavitisamraiyamu (1936).

23. Jakkana - Vikramarka Charitramu (1928) Madras.

24. Kachabhupati and Vithalaraju - Ranganath Ramayanamu (Uttarakanda) 1920 (Chitradu)-Amudritandhrasarvasvamu, No. 5.

25. Keith, A.B. - A History of Sanskrit Literature (1928) Oxford.

26. Krishna Rao, B.V. - Edited Sri Rajarajanarendra Pattabhisheka Sanchika (1923) Rajahmundry.

27. Ketana - Bhsdhsbhushanam, (1901) Madras.

28. Ketana - Dasakumaracharitramu, (1925) Madras.

29. Ketana - Vijnanesvaram (chintamani series No. 22) 1995 Rajahmundry.

30. Lakshamana Rao, K.V. (Editor) Andhravijnan sarvasvamu. Vols. I and II published by K. Nagesvara Rao (Madras).

31. Lakshmanarayavyasavali, Vol. I (No. 31) Vijnana Chandrika Granthamala) 1923 (Madras).

32. Manchana-Keyurabhahu charitramu (1902) (Sarasvati series No. 26) published by Editor Sarasvati, Coconada.

33. Mavanakavi - Markandayapuranamu, (1903) Madras, 2nd Edition.

34. Minakshi, Dr. C. -Administration and Social Life under the Pallavas.

35. Maltby - The Ganjam District Manual (1918) Madras.

36. Mackenzio, G. - The Kistna District Manual (1883).

37. Morris, H. - The Godavari District (1878).

38. Mysore Gazetteer, Vol. II Part II.

39. Mannichoda - Kumarasambhavamu Part I (The Forgotten poets series No. 2) published by M.R. Kavi (1909) Madras.

40. Nannichoda - Kumarasambhavamu Part II (The Forgotten poets series No. 9 1914).

41. Narayanakavi, Dubagunta - Panchatantramu (1924) Madras.

42. Narayana Rao Dr. C. - History of Telugu Language Parts I and II (1937) Waltair. Andhra University series No. 18.

43. Narasimhachari - Narantaka Kavicharitra Vols. I and II Edition (1928).

44. Nilakantha Sastri, Prof. K.A. - The Colas Vols. I and II,. Madras University Historical Series No. 9 and 10.

45. Nilakantha Sastri, Prof. K.A. The Pandyan Kingdom.

46. " - The Foreign Notices of South India.

47. " - Studies in Cola History and Administration.

48. " - The Chalukyas of Kalyani.

49. Nandalal Dev - The Geographical Dictionary of Ancient and Medieval India.

50. Panditaradhya, Mallikarjuna - Sivatatvasaramu (1920) Telugu Academy Publication No. 10 (1920) Madras.

51. Peddana, Allasani - Manucharitramu.

52. Peddanakavi, Vinnaketa - Kavyalankarachudamnai cantos 8 and 9. Telugu Academy Publication No. 10 (1920) Madras.

53. Peddanakavi, vinnaketa - Kavyalankarachudamanai, First seven cantees. Edited and published by V. Venkatarayasastri. Third edition (1929).

54. Pichchayya Sastri, D. - Chatupadyaratnakaramu (1927). Kelanidhi Granthamala No. 1.

55. Potana, Bammera-virabhadravijayamu, (1924) Madras.

56. Prabhakara Sastri, V. - Chatupadyamanimanjari (1920) Madras.

57. Prabhakara Sastri, V. - Prabhadha Ratanvali, Singarasrinathamu.

58. Ramakrishnayya K. - Studies in Mahabharata.

59. Ramayya, J. - Basana Padyamanjari (1930) Coconada.

60. Rama Rao M. - (Editor) Kakatiya Sanchika (1935)—Rajahmundry.

61. Ray; H.C. - the Dynastic History of North India Vol. I and II.

62. Reddi, Dr. C.R. - Kavitvatatva Vicharamu (1923), Andhra University series No. 8.

63. Reddi, Dr. C.R. - Vyasamanjari (1929) Waltair, Andhra University series No. 21.

64. Sarrangadeva - Sangitaratnakara Vol. I (1943) Edited by E. Subramanaya Sastri.

65. Sewell, R. - List of Antiquarian Remains in the residency of Madras Vol. I (1882) and Vol. I List of Inscriptions (1884) Archaeological Survey.

66. Somanatha, Nachana - Uttarautaruvamsamu.

67. " - Palkuriki - Basavapuranamu (1926) Madras, Andhra Granthamala No. 2.

68. Somanatha - Sri Mallikarjuna Panditaradhya Charitra, (1939) Andhra Granthamala No. 30.

69. Srinatha - Palanativiranacharitramu, (1911) Edited by A. Umakaram.

70. Srinatha - Kasikhandam.

71. " - Bhimesvarapuranam.

72 " - Sringaranaishaddama.

73. " - Krilabhiramamu, Ed. By V.P. Sastri.

74. Sri Rama Murthi, G. - Kaviuitamulu (1923) Fourth Edition, Madras.

75. Stewari, Charles - the History of Bengal (1813).

76. Subbayya, G.V. Bhattumurti, Ramarajabhushana (1940) Tenali.

77. Subbayya, G.V. -Kavitraya Kavitavimarsanamu, (1937) Madras, Vanilla Edition.

78. Subha Rao, R. (Editor - Kaligadesa Charitra (1930) Andhra Historical Research Society Telugu Granthamala No. 2. (Rajahmundry) Sir Asutishu Mukharji Silverjubilee Vols. III, Part III.

79. Sir Asutoshu Mukharji Silver jubilees Volumes III, Part III.

80. Tikkana-Nirva Chanottararamayanamu (1927) Madras.

81. " -Srimadardhra Bharatamu, Vols. III to VIII Published by V Ramaswamy Sastri and Sons (Madras).

82. Timmanakavi-Mahabharata Ashtaparvavu, edition 1928-Bangalore.

83. The Malaviya - Commemoration Volume (1932).

84. The Cambridge History of India Vol. III.

85. Viresalingam K. - The Complete Works Vol. X Telugu Poets Part I (1917) Rajahmundry.

86. Venkata Ramanayya, N.N. - Velugotivarivamsavali.

87. Virabhadra Rao Ch. AndrulaCharitramu Vols. I, III, V-VI.

88. Virabhadra Rao, Ch. Srinatha Kavi.

89. Venkata Ramanappa K. Telugu Chetupadyagalu, Mysore University Pracherapustakamela Series No. 43 (1942).

90. Yerrapregada - Hari Vamsamu.

# Index